Rhythmic Gymnastics

Nadejda Jastrjembskaia, PhD
Yuri Titov, PhD

International Federation of Gymnastics (FIG)

WILLARD LIBRARY, BATTLE CREEK, MI

Human Kinetics
Web site: http://www.humankinetics.com/

United States: Human Kinetics, P.O. Box 5076, Champaign, IL 61825-5076
1-800-747-4457
e-mail: humank@hkusa.com

Canada: Human Kinetics, 475 Devonshire Road Unit 100, Windsor, ON N8Y 2L5
1-800-465-7301 (in Canada only)
e-mail: humank@hkcanada.com

Europe: Human Kinetics, P.O. Box IW14, Leeds LS16 6TR, United Kingdom
(44) 1132 781708
e-mail: humank@hkeurope.com

Australia: Human Kinetics, 57A Price Avenue, Lower Mitcham, South Australia 5062
(088) 277 1555
e-mail: humank@hkaustralia.com

New Zealand: Human Kinetics, P.O. Box 105-231, Auckland 1
(09) 523 3462
e-mail: humank@hknewz.com

A Note on Terminology
Since *Rhythmic Gymnastics* was first published in 1999 a few of the terms used in this book have changed. Please be aware that "RSG" ("Rhythmic Sportive Gymnastics") is now properly "RG" ("Rhythmic Gymnastics"), and, similarly, the terms "rhythmic sportive gymnastics" and "rhythmic sportive gymnast's" are now "rhythmic gymnastics" and "rhythmic gymnast's, respectively, in current usage.

Published by Echo Point Books & Media
Brattleboro, Vermont
www.EchoPointBooks.com

All rights reserved.
Neither this work nor any portions thereof may be reproduced, stored in a retrieval system, or transmitted in any capacity without written permission from the publisher.

Copyright © 1999, 2016 by Nadejda Jastrjembskaia and Yuri Titov

Rhythmic Gymnastics
ISBN: 978-1-62654-478-9 (paperback)

Editorial assistance by Teh Lah Hoong
Interior design by Nancy Rasmus
Interior art by Sandra Meier, Joe Bellis, Tom Roberts, Kevin Chua

Cover photograph: Girl engaged art gymnastics isolated, by Boris Ryaposov /Shutterstock
Cover design by Adrienne Núñez
Echo Point Books & Media

To Kate and Jouri, Mom and Dad

Contents

Preface vii
Acknowledgments ix

Part I: Technique

Chapter 1: Developing Technique 3
Chapter 2: Body Movements 11
Chapter 3: Apparatus Handling Techniques 63
Chapter 4: Mastering Technique 119

Part II: Training

Chapter 5: Developing Flexibility and Coordination 129
Chapter 6: Developing Speed, Strength, and Endurance 147
Chapter 7: Structuring Workouts 161
Chapter 8: Creating a Training Program 169
Chapter 9: Dance 191

Part III: Competition

Chapter 10: Composing a Routine 223
Chapter 11: Preparing for Competitions 233
Appendix: Barre Exercises 245

References 253
Index 255
About the Authors 261

Preface

> There is nothing more practical than a good theory.
> —K. Boltzmann

The phenomenal success of rhythmic gymnastics (RG) has made it the most important sport available for girls and women today. Thousands of gymnasts train for RG worldwide. Its popularity is due to its many benefits, such as the enjoyment of movement using hand apparatus set to music. It is an art in which the gymnast has the power to captivate an audience using her originality, flexibility, strength, and coordination.

Rhythmic gymnastics is a rapidly growing gymnastic discipline under the International Gymnastics Federation (FIG) umbrella. The FIG formally recognized this discipline in 1961, first as modern gymnastics, then as rhythmic sportive gymnastics, before finally addressing it as rhythmic gymnastics. Started as a sport in the Soviet Union during the 1940s, it became popular in Eastern European countries during the 1950s and was recognized by the FIG in 1961. RG World Championships have been conducted since 1963, and the Olympic Games have included RG since 1984.

RG is popular around the world with more than 40 nations participating in the annual RG World Championships. Gymnasts from European countries continue to dominate in RG competitions due to strong tradition and unparalleled development. Other countries welcome coaches from Russia, Ukraine, Bulgaria, and Belarus because of their special systems for training gymnasts, coaches, and judges.

The goal of this book is to acquaint readers with RG as a sport. It discusses specific exercise techniques, modern approaches to training management, and specific types of training for competitions. It is intended for active and student RG coaches and physical educators who want to expand their knowledge in this sport and make gymnasts' learning more meaningful. It will also help gymnasts' parents better understand rhythmic sportive gymnastics. Finally, senior gymnasts will find a wealth of interesting and helpful information on RG techniques and training.

This book summarizes theories, methodologies, methods, and coaches' trade secrets for training top RG gymnasts. We have carefully reviewed all the literature and experience available to us concerning both RG and coaching science to extract the most valuable information. We made every effort to ensure that our information is current to make it useful to practicing coaches.

This book consists of three parts. Part I, chapters 1 through 4, covers RG techniques, including body movements and handling of apparatus, based on the classifications developed by the authors. Part II, chapters 5 through 9, discusses athletic training, including fitness, workouts, training programs, and dance preparation. Part I, chapters 10 and 11, concerns RG competition, including the elements of artistic expression, how to prepare for competition, and the components of successful performances.

Nadejda Jastrjembskaia wrote chapters 1, 2, 3, 9, and 11. Yuri Titov wrote chapter 4. The authors worked together on chapters 5, 6, 7, 8, and 10.

Acknowledgments

We wish to thank Nadejda's husband, Jouri Jastrjembski, for his invaluable assistance with the preparation of this manuscript during the last four years, and her daughter, Kate, who served as Nadejda's RSG teaching subject.

We also wish to give special thanks to others who supported us: Dr. Zakaria Ahmad, University Kenbangsaam, Malaysia and President, Malaysian Gymnastic Federation; and N. Shanmuhgarajah, Secretary General of the Malaysian Gymnastic Federation; Teh Lah Hoong, former RSG Project Manager of the Malaysian Sports Council; as well as A. Shaprawi, officer; and Dato' Maslan, Director General, Malaysian Sports Council.

We are also grateful to Professor Ludmila Shapkova of P.F. Lesgaft's Academy of Physical Culture and Sport, St. Petersburg, for her feedback; and to coach Mazieva Galina, Honor Educator from Russia; ballet master, Kostromitina Elvira, former dancer; and officer Chaikovskaia Tatiana, Director, RSG Sports School, Kaliningrad, Russia for their special attention and care.

We also thank all the kind people at Human Kinetics, especially Laura Casey Mast and Martin Barnard. Special thanks also go to the USA Gymnastics Federation for their positive support.

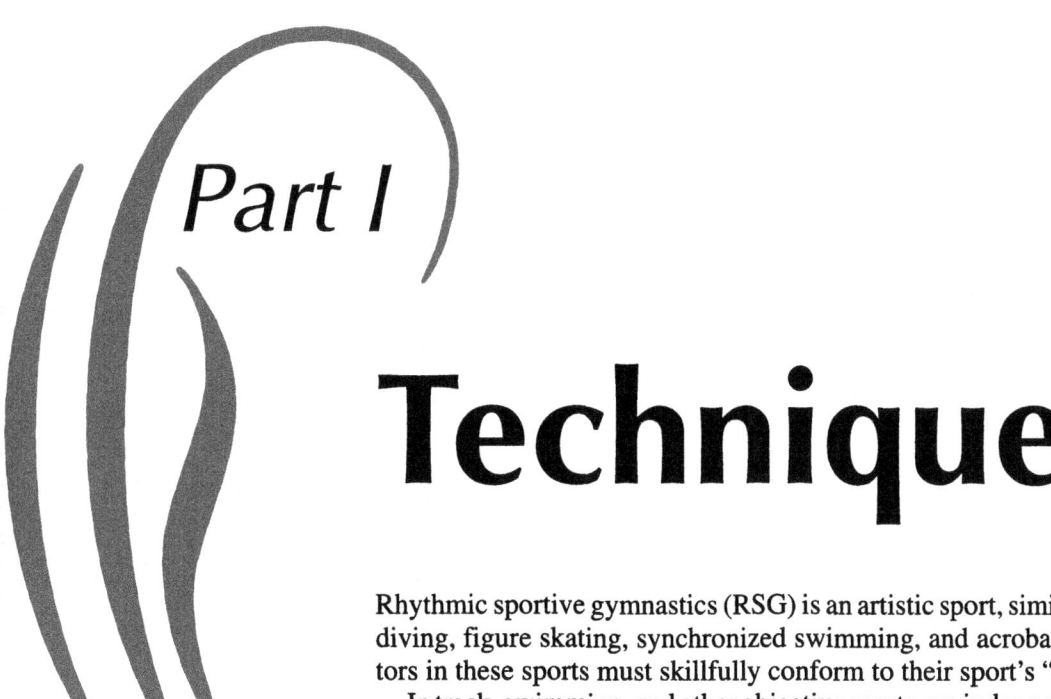

Part I

Technique

Rhythmic sportive gymnastics (RSG) is an artistic sport, similar to artistic gymnastics, diving, figure skating, synchronized swimming, and acrobatics. Successful competitors in these sports must skillfully conform to their sport's "Code of Points."

In track, swimming, and other objective sports, we judge a competitor's performance by the objective results. Of course, understanding "How did you run?" or "How did you swim?" is very important as well, but the results of the running or swimming remain paramount. In contrast, in artistic sports, the main questions are "What did you perform?" and "How did you perform?" Thus, technique is the main part of an athlete's training in artistic sports.

Developing technique is a very long and difficult process. It is vital to choose both the right elements to master and the correct way of performing them. Therefore, a coach must have up-to-date and accurate knowledge of technique to help the athlete succeed.

Of course, every artistic sport has its own particular techniques. Rhythmic sportive gymnastics involves two kinds of techniques: body movement and apparatus handling. The involvement of apparatus makes mastering RSG more difficult. These apparatus include the hoop, the ball, the clubs, the ribbon, and the rope. Each apparatus has its own history.

- The hoop became popular in the 1930s after a demonstration in the 1936 Olympic Games. The FIG recognized it as an RSG apparatus in 1963.
- The ball has been widely used in physical education since the 19th century. Participants included it in the first RSG World Championships in 1963.
- Of course, manipulating a rope is a very old children's activity. The FIG recognized its use in 1965. However, in 2011, the FIG decided to remove the use of rope in senior individual rhythmic gymnastics competitions.
- The ribbon on a bamboo stick is widely used in traditional Chinese dance. It became popular among RSG gymnasts in the 1940s, and participants first included it in the RSG World Championships program in 1971.
- Clubs were weapons and later a symbol of authority in Eastern Europe. Participants have used them as gymnastics apparatus since the mid-19th century. They have appeared in the RSG World Championships since 1973.

Rhythmic sportive gymnastics differs from other sports because it is specially designed for females. It is more oriented toward developing grace, smoothness, and connection with musical accompaniment than are other artistic sports. Therefore, participants may not include elements that require muscular strength or acrobatic exercises with flight in competitive compositions.

In part I, we will examine the basic components of RSG: developing technique (chapter 1); body movements (chapter 2); handling the apparatus (chapter 3); and mastering technique (chapter 4).

The Olympic History of Rhythmic Gymnastics

The Olympic debut of rhythmic gymnastics occurred in 1984 at the XXIII Olympic Games in Los Angeles, California, USA. The individual all-around competition included the hoop, ball, clubs, and ribbon. Lori Fung of Canada was awarded the gold medal with a final score of 57.950. (Until 1996, final scores were determined by adding the scores from the preliminary round to the scores awarded during the final round.) Doina Staiculescu of Romania won the silver medal, and Regina Weber of Germany won the bronze medal.

Spectators at the 1988 Olympic Games in Seoul, South Korea, witnessed a boost in scoring. Marina Lobatch of the USSR swept the preliminary and final rounds, scoring perfect 10s in all four apparatus (rope, hoop, clubs, and ribbon) in both rounds. She won the gold with a perfect score of 60.00. Adriana Dounavska of Bulgaria also scored four perfect 10s in the final round, but finished with the silver medal because of a 9.900 score in clubs in the preliminary round. The bronze medal was awarded to Alexandra Timochenko of the USSR, who also scored four perfect 10s in the final round, but was crippled by a 9.750 in the clubs in the preliminary round.

The judges at the 1992 Olympic Games in Barcelona, Spain, were not as generous. Bronze medalist in 1988, Alexandra Timochenko, now of the Ukraine, won the gold medal with a final score of 59.037. Carolina Pascual of Spain won the silver with a score of 58.100, and Oksana Skaldina of the Ukraine was awarded the bronze with a score of 57.912.

At the XXVI Olympic Games in Atlanta, Georgia, USA, in 1996, the scoring procedures were changed. For the first time in the Olympic Games, the preliminary scores were not added to the scores awarded in the final round. The individual all-around competition included the rope, ball, clubs, and ribbon. With a score of 39.683, Ekaterina Serebrianskaya of the Ukraine won the gold medal. Yana Batyrchina of Russia was the silver medalist with a final round score of 39.383. Elena Vitrichenko of the Ukraine, who would later sweep the 21st World Championships in 1997, won the bronze medal with a final round score of 38.365.

Group competition was added as a medal event for the 1996 Olympic Games in Atlanta. Nine countries (France, Spain, Belarus, China, Germany, Italy, Russia, Bulgaria, and the United States) competed in two group events, the five hoops competition and the three balls, two ribbons competition. Spain won the first Olympic gold medal awarded to a rhythmic gymnastics group with a final score of 38.933. The silver medal was awarded to Bulgaria for their score of 38.866. Russia won the bronze with a final score of 38.365.

Chapter 1
Developing Technique

A rhythmic sportive gymnast's movements in a competitive composition barely resemble the natural movements of walking, jumping, and running. Moreover, unlike natural movements, the gymnast executes her movements at various tempos and creates an optimum (sometimes maximum) display of physical abilities. In this chapter, we'll explore the various characteristics of motor activity, explain exercise technique, examine the structure of RSG exercises, and describe the kinematic, dynamic, and rhythmic characteristics of exercise technique.

Motor Activity

The exercises of RSG are complex as they involve coordinating different body parts with the apparatus: the ball, hoop, clubs, ribbon, and rope. Naturally, this complex coordination makes RSG difficult to master. Specifically, the gymnast must combine two motor tasks simultaneously. She must handle the apparatus while performing an element, moving various parts of her body. In this section, we will define the various components of an RSG composition and describe the characteristics the judges look for.

Composition Components

Many distinct components work together to create a successful RSG composition. Let's look at each closely.

Handling, or manipulation, is the coordination of the apparatus movement. It can involve the arms and other parts of the body, for example the leg, trunk, head, or neck.

An element is the shortest gymnastic exercise, as specified in RSG, that is complete. Each element consists of various movements by some part of the body (with or without apparatus) that form a particular shape. A movement is a change in the position of the body or one or more of its parts. A physical exercise is a system of movements used for the purposes of physical education and sport. An element is a physical exercise too, but it is specific to RSG and used in competitive compositions. Thus, in general, the term "physical exercise" is more widely used than "element." But in this book, we use "element" and "physical exercise" (or "exercise") interchangeably.

The connection of elements is usually a set of two or three consecutively and continuously performed elements. The combination of elements is the connection of a few different elements, usually longer than a connection, which the gymnast may perform with or without musical accompaniment.

A competitive RSG composition is the construction and performance of all elements by a gymnast. The composition reflects the characteristics of the musical accompaniment, adheres to the requirements of technical mastery as specified in the Code of Points, and creates a positive aesthetic impression (see chapter 10).

Specific Characteristics

The judges evaluate every element according to the following characteristics:

- degree of difficulty,
- apparatus mastery,
- rhythmic components,
- originality,
- virtuosity of performance

Degree of Difficulty

Difficulty of an element refers to the objective and subjective demands on the technical, physical, and psychological capabilities of a gymnast.

Technical Objective Difficulty We can define technical objective difficulty of an element by:

- the difficulty it presents in coordinating the movements to form an element;
- the tempo at which the gymnast performs the movements; and
- the combination of the movements to create a certain shape.

The judges rate the objective difficulties of elements according to the Code of Points.

Technical Subjective Difficulty The technical subjective difficulty of an element is determined by how much the element uses all the gymnast's physical and psychological abilities, including coordination, flexibility, power, speed, strength, and endurance. For example, a successful vertical back balance with the free leg in split position requires the gymnast to have developed vestibular stability (a sense of balance maintained by the middle ear), flexibility in the hips, and muscular strength in the stomach and back.

Psychological Difficulty The psychological difficulty of an element is determined by psychological intensity, which, of course, varies among individuals. This intensity subjectively influences a gymnast's performance. Psychological difficulty is influenced by the technical and physical difficulty of an element, the level of risk (the potential for dropping or tangling the apparatus), and the need for increased concentration.

Apparatus Mastery

Apparatus mastery refers to the flawless execution of apparatus handling together with body movements. Handling must be displayed in a variety of ways, such as in different directions, magnitudes, planes, levels, speeds or using different parts of the body. As a rule, the apparatus should be in constant motion and not handled as a decorative accessory. Points are also awarded to the performance of unusual or unique apparatus handling in conjunction with body movement that meets the criteria for apparatus mastery.

Rhythmic Components

Fundamentally, the discipline of rhythmic gymnastics uses dance elements to develop aesthetic expression and grace in the female body. (There are also several men's groups practising the discipline in Japan and a few other countries.) Out of respect for the essence of the discipline, the Code of Points has placed an emphasis on the rhythmic components, awarding points for series of rhythmic dance steps and deducting points when the rhythm and character of the music used are not harmonious with the movements of the gymnast.

Originality

Originality is the nonstandard construction of an element by moving the body, handling the apparatus, or both, differently. It requires an application of the gymnast's (or choreographer's) creativity to those elements found in the Code of Points. For example, constructing a jump currently not in use, or performing a standard jump in a different body position may offer an opportunity for the gymnast to gain significant points for originality upon the approval of the FIG RG Technical Committee. Originality can also come from a combination of elements rarely seen together.

Virtuosity

Virtuosity refers to the perfect performance of an element, including correct technique, form, apparatus handling, and amplitude. Non-conformance to these standards will result in the deduction of points under execution penalties. For example, the loss of balance during a pivot will result in the deduction of precious points.

Nutrition: Minerals

Minerals, a vital component of a gymnast's diet, promote growth and activity. Minerals have important and diverse functions.

Calcium and phosphorus are components of the bones, and phosphorus is found in every living cell of the body. Both are necessary for the heart, muscles, and nerves to work. The main sources for calcium and phosphorus are high protein milk products. A gymnast needs approximately 2 grams (2000 milligrams) of phosphorus and 1.2 grams (1200 milligrams) of calcium each day. Three one-cup servings of low-fat milk, plus one cup of low-fat yogurt, one-half cup of low-fat cottage cheese, or one ounce of cheese per day would supply 1200 mg of calcium and 1000 mg of phosphorus.

Sodium is necessary for the maintenance of fluid levels and occurs in animal products and kitchen salt. A gymnast needs about 2 grams (2000 milligrams) of sodium each day. That's less than one teaspoon in all foods consumed, all day long! Many foods have naturally occurring sodium in them, like milk, eggs, meats, cheese, and breads, so adding kitchen salt to foods isn't really necesssary!

Potassium alleviates water retention by helping remove excess water through the kidneys, regulates heartbeat, and sends oxygen to the brain. Potassium can be obtained from rye, wheat, beans, beets, tomatoes, and cheese. Many fruits are also good sources. Gymnasts need 2.5-5 grams (2500-5000 milligrams) each day. Eating one banana, one orange, four slices of whole wheat bread, one baked potato, one raw tomato, one raw carrot, and one green pepper would supply 2600 milligrams of potassium for one day.

Magnesium helps regulate proper nerve function and muscle contraction and assists in bone formation. Magnesium is a mineral particularly plentiful in raw green leafy vegetables, nuts, whole grains, milk, corn, and apples. A gymnast should have approximately 500 milligrams of magnesium each day. Three cups of low-fat milk, one cup of brown rice, one banana, one orange, and a five ounce fresh spinach salad would provide a gymnast with most of her magnesium for one day.

Iron helps to transfer oxygen to the muscles. Raisins, dried apricots, nuts, cacao, liver, dark meat poultry, and red meats are good sources of iron. A gymnast needs about 20-22 milligrams of iron each day. Four ounces of roast beef, two eggs, 1/3 cup raisins, 12 halves dried apricots, one cup cooked spinach, one cup cooked broccoli, and one cup kidney beans would provide a gymnast with 21 milligrams of iron for one day.

Exercise Element Technique

Each RSG exercise element has a certain inherent technique. An element technique means the method of its performance as expressed by a particular gymnast's movements. The essence of a technique is the gymnast correctly using her physical abilities to properly complete a particular element, such as catching the apparatus, leaping, or pivoting.

RSG element techniques are ways of performing movements that a gymnast subsequently incorporates into a whole system. The system is like a chain in which each link consists of one or several movements. Thus, the whole system is influenced by each individual movement.

Furthermore, the gymnast can execute each element in different ways. With only a few exceptions, however, only one way is technically correct, and that is the performance that gives the best result (a good shape). This best result is a beautiful, correct representation of the technique under the current standard, but beware: the standard may change in the future! The Code of Points describes the standards for RSG element techniques.

In practice, though, each gymnast uses her individual technique corresponding to the standard. To create individual technique, the coach and the gymnast have adapted the standard technique to the gymnast's own physical development and abilities, such as her height, her level of flexibility, and so on. Therefore, when the gymnast improves her physical, dance, and musical-motor abilities, her RSG element techniques will also improve.

Element Structure

Each element technique has its own basis and details. The basis of a technique is the exercise's movements, which determine its shape (form), distinguishing it from others. The basis of a technique develops from relatively independent phases: preparatory, main, and finishing.

In the preparatory phase, the technique is concerned with all the movements by the body and apparatus that prepare the way for realizing the main phase, for example, good speed or rotation, or both. For instance, a gymnast needs the preparatory phase to be ready to make the swinging movement necessary to throw an apparatus.

The main phase consists of all the movements accomplished, according to the objective of the element. Thus, in jumps and leaps, the objective is the gymnast's flight. In throwing an apparatus, the objective is the apparatus's flight.

In the finishing phase, the gymnast completes the movements she began to execute in the main phase. But not only does she conclude the main phase, she also changes her speed or direction of motion. For example, in landing from a jump or leap, the finishing phase consists of stopping the momentum and speed needed for the jump or leap. When elements are combined, the finishing phase creates the conditions necessary for performing subsequent elements. For example, when the gymnast catches the ball by rolling it over her arms, the finishing phase for catching consists of changing the direction of the ball's movement.

The details of a technique are concerned with the movements needed to best perform the element. For example, a gymnast can take off from both legs for a stag jump by swinging one or both arms. The details of technique are very important. They reflect the individual's level of mastery, which, in turn, affects her level of success. Thus, refining the details of a technique directly leads to perfecting performance.

Characteristics of Element Technique

We can describe element technique from several different angles. The kinematic point of view (from the Greek "kinema") concerns movement; the dynamic point of view (from the Greek "dinamis") concerns strength; and the rhythmic point of view (from the Greek "rhythmos") concerns alternating movements. In each of the following sections, we will examine each of these points of view.

Kinematic Characteristics

In RSG, an element executed by a gymnast must conform to certain standards specified in the Code

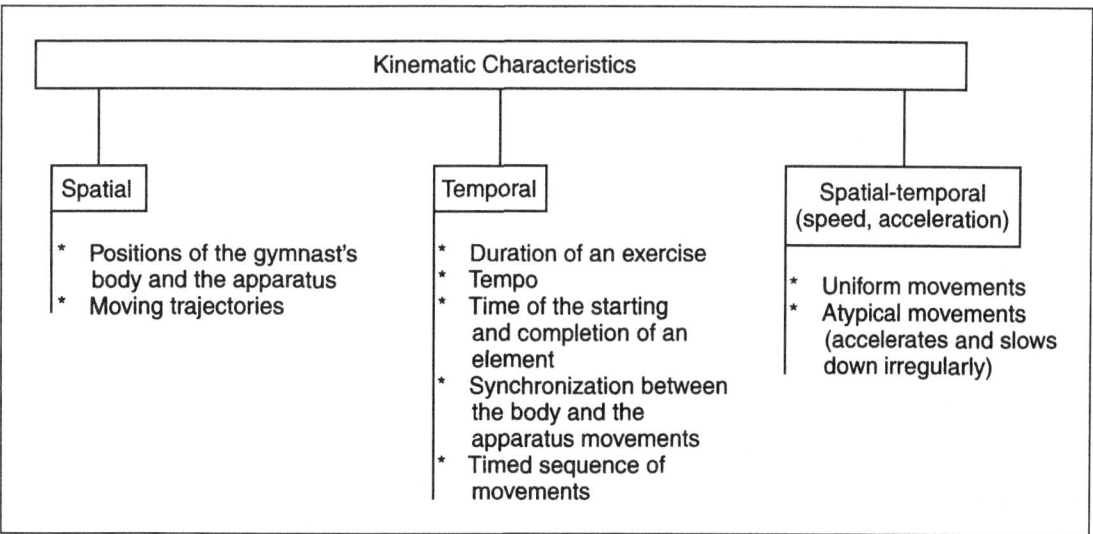

Figure 1.1 Kinematic characteristics of RSG elements.

of Points. When judging different gymnasts' performances, the base comparison lies in the kinematic characteristics, such as the body's position in space and the rhythm and tempo of movements (figure 1.1).

Spatial Characteristics The spatial characteristics of the apparatus and the gymnast's body while performing an element are determined by technique. Technique is influenced by the positions of the body (for example, shape or pose; see chapter 2) and apparatus as well as the moving trajectories of the body and apparatus.

The gymnast changes her poses many times during the execution of an element. These poses parallel the preparatory, main, and finishing phases of technique and involve the gymnast's positions within the element:

- The gymnast's location relative to a support such as the floor at the start of an element (the starting position [SP]).
- The gymnast's location relative to a support during an element; the shape of the element must be fixed by the gymnast and well-defined.
- The gymnast's location relative to a support at the conclusion of an element.

Before performing an element, the gymnast and her apparatus should be in the starting position that creates the best preconditions for executing an element. The positions of the body and the apparatus and their changes during an element should correspond to the Code of Points, biomechanics laws, and the aesthetic requirements of RSG.

The moving trajectory means the path of the total center of gravity (TCG) and the centers of gravity of each part of the body and the apparatus. The characteristics of a moving trajectory are its form and direction. The form of a trajectory is either rectilinear, following a straight line (such as a vertical jump), or curvilinear, following a curved line (such as a circular arm movement). The direction of the moving trajectory is defined relative to the gymnast's initial orientation (facing forward, backward, sideways, upward, downward, or oblique). In training, a gymnast and her coach may determine directions for movements with the help of external spatial reference points (visual marks), for example, by noting sections of the gym or by suspending apparatus.

Temporal Characteristics The temporal aspect of kinematic characteristics of RSG elements are the duration, tempo, timing of starting and completion, coordination between the various movements of the body parts and apparatus, and sequencing of movements.

Duration of element is the time from the first movement in the preparatory phase to the last one in the finishing phase. The duration must be enough for fixing and defining the necessary shape during the main phase. The Code of Points defines special requirements for the duration of some balances, requiring a minimum of one second.

Tempo, from the Latin *tempus*, meaning time, is the degree of quickness in a movement and the quantity of movements in a unit of time. The tempo of movements of the body part or apparatus depends upon its weight: the heavier the body part, the slower the tempo. The quickest movements are made by the fingers and wrists; slower movements are made by the shoulders and elbows; and the slowest movements, by the trunk. The tempo of a movement can be at the minimum or maximum capability of the joint. As such, each gymnast has her own physical abilities, yet each element has an optimum tempo associated with it. Thus, the tempo ranges between the minimum and maximum according to the gymnast's abilities.

Timing of the beginning and end of an element, or starting and finishing properly according to a cue or musical accompaniment, is very important when performing compositions, because musical accompaniment is recorded and therefore cannot be changed midexercise.

Coordination between the body and apparatus movements is crucial. Every movement must start only at an optimum time during an element. Early or late movements may change the other kinematic characteristics, possibly leading to errors.

Sequence of movements refers to following the standard order of movements of an element, thereby affecting timing. For example, a change in the order may result in a change in the shape of an element.

Spatial-Temporal Characteristics The spatial-temporal characteristics of RSG exercises are expressed in terms of speed and changing of speed.

The speed of a movement is determined by the amount of time it takes for certain parts of the body, the whole body, or an apparatus to move through space; it can be either uniform or nonuniform.

We refer to the change of speed in a unit of time as acceleration (increased speed) or deceleration (decreased speed). Movements without abrupt changes of speed are referred to as smooth. But fast movements with significant changes of speeds are referred to as abrupt (or sharp). The gymnast should be capable of changing the speed of her movements. She should be able to differentiate between movements that are executed slowly and those that are not. Indeed, a gymnast should seldom execute the different movements comprising an element at a constant speed. More often than not, proper execution requires a gymnast to combine decelerating and accelerating certain parts of the body while performing the total element.

Dynamic Characteristics

We can divide the dynamic characteristics of biomechanical forces and inertia that affect the movements of the gymnast into internal and external components (for instance, when outspread arms decelerate a pivot). The internal forces (the pull of the muscles and ligaments) and inertia (arising from the mass and position of body limbs) include the following:

- reaction of a support (e.g., the upward force of the floor),
- gravity,
- friction,
- external environmental resistance (e.g., air resistance), and
- inertia due to the mass of the apparatus.

Interaction of internal and external forces and inertia creates the dynamic structure of an exercise. The efficiency of a technique in RSG is determined by how well the gymnast uses these internal and external forces and inertia. A number of rules laid down in the science of biomechanics specify the effective use of these forces in combination with inertia. Thus, knowledge of biomechanics will help a gymnast perform the RSG exercises efficiently. But even top level gymnasts differ in how skillfully they use these forces, affecting technique and therefore their performances.

Rhythmic Characteristics

Rhythmic characteristics form a complex aspect of the technique of an RSG element. Indeed, the term "rhythm" itself has various meanings. For example, while the layman may only think of rhythm in relationship to music, rhythm is also present in the emotions of a gymnast and in her compositions, such as mood changes in a gymnast following a rhythmic pattern.

The essence of rhythm in an RSG element consists of alternating active muscular tension with less tension in other groups of muscles. But don't confuse rhythm in this sense with tempo, which is the frequency of movements within a certain length of time. Rhythm, as a complex characteristic of technique, reflects the natural order of distribution of efforts in time and space as well as the degree of the increase and decrease of muscular change in the movement.

Ultimately, the rhythm of an element unites the rhythm of movements in all phases. So—not surprisingly—if rhythm is optimal, it promotes superior performance. Likewise, the wrong rhythm can cause inferior performance. But if an element is repeated many times by a gymnast, she can recognize and optimize the rhythm. In summary, an optimal rhythm reflects the best increase and decrease of efforts and the optimal duration of phases in tensing and relaxing the muscles alternately.

The technique of RSG elements, such as jumps, leaps, and throws of the apparatus, is built on the continuous escalation of the capacity of the movements, culminating in the main phase of an element. At the same time, a gymnast might modify the rhythm in an element that changes according to external conditions (such as the rhythm of throwing a hoop or ribbon) simply by virtue of the physical characteristics of the apparatus.

Although an optimal range or objective limit to the rhythm in each movement exists, within this range the gymnast can apply her own optimum rhythm to perform the element at her best. In this way, every gymnast finds her own optimal individual performance rhythm.

Summary

In this chapter, we have discussed the avenues along which a gymnast may develop technique in RSG. We have examined the various aspects of motor activity, including the components of composition, and the specific components of individual exercise technique, including exercise structure and particular characteristics of exercise technique (kinematic, dynamic, and rhythmic). Every part of an individual element occurs in a logical chain. Thus, perfecting one aspect helps perfect the others in the chain. In chapter 2, we will take this discussion further as we look at body elements and the physics behind them.

Chapter 2

Body Movements

A gymnast performs the elements of body movements (also called freehand, or without apparatus) with all or part of her body. These elements, together with the elements with apparatus, form the essence of RSG as a sport. Therefore, we can consider all freehand elements to be the basis of RSG elements. In this chapter, we will describe the basic types of freehand elements, including jumps and leaps, balances, turns and pivots, body waves and swings, and modal (linking) elements. First, however, we will discuss the basic characteristics of all body movements, including how they are classified in RSG and their essential principles.

Characteristics of Body Movements

The elements of body movements include all possible body actions that are suitable for rhythmic sportive gymnastics: jumps, leaps, balances, turns, pivots, waves, swings, steps, poses, rolls, some handstands, crawling, and so on. Each of these kinds of movement has its own distinct technique.

Classification of Body Movements

We can classify body movements in many different ways. One way is represented in the Code of Points, which is intended to create more objective judging in competitions by defining and classifying difficult RG elements. The Code of Points splits all body movements into body movement groups (jumps and leaps, balances and rotations) and other groups including dance step combinations, dynamic elements (with rotation and throw), and mastery elements. The Code of Points further divides all elements from the body movement groups into various levels of difficulty with values ranging from 0.1 to 0.5. The Code of Points allows multiple rotations and mixed difficulty, wherein two or more movements with differing value of difficulty are performed. Repetition of the same difficulty in a competitive routine is not tolerated except in certain cases such as successive leaps or jumps. The Code of Points, however, is not exhaustive and does not include many of the simpler RG movement elements in its list.

In contrast, this book includes all elements of body movements in the educational classification. Thus, it is wider than the Code of Points, describing more elements. The objective of educational classification is to understand the technique of elements from the teaching point of view coaches and gymnasts themselves need to assume.

Educational classification is based on two educational and biomechanical principles, dividing all elements of body movements into two large groups (basic and modal) according to their significance in compositions and describing elements according to the body support in the main phase.

The following groups of elements are basic elements because they function independently in compositions (figure 2.1):

- Jumps and leaps
- Balances
- Turns and pivots
- Body waves and swings
- Floor elements (rolls, walkovers, cartwheels, passing supports, grovels, turns, lying positions, and so on)

We can divide all basic elements into two general groups, depending on what support the element needs from different parts of the body. The first group includes all basic elements performed while supported by the legs, whether standing or kneeling. In turn, we can further divide the basic elements with leg support into subgroups according to the characteristics of the main phase:

- The main phase does not have contact with the floor (jumps and leaps).
- The main phase has contact with the floor:
  — One or both legs do not move relative to the floor (balances).
  — One or both legs move on the floor and form the axis for body rotation (turns and pivots).
  — One or both legs move on the floor without rotation (body waves and swings).

The second group of basic elements are those whose main phase involves contact with the floor but are supported by different parts of the body other than the legs (but note that this group may include combination elements involving leg support).

- Static body position (floor balancing).
- Dynamic (moving) body position:
  — With rotation (rolls, passing supports, grovels, turns).
  — Without rotation (jumps, lying positions, slides, wave-like motions).

Modal, or linking, elements include poses (starting and finishing), traveling (running and walking),

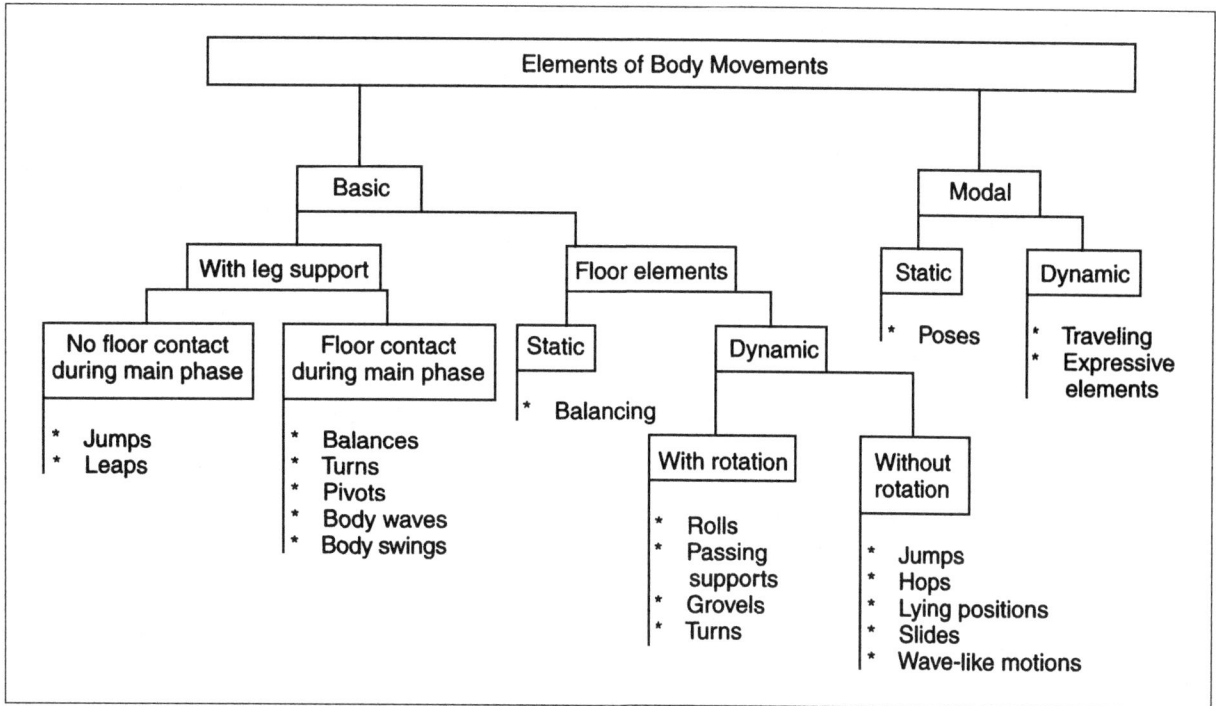

Figure 2.1 Classification of body movement elements.

and expressive elements (arm waves and swings), all of which function as connective and expressive elements. There are two groups of modal elements, which, once again, we can classify according to the characteristics of the main phase:

- Static main phase (poses)
- Dynamic main phase
  — Traveling
  — Expressive movements

Keep in mind as you study this book that we will describe all elements of body movements according to the aspects of educational classification we have outlined in this section.

Essential Principles of Body Movements

Rhythmic sportive gymnasts must perform all elements of body movements in the gymnastic style (figure 2.2), which consists of the following:

- Demonstration of correct shape (pose);
- Both legs turned outward;
- Correct stand on toes, if the gymnast is using toes for support of the element;

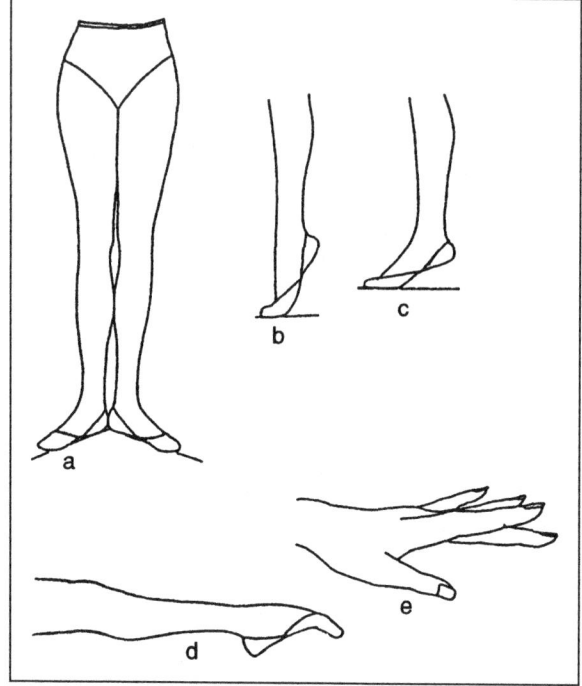

Figure 2.2 Body positions in the gymnastic style: (a) turned-out feet, (b) stand on high toes, (c) stand on low toes, (d) straight line of the leg with pointed toe, (e) poised hand.

- Straight line of the leg if necessary to give the element a good shape;
- Correct body posture if an erect position is necessary for good shape; and
- Good amplitude.

Each element of body movement differs from others due to its pose, or shape, which must be demonstrated by a gymnast during the performance. The shape, or pose, is the arrangement of the body parts (legs, arms, head, and trunk) relative to the floor (support). The purpose of each RSG element is to hold the gymnast's body in a certain pose—to demonstrate the shape relative to the floor. Poses may be static or dynamic. The static shapes or proper poses (from the Greek "statike" meaning "standing") are poses in which the body remains in a fixed position. Dynamic shapes are poses in which the body parts move along given trajectories with a certain speed to demonstrate the shape.

Rhythmic sportive gymnasts must perform practically all elements of body movements with turn-out leg positions. Turn-out (figure 2.2a) means a rotation outward of the legs at the hips. Coaches should focus on having gymnasts rotate their legs from their hips, because gymnasts often turn out only their feet and shins, leaving their thighs and knees rotating inward. For further discussion of turn-out, see Classical Drills in chapter 9.

A correct stand on toes is necessary to perform an element correctly. There are two types of stands on toes, a high stand on toes (figure 2.2b), for which the gymnast lifts her heel to the maximum so the foothold and area of support are smaller than in a low stand on toes, and a low stand on toes (figure 2.2c), for which the gymnast lowers her heel so the foothold and the area of support is greater than in a high stand on toes.

Rhythmic sportive gymnasts perform practically all RSG elements using the high stand on toes. That is why the term "stand on toes" is understood in RSG as "stand on high toes." The high stand on toes is used more widely because it is more aesthetically pleasing because the high stand on toes produces a straight line of the leg, making the body look tight.

The gymnast must distribute her body weight between both legs equally when she stands on high toes. The first three toes must press equally on the floor. The center of gravity remains between the heels and the middle of the support area. For more information, see the section on *relevé* in chapter 9.

Straight line of the leg (figure 2.2d) means that the knee does not project above the thigh and shin, but "drowns" in. This requires good knee flexibility.

Pointed toes (figure 2.2d) result when the gymnast straightens and rounds her instep, keeps her toes straight, and tightens her shin, ankle, and foot. The toes should be grouped around the third toe. The common mistakes with pointed toes are grouping around the first toe, lowering the braced big toe, turning in the foot, and relaxing the shin and ankle. To prevent this last mistake, the coach should check for sufficient tightening of the gymnast's Achilles tendon as often as possible.

In the poised hand position (figure 2.2e), the gymnast closes her middle finger and thumb and barely lifts up her little finger.

Correct body posture, or body alignment (figure 2.3a), in a vertical (erect) position results when the back of the head, shoulder blades, buttocks, and heels are aligned. The shoulders and shoulder blades must be in two parallel lines (figure 2.3b). The gymnast should tighten her stomach muscles and buttocks.

The amplitude of elements refers to the ability to perform to the highest degree of flexibility in the

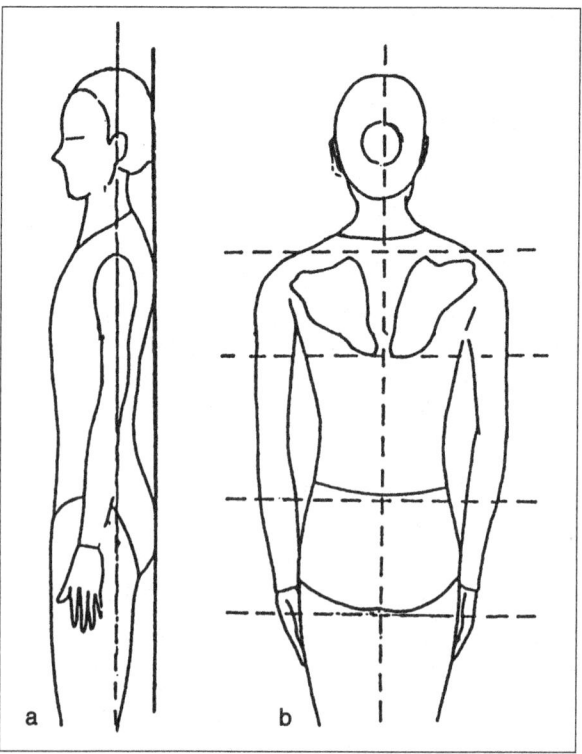

Figure 2.3 Correct body alignment: (a) from the side, (b) from the back.

involved joint or joints. The spine and hips display exceptional amplitude when performing RSG elements. See chapter 5 for more details on flexibility.

Basic Body Movements

Now, we will look more closely at what each of the basic elements of body movements entails. We will carefully note the phases, essential principles, and classification of performing each element. Then, we will outline the specific techniques of selected examples of each element to help the reader better understand and apply the information.

Jumps and Leaps

In RSG, proper jumps and leaps refer to elements of body movements in certain dynamic poses in the unsupported position (flight) after a takeoff from one or both legs. The gymnast can lift her body over the support at takeoff. We call jumps or hops involving takeoff from other parts of the body, mostly from the buttocks, floor jumps or hops.

What are the differences between jumps and leaps from one or both legs? Jumps direct their takeoff power mainly upward. So, more often than not, a gymnast takes off from both legs from a place on the floor, mount, or preliminary vertical jump. That is why the body flight trajectories are steep. In contrast, leaps direct their takeoff power away from the vertical—upward and forward, sideways, or backward. Gymnasts usually leap by taking off from one leg and swinging with the other leg. In such leaps, the body flight trajectories are much more curved (figure 2.4).

Essential Principles of Jumps and Leaps

RSG jumps and leaps have three phases: preparatory, main, and finishing. The distribution of the gymnast's attention during each phase of jumping and leaping is not equal. Attention is higher during approach and flight and lower during takeoff and landing. This is because, naturally, a better preparatory phase helps the gymnast better control her movements during flight. She usually takes off and lands automatically.

Preparatory Phase We can divide the preparatory phase of a jump or leap into two parts: the preliminary subphase and the takeoff subphase. Both work together to create the best possible conditions for the jump or leap itself.

Preliminary Subphase The preliminary subphase consists of the movements preceding the takeoff. A proficient preliminary subphase promotes a quality performance. The preliminary subphase should begin with a semisquat (the spring movement) before the takeoff. To increase the height of the flight, the gymnast can use a mount (or mount after the approach), as in figure 2.5a, illustration 2, or a vertical jump (or the vertical jump from the approach), as in figure 2.5b, illustration 2, before the semisquat (illustration 3, both a and b). These movements are essential for providing the gymnast with the amount of momentum that she needs to achieve high elevation.

Figure 2.4 Body flight trajectories: jumps and leaps.

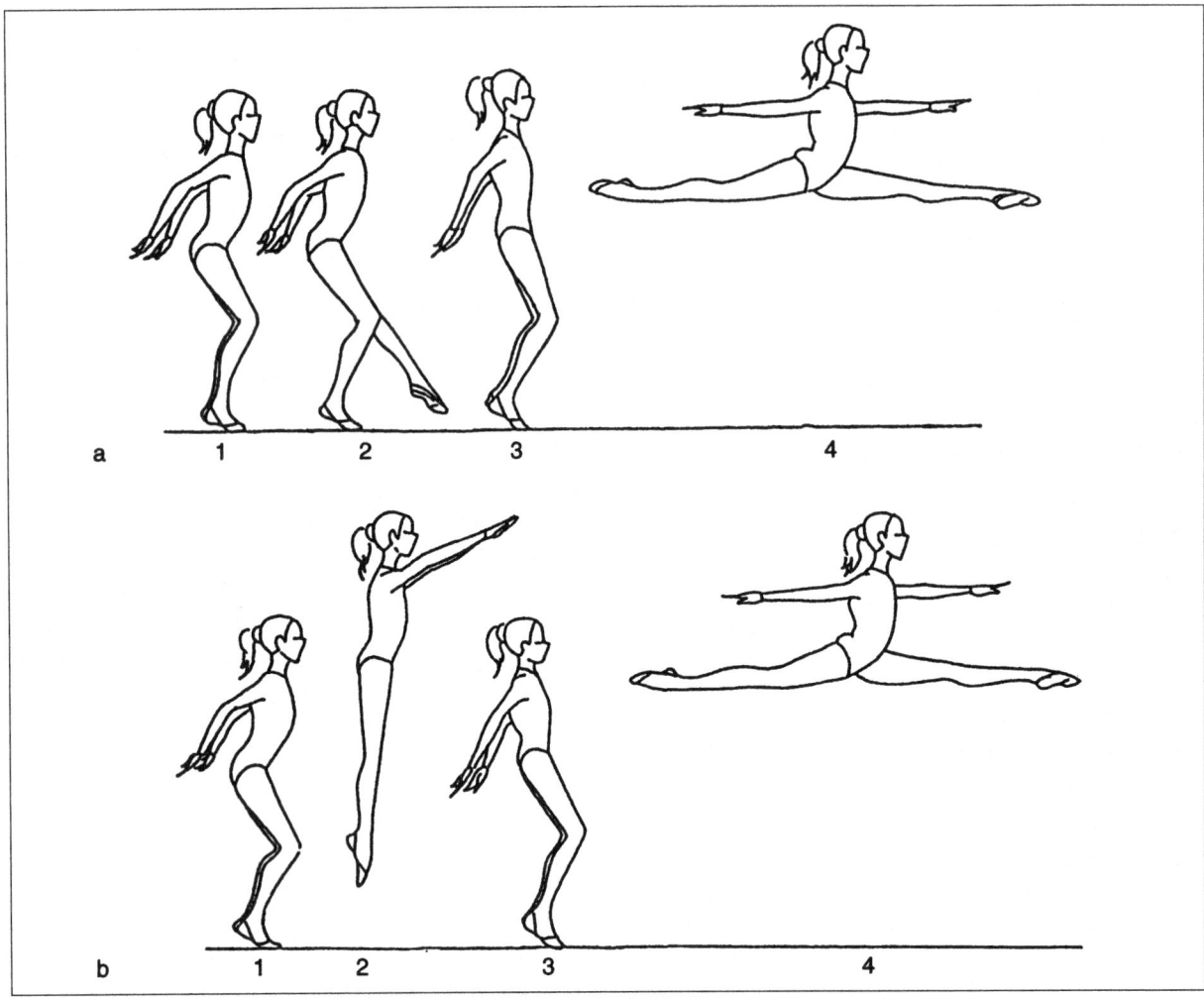

Figure 2.5 Preliminary subphase of jumps and leaps: (a) the mount, (b) the vertical jump.

During the semisquat, the gymnast should press her heel very fast into the floor in an elastic manner to quickly transfer her body weight. Passing the body weight through the heel during takeoff produces high elevation for the following reasons: it gives a larger surface from which to take off than the ball of the foot alone, and the Achilles tendon is forced to perform to the maximum extent of which it is capable, both in stretching and then contracting fully.

Gymnasts use various approach steps including dance (such as the gallop or the polka), running, and vertical jumps. Of course, the approach speed influences the power of the takeoff. In RSG, the best approach is of average intensity. The mount and the vertical jumps are the low preliminary jumps before the main jump or leap. The gymnast executes the mount (figure 2.5a) by swinging one leg and subsequently taking off from the other leg, connecting both legs in flight and landing onto both legs simultaneously. The gymnast then takes off from both legs for a gymnastic jump or leap. She may also use a vertical jump with both legs as a preliminary jump (figure 2.5b).

In any case, the gymnast finishes the preliminary subphase with a semisquat (figure 2.5, illustration 3 for both a and b), during which the muscles are spread, ready for active contraction in the takeoff subphase.

Certainly, the semisquat is very important. Indeed, the height of a jump or leap depends on the depth of the semisquat. Increasing the depth of the semisquat, up to the optimal value, increases the height of the jump or leap, although too great a semisquat decreases the resulting height.

The most important factor in semisquat depth is the angle of the knees. For top level gymnasts, the semisquat depth is less than for beginners. The optimal semisquat depth is 112 degrees—the gymnast should squat to 93 percent of her full height. Varying more than 20 degrees from the optimum reduces the resulting height.

Semisquat depth also depends on the strength of the leg flexor muscles. We recommend classical ballet drills to strengthen these muscles. Gymnasts frequently err by taking off from their heels before they are able to perform the semisquat at an optimal level. This reduces the height of the jump or leap. To correct this error, the gymnast may perform a *demi-plié* (see chapter 9).

Takeoff Subphase The takeoff subphase gives the gymnast's center of gravity vertical speed, resulting in its rise. The greater this speed, the greater the flight's height. The takeoff begins with a change in the angle of the hips, followed by the knees, and finally the ankles. The foot leaves the floor starting with the heel and finishing with the tips of the toes. At this moment, the gymnast must straighten her legs and stretch her toes. The gymnast must focus all her efforts on her foot (or feet), because strong foot muscles help create strong takeoffs. Thus, the height of the jump or leap depends on the strength and elasticity of the leg muscles, the foot and knee ligaments, and the Achilles tendon. A great jump or leap requires the gymnast to perform a takeoff precisely, strongly, quickly, and in the right direction.

The efficiency of the jump or leap depends on coordinating the leg and arm movements. The arms should help the gymnast form "wings" as well as provide momentum for an effective takeoff. As a rule, beginners are not able to use swinging movements of the arms effectively. Instead, their arms "run" ahead or behind their takeoffs. Keep in mind that the higher the jump or leap, the stronger the arm swing needed. Moreover, during takeoff it is very important to hold the trunk in the correct position with tightened back muscles, especially in the lower back.

Biomechanics research (Lazarenko, 1991) shows that there are three types of takeoffs (figure 2.6):

- The elastic takeoff (figure 2.6a) has the single-peaked form and a short time of takeoff; $t_{takeoff} = 0.15 - 0.26$ seconds.
- The powerful takeoff (figure 2.6b) has a wide double-peaked form and a greater time of takeoff; $t_{takeoff} = 0.31 - 0.42$ seconds.
- The intermediate takeoff (figure 2.6c) is an unstable form.

A scientific study by Lazarenko (1991) found that members of the USSR national team used the steady elastic form for takeoffs. Their average takeoff time ($t_{takeoff}$) was 0.234 seconds, and their average flight time (t_{fl}) was 0.520 seconds. The same study found that the dynamics of less-proficient gymnasts (1st Grade) were unstable (intermediate takeoff); their average takeoff time was 0.283 seconds, and their average flight time was 0.456 seconds.

RSG encompasses two main kinds of takeoff: the takeoff from two legs and the takeoff from one leg while swinging the other. But a gymnast may execute several jumps and leaps, such as the stag leap and jump, with either kind of takeoff.

Main Phase (Flight) As mentioned, the duration and height of the flight are mainly determined by the takeoff subphase. The shape of the jump or leap, however, also affects height. The more difficult the shape, the greater the time of takeoff, and the time of flight decreases. The flight duration of the high jumps and leaps is close to 0.5 seconds. A gymnast performs higher jumps from a mount. In contrast, she performs lower leaps from an approach, because she can execute them while moving forward. By knowing the time of the flight, it is possible to calculate the increase in height (elevation) of the gymnast's center of gravity:

$$H = \frac{g \cdot t_{rise}}{2}$$

Here H is height of elevation (meters), g is the acceleration due to gravity (meters per second), and t_{rise} is the time taken to rise (seconds).

As can be seen from the formula, a large flight height results from a lengthy duration of rising, which, in turn, results in a greater flight time and a correspondingly greater opportunity for the gymnast to establish her pose during flight. In flight, the gymnast reaches a necessary shape at first (rising time) (figure 2.7, illustration 6), then demonstrates it (illustrations 7-9) and prepares for landing (illustration 10). The duration of the shape depends on the duration of the flight and the time taken to reach the pose. The less time lost in reaching the pose (takeoff time), the more time there is for demonstrating this shape in flight, which is what will be evaluated by the judges. The time taken to reach the pose can only be reduced by increasing the speed of the center of gravity at takeoff.

Not surprisingly, arm movements help produce additional elevation during flight. Normally, when

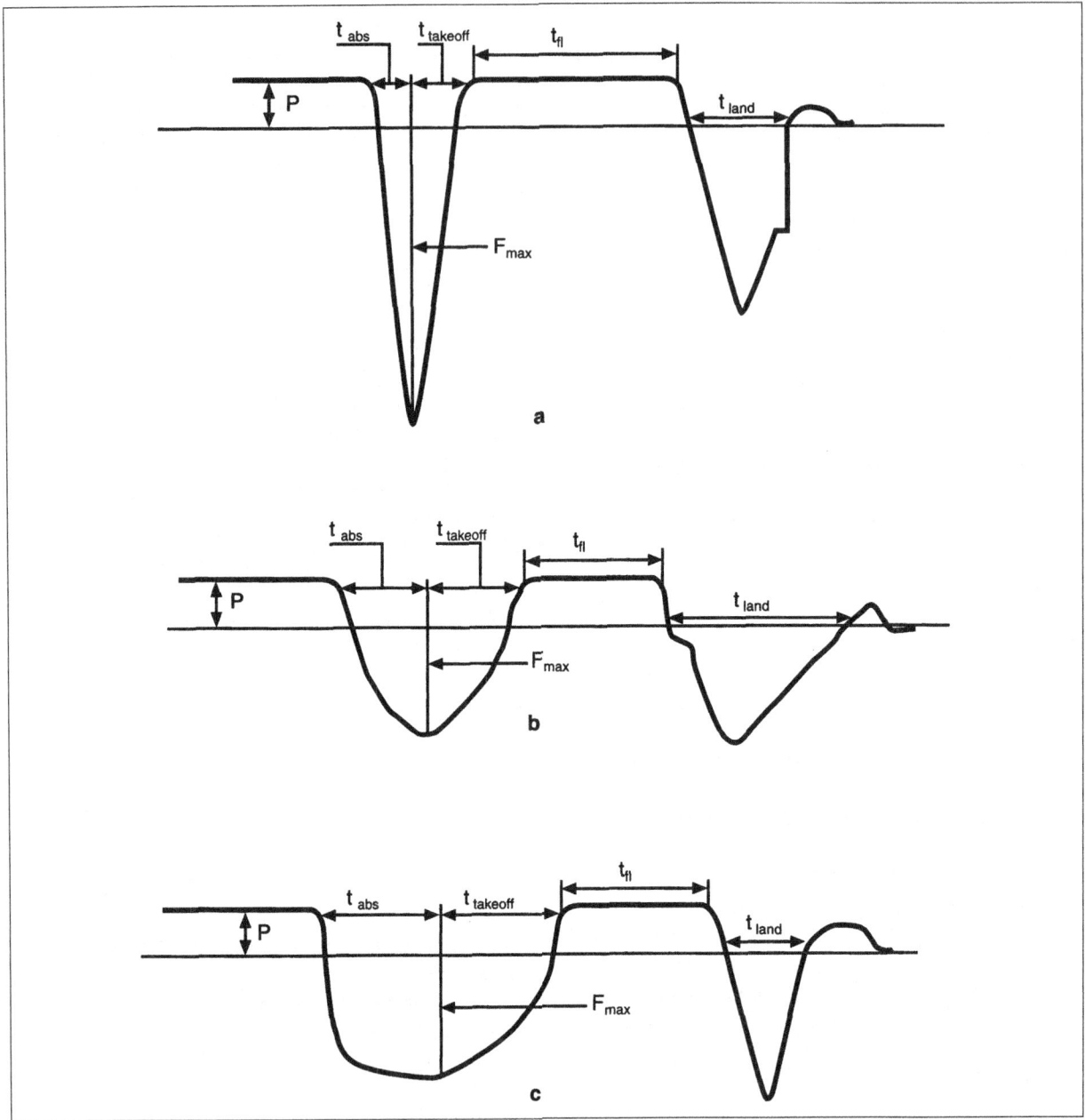

Figure 2.6 Sample dynamograms for different types of takeoff: (a) elastic, (b) powerful, (c) intermediate; P marks the preparatory phase, t_{abs} is the time of semisquat, F_{max} shows maximum force, $t_{takeoff}$ is the time of takeoff, t_{fl} is the time of flight, and t_{land} is the time of landing.

From "Quantitative Evaluation of the Qualitative Parameters of Jumps and Leaps Preparation in RSG" by Lazarenko, T. (1991). Unpubl. doct. diss., Moscow. Reprinted by permission.

the legs are split, the arms are open and to the sides, or one in front and the other to the side. When the legs are closed, the arms are more often in front. At the same time, however, the gymnast should avoid tension in her upper body. Keep in mind that well-controlled yet tension-free arms give the impression of freedom and airiness.

During flight, the gymnast should tighten her leg muscles and point her toes. She should be especially careful to control the tightening of her buttocks and to turn out her upper legs as far as possible. A gymnast can control her body position during flight very well, but controlling the amplitude of movements during flight is more difficult.

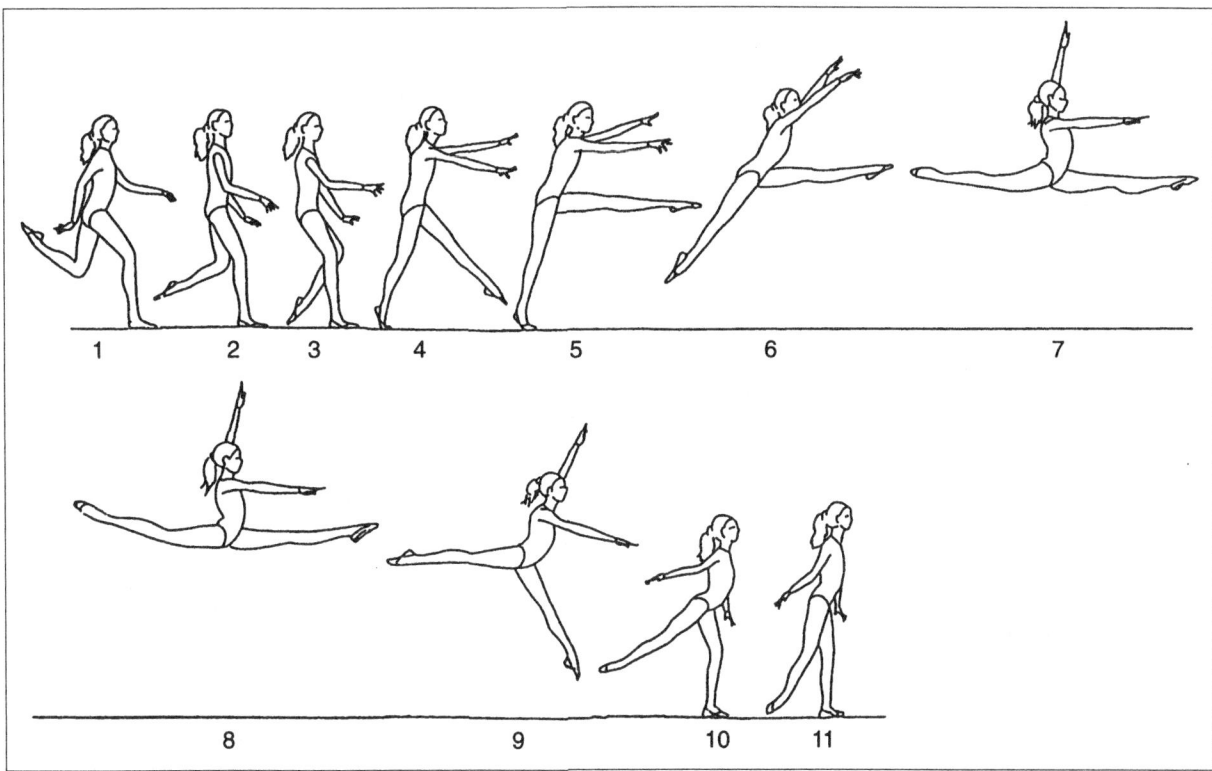

Figure 2.7 The split leap.

Finishing (Landing) Phase The purpose of this phase of the jump or leap is to decrease the speed that the gymnast has acquired. Specifically, the kinetic energy accumulated up to the moment of landing is dissipated by the shock-absorbing properties of the gymnast's musculoskeletal system and the floor (figure 2.7, illustration 10). Stability during the landing depends upon the trajectory of the gymnast's body during the flight, the gymnast's ability to correct an inaccurate landing with her arms, head, and trunk movements, and her leg muscle strength. Of course, poor landing technique and hard floors increase the load on the gymnast's musculoskeletal system.

The gymnast should achieve a soft, springy, silent landing by rolling from her toes to her heels. She should gently bend her knees, then quickly straighten them. In this way, a good landing reduces the negative acceleration arising at the moment of floor contact and eases the abrupt impact.

It is easier to land on two legs in a semisquat than to land on one leg. To use only one leg, the gymnast needs both strong and elastic leg muscles to maintain her stability. Furthermore, landing after several jumps or leaps repeated in fast tempo is also difficult.

It comes as no surprise that the landing phase presents the greatest risk of injury in a jump or leap. It is thought that 34 percent of all gymnastics injuries (including nonflight elements) occur during a landing. To help her learn to protect herself, the gymnast must pay attention to the sounds of landing. A knock (heavy landing) indicates poor absorption of force, which could negatively affect the gymnast's motor system.

Classification of Jumps and Leaps

Several methods exist for classifying jumps and leaps. The traditional method is based on describing the takeoff and landing. This method defines three main groups of jumps and leaps: takeoff from both legs landing on both legs, takeoff from one leg landing on the same leg, and takeoff from one leg landing on the opposite (swinging) leg. Other possible combinations include the takeoff from both legs with landing on one leg and the takeoff from one leg with landing on both legs.

We use a different classification method in this book (table 2.1). It is based on analyzing the pose during the flight phase. The following shapes may be used by a gymnast in flight:

- Vertical trunk and leg positions.
- Vertical trunk with change of flexed legs at the hips (cat jump).
- Vertical trunk with change of stretched legs (scissors jump).
- Vertical trunk with flexed legs at the hip joint (tuck jump).
- Vertical trunk with one leg stretched, other leg bent (Cossack jump).
- Vertical trunk with one leg stretched vertically, other leg flexed at the knee (hop).
- Arched body position with stretched legs (arch jump).
- Vertical or leaned trunk with stretched and bent legs (*cabriole*).
- Bent trunk with stretched legs (pike).
- Vertical or leaned trunk with separated legs below horizontal (straddle or stride).
- Vertical trunk with a half-split position (stag).
- Ring position (ring).
- Split position (split).
- Vertical body with one leg vertical and the other horizontal (open).
- Horizontal trunk with a change of stretched legs (butterfly).

Analyzing the flight-phase poses reveals six main movements from which it is possible to compose any dynamic shape in the flight phase:

- Hip (step) amplitude
- Legs bending-extending at the knees
- Legs bending-extending at the hips
- Trunk position
- Leg movement during flight
- Turning movements

Knowing these movements, it is possible to construct a jump or leap even if it is not now in use. To be even more creative, each movement can be varied as shown in figure 2.8.

Knowing the various jump and leap movements will help the coach develop a harmonious system of jump and leap training, moving from the easy to the difficult by changing some movements. Here are a few in more detail.

- Hip (step) amplitude (figure 2.8a) may range from absent to anatomical maximum or minimum.
- The legs bending-extending at the knees (figure 2.8b) may have a large range of amplitudes. The leg can be fully straightened, bent about 90 degrees, bent less than 90 degrees, or fully bent. Combining bending-extending at the knees of both legs creates a large variety of movements.
- The bending-extending at the hips (figure 2.8c) has four main variations: maximum bending, bending about 45 degrees, vertical leg position, and maximum extension.
- The trunk position (figure 2.8d) is characterized by the bend forward, the vertical position, the back bend, and the side bend.
- In flight the gymnast can execute additional movements with her legs (figure 2.8e): she may change legs or one leg may contact the other.
- In the jump and leap, a gymnast can turn vertically at the axis, usually from 90 to 360 degrees. Some jumps, for example, vertical ones, can be executed with greater rotation (turns in the vertical plane, figure 2.8f).

Techniques of Selected Jumps and Leaps

Rhythmic sportive gymnasts most commonly use one of three poses during flight: the split position, the ring position, or the stag position.

The split position requires the following:

- The legs are apart and aligned with each other.
- The legs are horizontal to the floor.
- The legs are straightened with drawn-in knees.
- A fixed-split position during flight, allowing clear evaluation of the split position.
- A vertical trunk position.

The ring position requires the following:

- The thigh is higher than horizontal.
- The knee is slightly turned out and bent under at an obtuse angle.
- The shin is held upward and slightly turned outward.
- The back of the head meets the knee or middle of the shin.
- The spine is fully arched backward.
- The shoulders are aligned.
- The head is tilted back fully.

TABLE 2.1
Classification of Jumps and Leaps in Rhythmic Sportive Gymnastics

Shape in flight (position)	Type of jump or leap	Type of takeoff (one or both legs)
Vertical	Vertical jump on the spot or with traveling	Both
	Vertical jump with a half- or full-turn	Both
Cat	Front or back cat jump	One
	Front or back cat jump with a half- or full-turn	One
Scissors	Front or back scissors jump	One
	Front or back scissors jump with a half- or full-turn	One
Tuck	Tuck jump	Both
	Tuck jump with a half- or full-turn	Both
Cossack	Front or side Cossack jump	One, both
	Front or side Cossack jump with a half- or full-turn	One, both
Hop	Front or side hop jump	One
	Front or side hop jump with a half- or full-turn	One
Arch	Arched jump	Both
	Arched jump with a half- or full-turn	Both
Cabriole	Front, side, or back *cabriole* jump	One
	Front, side, or back *cabriole* jump with a half- or full-turn	One
	Cabriole with a turn through the split position	One
Pike	Pike jump	Both
	Front or side pike straddle jump	Both
Straddle or stride	Star jump (straddle jump with stretched legs)	Both
	Straddle leap with stretched legs	One
	Straddle jump or leap with flexed legs	One, both
	Stride jump or leap with stretched or flexed legs	One, both
Stag	Front or side stag leap or jump	One, both
	Front or side stag leap or jump with a half- or full-turn	One, both
	Front stag leap or jump with change of legs	One, both
Ring	Ring jump with one leg	Both
	Ring jump with one leg with a half- or full-turn	Both
	Ring jump with both legs	Both

(continued)

TABLE 2.1 (continued)

Shape in flight (position)	Type of jump or leap	Type of takeoff (one or both legs)
Ring (continued)	Stag ring leap or jump	One, both
	Split ring leap	One
	Split ring leap or jump with a half- or full-turn	One, both
	Stag ring leap or jump with a half- or full-turn	One, both
	Stag ring leap with change of legs	One
	Split leap with change of legs in ring	One
	Split leap and a half-turn with change of legs in ring	One
	Ring Cossack jump	One
Split	Front or side split leap or jump with stretched or flexed legs	One, both
	Front or side split leap or jump with a half-turn of the trunk	One, both
	Front split leap with stretched or flexed legs and a turn	One
	Front split leap with change of legs	One
	Front split leap with change of legs with a half- or full-turn	One
	Front split leap with back bend	One
	Front split leap with double change of legs	One
	Knocking split leap	One
Open*	Jump or leap in *arabesque* (open jump or leap)	One, both
	Jump or leap in back *attitude*	One, both
	Front open jump with stretched legs	One, both
	Front open jump with a half-turn of the trunk	One, both
	Tour jeté (front open jump and a half-turn with stretched legs)	One
	Jump in front *attitude*	One, both
	Side open jump with stretched or flexed leg	One, both
	Jump in *arabesque* with a half- or full-turn	One
	Jump in back *attitude* with a half- or full-turn	One
	Front open jump with stretched or flexed leg and a half- or full-turn	One
	Jump in front *attitude* with a half- or full-turn	One
	Side open jump with stretched or flexed leg and a half- or full-turn	One
Butterfly	Butterfly jump	One

*In an open position, the body is erect with one leg vertical (upward) and the other leg horizontal.

Body Movements 23

Figure 2.8 The gymnast's body in flight during RSG jumps and leaps: (a) hip amplitude, (b) legs bending and extending at the knees, (c) legs bending and extending at the hips, (d) trunk position, (e) leg movement in flight, (f) turns in the vertical plane.

The stag shape requires the following:

- One leg is bent forward or sideways at the knee.
- The other leg is stretched backward or to the other side horizontally.
- The trunk is straightened.
- The gymnast must demonstrate the half-split position—the toes of one leg touch the thigh of the other leg.

Stag Jump or Leap

The stag jump or leap (figure 2.9a) is the principal one for the stag group of jumps and leaps. The gymnast executes it either by taking off from two legs from a mount (stag jump) or from one leg after an approach while swinging the other leg (stag leap).

Stag Ring Jump or Leap

In the stag ring jump or leap (figure 2.9b), one leg is bent in a half-split position, the other leg is bent backward by the ring, and the trunk is arched backward. A gymnast must demonstrate the half-split and ring position at the same time. Similar to the stag jump or leap, the gymnast executes the stag ring either by taking off from two legs from a mount (stag ring jump) or from one leg after an approach (stag ring leap).

Stag Ring Jump or Leap With a Half- or Full-Turn

The gymnast executes the stag ring jump or leap with a half- or full-turn like the stag ring jump or leap, but she turns 180 degrees to 360 degrees in flight.

Stag Ring Jump or Leap With a Change of Legs

In the stag ring jump or leap with a change of legs, the flight phase begins with one leg moved forward and the other stretched backward. The gymnast then abruptly moves her front leg backward to the ring and moves her back leg to a stag position in the front.

Front Split Jump or Leap

The front split jump or leap (figure 2.9c) is the main leap in the split group. The gymnast executes the front split leap by swinging one leg and taking off from the other leg while moving up and forward. During flight, the gymnast demonstrates the split pose and reaches a horizontal position. During the takeoff, her trunk is slightly inclined forward but is straight during flight. The gymnast lands on her swinging leg. She may also perform the front split jump by taking off from both legs and striding her legs quickly.

Split Ring Leap

The gymnast performs the split ring leap (figure 2.9d) by swinging one leg up and forward and taking off from the other one. She spreads her legs to create the split, bends the trailing leg to the ring position, and bends the trunk backward, creating a strong arch with the chest, abdomen, and pelvis.

Side Split Leap

The gymnast executes the side split leap (figure 2.9e) with a one-legged side swing. In flight, the gymnast demonstrates the side split pose. On the last step of the approach, she places her takeoff foot in the outside position and turns her trunk to the side of the takeoff leg, facing forward. To perform the side split jump, the gymnast takes off from both legs and straddles her legs quickly.

Split Leap With Half-Turn During Flight

In the front split leap with a turn of the trunk (figure 2.9f), the gymnast executes a split leap, taking off from one leg and swinging her other leg. She then makes a half-turn with her trunk during the flight phase.

Split Leap With a Change of Legs

The gymnast performs this leap by swinging one leg and taking off from the other leg, upward and forward. During the flight, she demonstrates a split leap, then abruptly changes to the split position by swinging her legs.

Knocking Split Leap

The gymnast executes the knocking split leap (front split leap with swinging leg, which bends and contacts the takeoff leg; figure 2.9g) by swinging one leg forward and taking off with the other leg up and forward. During flight, the gymnast demonstrates the split, then quickly flexes the swinging leg at the knee and contacts the takeoff leg with her toes. After this,

Figure 2.9 RSG jumps and leaps: (a) stag jump or leap, (b) stag ring jump or leap, (c) front split jump or leap, (d) split ring leap, (e) side split leap, (f) front split leap with trunk turn, (g) knocking split leap, (h) ring jump with one leg (first and second variations), (i) ring jump with both legs, (j) pike straddle jump, (k) scissors jump, (l) open jump in *arabesque*, (m) side *cabriole* jump, (n) Cossack ring jump.

some elite gymnasts stretch the knocking leg forward to the split position and land on it. Less skillful gymnasts can land immediately after knocking.

Knocking Leap With a Ring

This leap begins exactly like a split ring leap. During flight, the gymnast bends her swinging leg at the knee and knocks the middle of the thigh of her takeoff leg. She lands on the swinging leg.

Ring Jump With One Leg

The gymnast performs this jump (figure 2.9h) by taking off from both legs and landing on one. Then she moves one leg forward and bends the other leg back to the ring position. There are two variations of this jump. In the classical variation, the gymnast maintains a bent swinging leg. A gymnast with good flexibility in the spine and hips, however, may perform the second variation by keeping her swinging leg straight or only slightly bent.

Ring Jump With Both Legs

A gymnast performs this jump (figure 2.9i) by taking off and landing on both legs. During flight, she moves her legs backward and bends her knees to touch her head with her toes or heels while bending her trunk fully backward.

Pike Straddle Jump

The gymnast executes this jump (figure 2.9j) by taking off and landing on both legs. During flight, she separates her legs sideways and bends her trunk forward.

Scissors Jump

The gymnast performs this jump (figure 2.9k) by taking off from one leg and swinging the other leg forward. During flight, the gymnast changes legs, so that she lands on her swinging leg.

Cat Jump

The gymnast performs this jump in the same way as the scissors jump, but with her legs bent and turned out.

Jump in *Arabesque*

The jump in *arabesque* (open or vertical jump, figure 2.9l) is the basis for group jumps with one leg horizontal, takeoff from one leg, backward swing by the other leg, and landing on the takeoff leg. It needs to be executed at a great height with legs separated at a 90 to 135 degree angle.

Cabriole

This is the arch beat jump (figure 2.9m shows the side *cabriole*). The gymnast executes it by swinging one leg and taking off from the other leg. During flight, the gymnast beats her swinging leg with her takeoff leg. She can execute this jump with both forward and backward leg movements.

Cossack Jump

The gymnast executes the Cossack jump by swinging forward with one leg straightened and taking off from the other one. During flight, the gymnast bends her takeoff leg into a tuck position and stretches her swinging leg horizontally, keeping her trunk vertical. This jump requires a good takeoff and high elevation, so the gymnast can stay in the Cossack position longer.

Cossack Ring Jump

The Cossack ring jump (figure 2.9n) requires good technique and physical fitness. The shape of this jump during flight is similar to the split ring leap, but there are substantial differences in technique. In the split ring leap, the gymnast jumps upward and forward, but in the Cossack ring jump, she jumps upward only. The gymnast achieves the desired ring position by bending her back and arching her chest, abdomen, and pelvis.

Split Leap and Half-Turn With Change of Leg in a Split Position

The gymnast performs this leap (figure 2.10) with an upward takeoff from one leg and forward swing of the other one, followed by a turn of the trunk and a backward movement of the takeoff leg. The gymnast must move her shoulders slightly backward and put her feet in front of the trunk, starting with her toes, on the last steps of the approach. At takeoff, she makes an active forward swing with her leg and swings her arms to increase upward lift. During flight, her trunk makes a half-turn, her legs pass each other, not touching one another (the takeoff leg moves backward, the swinging leg moves forward). The gymnast lands on her swinging leg.

Figure 2.10 Split leap and half-turn with change of leg in a split position.

Jeté With a Turn and Legs in the Split Position

This leap is performed by swinging one leg forward and turning it to the side. The trunk is turned to the same side immediately. The takeoff leg is then lifted behind to the horizontal, while the arms support the turn. At the peak of the leap the gymnast must elevate maximally, as well as demonstrate a split position at 180 degrees. The takeoff leg should be strongly stretched backward. Landing takes place on the swinging leg.

Split Leap and a Half-Turn With a Change of Legs in the Ring

This leap is also similar to the split leap and half-turn with change of legs in a split position. The gymnast must pay attention to the vertical takeoff and ensure an efficient trunk turn, thereby helping her swing her leg to the ring.

Butterfly

The butterfly (figure 2.11) is made up of two parts. First, the gymnast stands with her takeoff leg pointed outward. She then swings her arms and trunk in a circular motion (by bending at the waist) toward the takeoff leg. Next, she moves the swinging leg around and pushes off the takeoff leg. The two legs pass each other (see figure 2.10) while the gymnast's trunk continues to move from its position parallel to the floor, back to an upright position. The takeoff occurs on one leg, while the landing occurs on the opposite (swinging) leg.

Balances

Balance refers to keeping the body in various poses (shapes) on limited support, executed using various parts of the body.

Proper balances are balances executed while standing on one or both legs (and no other body part), requiring skill to maintain the stability of various positions of the trunk, arms, and legs. The leg on which the gymnast balances is called the "supporting leg"; the other leg is called the "free leg."

While performing balances, a gymnast must do the following:

- Maintain a well-defined shape for one second, according to the Code of Points.
- Demonstrate good amplitude in the shape.
- Not step or hop on the supporting leg.
- Not support herself on one or both hands or on an apparatus.

A gymnast must perform most balances on her toes, raising the heel of her supporting leg as high as possible.

Phases of Balances

The execution of a balance involves three phases:

1. The preparatory phase: posing and restricting the support. In balances on both legs, the

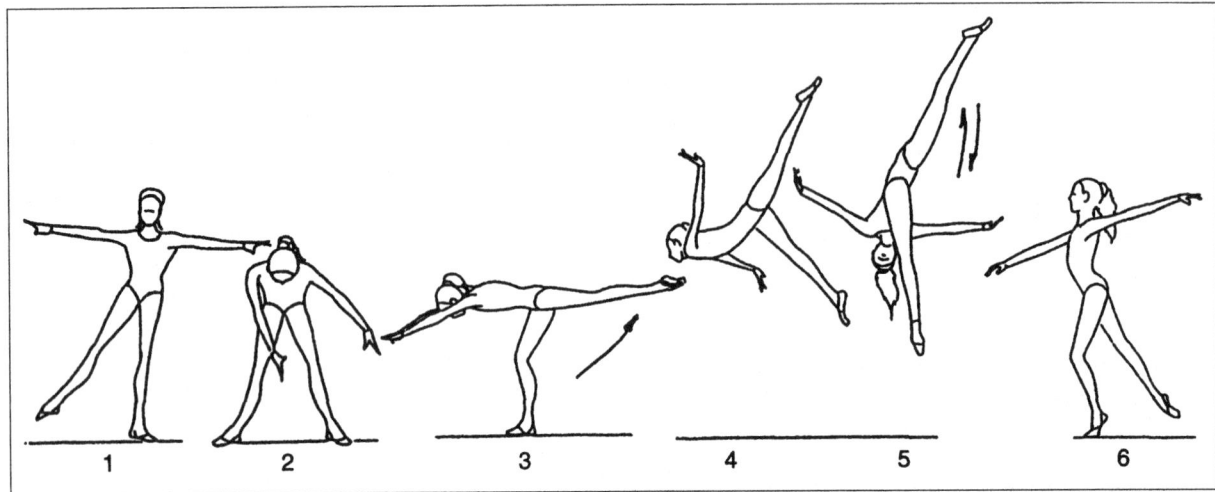

Figure 2.11 The butterfly.

Figure 2.12 Conditions for balancing: (a) location of the gymnast's center of gravity (*CG*) over the support area, (b) kinds of stability at the various heights of the center of gravity.

restriction of a support may be to rise onto the toes; in balances on one leg, to raise the free leg, either straight, in an arch, or through *passé*, slowly or quickly (swinging).

2. The main (realization) phase: maintaining the necessary pose.
3. The finishing phase: exiting from the balance.

Essential Principles of Balances

Biomechanics and physiology help a gymnast balance steadily.

From the biomechanical point of view, putting the center of gravity over the support area is the main condition for maintaining a balance. As shown in figure 2.12a, displacing the center of gravity from the limits of the support area causes the gymnast to lose her balance. The gymnast's stability is determined by the size of the support area, the height of the center of gravity above the support, and the alignment of the center of gravity.

Of course, a larger support area results in better stability. Stability is also better when the gymnast's center of gravity is low. That is why balances on the knees are more stable than balances on the toes. Angle α_1 must be less than angle α_2 (figure 2.12b), where angle α_2 is the ideal angle of fluctuation of the gymnast's center of gravity (CG) over the support area. The gymnast with a higher center of gravity can lose her balance with a smaller angular amplitude of fluctuation than a gymnast with a lower center of gravity. Therefore, when standing on the toes, it is more difficult to maintain balance than when on the entire foot, both because the support area is less and the center of gravity is higher.

A gymnast's body is a complex biomechanical system, consisting of many parts connected by joints (leg, thigh, spine, pelvis, and so on). This explains the physiological difficulty of managing a balance. Specifically, physiology's role in maintaining a balance stems from three senses: vision, motor sensation (sensing the body's position in space), and vestibular balance. Thus, the better the gymnast is prepared technically, physically, and psychologically, the better her balances will be.

Deviation from a steady position causes movements that affect the pose (shape). During a poorly balanced pose, gymnasts generally overcompensate, moving the center of gravity beyond the necessary position, marking them clearly as beginners. Yet, compensatory movements by the arms, free leg, trunk, or head help to preserve a pose. A gymnast demonstrates the highest mastery when such compensation comes from an almost imperceptible use of muscles that enable her to reduce the amplitude of her body fluctuations as she repositions her center of gravity over the support area. Gymnasts should remember that they must especially focus on developing these groups of muscles to be able to subtly hide any problems.

A gymnast should have strong legs so she can make invisible compensatory movements to keep her center of gravity over her support area, thus helping her keep her balance. She should focus on uniformly distributing her weight over the support area (the knee, flat foot, or toes). She should not allow her leg and trunk muscles to relax. In these ways, she will learn to balance her body properly, so that it is easy for her to preserve a gymnastic balance. If all else fails, however, she can swing her arms, presenting the swinging as expressive movements.

A gymnast who does not equally distribute her attention while practicing her balances tends to give most of her attention to the main phase and pay less attention to the preparatory and finishing phases. This explains why the finishing phase tends to reveal the most mistakes.

Classification of Balances

Balances (figure 2.13) can be executed on one or both legs or on one knee.

We can further divide entire leg balances into two subgroups: on both legs and on one leg. But no matter if the gymnast uses one or both legs, she can balance in one of two ways. Regular balances do not change the shape of the balance. Combination balances change the shape of the balance in the trunk position, free-leg position, or both. In either case, the supporting leg cannot change its position, but can move slightly by either changing between a flat foot and a toe-stand or bending or straightening the knee.

We can further classify balances according to the trunk position relative to the supporting leg: front, back, side (lateral), or vertical (high). In all balances except vertical, the trunk may be at any angle to the supporting leg. The gymnast may move her trunk while changing position by raising from the front,

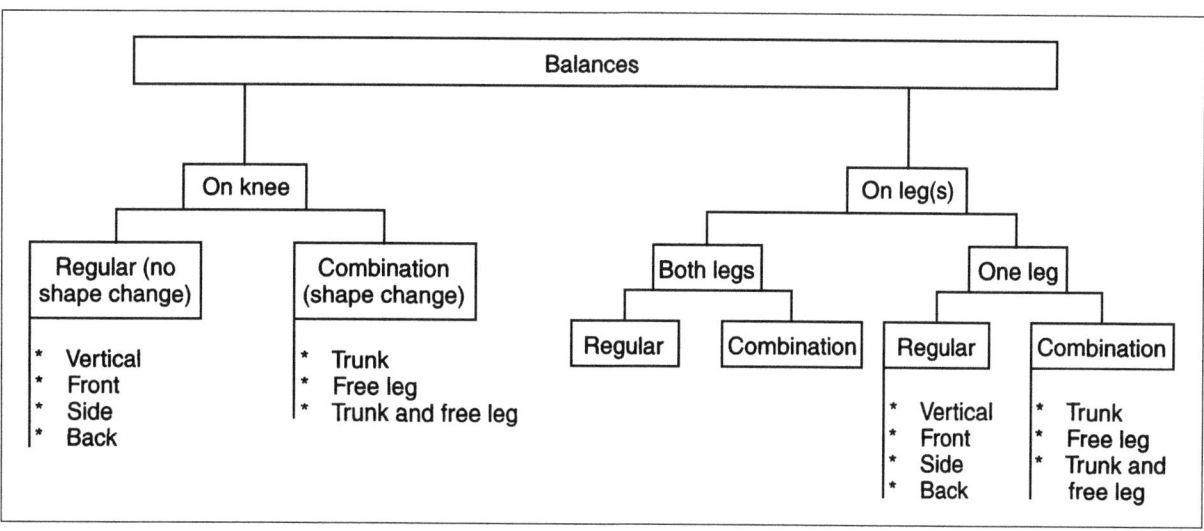

Figure 2.13 Classification of balances on one knee or on one or two legs.

back, or side position up to the vertical position (increasing the angle of the supporting leg) or lowering her trunk from vertical to forward, backward, or sideways (decreasing the angle of the supporting leg).

The gymnast can lift her free leg sideways, forward, or backward at any angle to the supporting leg. The limiting factors are an individual's hip mobility and muscular elasticity. Her leg can be straight or bent at the knee at any angle: acute, right, or obtuse in a ring (figure 2.14).

The gymnast may change her free-leg position around her body: for example, forward-sideways, sideways-backward, or forward-sideways-backward. Sometimes she may change the shape of a balance by bending or stretching her free leg; for example, a vertical balance with the free leg behind, then bending the free leg at the knee through the *passé* position, then going into a back balance (or in the reverse order).

A gymnast may hold her free leg with one or both hands forward, sideways, or backward (see figure 2.15 for one-handed holds). She may choose to raise her free leg with one or both hands, then straighten her arms, and perform the balance without holding her leg. Combined balances may be associated with trunk bends and changing the position of the free leg. The gymnast may also keep moving her arms to create a pose, especially when handling apparatus during compositions.

Techniques of Selected Balances

In the following sections, we'll look closely at several commonly used balances. These descriptions can be used to teach gymnasts the basics. Mastering the basics is a vital step for those gymnasts wishing to progress to more difficult skills later in their training.

Balances on One Knee

These balances are performed in a kneeling position, using the knee for support and keeping the thigh at vertical (figure 2.16). The hip should be over the supporting knee. The gymnast should ensure that she holds her hips and pelvis straight, tightens the muscles in her thighs, buttocks, back, stomach, and free leg, and points the toes of both feet.

While balancing on one knee, the gymnast may raise her free leg forward, sideways, or backward, bending or stretching it at various heights, including the horizontal and split positions. She may also hold her free leg with one or both hands. Finally, she may bend her trunk sideways (figure 2.16b), backward (figure 2.16c), or forward (figure 2.16d).

Balances on Both Legs

These balances are performed by standing on the toes. The gymnast must tighten her leg and trunk muscles and keep her heels together. She may bend

Figure 2.14 Various positions of the free leg for balances on one leg: (a) sideways at an acute angle (*passé*), (b) forward at an angle (turned-in *passé*), (c) obtuse in a ring.

her trunk forward, backward, or sideways during this balance. The steadiest position is with the trunk bent forward, because humans have greater flexibility to curl the spine forward than backward. For vestibular analysis, the forward bend is also more natural than the back one. While balancing with her trunk bent back, the gymnast should focus on locating her hips over the support area and tightening her leg and trunk muscles.

Regular Balances on One Leg

In vertical balances, the gymnast keeps her trunk perpendicular to the floor. She may place her free leg forward, sideways, or backward at different heights, hold her free leg with one or both hands (or not), and stand on her flat foot or her toes. She may bend her supporting leg at the knee, in which case it is vital to raise the heel of her supporting leg as high as possible.

• In the vertical balance, with a front split (figure 2.17a), the gymnast turns the toes of her supporting foot slightly outward; the leg should be straight. The gymnast should focus on the vertical position of her trunk: her shoulders must be aligned with each other and may not move forward. She should tighten her stomach and bring her shoulder blades together.

Figure 2.15 One-handed holds of the free leg: (a) forward, (b) backward in a ring, (c) sideways.

Figure 2.16 Balances on one knee: (a) vertical with free leg forward, (b) side with free leg sideways, (c) back with free leg forward, (d) front with free leg backward.

Figure 2.17 Vertical balances with a free leg: (a) forward, (b) sideways, (c) backward.

The free leg must be turned out from the hip and straightened, with pointed toes. The gymnast may hold her free leg horizontally, especially if she is a beginner.

• In the vertical balance, side splits (figure 2.17b), the gymnast keeps her trunk straight and her free leg at her side at the required height, turned out at the hip and downward. She brings her shoulder blades together in one line, keeps her shoulders horizontal and lowered, tightens her stomach, and turns the foot of her supporting leg slightly outward. She may hold her free leg at the horizontal, especially if she is a beginner. The gymnast must focus on ensuring that her pelvis and supporting leg are aligned, keeping her hips straight, and preventing her trunk from arching toward the side of her free leg.

• In the vertical balance, free leg backward (or *arabesque*, figure 2.17c), the gymnast lifts her free leg above 90 degrees, with her trunk slightly tilted forward. This balance comes to RSG from classical ballet.

Arabesques and Attitudes

A gymnast should learn *arabesques* and *attitudes* from classical ballet to enhance her stability—what classical ballet calls "aplomb." They help to develop leg strength and accustom a gymnast to uniformly distribute her weight on her supporting leg. Both *attitudes* and *arabesques* are balances performed on one leg. To perform *attitudes*, the gymnast lifts her free leg with her knee bent behind or in front of her body. In contrast, in *arabesques*, she fully stretches her free leg as she lifts it behind herself.

In *arabesques*, the gymnast's arms may be in different positions, but they must be stretched with her palms turned downward. The shoulders in all *arabesques* must remain at the same level. The back has the main role in an *arabesque*: if a gymnast holds her back correctly, she can produce a nice line with her body. Thus, the gymnast should focus on tightening the muscles in her back and buttocks. We recommend that RSG lessons include plenty of *arabesques*. The gymnast may bend the supporting leg in *demi-plié* or move one or both arms above her head or to the front, side, or back after acquiring the classical *arabesque* (according to the Russian school of thought).

• The first *arabesque* (figure 2.18a) requires lifting the free leg above 90 degrees. The legs are turned out. The arm on the same side as the supporting leg is extended with palms downward. The trunk is bent slightly forward or kept vertical. As in all *arabesques*, the gymnast keeps her head in profile to the direction her trunk points.

• The second *arabesque* (figure 2.18b) is similar to the first *arabesque*, but the positions of the arms differ. The arm opposite the supporting leg is extended in front, and the other arm is to the back. The gymnast looks directly in front of herself.

• The third *arabesque* (figure 2.18c) is on one leg with the free leg lifted high and backward at over 90 degrees from the vertical leg. The gymnast arches her trunk and bends it slightly forward. She extends the arm on the side of her free leg forward and keeps her other arm out to the side. The gymnast turns her head so that it faces the same direction as her trunk.

Figure 2.18 *Arabesque* from classical ballet: (a) first, (b) second, (c) third, (d) fourth.

- The fourth *arabesque* (figure 2.18d) uses the same leg positions as the third *arabesque*. However, the gymnast extends her arm on the side of the supporting leg forward, holding the arm on the side of her free leg backward, parallel to the raised leg. The gymnast strongly arches her spine and looks directly to the front.

- The back *attitude* (usually used without the word "back"; see figure 2.19a) is a balance on one leg in which the gymnast bends her free leg behind her body, holding her knee at an obtuse angle. Her legs are turned out. She should focus on the position of her free leg: its knee must turn to the side, and the thigh must turn out at the hip. It is incorrect to turn the free knee downward. There are two types of back *attitude*. In the classical (ballet) back *attitude*, the gymnast keeps her shin and foot parallel to the floor. In the gymnastic back *attitude*, she turns her shin slightly upward at the knee, turned out to the side, and points her toes upward as well. The gymnast's arms should be in the following positions: the arm opposite the free leg is in third position (see chapter 9), and the other arm is in second position. She holds her shoulders horizontal, arching her spine and turning her head to the side. While performing the *attitude*, the trunk leans toward the free leg. If the gymnast tightens her back muscles and raises her free leg correctly, her shoulders stay aligned, creating the correct shape of the *attitude*. When a gymnast has learned the basic kind of *attitude*, she can change her arm positions.

- The front *attitude* (*attitude croisée devant*; see figure 2.19b) involves balancing on one leg and bending the free leg in front of the body with the knee turned out and the foot as high as possible. In this position, the high arm is on the same side as the supporting leg and the other arm is to the side.

Figure 2.19 *Attitudes*: (a) back, (b) front.

Balance in *Passé*

The balance in *passé* (figure 2.14a, page 30) is a vertical balance, with the free leg bent at the knee at an acute angle and turned out to the side. The gymnast holds the free leg to the side, aligned with the supporting leg. To accomplish this, the gymnast must tighten her leg and trunk muscles. She should also focus on placing her hips over the support area and ensuring the vertical position of her trunk. RSG now uses the turned in variation of the *passé* position, in which the gymnast bends her free leg at the knee and extends her thigh straight forward.

Vertical Split Balances With the Free Leg Held by the Hands

These (figure 2.15, page 31) are balances in which the gymnast stands on one leg and raises her free leg forward, sideways, or backward, holding her foot with one or both hands. She stretches the free leg into the split position and fixes this shape. She should focus on ensuring that her supporting leg is slightly turned out, holding her trunk properly (vertically, with forward or sideways split balances, but fully arched in the low back with the backward split), and turning out her free leg at the hip and her knee to the side. She must also ensure that one shoulder or part of the body cannot move forward, backward, or sideways, and she needs to bring her shoulder blades together.

• Figure 2.20 shows the vertical split balance, free leg behind, held with both hands (or back split with help). In this case, the gymnast fully arches her low back. Her head must be turned upward.

• The vertical ring balance, free leg held behind with one or both hands (or ring balance with help, figure 2.15b, page 31) is performed like the split balance with the free leg behind the body, bent at the knee and turned out.

Side Balances

Side balances require the gymnast to raise her free leg to the side. She bends her trunk to the side in the opposite or same direction as the supporting leg (figure 2.21). There are several kinds of side balances, including raising the free leg up to split and bending the trunk to the other side (figure 2.21a); raising the free leg to horizontal or above and bending the trunk to the other side (called a "side scale") (figure 2.21b); and raising the free leg to horizontal or below and bending the trunk to the same side (figure 2.21c).

A gymnast frequently executes the side balance by holding her free leg in one or both hands during the split. She turns the foot of her supporting leg slightly outward and brings her shoulder blades together. The coach should ensure that the gymnast's buttocks do not move backward, that her buttock muscles are tense, and that her stomach muscles are tight. The gymnast's free leg should remain to the outside with the heel downward, raised to the necessary height.

Front Balances

In front balances (figure 2.22), the gymnast may bend her trunk forward at any angle to the supporting leg, including the following:

• The basic front balance, in which the gymnast bends her trunk parallel to the floor and raises her free leg up to the split position (figure 2.22a). This balance is often performed while holding the free leg with one or both hands. During this balance, the gymnast arches her trunk and holds her shoulders level.

• The front scale, in which the gymnast bends her trunk parallel to the floor and raises her free leg up to a horizontal level or above (figure 2.22b).

• The *pencheé*, in which the gymnast bends her straight trunk downward, touching it to the supporting leg, while she raises her free leg up to the split position (figure 2.22c).

Balances of this group are the most stable, because they give the gymnast the greatest opportunity for using her trunk to assist. The gymnast turns the

Figure 2.20 Vertical split balance, free leg behind, held with the hands.

Figure 2.21 Side balances: (a) split, trunk bent to opposite side, (b) scale, with leg at horizontal and trunk bent to opposite side, (c) free leg below horizontal with trunk bent to same side.

Figure 2.22 Front balances: (a) basic front balance, (b) front scale, (c) *pencheé*.

foot of her supporting leg slightly outward and maintains her free leg in a turned-out position. She also keeps her shoulders level and brings her shoulder blades together.

Back Balances

These are balances with the trunk bent backward. They include the following:

- The back scale, in which the gymnast bends her trunk backward horizontally and raises her free leg forward to horizontal or above.

- The gymnast bends her trunk backward horizontally and raises her free leg forward and upward to the split position.

- The back balance (figure 2.23), in which the gymnast bends her trunk backward vertically

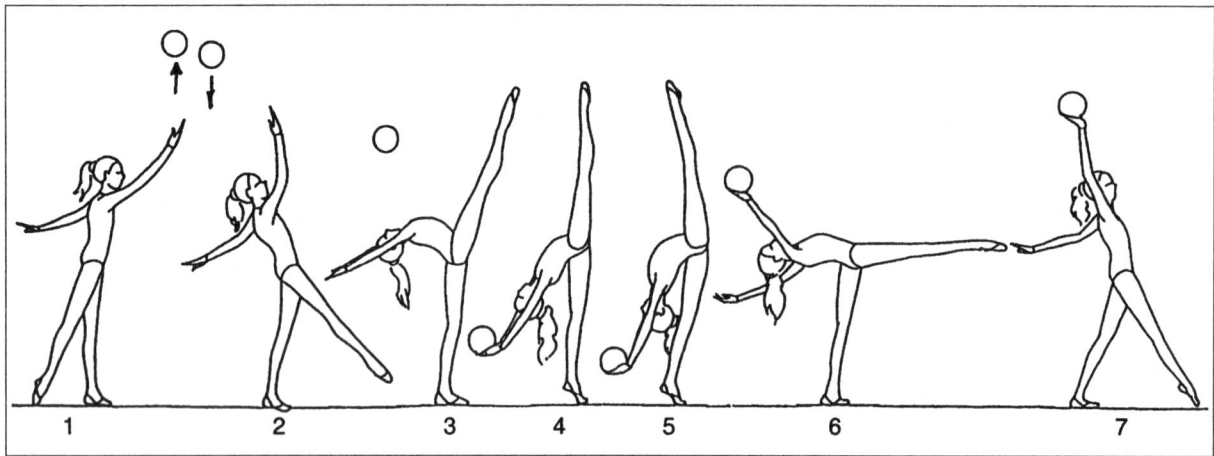

Figure 2.23 Back balance while catching the ball.

and raises her free leg forward and upward to the split position.

- The gymnast bends her trunk backward horizontally or vertically and bends her free leg at the knee and raises it to the turned-in *passé* position forward, with or without contacting the supporting leg.

If her trunk is bent backward horizontally, the gymnast can fix the position of the balance. If she bends her trunk backward vertically, she can demonstrate the back balance in the dynamic shape (figure 2.23, illustrations 5 and 6). She must move her trunk downward without tension by swinging it, keep her shoulders aligned, and move her head back without tension. She must turn her free leg out at the hip and tighten its muscles. She must keep her supporting leg straightened and turned out as well. She should turn her pelvis slightly to the side, opposite the raised leg and to the front. This position places her center of gravity over the support area. She may perform the back balance on her toes with her heel fully raised or on a flat foot.

Combination Balances

A gymnast can create many balances by combining simpler balances. In the following sections, we will describe several of the more common combination balances.

Balances With a Change in the Trunk's Position

In these balances, the free leg stays in its previous position. These balances are performed by shifting the trunk among the vertical, horizontal, and oblique planes. For example, the gymnast might shift from

- a vertical balance with a front split to a back balance,
- a vertical balance with her free leg at the horizontal in front to a back balance with her trunk horizontal,
- a front scale to *arabesque*,
- a vertical balance with side split to a side split balance, or
- a front balance to a balance in *pencheé*.

Balances With a Change of Position of the Free Leg

These balances usually begin from a vertical balance. The gymnast might shift from

- a balance in *passé* to a vertical balance with a side split,
- an arabesque balance to a vertical ring balance,
- a vertical balance with a side split to a balance in *attitude*, or
- a vertical balance with a front split to a vertical balance with a side split.

Balances With a Change in the Position of Both the Trunk and the Free Leg

These balances form the largest group of combined balances. Typically, a gymnast combines two balances. For example, she could shift as follows:

- Starting from a front scale balance, she could bend her trunk back and swing the free leg forward to create a back balance.
- Starting from an *arabesque*, she could bend her trunk forward to balance in *pencheé* with her free leg raised to the split position.
- Starting from a vertical balance with a front split, she could shift to a balance in *pencheé* while bending the trunk forward and lifting the free leg backward.
- Starting from a vertical balance with her free leg in *passé*, she could shift to a side balance with a side split.

Combination balances require a gymnast to possess a high level of proficiency in the regular balances and well-developed vestibular stability.

Turns and Pivots

Turns and pivots are rotational movements executed on one or both feet around the vertical axis of the gymnast's body. Both balancing and rotating components are involved, essentially creating dynamic balances.

A turn is a rotation of the gymnast's body on both feet with a smaller number of rotations than a pivot (a maximum of 720 degrees). A pivot (or pirouette) involves rotating on the supporting leg, in different poses, from a half-turn up to seven or eight rotations.

The Code of Points offers the following criteria for pivots:

- They must have well-defined shapes.
- They must be performed only on the toes. The judges will usually penalize the gymnast who supports her weight by rotating on her heel, although there are special cases of combination pivots for which lowering onto the heel is permitted.
- They must be of good amplitude.
- The gymnast must keep her balance while rotating.

Phases of Turns and Pivots

During turns and pivots, the main task of a gymnast is to maintain her stability throughout the three phases: the preparatory phase, which consists of the preliminary subphase and the momentum subphase, the main phase, which involves the actual rotation, and the finishing phase, which completes the element.

Essential Principles of Turns and Pivots

A gymnast may distribute her attention unequally when practicing turns and pivots. Specifically, she may control her movements very well during the preliminary subphase and the actual rotation (the main phase). She may have less control, however, in the momentum subphase, and her control may be almost nonexistent in the finishing phase. Not surprisingly, then, judges see many mistakes in turns and pivots at the end of the rotation. In the following sections, we will examine each phase to help both the coach and gymnast overcome common errors.

Preparatory Phase As mentioned, the preparatory phase of the turn and pivot occurs in two subphases. The purpose of the preliminary subphase is to create the necessary conditions that will produce a rotation. In other words, the gymnast prepares her arms, legs, and trunk for the pivot or turn. She strives to reach the optimum position with her body that will enable her to reach the necessary speed, so she can move her body parts with sufficient energy to execute the turn or pivot. So, when executing a large pivot, it is necessary for the gymnast to bend her swinging arm at the elbow, moving it to the side opposite the movement, move her free leg forward and backward, and bend her supporting leg (see figure 2.24, illustration 1).

The momentum subphase creates inertia in the turn or pivot as the gymnast swings her arms, rotating her trunk, pushing her legs, and/or swinging her free leg. A gymnast may start turns and pivots (for example, in *passé*) by stepping directly onto the ball of the foot (*relevé*) without a preliminary semisquat.

With a quick swing of her arms, the gymnast generates the maximum acceleration of her arms, trunk, and legs, producing the strength necessary for her rotation (figure 2.24, illustrations 2 and 3). In the momentum subphase, the arms and trunk move at different times with the trunk moving forward first, then the arms.

If the gymnast pivots with a swing of her free leg, the swing gives her body its main rotational force. The larger the radius of the swing of the leg, the greater the force generated for the rotation. Therefore, it is better to swing with a straight leg. In fact, all swings of the arm and leg will be more effective if they reach closer to the horizontal plane. The gymnast must focus on swinging the arm or leg only, keeping her trunk and shoulders motionless.

At the end of the momentum subphase, the gymnast should transfer her body weight onto the toes of

Figure 2.24 Combination turn with change of position of the free leg from front to back in *attitude*.

her supporting leg quickly and precisely. Not only is standing on the toes a required turn and pivot technique, it also reduces the friction between the feet and the floor. Some parts of the body should maintain a certain position to keep the body rotating around its axis. For example, in some turns the gymnast may need to keep the chest lifted and the shoulders down in order to maintain rotation.

Main Phase After slowing down the swing of her arm and leg at the end of the momentum subphase, the gymnast moves into the rotational (main) phase (figure 2.24, illustrations 5-7). Here, inertia makes the gymnast's body rotate around a longitudinal axis. Depending on the turn or pivot and skill of the gymnast, the intensity of the rotation can vary. The fastest rotation occurs in a pose in which the gymnast straightens her trunk, swings her free leg close to her supporting leg in the *passé* position, and holds her arms close to her body. Any diversion of the arms and legs from the described position during rotation will reduce the speed of the turn or pivot. To create a pivot with the slowest rotation, the gymnast arches her back or bends forward, keeps the swinging of her leg to a minimum in the subphase, and holds her arms horizontally. Moreover, to pivot slowly, the gymnast should estimate the strength of her momentum so that the inertia is sufficient to complete the pivot.

During fast-rotating pivots, the gymnast should keep her body erect. Any excessive bending or arching of the body, or irrational movements of the arms or the free leg can cause centrifugal force, causing "throwing." This is when inertia abruptly throws a gymnast to the side, making her lose her balance. Therefore, while pivoting, the gymnast must pay more attention to her body posture and body steadiness relative to the floor. When pivoting, the projection of the center of gravity of a gymnast's body (CG) must pass without fail through the support area. A gymnast may, however, perform some pivots, especially those with a low number of rotations, with her back rounded.

Another common pivot and turn fault occurs when a gymnast relaxes her arms prematurely. Inevitably, this mistake also involves relaxing the rest of the body and, as a consequence, the gymnast loses stability. To hold her trunk tensely enough so she can stand high on her toes, the gymnast should tighten certain groups of muscles, especially along her spine and in her buttocks.

The successful turn or pivot also depends on the correct turn of the head. The head is the last part to rotate, but it is the first part of the body to complete the turn or pivot. This is basically the process of "spotting," a technique in which the gymnast focuses her eyes on a fixed point in front of her for as long as possible. Then her head turns around as quickly as possible toward the end of the turn to focus once again on the same fixed point. This technique gives the impression that her head always faces forward. But the gymnast must ensure that her head does not go outside the axis of rotation. If her head loses its erect position, she may lose stability during the rotation.

Finishing Phase This phase, true to its name, simply stops the rotation. The gymnast puts the foot of her free leg on the floor, and stretches her arms sideways or moves her arms and free leg from the axis of rotation. A passive stop is possible if the rotation gradually fades due to the friction between the toes and the floor.

To effectively finish a pivot or turn, the gymnast must ensure that she does not relax her supporting leg immediately, that she gently places her free leg close to her supporting leg, and that she does not "fall down" on the flat foot suddenly. In some cases, especially after multiple fast-rotating pivots, the gymnast should lower the center of gravity by bending her knees and moving to any kneeling position on the floor. In conjunction with music, this produces a very nice aesthetic effect.

Classification of Turns and Pivots

The difficulty of each turn and pivot depends on how difficult it is for the gymnast both to remain steady and maintain an appropriate rotational speed (i.e., angular speed or number of rotations). Along these lines, we can define turns as those elements executed on both legs and pivots as those elements executed on one leg (figure 2.25).

To maintain a steady position, it is easier to perform the following turns: the *chaîné*, step, and cross on toes. A spiral turn is more difficult as it is close to the structure of waves. One exception is found among turns: a stepping turn on one foot with the free leg forward, backward, or sideways.

A gymnast can pivot on one leg with or without changing her pose, swinging her free leg inward or outward. The direction of a pivot may be outward, or rotate in the same direction as the supporting leg (for example, a pivot with the left leg providing support, rotating in the direction of the supporting [left] leg, is an outward or "left pivot"). Or the direction of the pivot may be inward, or go in the direction opposite the supporting leg, rotating in the direction of the free leg (for example, a pivot with the left leg providing support, rotating in the direction of the free [right] leg, is an inward or "right pivot").

Pivots, as with balances, may be regular or combination. Regular pivots are those for which the gymnast does not change the position of her legs or trunk. In contrast, combination pivots are those for which the gymnast does change the position of her legs or trunk.

A gymnast may turn and pivot to different degrees: a half-turn (180 degrees), full-turn (360 degrees), double-turn (720 degrees), triple-turn (1080 degrees), and so on. The number of turns

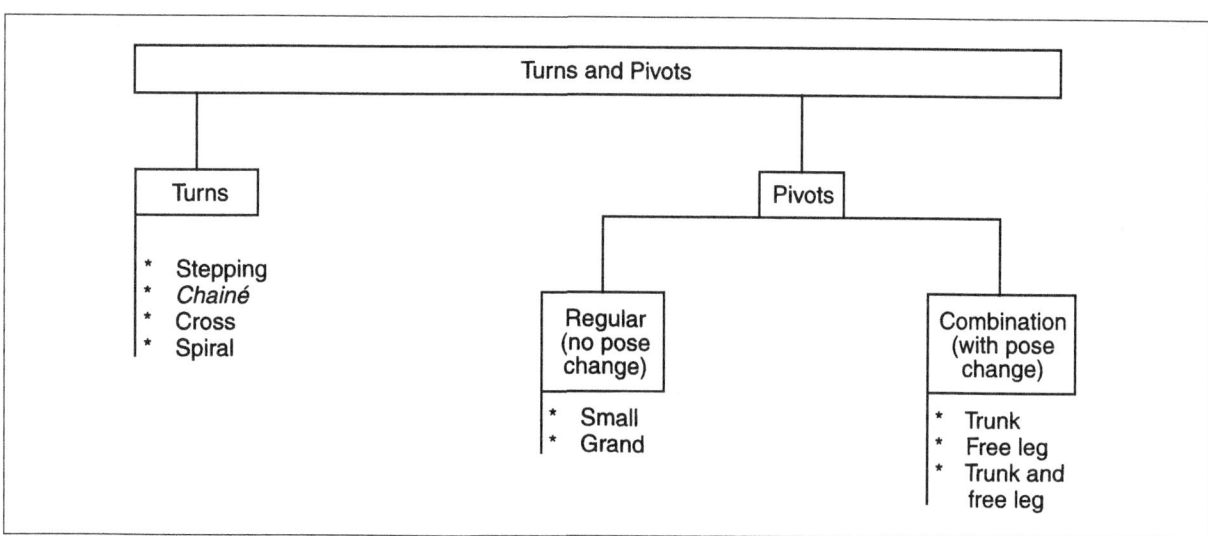

Figure 2.25 Classification of turns and pivots.

depends on such factors as the shape of the pivot, gymnast's mastery, strength of the supporting leg, ability to tighten the involved muscles, and vestibular stability.

A gymnast may vary the positions of her trunk, arms, and head while turning or pivoting. Moreover, she may extend her free leg forward, sideways, or backward, either straight or bent.

Techniques of Selected Turns and Pivots

In the following sections, we will describe several turns, then several pivots. These are some of the most commonly seen turns and pivots at competitions. The reader should find these descriptions to be a helpful guide.

Chaîné Turn

The *chaîné* turn (figure 2.26a) is performed at 180 degrees, 360 degrees, or 720 degrees with a turn on the toes of one leg, ended by closing the free leg to the supporting leg. Typically, a gymnast makes this a 360 degree turn as a series in a straight line or circle with one foot pointed forward or sideways. Then she steps quickly on her toes with this foot. The gymnast's body turns, and she brings the toes of the other foot near the toes of the first foot, heels almost touching. The gymnast usually holds her arms straight out to the sides on the first step and close to her body or brings them to the first position (see chapter 9) during the rotational phase. In a series of *chaîné* turns, the arms alternately open and close when moving from the second to the first position. The gymnast's eyes maintain contact with the "spot" in the direction of turning for as long as possible, until her head finally whips around, completing the turn ahead of the body.

Stepping Turn

A gymnast executes a stepping turn by overstepping on her toes to the right or left, traveling at a diagonal or in an arch or circle. She takes the first step on her toes in the direction she wants to travel in.

Stepping Turn on One Foot With the Free Leg Forward, Backward, or Sideways

A gymnast performs this turn by sliding her supporting foot. It is very important to maintain the correct balance shape while turning: motionless free leg in the front, side, or back split position, executed with or without the help of one hand. The gymnast must be sure to tighten the muscles of her legs and trunk.

Cross Turn

A gymnast executes a cross turn (figure 2.26b) by taking a cross step of one leg in front or behind the other leg and turning 180 degrees or 360 degrees. The turn should align the toes as the heels touch one another. Mounting on her toes, the gymnast executes the turn, distributing her body weight evenly

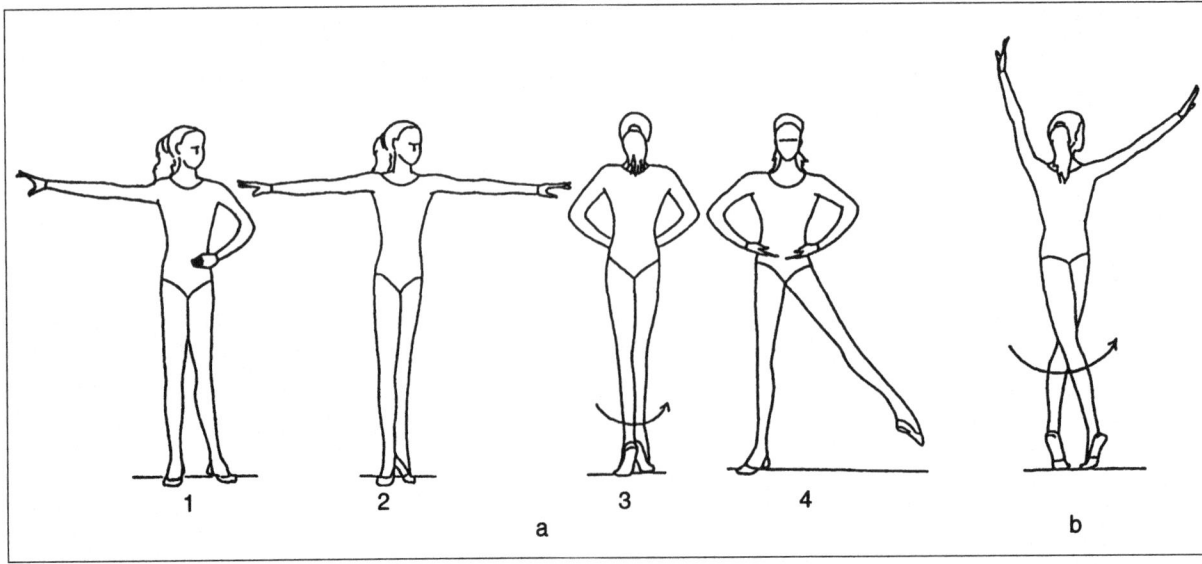

Figure 2.26 Turns: (a) *chaîné*, (b) cross.

on both legs. In the finishing phase, she may lower her heels.

Spiral Turn

The spiral turn (figure 2.27) connects a cross turn with a body wave. To begin the turn, the gymnast stands on her toes, holding her arms sideways. Next, she puts one leg in front of the other leg. Then, she makes a 90 degree turn, using her knees and feet, "twisting" in transition in a round semisquat (figure 2.27, illustration 2). Continuing the turn with the knees at 45 degrees or more, she moves her thighs and pelvis forward. While leaning in one direction, she begins to turn her shoulder to the other; at this point, the top half of her body is behind the bottom half, forming a right angle (figure 2.27, illustrations 3 and 4). Continuing the turn, she moves her chest forward. While leaning forward very far, her head lags behind the turning of her shoulders. Meanwhile, her chin almost touches her clavicles (collarbones). She finishes the turn by standing erect on her toes with her arms extended to her sides.

Regular Pivots

Regular pivots can be small, in which the gymnast raises her free leg to below horizontal, and grand (large), in which the gymnast may (1) straighten her free leg in *arabesque*, (2) bend her knee into *attitudes*, (3) hold her free leg straight forward, sideways, or backward at different angles to her supporting leg with or without holding her free leg with one or both hands, or (4) bend her free leg behind her to the ring position.

Small Pivots

There are many different kinds of small pivots. Here, we will describe several of the most commonly performed:

- Keeping her support leg straight, the gymnast bends her free leg at the knee in the *passé* (figure 2.28a) or *sur le cou-de-pied* position behind the support leg.
- With her support leg straight, the gymnast bends her free leg slightly, or straightens and

Figure 2.27 *Spiral turn.*

Figure 2.28 Small pivots: (a) in *passé*, (b) with the free leg raised below horizontal, (c) while leaning forward with the free leg bent near the supporting leg, (d) with arched back and free leg bent, raised below horizontal, (e) in a semisquat with the free leg in front *attitude*, (f) in a semisquat with the free leg below horizontal.

raises it to below horizontal (figure 2.28, b and d).

- The gymnast bends her support leg down to a semisquat and bends her free leg or straightens and raises it to below horizontal (figure 2.28, e and f).
- The gymnast may also bend her trunk while performing small pivots (figure 2.28c).

The gymnast pivots in *passé* on a straightened supporting leg. She bends her free leg in *passé*, keeping her trunk vertical. She may perform this pivot in one of two ways: by semisquatting, then standing onto her toes in the preparatory phase, focused on standing quickly onto her toes with a "sharp" movement, bringing the heel of her supporting leg to the maximum height above the floor; or, by standing on the toes of her straightened supporting leg without semisquatting, tightening the muscles of her supporting leg, raising her heel as high as possible above the floor, and shifting her body weight quickly onto her supporting leg.

— It is necessary to raise the bent free leg in the *passé* position and fix this shape after shifting the body weight onto the supporting leg. A gymnast should understand the stability of this position is due to tightened trunk and leg muscles.

— While performing this pivot, her back should be straight, her shoulders must be aligned, her buttock muscles must be tight, and her shoulder blades must come together.

— When finishing, her free leg must be near her supporting leg.

The pivot in *sur le cou-de-pied* positions are performed the same way as in *passé*, but the position of the free leg is different.

The gymnast may perform small pivots while leaning forward or arching backward (figure 2.28, c and d). In this case, she tightens her trunk muscles, especially those in her back and stomach. While performing small pivots on a bent supporting leg, the supporting knee must be fixed by the tightened muscles, and the heel must be as high as possible above the floor.

Grand Pivots

Grand pivots refer to pivots for which the gymnast raises her free leg to and above horizontal. As has already been mentioned, the grand pivots have the slowest speed of rotation. Therefore, the gymnast should give her body maximum acceleration by swinging her arms, pushing from the floor with her free leg, and making quick transitions onto the toes of her supporting leg. When pivoting while handling an apparatus, it is better to swing the apparatus as a continuation of the arm, increasing the radius of the pivot's rotation, thereby increasing the strength of the pivot. While rotating, it is desirable to move the arm or arms holding the apparatus as far as possible from the horizontal line, that is, to raise or lower the arm or arms.

The speed of rotation will be increased if the gymnast raises her free leg to a split position and holds it with one or both hands. This is because the free leg is closer to vertical. When performing grand pivots, especially with double rotations, the gymnast needs to pay attention to how she swings her arm: she must not move it back and down, and she must not move her shoulders forward.

Pivots in *arabesque* are, of course, performed in the *arabesque* position. To create a good pivot in *arabesque*, the gymnast must do the following:

- During the preparatory phase, the semisquat must not be too deep; instead, a gymnast should push off from the floor with the heel of her supporting leg and stand on her toes.
- She must swing her arms sufficiently to help her rotate.
- She must tighten her free leg and stretch it behind her, keeping the leg at that height during the entire rotation.

- She must keep her trunk straight by tightening the muscles of her back, abdomen, and pelvis when in a vertical position.
- She must stretch and tighten her supporting leg, which is turned out, creating a straight line from her support foot, through her leg and trunk, to her head.
- She must keep her head erect without leaning at the start of the rotation and quickly return it to the forward-facing position.

A gymnast pivots in back *attitude* (figure 2.29a) in the *attitude* position while maintaining the pivot's shape during rotation. Most of the time, the demands are the same as for pivots in *arabesque*, but the gymnast must focus on the position of her free leg and trunk.

There are two ways of raising the free leg: (1) lift it to the *attitude* position at the same time as standing onto the toes of the supporting leg (if the gymnast does not sense the tightened muscles of her free leg or her muscles are weak, she lowers her knee and loses the pivot's shape), or (2) lift it to the *arabesque* position, standing on the supporting leg's toes and, at the start of the rotation, bending the free leg in *attitude*. For the back *attitude*, the trunk and head must be erect, and the shoulders must be aligned with each other. Special attention should be paid to the position of the free leg while rotating. If the gymnast does not hold her back and free leg securely, her free leg may move to the side, and the shape of the *attitude* will change.

Pivots with the free leg sideways (figure 2.29b) have the same requirements for acceptable performance as pivots in *arabesque*. The gymnast should raise her free leg to horizontal and above, straightening it with tightened muscles and fixing it in place from the hip. The gymnast should turn the knee upward and turn the heel downward. In this position, the free leg should not lose height while the gymnast rotates. For this, special attention should be paid to the side muscles tightening. When a gymnast starts to learn this pivot in slow motion, her free leg should be aligned with her trunk. When she can perform it at a fast tempo, her free leg should be a little bit forward of her trunk. She should hold her free leg such that any bending, as well as non-fixed motion (turning far ahead of or behind the rest of the body), is not visible. If a gymnast holds her free leg straight to the side while rotating quickly, her trunk will deviate backward involuntarily, losing stability.

Grand pivots with the free leg held with the hands differ from other grand pivots in which the gymnast

Figure 2.29 Grand pivots: (a) in back *attitude*, (b) with the free leg sideways, (c) with the free leg forward held by a hand, (d) with free leg sideways held by a hand, (e) with the free leg backward in a ring held by the hands.

does not hold her free leg with one or both hands, because she does not swing her arms in the preparatory phase. Instead, in the preliminary subphase, she semisquats and grasps her bent free leg with her hand, forward of the supporting leg. Then during the momentum subphase, she stands on her toes, stretches her free leg, and swings it. That is why it is easy to perform this kind of pivot with the free leg sideways (figure 2.29d). When a gymnast pivots with her free leg forward (figure 2.29c), she cannot swing her free leg. It is difficult for a gymnast to perform a half-turn swing in a pivot with her free leg behind (figure 2.29e), because she must have good flexibility in her hips and back. At the end of the momentum subphase, the gymnast must stand on her toes quickly to produce the main energy for the rotation. During the rotational (main) phase, she must keep her free leg vertical, near her trunk. The greater the angle between the trunk and the free leg, the slower the rotation. The gymnast should focus on the position of her trunk: straight on the vertical, buttocks under the shoulder blades, and the shoulders aligned with each other. In the finishing phase, she must not relax her free leg or allow it to fall.

The pivot in a back balance position is also a grand pivot. In this pivot, it is very important to lift the free leg to vertical and lower the back during the momentum subphase quickly, thereby helping to increase the duration of the rotation. If the gymnast lowers her free leg and raises off her body slightly in the rotational phase, she immediately decreases the speed and loses the shape of the pivot. In the finishing phase, it is very important to lift the body up, then hold the free leg as long as possible.

Combination Pivots

These are pivots with a change of pose during the rotation. It is advisable to divide them according to the change of position of the leg, the trunk, or the leg and trunk together. There are two ways of performing combination pivots: by lowering the heel of the supporting leg and without lowering the heel of the supporting leg.

Of course, pivoting without lowering the heel is more difficult than with it, because lowering gives additional energy for rotating. The lowering must be very fast, and the heel must return to the starting position. Lowering the heel may be accompanied by a small bending of the supporting leg. The gymnast must be sure to straighten her supporting foot.

Combination pivots with a change of the free leg position include the following:

- Rotating 360 or 720 degrees, free leg moving horizontally, from front to back or vice versa, or from *passé* to *arabesque* without lowering the heel.

- *Fouette* (360 degrees + 360 degrees or 360 degrees + 360 degrees + 360 degrees), the free leg bent and extended horizontally after each intermediary heel support.
- Double pivot in *passé* and a pivot with a front split and intermediary heel support.
- Pivot (360 degrees) in *arabesque* and a double pivot (720 degrees) in *passé*.
- *Fouette* pivot (three times) and a pivot (360 degrees) in *attitude* with intermediary heel support.

Figure 2.24 (page 38) shows the pivot with a change of position of the free leg raised forward (illustrations 4-6) and backward in *attitude* (illustration 7). See the Code of Points for other examples.

A gymnast may create a combination pivot with a change of the trunk position, as follows:

- A pivot (360 degrees) in *passé* with the trunk leaning toward the front with free leg and a pivot (360 degrees) in *passé* with a vertical trunk position and with or without intermediary heel support (the trunk changes position in relation to the vertical).
- A pivot (360 degrees) with trunk arched back, free leg below horizontal, and a pivot (360 degrees) with a straight trunk.

Combination pivots with a change of both the trunk and free leg positions, such as "illusion," come to RSG from figure skating. This is a real pivot on one leg, because it has all the parts of a pivot, including the preparatory, rotational, and finishing phases. Its unique features involve the moving shape of the trunk and free leg. A gymnast performs this pivot by swinging her free leg and moving her trunk in a circular motion (figure 2.30). The pivot begins by stepping forward with the supporting leg, swinging the free leg, and leaning the trunk forward. The gymnast straightens after moving her free leg into the vertical split position with or without using hand support.

Figure 2.30 The illusion pivot.

Body Waves and Swings

Body waves and swings are specific RSG elements that display the flow of the gymnast's body movements. Correct performance depends on the gymnast's coordination and joint flexibility.

Principles of Body Waves and Swings

The wave (see figure 2.31) consists of bending and extending the joints. The muscles should be relatively relaxed. Tension increases only in those muscles that are necessary for smoothly bending and extending the joint. Changing the degree of tension in the muscles continuously coordinates the movements. A gymnast should pay special attention to the sequential movement of her body parts. The speed and amplitude of the wave, that is, the height of a "crest," can vary from very slight to very great, depending on the flexibility of the joints through which the wave passes.

The total body swing (figure 2.32) is a fast successive bending and extending of the joints, initially performed with acceleration, followed by reduced tension as inertia takes over. The swing is characterized by this abrupt initial movement, which is transmitted to the succeeding joints. Total body swings

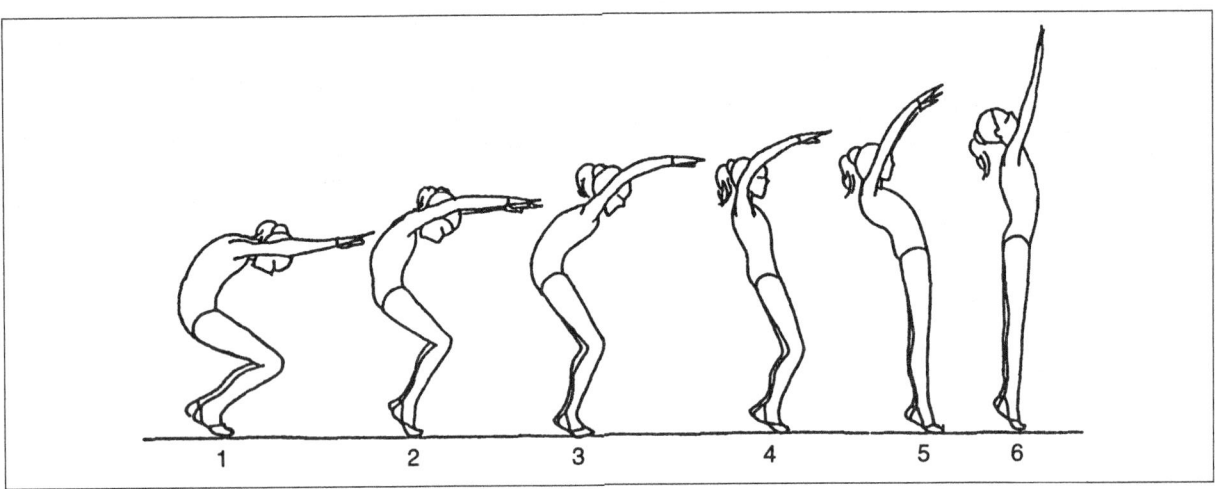

Figure 2.31 Total body wave forward from a round semisquat (classical variation).

Figure 2.32 Total body swing to a vertical balance.

help a gymnast develop a feel for muscular tension as she learns to control the strength and speed at which the muscular tension travels through her body.

Classification of Body Waves and Swings

Depending on which parts of the body participate in waves and swings, we can divide them into total body waves and swings and trunk waves and swings (figure 2.33).

Waves and swings of the arms are group elements that give expression to compositions. In this chapter, however, we will concentrate on waves and swings that move more body parts, including three types: forward, performed from bottom to top; reverse, performed from top to bottom; and side, performed from side to side.

Techniques of Selected Waves and Swings

Here, we will describe several waves and several swings to give the reader a broad base of techniques.

Waves

The first variation of the total body wave forward (classical variation; figure 2.31, page 46) is performed from a "round" semisquat on the toes or flat feet. In this position, the body weight is on the toes, the legs are in a semisquat, the pelvis is over the heels, the spine is rounded, and the head is between the arms. The gymnast consecutively extends her knees (figure 2.31, illustrations 1-2), pelvis, abdomen, chest, and head forward (figure 2.31, illustrations 3-6). She should make sure she does not bend her knees strongly at the start of the wave, does not straighten the knees and elbows prematurely when moving her thighs forward, and that she does perform a smooth circle with her arms when her thighs move forward: arms downward, palms outward, then behind her as she arches her back.

To perform the second variation of the total body wave forward (new variation; see figure 2.34), the gymnast stands on her toes, holding her arms upward. To start, she rounds her trunk forward (illustrations 2-3), then she performs a round semisquat (illustration 4). Next, she executes the classical variation (described in the previous paragraph),

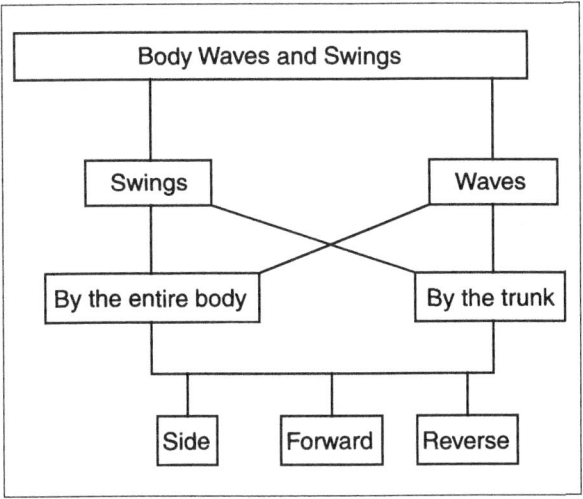

Figure 2.33 Classification of body waves and swings.

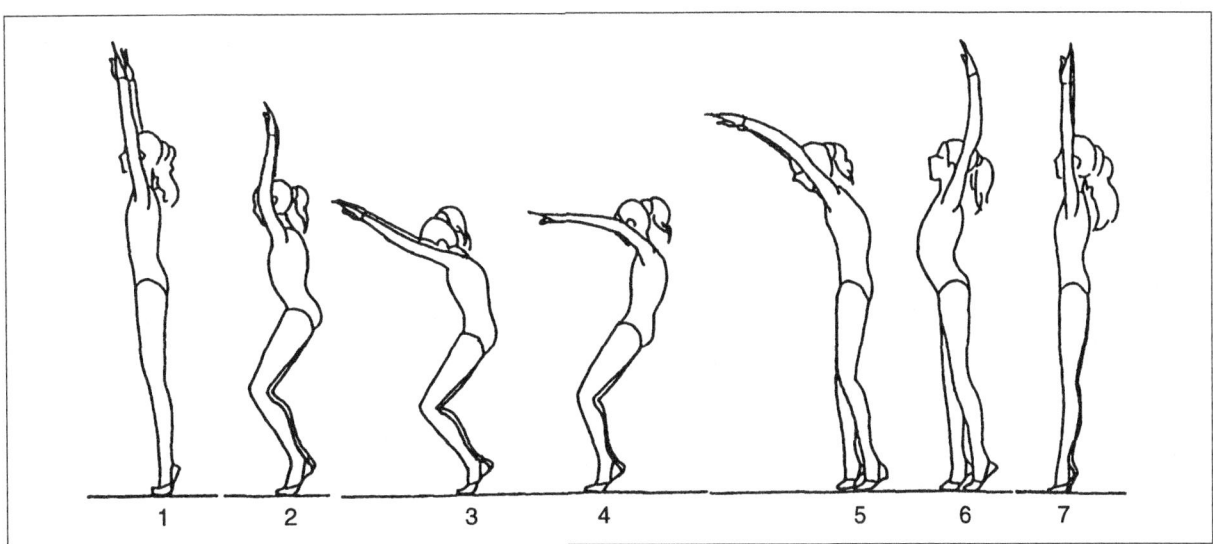

Figure 2.34 Total body wave forward from standing on toes, with the arms raised upward (new variation).

moving her body parts forward in the following sequence: the thighs, pelvis, stomach, shoulders, and head (figure 2.34, illustrations 5-7). But for this second variation, the gymnast moves her arms differently. She should continue to hold them up, making them move forward, using wave-like motions.

The reverse total body wave begins with a back bend from above (figure 2.35, illustration 2). Then the knee (illustration 3) and the chest (illustration 4) join in the movement. Finally, the gymnast rounds her upper back to create a round semisquat.

For the side total body wave (figure 2.36), the gymnast maintains all the main positions of the total body wave in that she sequentially straightens all the joints of her body. But to perform the side total body wave, the gymnast stands on her toes or the flat foot of one leg with the other toes to the side, transferring her body weight from one leg onto the other. In illustration 2, the gymnast semisquats, bending to the right, with her pelvis displaced to the left. Next, she transfers her body weight onto both legs and displaces her pelvis to the right (illustrations 3-4). Then, she transfers her body weight onto her right leg and moves her pelvis to the right and upward (illustration 5). Bending to the right, the gymnast moves her knees, pelvis, and chest in sequence to the right. Then she lowers her arms and moves to the right as the wave reaches her chest (illustration 6). Finally, she finishes the wave by standing on her toes.

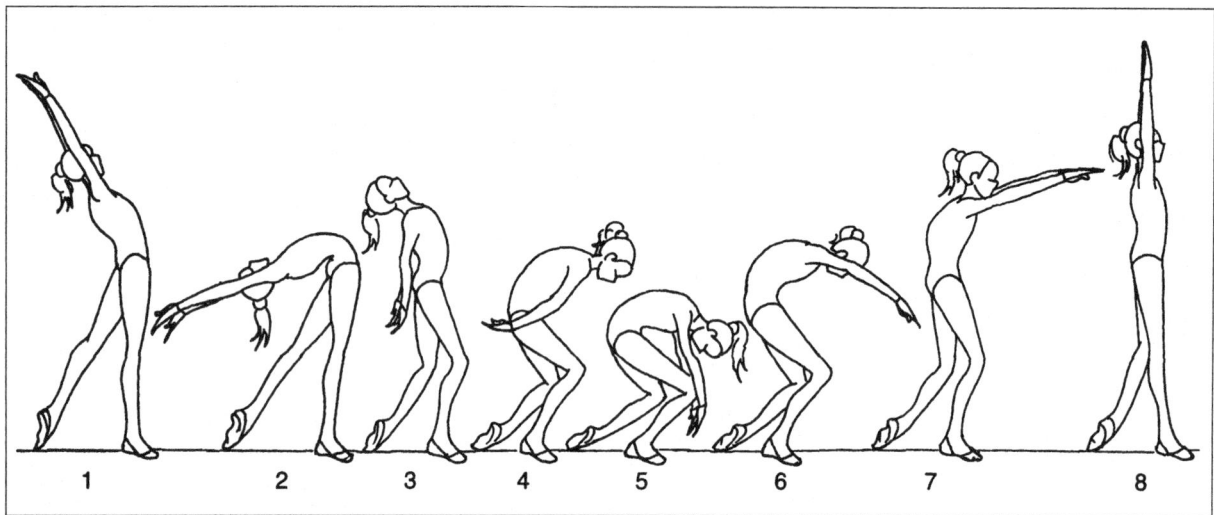

Figure 2.35 Reverse total body wave.

Figure 2.36 Side total body wave.

The total body wave from the knees (figure 2.37) is an unusual body wave, because there is no round semisquat; instead, the gymnast passes support through her insteps. She makes the wave shape only through moving the parts of her body forward in sequence, pushing and stretching her pelvis and thighs. Thus, it is necessary to move the pelvis forward before the stomach and chest. We recommend this wave only for gymnasts with good flexibility in their feet. When a gymnast is learning this wave, she should focus on quickly pushing and stretching her thighs and pelvis, standing on her insteps, and arching her back.

The gymnast may practice the trunk wave to prepare her to learn the total body wave. The trunk wave has the following variations:

1. Moving forward from the kneeling sit (figure 2.38a), the gymnast leans forward with her spine arched and then returns to the starting position with her spine rounded. The movement begins in the loins and is transferred from vertebra to vertebra to the chest through the neck.

2. Moving forward from the kneeling sit with a rounded spine (figure 2.38b), the gymnast lowers her head; then rising from the kneeling position, the gymnast moves her pelvis forward, her shoulders lagging back and staying in line with her heels. Then she lowers her head onto her chest and, finally, straightens her chest and neck in sequence.

3. Moving in reverse from a kneeling position (figure 2.38c), the gymnast arches her back, bends her hips by circling her arms down, and sits on her heels with her spine rounded.

Swings

The total body swing differs from the total body wave in that the wave proceeds at regular intervals but the swing begins with an abrupt movement, proceeds with accelerated movements, and subsequently slows down, passing upward as an undulation through a relaxed body. The gymnast moves her arms freely together with her body and then raises them in front of her body at the end of the swing. The gynmast finishes in a position higher than the starting position by straightening her body or moving forward. Figure 2.32 (page 46) illustrates a total body swing to a vertical balance on the toes.

Floor Elements

Floor elements are a varied group of RSG elements that a gymnast performs using supports other than her legs. This group includes elements that are performed while sitting or passing support of the body on one or both hands, the shoulders, chest, and spine, and one or more parts of one or both legs in combination with one or more other supports.

Some of the floor elements in RSG come from artistic gymnastics. These are classified in the Code of Points as "acrobatic" elements. Some of the easier floor elements are not classified by the Code of Points as being difficult or as being acrobatic elements.

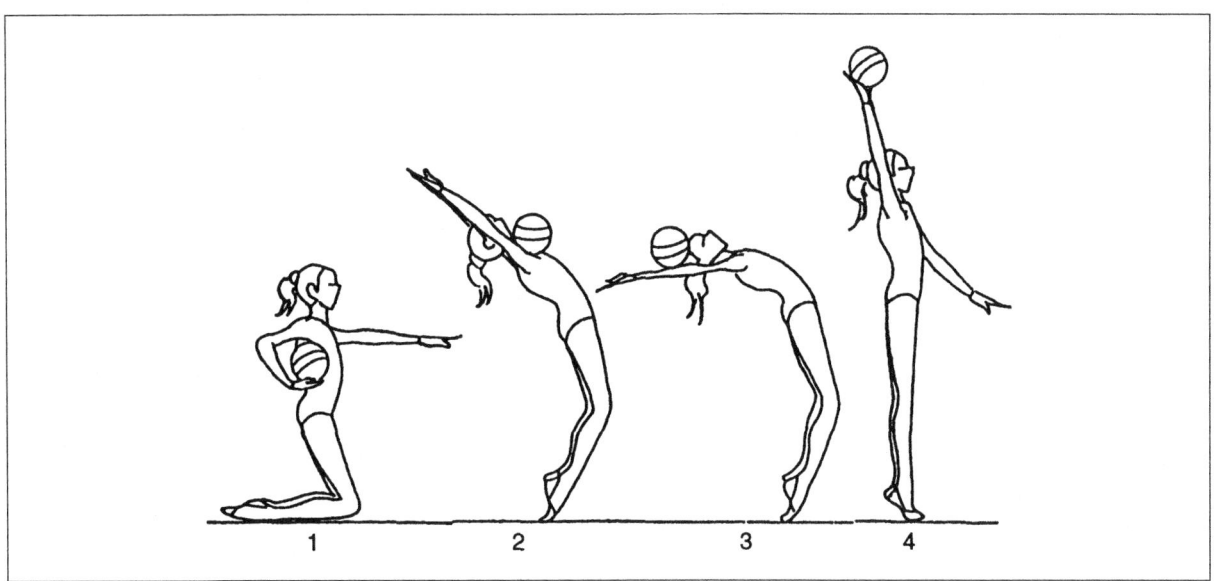

Figure 2.37 Total body wave from the knees.

Figure 2.38 Trunk waves: (a) forward from a kneeling sit, (b) forward from a kneeling sit with a rounded spine, (c) reverse from kneeling.

Floor elements in compositions help gymnasts meet the following requirements of the Code of Points:

- change levels in space,
- change the dynamics of the performance (using floor elements diversifies the composition), and
- meet special requirements for apparatus elements since floor elements are sometimes simpler and steadier than elements of body movements performed while standing on one or both legs.

Classification of Floor Elements

Each floor element can have many different shades depending on the individual and the apparatus. That is why there are many different elements with different techniques. The following are subgroups of the floor elements:

- Rolls
- Walkovers and cartwheels
- Passing supports
- Grovels
- Lying positions

- Floor balancing
- Floor turns
- Slides on the floor
- Wave-like motions
- Floor jumps

Techniques of Selected Floor Elements

In the following sections, we will look closely at representative examples of the various floor elements. Note carefully the steps each requires to create the perfect addition to a competitive composition.

Rolls

A roll is simply a rotary motion of the gymnast in the tucked or untucked position while touching the floor with her body sequentially. In the tuck position, the gymnast bends her legs, draws her knees toward her chest, presses her elbows to her body, and bends her head forward. The knees should be 15 to 20 centimeters from each other. When rolling, the gymnast should pay attention to creating a compact tuck position; this will help her roll as fast as possible.

A gymnast can roll forward, backward, and to the side (laterally) as long as she rolls with a good rotational speed. Compact and therefore fast tucking will give the gymnast enough momentum to rotate her body. When rolling, however, the gymnast cannot stop to push off the floor to keep rolling during the main phase. She may roll from a squat support, straddle stand, or semisquat or after steps, including dance steps. In the last instance, the momentum for body rotation is higher than for starting from a standing position. Common errors include the gymnast stopping after the approach before starting the roll and the gymnast's body not rotating.

Forward Roll Through the Neck

The gymnast may perform this roll with or without the support of one or both hands. Typically, this roll forward is performed in a composition after an approach (for example, steps, split leap). Figure 2.39 shows a forward roll with hand support. The gymnast transfers her body weight onto her hands. Next, as she continues to straighten her legs and push off on them, she lowers her head. Then, she touches the back of her head to the floor and rolls forward into the tuck position. The gymnast should focus on avoiding stopping after the approach. She should be sure to stand on her hands and move her head forward quickly. Finally, she should ensure that she balances on her head at the same moment as on her hands, not raising her head even a little; by raising her head, a gymnast disrupts the sequence through which she touches the floor with her body.

Backward Roll Through the Neck

This roll, as a rule, begins from a squat support. The gymnast should assume the tuck position by pushing her arms and pulling her knees to her shoulders. Her head should be bent forward. Then she rolls onto her shoulder blades, placing her palms on the floor beside her head. With her fingers close to her shoulders, the gymnast supports herself with her hands and rotates to a squat support. During this roll, the gymnast should try not to straighten her legs.

Forward Roll Through One Shoulder

A gymnast performs this roll using different techniques than with the forward roll through the neck (figure 2.39, illustrations 12-17). In the first phase of this roll, the gymnast bends her shoulder downward and rotates through her shoulder. This moves her head down to touch her chest. Then the gymnast rolls through the same side of the spine as the support shoulder. The other principles of the technique are the same as for rolls through the neck: consecutive rotation from the shoulder onto the spine into the tuck position.

Lateral Roll in the Tuck Position

This roll may begin from standing on one or both legs, kneeling, or the kneeling sit. The gymnast starts by bending her trunk to the side and then bending her legs, if necessary. She then tucks after contacting the floor to the side, increasing the rotational speed. This moment is very important if the gymnast began in a kneeling sit, because in this position a gymnast does not have enough momentum to push off from the floor. If a gymnast begins from a standing or kneeling position, descending to the floor and pushing will give her more momentum for rolling. While rotating she must not open her body early; she should save energy to be able to finish rotating and kneel again.

Lateral Roll Through the Split Position

To perform this roll (figure 2.40), the gymnast rotates from a split position with her trunk bent

52 Rhythmic Gymnastics

Figure 2.39 Forward rolls through the neck and shoulder with consecutive club throws with the feet and hands.

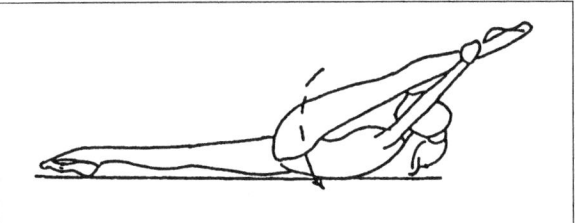

Figure 2.40 Lateral roll through the split position.

forward to the floor and one leg held by her hand. She must concentrate on maintaining contact with the floor with her stretched leg and pelvis.

Walkovers

Walkovers are a handspring movement, performed without stopping in a handstand position. There are several types of walkovers: forward, backward, and arabian.

Cartwheels

A cartwheel is a sideways traveling movement in which the gymnast's arms and legs represent the spokes of a wheel in the sequence hand to hand and foot to foot.

Passing Supports

Passing supports refer to the gymnast's movements in an untucked position with one or both legs lifted. A gymnast may perform passing supports on one, or both hands or forearms, and her chest, either forward, backward, or sideways. No stopping and no flight are allowed during passing supports.

Passing Support on One Hand With a Split

The gymnast performs this passing support by pushing off with both legs (figure 2.41, illustration 2), then she demonstrates the split without stopping (illustration 3), and returns to the starting position.

A gymnast can create many interesting elements with the apparatus while performing a passing support on one hand. In figure 2.42, for example, a gymnast turns the rope, her hand supporting her on the floor, her shoulders perpendicular to the floor. Note that her legs are bent.

Backward Passing Support on One Hand

Figure 2.43 illustrates this passing support. The gymnast pushes with her left leg and swings with her right leg. Meanwhile, she supports herself on her arm on the same side as her swinging leg (illustrations 2-5). In illustration 4, the gymnast demonstrates the split without stopping. When the split ends, she puts her swinging leg on the floor while holding the leg she pushed with aloft (illustration 5).

Passing Support on the Shoulder

A gymnast performs this element by moving onto her shoulders from a sitting position (figure 2.44). She must move very fast to create the energy she needs to pass through the shoulder. If she goes too slowly, she will not be able to pass through her shoulder later. When her legs move through the vertical position, she should shift her body weight onto the passing shoulder, raising the opposite shoulder and arm a little. The gymnast should focus on

Figure 2.41 Passing support on one hand with a split.

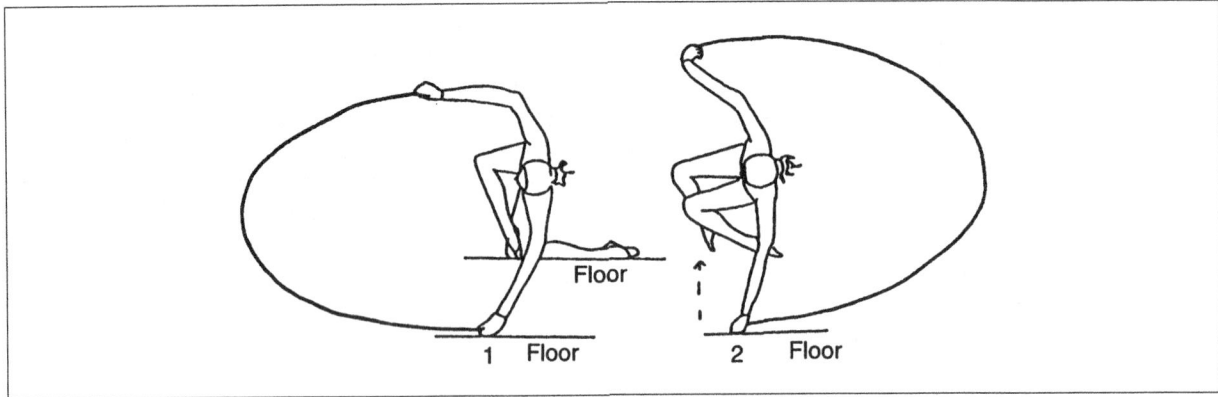

Figure 2.42 Passing support on one hand through a rope, turned forward.

Figure 2.43 Backward passing support on one hand.

rolling from her chest to her stomach in sequence after passing through her shoulder. Thus, she should not relax her leg muscles after passing support.

Grovels

Similar to lateral rolls, a gymnast grovels when she rotates in an untucked position sideways through her thighs, pelvis, or chest with the help of one or both arms. Grovels differ from lateral rolls in that in grovels, the arms support the gymnast's body. Figure 2.45 shows the grovel through the legs and pelvis with a helping arm. Figure 2.46 shows the grovel through the back with the help of both arms (illustrations 5-6).

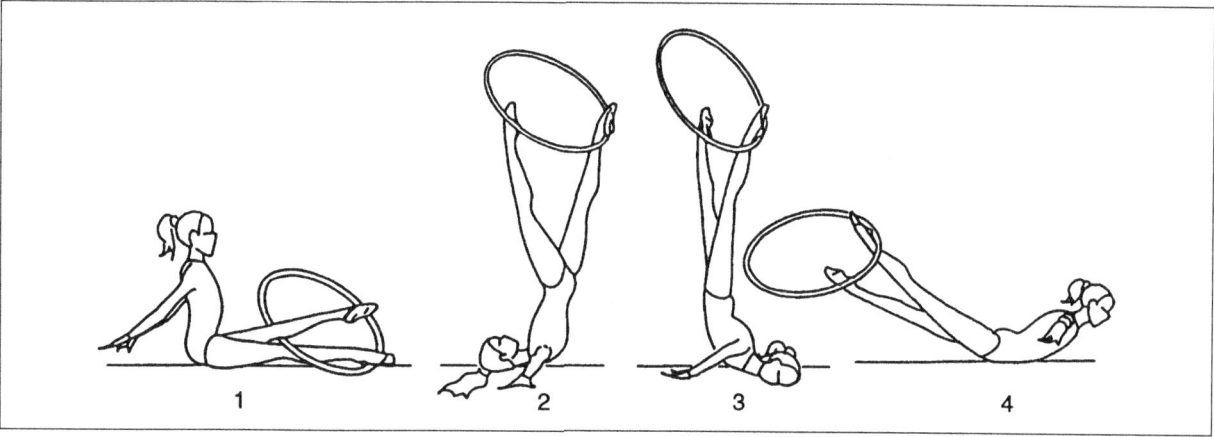

Figure 2.44 Passing support forward on the shoulder with the hoop on the legs.

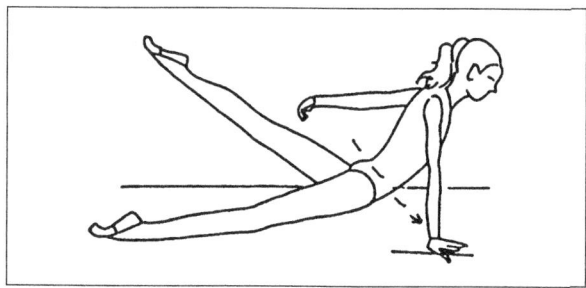

Figure 2.45 Grovel through the legs and pelvis with a helping arm.

Lying Positions

This is a steady position of the body on the back or stomach and chest. Figures 2.46 and 2.47 show two examples of gymnasts moving to a lying position. Because lying is very comfortable when handling apparatus, gymnasts often use it when performing original elements.

Floor Balancing

Floor balancing, or support, involves trying to steady positions of the body on one or more parts of the body other than the legs: in a V-sit position (figure 2.48a), on the chest (figure 2.48b), or with an arched back (figure 2.48 c, d). To hold all these positions, a gymnast must tighten her muscles to project the center of gravity (CG) over the support. Balances on these supports are steadier than on the legs, because the center of gravity is lower, but floor balancing poses are inconvenient because they demand more muscle tension.

Floor Turns

These are turns on the back, buttocks, chest, or stomach. Figure 2.49 shows the turn on the spine, performed by swinging one leg.

Slides on the Floor

Slides on the floor involve motions forward, backward, or passing through the split position while in contact with the floor. In figure 2.50, a gymnast demonstrates the slide forward with the help of both arms. A slide through the side split begins from sitting (backward) or lying on the legs (forward). The gymnast straddles her legs and passes through a side split with or without the help of one or both arms. She must not stop in this position; the slide must be continuous and smooth.

Wave-Like Motions on the Floor

Wave-like motions on the floor involve sequential bending and extending of the joints while lying or sitting. These exercises differ from proper waves because the starting position does not allow a real body wave. Wave-like elements help a gymnast vary her composition. Figure 2.51 shows an example of a wave-like element.

Floor Jumps

These are jumps on the buttocks (figure 2.52) or spine. They are not specific to RSG, but they are used by some gymnasts because they are very showy, deeply impressing spectators.

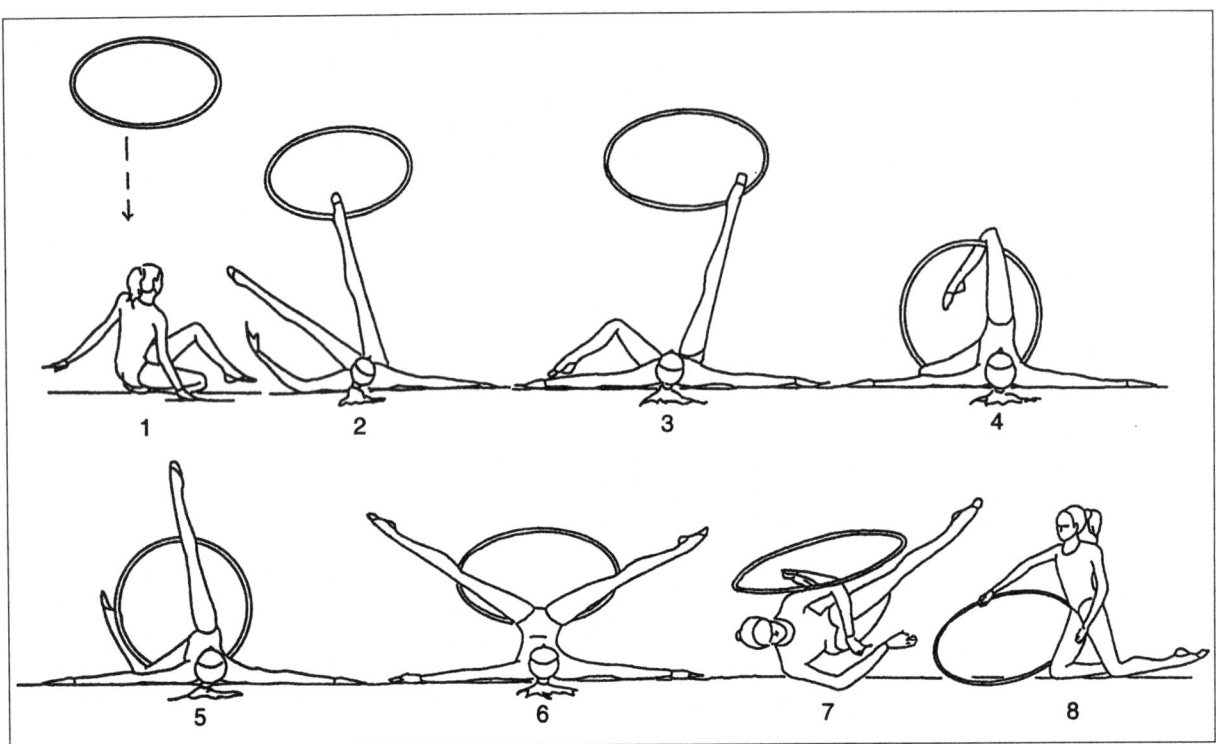

Figure 2.46 Lying on the back, catching a hoop with the legs, then groveling into kneeling.

Figure 2.47 Lying on the back, catching a rope and spinning it on a foot.

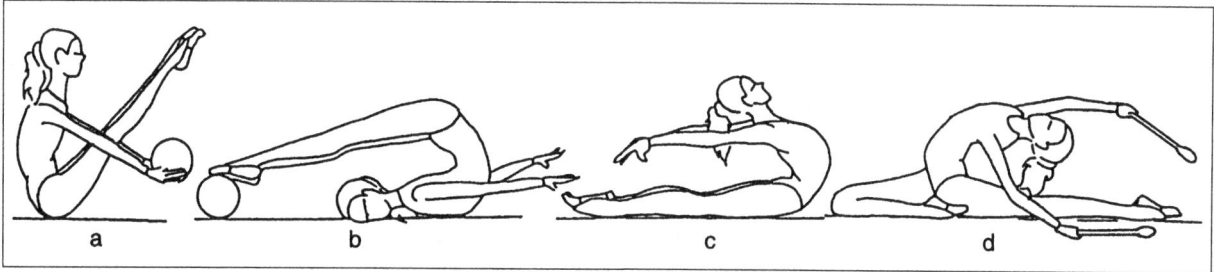

Figure 2.48 Floor balances: (a) balancing in a V-sit, (b) arched back with support on the chest, (c) arched back with support on the legs, (d) half-split support with an arched back.

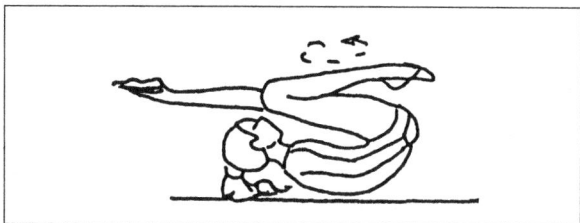

Figure 2.49 Turn on the spine.

Thus far, we have looked closely at the basic elements of body movements. Now, in the following sections, we will examine modal, or linking, body movements. This information will help coaches and gymnasts make competitive compositions smoother.

Modal Body Movements

As mentioned early in this chapter, the modal group of elements, also known as linking elements, help a gymnast interpret the character of the music and connect elements of other groups. In this section, we will describe how modal elements are classified and the specific techniques of selected modal elements.

Classification of Modal Body Elements

We can divide the modal group into static elements, or poses, and dynamic elements, or traveling and

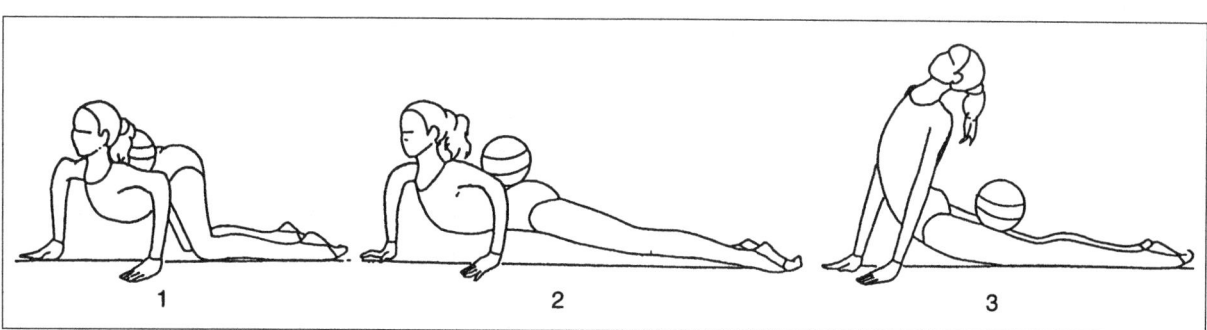

Figure 2.50 Sliding on the floor, then rolling the ball over the back.

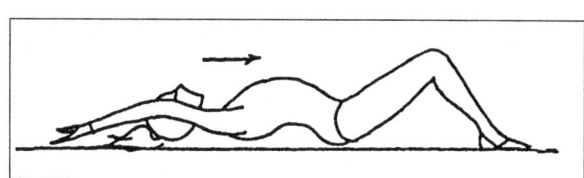

Figure 2.51 Wave-like motion of the body.

Figure 2.52 Floor jump on the buttocks.

expression. A static pose, also known as a proper pose, is a momentary static fixing of the body in position. In RSG, traveling across the floor may involve walking or running. Running, of course, is faster than walking and involves a small flight phase. Walking in RSG simply means taking different types of steps, which are a variety of locomotions in different directions, shifting the body weight from one leg to the other. Finally, expressive elements involve motions with different body parts to kinesthetically express the gymnast's interpretation of the musical accompaniment, excluding elements of mime. In the following sections, we will describe the techniques of each of these aspects of static and dynamic modal elements.

Techniques of Selected Modal Elements

We will turn, now, to examining specific techniques needed to perform modal elements effectively. First we will look at static poses, then traveling, and, finally, at expressive elements.

Static Poses

There are two main types of poses in RSG: starting and finishing. Before beginning her composition, a gymnast takes a certain starting pose, which she fixes for the minimum time necessary before making her transition to moving. The finishing pose completes or "tops off" the composition. The gymnast should hold the starting and finishing poses for the spectators and judges. Moreover, the Code of Points requires a gymnast to be in contact with the apparatus during poses. The choice of these and other poses should depend on the following factors:

- Aesthetics.
- Plan of a composition.
- Character of the musical accompaniment.
- Subsequent or previous movements.
- Individuality of the gymnast.
- Imagination.

A gymnast can pose in the following positions:

- Standing on one or both legs.
- Kneeling on one or both knees.
- Sitting.
- Squatting or semisquatting.
- Lunging.
- Balancing on supports.
- Lying.

Figure 2.53 shows several examples of effective poses.

Traveling

A gymnast may walk and run forward, backward, or sideways in various patterns across the floor, moving her arms and trunk in various positions. In the preparatory phase of training lessons, a gymnast can walk and run to warm up her legs, especially her feet. There are two types of steps used in RSG: dance steps (folk, historical, modern, jazz, and so on) and gymnastic steps (on the toes, soft, high, sharp, wide, spring, cross; see figure 2.54).

Chapter 9 describes the dance steps appropriate in RSG. Here, we will concentrate on gymnastic steps only. All of the steps we will describe are performed while assuming an erect body position.

Steps on Toes

This is simply walking on the toes with or without slightly bending the knees.

Soft Steps

A gymnast takes soft steps by shifting her body weight from her toes while rolling gradually onto flat feet (figure 2.54a).

High Step

To high step, the gymnast stands on one leg on her toes and steps to a flat foot or onto her toes again. She raises her free leg forward, bending it at the knee at a right angle and pointing her toes (figure 2.54b).

Sharp Step

To sharp step, the gymnast stands on one leg, rocking from her toes to lower her heel and flatten her foot, her free leg bent and supported on its toes vertically near the supporting leg (figure 2.54c). Then she changes her leg positions: the supporting leg becomes the free leg, and vice versa. To make the step "sharp," the gymnast should lower her heel quickly (with an "accent").

Wide Step

To wide step, the gymnast lunges on flat feet or toes while swinging her arms strongly (figure 2.54d).

Figure 2.53 Examples of static poses: (a) lying on the shoulders, (b) the lunge on the left leg, (c) the right kneeling while bending forward, (d) the kneeling sit on the heels, (e) stag ring position with the left leg forward, (f) lying support on one hand with the right leg bent, (g) lying on the thighs with bent legs and arched back, (h) kneeling sit on the left heel, right knee forward, with rope wound around the hands.

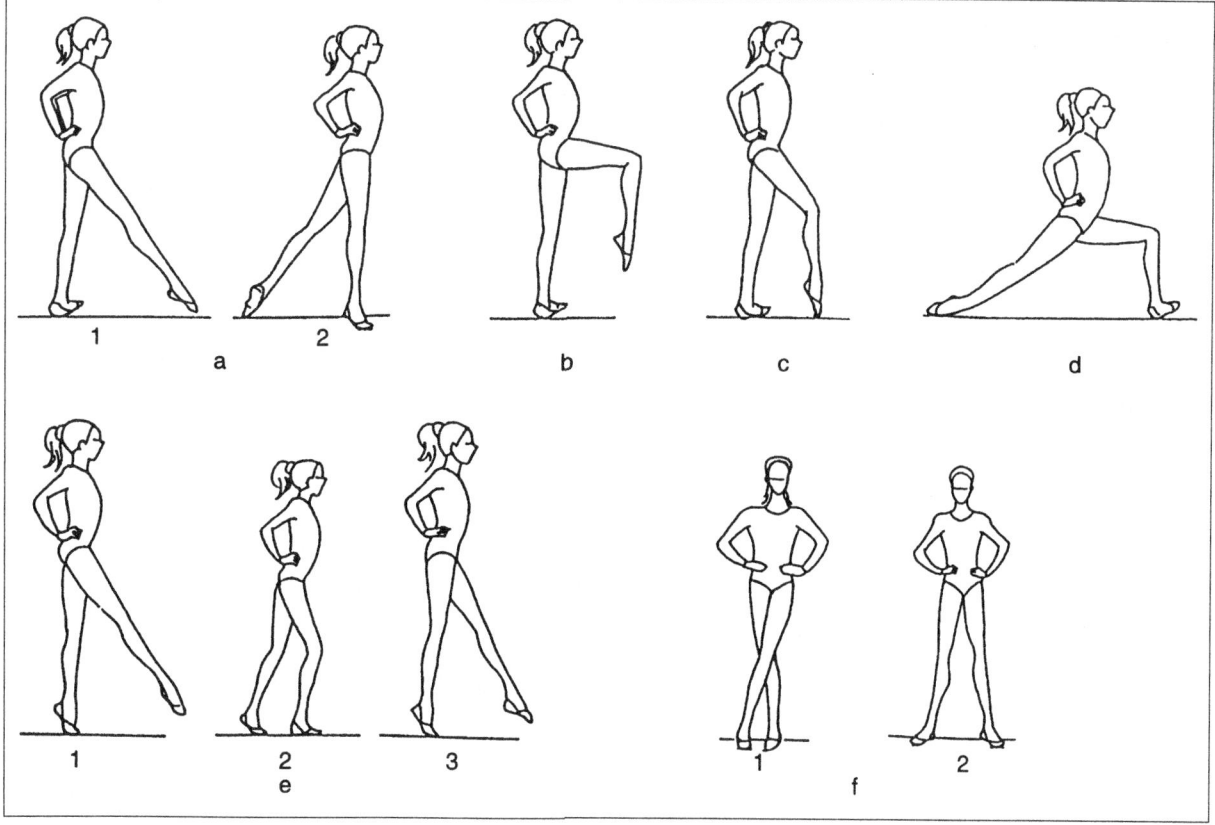

Figure 2.54 Gymnastic steps: (a) soft, (b) high, (c) sharp, (d) wide, (e) spring, (f) cross.

Spring Step

To spring step, the gymnast semisquats on the flat foot or toes of one leg and abruptly straightens the other leg (figure 2.54e).

Cross Step

Also known as the grapevine, the gymnast cross steps by placing one leg to the side, for example, a straight right leg to the right with the left leg extended to the side on the toes. Then the gymnast crosses her left foot in front of her right foot slightly bending her knee. Next she shifts her body weight onto her left foot, moves her right leg to the side, rests her right leg on its toes, and crosses her left leg behind and so on (figure 2.54f).

Running

This is simply stepping with small flight phases in which the gymnast repeats the movements of walking at a fast tempo, whether on the toes, high, wide, or crossed. The gymnast may also alternately bend her knees behind on flat feet or her toes.

Elements of Expression

Elements of expression include motions of different parts of the body to express the gymnast's interpretation of the musical accompaniment. Note, however, that the Code of Points does not recognize the elements of mime. The following is a list of elements of expression:

- Motions of the head, shoulders, arms, or trunk, borrowed from traditional folk, historical, or modern dances.
- Wave-like motions of the arms.
- Spring-like motions.
- Circles and swings of the arms, legs, or head.

There are many motions that a gymnast may borrow from traditional folk, historical, or modern dances. After choosing the musical accompaniment for the composition, the coach should select motions that will help the gymnast express her interpretation of the music. These elements cannot prevail over the other elements, however, because the composition may lose its gymnastic character. Instead, a coach should only incorporate a few elements in a gymnast's composition, giving it a uniqueness all its own. These elements work best alongside basic elements of body movements or handling of the apparatus.

Isolations

We will look, for example, at some movements borrowed from jazz. Isolations, as they are called, are very popular. Isolation means a motion of one body part in one direction while other parts of the body are moving in a different direction. A gymnast can isolate her head, shoulders, pelvis, or rib cage.

Head isolations may be front-to-back, side-to-side, looking side to side, turns, and swings. For a front-to-back isolation, the gymnast drops her head forward until her chin almost touches her chest and then backward as far her head can go. For a side-to-side isolation, a gymnast moves her head from one side to the other, bringing her ears as close as possible to her shoulders. (She must not raise her shoulders toward her ears.) When looking side to side, she turns her head over each shoulder, rotating her head sideways. For head swings, a gymnast lowers her head to the side and swings it straight to the other side or in a downward arch.

Shoulder isolations include up-and-down, forward-and-backward, and shoulder circles. They are performed similar to head isolations.

Wave-Like Motions

These movements of the arms include arm waves, swaying, hand waves, and swings. An arm wave (figure 2.55) can truly lend expression to a body movement. It begins from the shoulder, then smoothly and continuously passes to the elbow, then moves on to the wrist. When performing an arm wave, the gymnast should focus on the following:

- Feeling the connection of the scapulas when starting the movement.
- Proceeding with the correct sequence of movements.
- Allowing the muscles of the forearm and the hand to remain relaxed before extending the joints involved.
- Moving from joint to joint continuously with average tension through to the fingertips.
- Moving gently and smoothly, avoiding abruptly flexing and extending the joints, which can interfere with "passing" the wave.

At the moment the gymnast extends her hand, she contracts her shoulder blades again, then after the last movement of the first wave, the new wave begins. Thus, the gymnast does not straighten all the joints in her arm at any one movement. In serial waves, which are called arm swaying (figure 2.56), one arm begins the wave after the other arm finishes it.

To create a hand wave, the gymnast starts by bending her wrist joints, then sequentially bends all the small joints of the hand and ends at the fingertips. The hand wave requires great flexibility in all the hand joints.

To create arm swings (figure 2.57), the gymnast, reducing tension of the muscles and slightly flexing all the joints in her arms, swings her arms to the right with an abrupt downward movement. At the final point of the swing, the arms are straight but relaxed, and the hands are extended along the same line (straight out from the arms).

Spring-Like Motions

Spring-like motions involve uniform bending and extending the participating joints. Typically, gymnasts use their arms (figure 2.58) and legs as well as their whole bodies. In a composition, a gymnast employs spring-like motions to link elements, to create a "working" role, and to help her throw the apparatus. Similar purposes are served by spring-like motions during jump and leap takeoffs and landings.

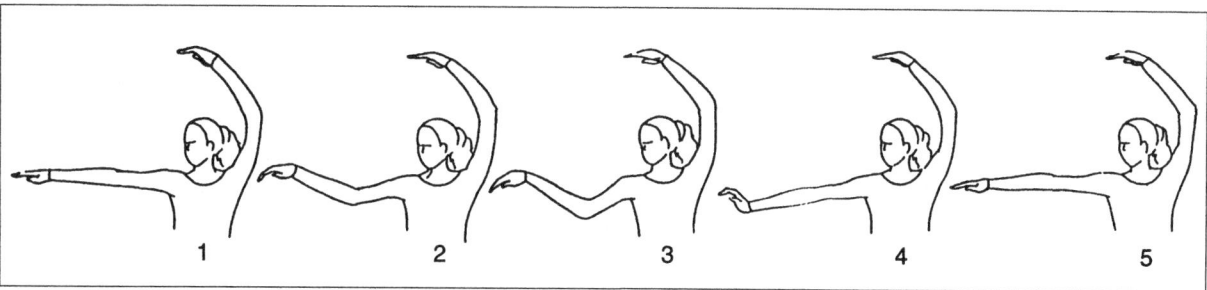

Figure 2.55 Arm wave.

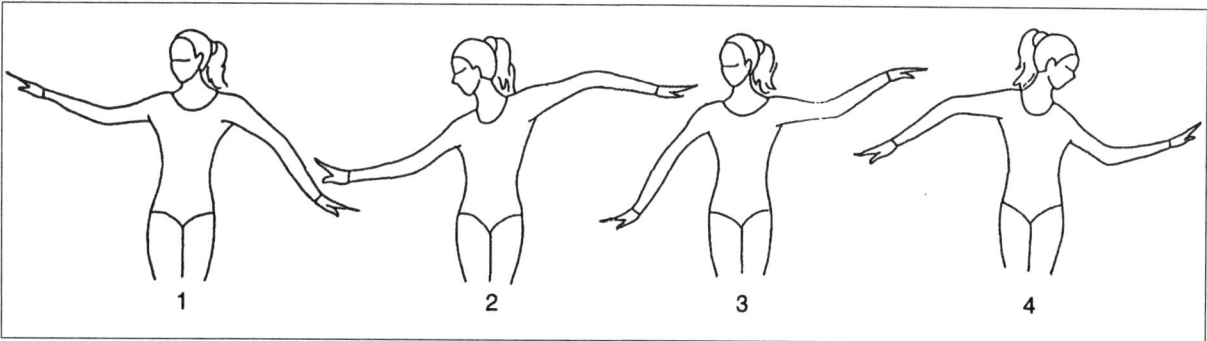

Figure 2.56 Arm swaying.

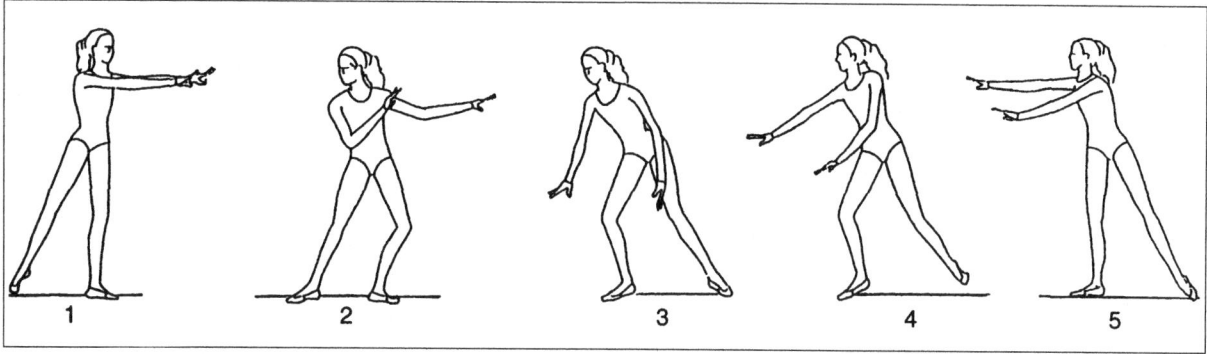

Figure 2.57 Arm swing.

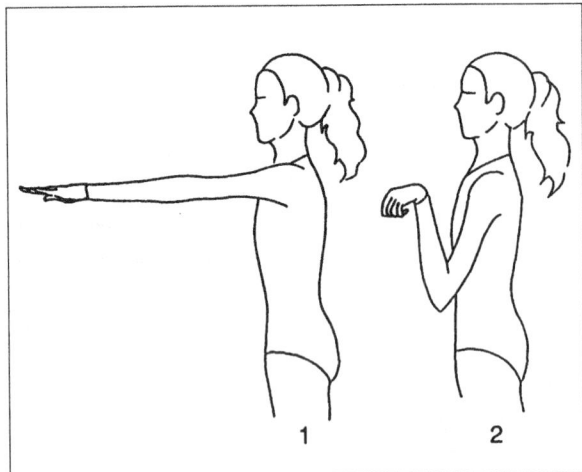

Figure 2.58 Spring-like arm motions.

Gymnasts can also use spring-like motions to reflect abrupt, dynamic characteristics of the music.

Circles

Circles are made by moving the arms, legs, trunk, or head in an arc. Like swings, gymnasts use circles as linking elements, in a working role, as part of a more complex movement, and as expressive elements (e.g., jazz circles with the head, shoulders, and so on). Moreover, circles can help gymnasts express their interpretation of the dynamics of the musical accompaniment.

Summary

In this chapter, we have looked closely at what each of the basic elements of body movements involves. We have carefully noted the phases, essential principles, and classification of performing each element. We have outlined the specific techniques of selected examples of each element. We encourage the reader to use this information to create successful competitive compositions.

Then we examined modal, or linking, body movements. We recommend that the reader use this information to make competitive compositions proceed more smoothly.

Now, in the following chapter, we will look at the same issues in regard to handling apparatus.

Chapter 3

Apparatus Handling Techniques

The techniques of handling apparatus are quite difficult to acquire because they require mastering many small movements, especially of the fingers. Therefore, every gymnast needs time to learn and polish every movement. Indeed, the gymnast who fully understands how to handle apparatus skillfully will certainly be more successful.

Apparatus Characteristics

Each hand apparatus is unique, distinguished by its own physical properties. It is, however, possible to separate apparatus into two groups: rigid (the hoop, ball, and clubs) and soft (the ribbon and rope).

In the following sections, we will look at both of these categories and each apparatus more closely.

Rigid Apparatus

Rigid apparatus acts differently from soft apparatus simply because it does not "give" much on contact with the gymnast or floor. This property affects how the apparatus responds to movements, and the gymnast must learn how to use these responses to her advantage. In the following sections, we will discuss the hoop, ball, and clubs.

Hoop

While the hoop can be wooden or plastic, it must not become deformed during movements. According to the Code of Points, the internal diameter of a hoop can vary from 80 to 90 centimeters; it must weigh at least 300 grams.

Form and material determine the movements of the hoop. The rim permits it to rotate, and its ability to quickly return the form of a circle allows the gymnast to use it as a spring. Such effective rebounds permit the gymnast a wide variety of movements. In addition, the gymnast can create a large rotary movement due to the great distance from the center of gravity to the hoop's rim (see "Catches," page 85, for more details). A large rotary movement also creates a stable trajectory in flight, allowing the gymnast to pass parts of her body into the hoop while catching it.

Ball

The ball can be rubber, synthetic, or plastic (if the plastic has elasticity similar to rubber). The Code of Points states that the diameter of the ball can vary from 18 to 20 centimeters and must weigh at least 400 grams. Although the ball can be of any color and feature a geometric design, the Code of Points does not permit the ball to have large figurative drawings.

Naturally, because of the material from which it is made, the ball has the highest elasticity of all the apparatus. And its spherical form makes it suitable for rotations, rolls, throws, bounces, and rebounds.

Clubs

Clubs can be made of wood or synthetic materials. According to the Code of Points, the length of a club can vary from 40 to 50 centimeters, and each club must weigh at least 150 grams. The shape of the club is like a bottle: the wide part is called the "body," the thinner part is the "neck." The neck ends in a ball-like shape called the "head" not more than 3 centimeters in diameter (figure 3.1). The gymnast may cover the club with tape or paint it completely or partially in one or more colors.

We call a pair of clubs "twin apparatus." Of course, this presents a unique challenge to the gymnast, requiring her to coordinate her movements with those of, not one, but two apparatus at once. It is helpful to know that the center of gravity of the club is toward the head as this fact makes it more difficult to handle. Catching clubs is especially

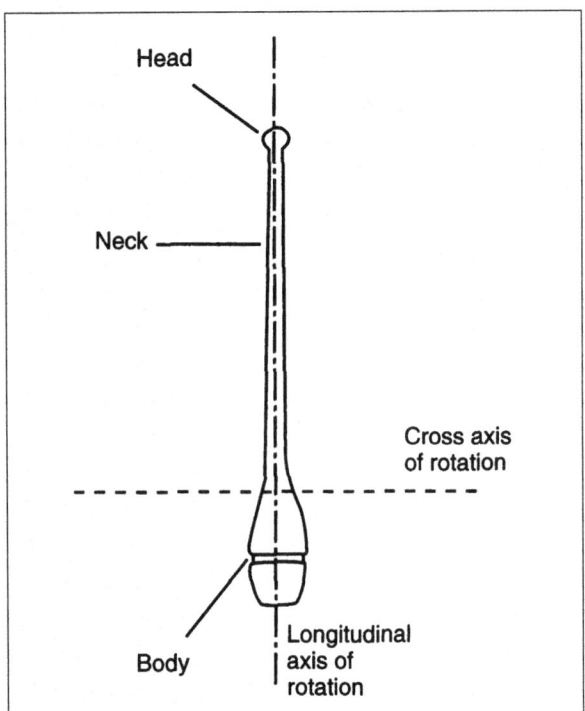

Figure 3.1 The RSG club.

difficult because their rotational planes are unstable during flight. Finally, unlike the other two rigid apparatus, the ball and the hoop, clubs do not really bounce because of their low elasticity and complex form.

Soft Apparatus

As the gymnast can use the rigid property of the hoop, ball, and clubs to her advantage, so too can she use the soft property of the rope and ribbon. In the following two sections, we will describe how a gymnast can use the rope and ribbon to add effective elements to her competitive composition.

Rope

The rope can be made from hemp or from a synthetic material, provided that it has the same weight (density) and elasticity as hemp. The rope should be proportional to the height of the gymnast: when she is standing on the middle of the rope, the ropes ends should reach her armpits. The rope should not have handles; instead, the Code of Points allows only one or two knots on the ends of the rope. The gymnast may cover the ends of the rope for a length of not more than 10 centimeters with an antislip material. The rope can be of a uniform diameter or gradually thicken toward the center, but the thicker parts should be made from the same material as the rest of the rope. The rope itself can be any color or partially painted.

As a soft apparatus, the rope differs from a ribbon in length and weight. The gymnast can, for example, use the rope's strong elasticity to create interesting elements (like bouncing the ends of the rope off the floor). Moreover, the tension the rope can hold permits the gymnast to rotate it at a high speed. This feature, however, makes it difficult to maintain a given shape in flight and while catching.

Ribbon

The ribbon (figure 3.2) consists of two main parts: stick and material. The stick can be of wood or a synthetic material, with a maximum diameter of 1 centimeter at its widest part. The shape of the stick may be cylindrical, conical, or a combination of these two, and its length must be 50 to 60 centimeters, including a ring to which the gymnast attaches the ribbon to the stick. The gymnast may cover the end of the stick she holds with an adhesive tape or antislip material for a maximum length of

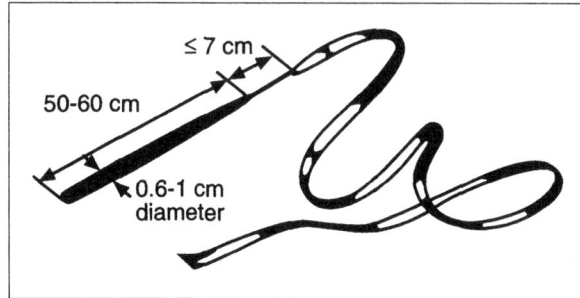

Figure 3.2 The ribbon.

10 centimeters. The ribbon should be of satin or any other similar unstarched material. It can be of one, two, or more colors. The weight of the material without the stick and attachment should be at least 35 grams; its width should be from 4 to 6 centimeters, and its length should be at least six meters. The end of the material attached to the stick may be doubled for a distance of not more than one meter and should be sewn together along both long edges. The ribbon is attached to the stick by a series of rings. The length of the given attachment may not be more than 7 centimeters (not counting the ring at the end of the stick).

The ribbon is the longest apparatus and the easiest to use. Its irregularity (stick and material), the opportunity it provides for constant movement and creation of various figures, and the stability of its shape in flight all make it easy to catch.

Classification of Apparatus Handling

All handling of apparatus falls into two main categories: static and dynamic (figure 3.3). In the following sections, we will examine each of these categories in detail.

Static Elements of Apparatus Handling

Static elements concern elements in which the apparatus is supported by any part of the gymnast's body that do not allow independent movements of the apparatus. The gymnast keeps the apparatus static using various grips. She uses static elements in combination with body poses only, except balances with the ball.

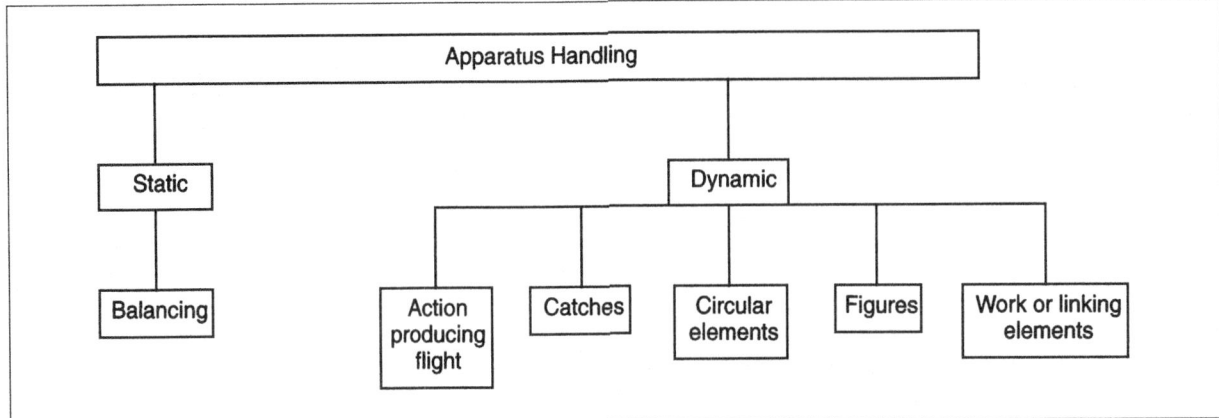

Figure 3.3 Classification of apparatus handling.

Dynamic Elements of Apparatus Handling

Dynamic elements are movements in which the apparatus executes motion, rotation, or a combination of the two with or without separation from the body of the gymnast. All dynamic apparatus actions are divided depending on the character of the executed elements. These are actions that lead to flight or unsupported positions (for example, throws, rebounds, bounces), catches, circular movements, figure elements, and linking elements.

Grips

It should come as no surprise that how a gymnast grips an apparatus can make or break her performance. Each specific way of holding an apparatus either adds to or detracts from the overall impression the gymnast makes on the judges. Thus, in the following sections, we will describe the types of grips from which the gymnast may choose to create the smoothest possible performance.

Types of Grips

The physical structure of each apparatus dictates the different ways the gymnast may use it. Apparatus with static, or rigid, grips do not have any degree of freedom as they are fixed in position by one or more parts of the body. Dynamic, or free, grips allow the apparatus to maintain a certain amount of latitude.

All grips are divided into two groups (figure 3.4). In many cases, the gymnast may use various parts of her body to grip the apparatus, but the majority of all movement of the apparatus is with the hands. Therefore, grips of the apparatus mainly concerning the hands are called main, or typical, grips. Grips made by other parts of the body (e.g., forearm, shoulder, foot, thigh, leg) are called nonmain, or atypical, grips.

As mentioned, the gymnast can execute main grips with one or both hands. She may either use her palms or the backs of her hands. Specifically, the hand may grip an apparatus in the following ways:

- From above the apparatus in an overgrip.
- From below the apparatus in an undergrip.
- From the side or sides of an apparatus in a "side grip."
- With the hand twisted 360 degrees in a reverse grip.
- With one or both arms in a straight grip.
- With crossed arms in a cross grip.

The creative gymnast may combine grips, having one hand effect one grip and the other hand, a different grip. Some two-handed grips are either straight, for which the gymnast straightens her arms, or crossed, for which the gymnast crosses her arms.

The position of the apparatus in different grips relative to the floor can be horizontal, vertical, or inclined. Relative to the gymnast's face the position of the apparatus may be in front, behind, or to the side.

Techniques of Grips

Naturally, the various apparatus both permit and dictate differing grips. In the following sections, we will describe the appropriate grips for each apparatus.

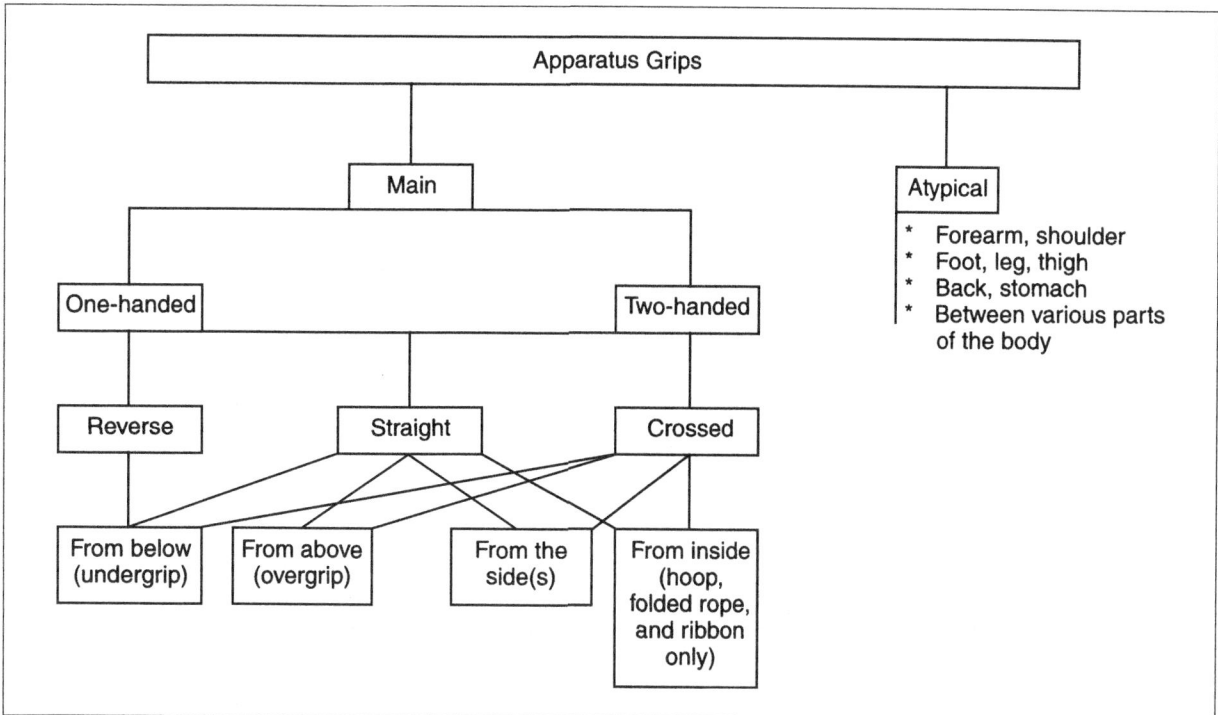

Figure 3.4 Classification of apparatus grips.

Hoop

To create a main grip, the gymnast holds the hoop with three fingers (thumb, forefinger, and middle finger) or four fingers (thumb in opposition to other fingers; see figure 3.5). In both cases, the fingers hold the hoop without tension, permitting the gymnast to go smoothly from performing one movement to another. A gymnast may execute a one-handed grip from above or below. A two-handed grip may be with the arms straight or crossed. Unique to all apparatus, the gymnast may grip the hoop from the inside, leading to some interesting two-handed grips: (1) both hands using the same grip, both from either outside (figure 3.5c) or inside (figure 3.5d) the rim and (2) both hands using different grips, one hand from inside the rim and one hand from outside the rim.

The free grips are performed with the hand, leg, or other body part, from inside the apparatus. This allows the gymnast to rotate the hoop.

Ball

A ball lends itself to all kinds of static grips (figure 3.6), including main grips (e.g., one-handed, two-handed, straight, crossed, reverse, from below, from above, from one or two sides) and nonmain, or atypical, grips, using one or more other body parts.

Gripping a ball is different from gripping other apparatus because the gymnast can hold the ball between both her hands in the same or different grips. The gymnast may use the following hand positions to create different grips:

- One from above, the other from one side.
- One from below, the other from one side.
- One from below, the other from above.

When the gymnast executes a main grip of the ball, she allows it to lie freely on her palm or palms. She separates her fingers, bending them slightly under the form of the ball without tension. The gymnast is not allowed to press the ball to her forearm or to compress it with her fingers. When gripping the ball from the sides, the gymnast also bends her fingers slightly. To grip the ball with the back of the hand, the gymnast must stretch her fingers as far as possible, forming a curved bowl of sorts (figure 3.6e).

Atypical grips are widely used in competitive compositions, mainly by elite gymnasts. They are usually concerned with balancing the ball on some part of the body, such as the neck, shoulder, forearm, back, or feet (figure 3.6f). An elite gymnast also uses an atypical grip to catch the ball.

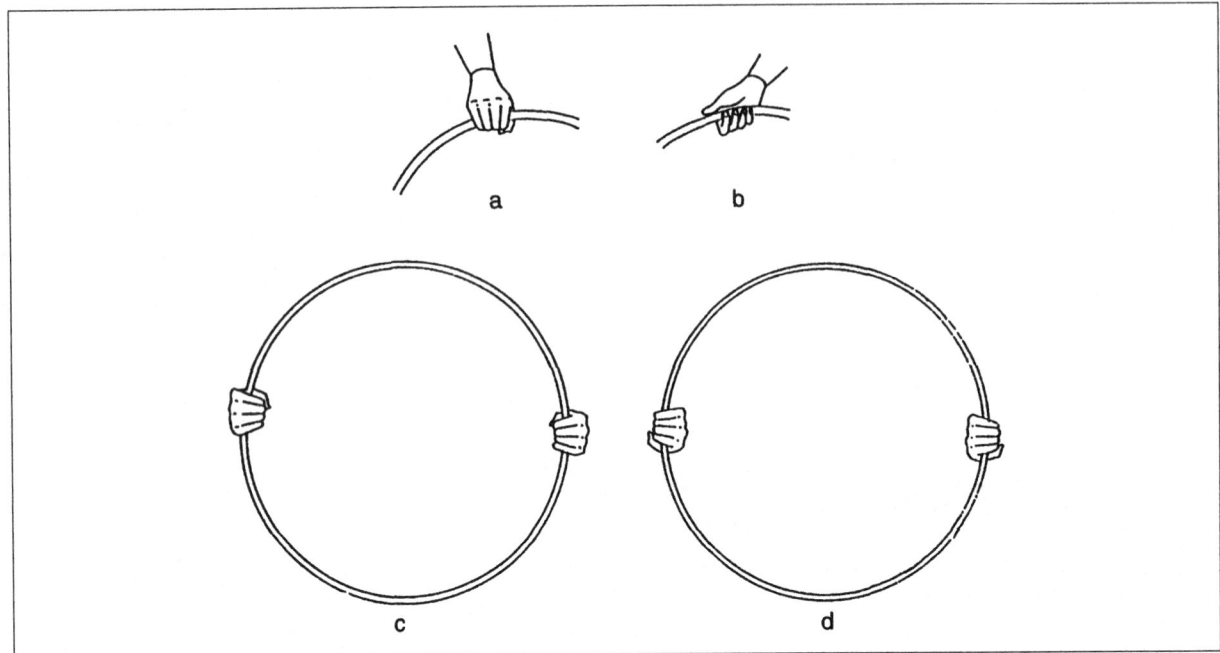

Figure 3.5 Sample hoop grips: (a) one-handed from above, (b) one-handed from below, (c) two-handed from outside, (d) two-handed from inside.

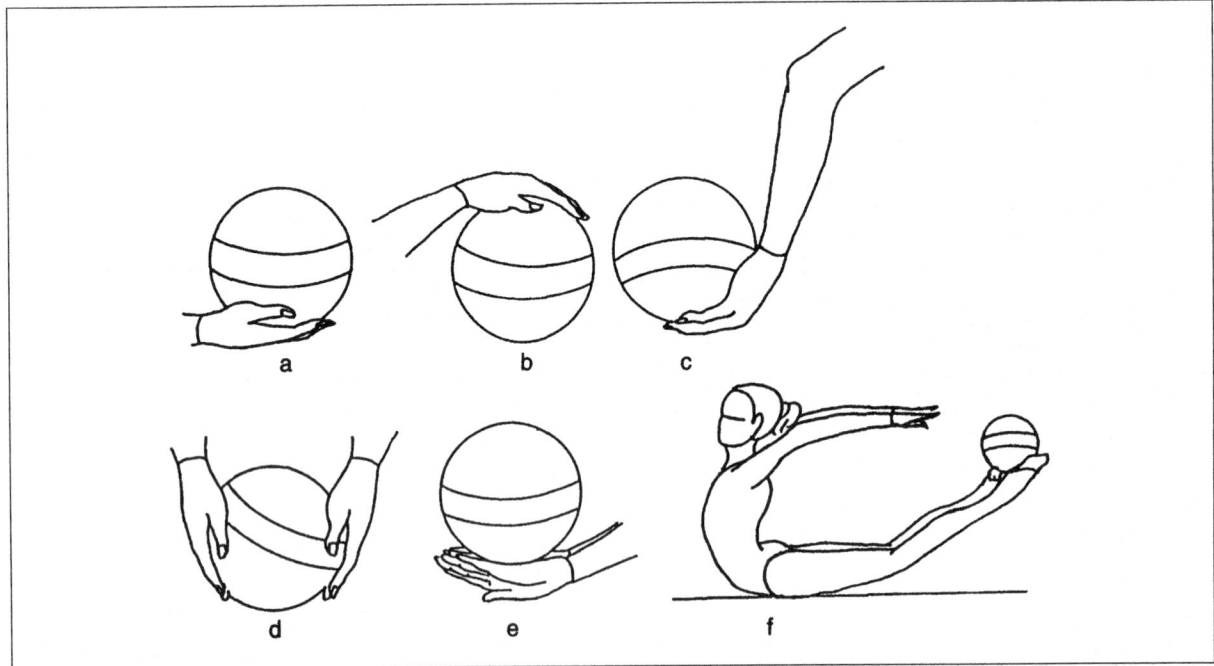

Figure 3.6 Ball grips: (a) one-handed from below, (b) one-handed from above, (c) one-handed in reverse, (d) two-handed from the sides, (e) on the backs of both hands, (f) with the feet.

Clubs

A gymnast may hold the clubs in main or atypical grips in three positions: by the club's head, its neck, or its body.

To create a main static grip of the club's head, the gymnast fixes it without tension in her palm, thumb, and middle finger to hold the club by the head; her forefinger may extend forward along the club's neck (figure 3.7a). In this grip, the club is aligned

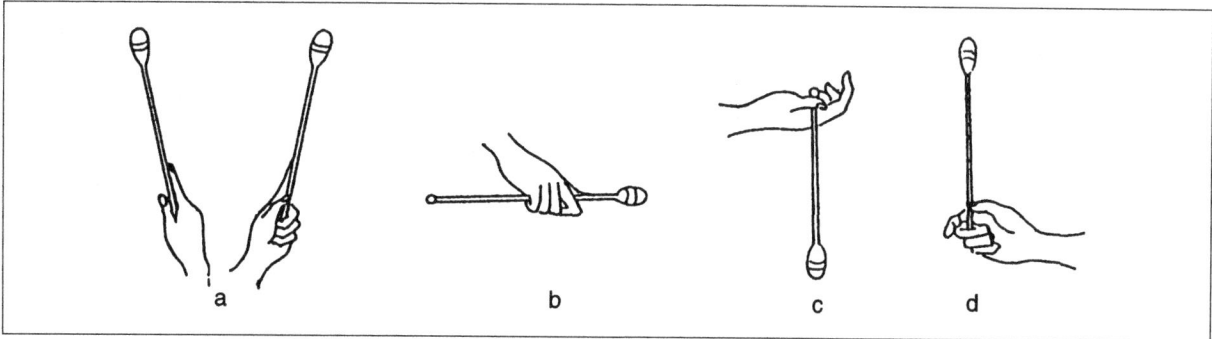

Figure 3.7 Main club grips: (a) rigid grip by the head with the forefinger extended along the neck, (b) rigid grip of the neck, (c) free grip of the head between the thumb and palm, (d) free grip of the head between fingers and palm.

with the forearm or hand. In all rigid grips, the movement of the club is solely determined by the movement of the gymnast's arm. When catching the club by its neck, the gymnast must grip the club rigidly without fixing her forefinger along the club's neck.

The gymnast may momentarily hold the club by its neck or body in main static grips from above or below, with or without keeping her thumb opposite to her other fingers (figure 3.7b). However, the Code of Points requires that gripping the club by its neck or body cannot predominate over the other grips in a competitive composition.

To create free grip of the club, the gymnast may only use one hand. Her fingers freely hold the club's head in one of two ways (figure 3.7, c and d): between her thumb and palm or between her fingers and palm.

Free grips help keep the club's rotation in a constant plane in the palm. So, during mills and small circles with the clubs, it is necessary to hold the clubs in a relaxed manner without tension or pressure.

The gymnast may hold the club momentarily in atypical static grips, too, for example, between her feet (figure 2.39, illustrations 1-4, page 52), between her calf and thigh, under her armpit, and so on.

Because the clubs are a twin apparatus, they can be held together or separately. The gymnast can combine them in parallel or nonparallel positions. There are two variations of the parallel position: (1) the head of one club touches the head of the other, and the body of the first touches the body of the other, or, (2) the head of one club touches the body of the other.

In nonparallel positions, the clubs may form a straight line (head with head, body with body) or an irregular (crooked) line along which the gymnast shifts the clubs relative to one another (the head of one to the neck of the other, and the body of the first to the neck of the other).

The grips of combined clubs can be: straight or crossed at different parts of the clubs, for example, one hand for the head, the other for the neck, from above, below, or the side.

To hold the clubs separately, the gymnast may use one of several grips:

- Two main grips in both hands.
- Two atypical grips with one or more other parts of the body.
- One main grip and the other atypical, for example, one club in the hand, the other on the foot.

Rope

The gymnast can hold the rope with either main or atypical grips. The rope can be either open or folded into halves, thirds, or fourths. Specifically, the gymnast may hold the rope in the following ways:

- Using one part of her body in a main grip using one hand, or in an atypical grip (for example, by using her neck).
- Using two parts of her body in two main grips using both hands, or in two atypical grips (for example, one end on her foot and the other on her forearm), or in one main and one atypical grip (for example, by placing one end on her foot and the other in her hand).

Gymnasts use straight, reversed, and crossed grips, from above and below, to hold either an open or a folded rope with main grips. A gymnast can effectively grip one-handed at the end or the middle of the rope. She can create a secure two-handed grip by holding the ends or middle or by holding with one hand at the middle and the other at the end.

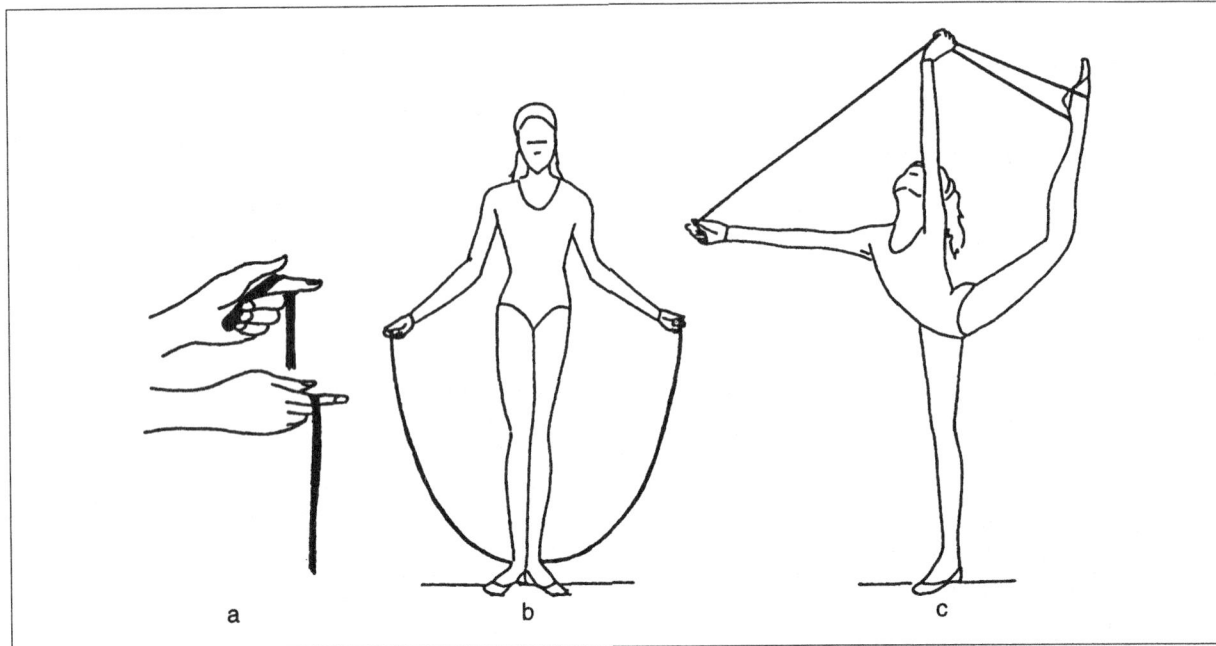

Figure 3.8 Sample rope grips: (a) in the hands, (b) with two hands at the ends, (c) with two hands and one foot.

In a main grip, the gymnast should hold the rope lightly by the ends so that she retains the mobility necessary to perform the elements. In jumps and leaps, the rope's ends lie in her palms and are easily supported by her thumbs from above and her forefingers and middle fingers from below without any pressing (figure 3.8a). The gymnast should bend her elbows slightly without tension. For swings, circles, and especially for throwing, the gymnast may hold the rope between her fingers either with (1) her second finger and forefinger, so her third finger is between the rope's ends or (2) her thumb and third finger, so her forefinger is between the rope's ends. The first position is better for throwing because the rope's ends receive equal initial velocity. In both grips, the gymnast fixes the rope's knots in the bases of her fingers and slightly presses with bent fingers from above.

Ribbon

As a rule, the ribbon is held by a stick. In certain cases, however, the Code of Points allows the gymnast to hold the ribbon with her hand momentarily or to use one arm for the ribbon and the other for the stick, at least in certain cases. A gymnast frequently uses this last position when throwing the ribbon. These grips may be straight or crossed and from above or below.

The gymnast should hold the stick freely with her thumb, forefinger, and middle finger so that the end rests lightly on her palm at the base of her thumb (figure 3.9). Her grip should be relaxed but strong enough to prevent slipping. If the grip is not too intense, the coach can easily pull the stick from it. But if the coach must tug hard, there is excessive tension in the gymnast's hand muscles.

Apparatus Flight

An apparatus's flight (unsupported position) may be the result of a gymnast's manipulation or a reaction of the apparatus with the floor area (support). Either way, the necessary energy for their transition to flight is built through throwing, bouncing, or rebounding.

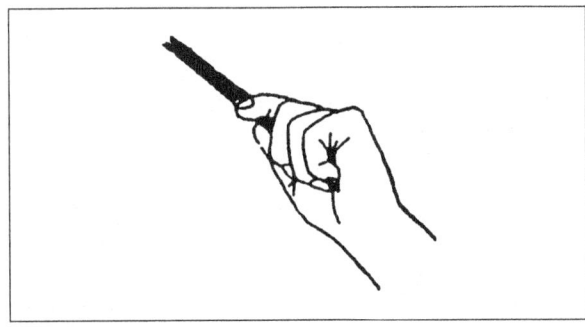

Figure 3.9 Grip of the ribbon stick.

General Physics of Apparatus Flight

The flight of a piece of apparatus depends upon three factors: the force (F) applied to the apparatus enabling it to fly; the mass (m) of the apparatus; and the time (t) during which the force F was applied.

A body's energy of movement, or momentum, is the product of a body's mass and its linear velocity:

$$F = m \cdot a$$

where F is the momentum, m is the apparatus's mass, and a is the apparatus's linear velocity.

The time interval Δt during which the force F was applied is the time from the starting t_S to the finishing of the act t_F:

$$\Delta t = t_F - t_S$$

The impulse (I) applied to the apparatus is the product of the (average) force applied to the apparatus and the amount of time over which that force is applied (figure 3.10):

$$I = F \cdot \Delta t$$

You can also understand impulse as the change in momentum of the apparatus as a result of applying the force.

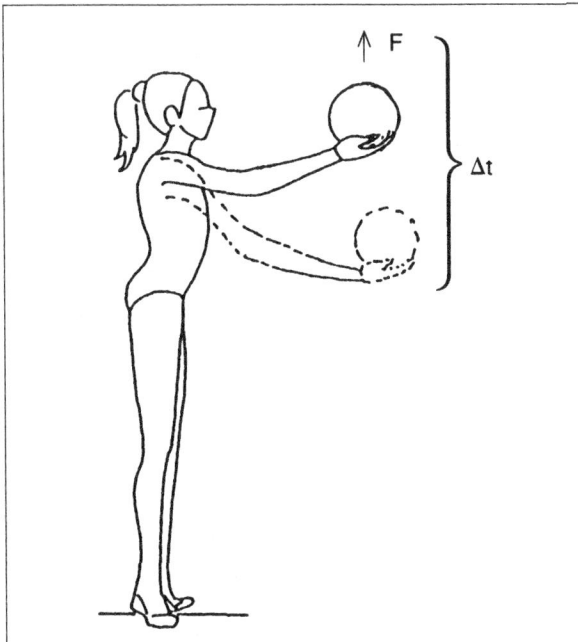

Figure 3.10 Impulse of the force formed when the ball is thrown, where F is the force applied to apparatus and Δt is the action time of this force.

Throws

A throw is an action taken by a gymnast that gives the apparatus the energy to move into an unsupported position (flight).

Physics of Throws

All throws are characterized by height and range, which depend on the initial velocity (V_0) of the apparatus. In turn, the velocity of the throw depends on the magnitude force (F) applied to the apparatus, and on the length of time (Δt) it is applied. It is possible to throw the apparatus to a certain height by applying a large force F in a short period of time Δt or by applying a smaller force F, but over a longer time Δt. Thus, the initial velocity V_0 of a thrown apparatus is

$$V_0 = \frac{F \cdot \Delta t}{m}$$

where F is the force applied to the apparatus, Δt is the action time, and m is the mass of the apparatus.

According to the initial velocity of apparatus V_0, throws can be executed in several ways: to apply a small force F over a long time Δt, it is necessary to execute a preliminary swinging movement, and to apply a large force F in a minimum Δt, the throw is executed with a push or small swing. In any case, to give an apparatus energy, momentum is necessary.

There are two main types of throws: (1) a proper throw, performed after a regular preparatory swing (in this book, "throw" implies "proper throw") and (2) a toss, which is simply a very small throw, performed with a preparatory push or small swing of the hand. A gymnast may use either a proper throw or a toss with all apparatus to change her grip.

The force F applied to the apparatus can be directed in every possible direction relative to the gymnast's face, typically, forward, backward, upward, sideways (right or left), or oblique. The trajectory of the flight of an apparatus depends on the magnitude of the force F and on the direction of this force. Changing the angle α of the throw and the velocity of the throw V_0 will change the trajectory of the flight.

Depending on the magnitude of the force F and its direction, both the height and range may be described in three ways: height of flight (high, medium-high, low), range of flight (near, medium-far, far).

The vertical height (H) of a throw of an apparatus is determined by the following formula:

$$H = \frac{V_0^2}{2g}$$

where V_0 is the initial velocity of the apparatus thrown and g is the acceleration due to gravity.

You can calculate the range of a flight using the following formula:

$$L = V_0^2 \cdot \mathrm{Sin}\, 2\alpha$$

where L is the range of the flight, V_0 is the initial velocity of the apparatus thrown, and α is the angle of the throw between the body part and the horizontal.

By increasing the angle of the throw α from 0 degrees at horizontal up to 45 degrees, the range of the flight will be increased. And by changing the angle of the throw α from 45 degrees up to 90 degrees, the range will decrease gradually, but the height will also be increased. In turn, the change of velocity V_0 influences the trajectory of the flight of the apparatus.

When teaching throws with apparatus, you should use space marks (on the walls or ceiling) for better space orientation. These help the gymnast understand how to create the correct throwing angle with her arm. When performing these elements, the gymnast must direct her apparatus to a concrete point and delay releasing the apparatus until she is sure she has formed the correct angle with her arm. After learning the correct angle of throwing α, it is not necessary to delay the arm position.

Combining the two factors of height and range yields a variety of throws. According to the requirements of the Code of Points, the minimum height of a gym hall is 8 meters, and floor size must be 13 by 13 meters. Thus, throws may be classified as follows:

- Height (vertical):
  — Up to 2 meters is classified as low.
  — From 2 up to 4 meters is classified as medium.
  — More than 4 meters is classified as high.
- Range (horizontal):
  — Up to 3 meters is classified as near.
  — From 3 up to 6 meters is classified as medium.
  — More than 6 meters is classified as far.

Thus, depending on the height and range, nine versions of throws are possible, created by the near, medium-far, and far ranges for each of the three heights.

It is necessary to apply a large force F for the medium ranges and especially for high and far throws. For these throws, the gymnast uses not only her arm muscles but also her trunk and leg muscles. Specifically, she must semisquat, then straighten her legs (figure 3.11). In this way, she transfers the energy from her muscles to the apparatus. Therefore, the apparatus will fly farther and higher than without using a semisquat.

To create a high or medium-high throw, the gymnast must use her entire arm from her shoulder to her hand, keeping her elbow slightly bent. In

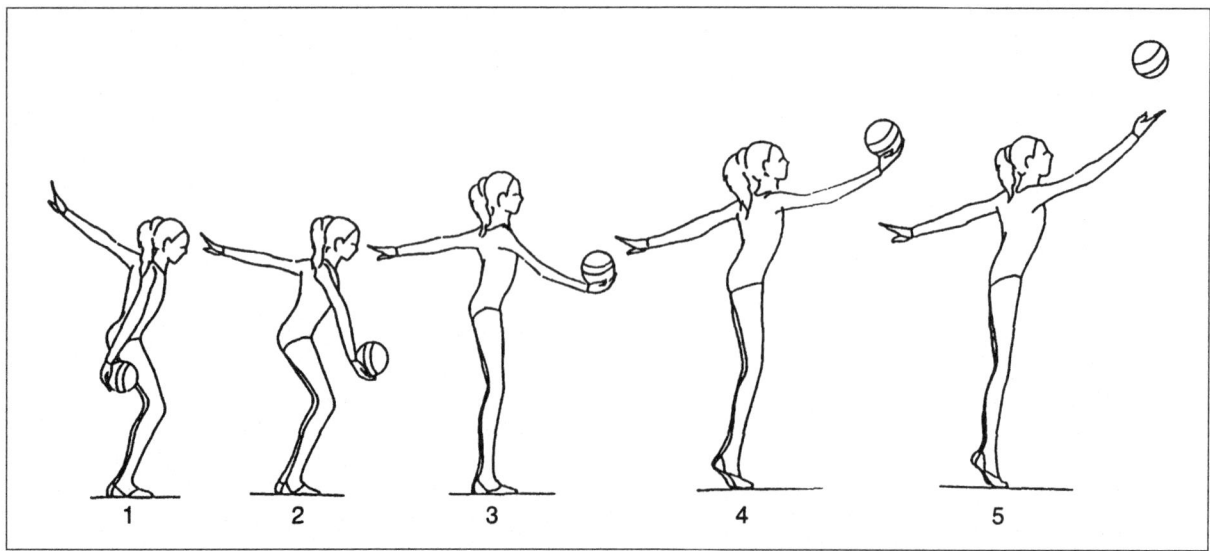

Figure 3.11 Ball throw with a preparatory swing and semisquat.

contrast, the gymnast tosses the apparatus from only her elbow and wrist.

Throws with rotations in flight involve physics as well. The gymnast can give each apparatus a trajectory such that it will not only fly but also rotate in various planes (figure 3.12a): horizontal, oblique, and vertical. To create rotating trajectories, it is necessary to apply the following forces F to the apparatus: the force, applied to it in the action time $F \times \Delta t$ (impulse of the force) and rotary moment M.

The rotary moment of force F at a distance e from the apparatus's axis of rotation is

$$M = F \cdot e$$

where F is the force applied to the apparatus and e is the arm force, the distance from the apparatus's axis of rotation to the point at which the force is applied (figure 3.12b).

The rotary moment depends on force F, which is applied to the apparatus and arm force e. The greater e is, the less force is needed. For the hoop, the arm force e necessary is greater than for the club or ball. Therefore, a smaller force F is necessary to rotate a hoop than to rotate another apparatus.

Depending on both the force F and the distance e from the axis of rotation, the apparatus will fly and rotate in different directions: forward, backward, sideways, and oblique. Differences in these two variables can create a variety of directions in which the apparatus may rotate. The three main types of rotations are as follows:

- Straight—the apparatus is in flight, rotating away from the gymnast.
- Return—the apparatus rotates in a direction toward the gymnast.
- Lateral—the apparatus is in flight and rotates in the horizontal plane from the right to the left or from the left to the right.

Naturally, throws of the soft apparatus (the rope and the ribbon) differ from throws of the rigid apparatus (the hoop, clubs, and ball) due to their physical properties. Specifically, the gymnast can throw soft apparatus whole or partly (for example, one end of the rope or the stick of the ribbon) and open or folded (for example, rolled up or twisted). But the gymnast must keep all throws of the soft apparatus in the necessary shape during flight. How? She must rotate and swing the rope or ribbon fast enough to create sufficient acceleration in the preparatory phase.

Phases of Throws

We can divide all types of throws into three main phases:

1. The preparatory phase gives the apparatus energy through a swing or push.
2. The main (release) phase is when the apparatus is moved from a supported to an unsupported position.

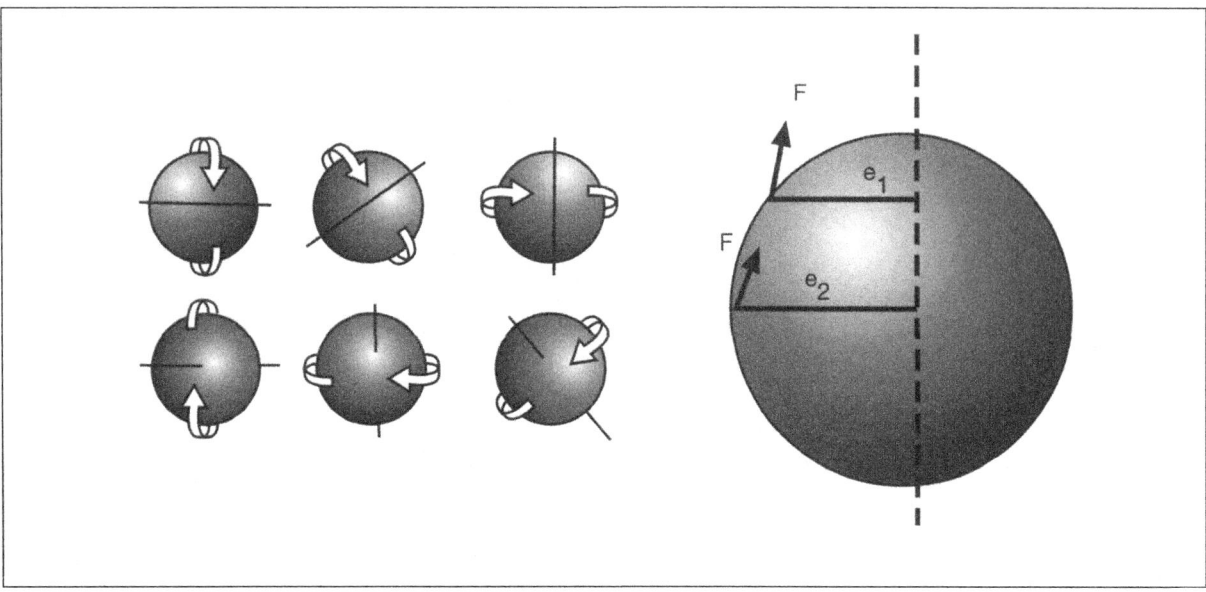

Figure 3.12 Rotation of apparatus in flight: (a) plane of rotation, (b) dependence of the rotary moment on length of the arm force e.

3. The finishing phase in which the flight of the apparatus and the part or parts of the body that performed the throw moves from the releasing position to prepare for the following element.

A gymnast can increase the difficulty of a throw in the way she grips the apparatus and the trajectory she sets in the preparatory phase. She may, for example, opt to use an atypical grip, perhaps with her legs. Or she may grip soft apparatus at the end, middle, or both. She may curve the trajectory of an apparatus in the preparatory phase if she throws the apparatus under an arm or leg (figure 3.13) or behind a shoulder or her back.

Techniques of Selected Throws

We will look, now, at specific techniques for throwing perfectly. We will discuss throwing each apparatus—its particular characteristics, its advantages, and its challenges.

Hoop The gymnast can perform the simplest throws using a static or dynamic (rotational) grip with one or both hands. To increase the difficulty, the gymnast can throw the hoop with other parts of her body, for example, with one or both arms, one or both legs, or her neck. During flight the hoop cannot alter or vibrate.

To throw correctly and high enough using any grip, the gymnast should rotate the hoop or swing it in the preparatory phase by slightly bending her arm. Then she should straighten her arm in the release (main) phase in the direction she wants it to fly. She should throw the hoop, not by abruptly flinging it, but by gently opening her hand. Excessive tension in the arm during throwing causes fatigue, especially in a composition with numerous throws. And if the gymnast becomes too tired, she loses her "feel" for an apparatus.

In throwing from a one-handed static grip, the gymnast should start from a semisquat and make a preparatory swing of the hoop (figure 3.14). During the release phase of throwing the hoop, the gymnast should straighten her legs and open her hand or hands, thereby increasing the height of the throw. In an upward throw, the preparatory swing should bring the arm right above the head. In oblique upward throws, the hand should be higher than the shoulders under angle α, close to 45 degrees. In forward throws, the hand must be at the same level as the shoulder (figure 3.14a). For variety, the gymnast may opt to throw bypass swings (under the shoulder and under the arm). Figure 3.14b shows a throw under the shoulder.

A preparatory rotation gives the hoop momentum when using a one-handed dynamic grip to throw. Such throws have two main advantages: they do not require significant additional effort and rotation in flight lends the hoop stability; in other words, it is

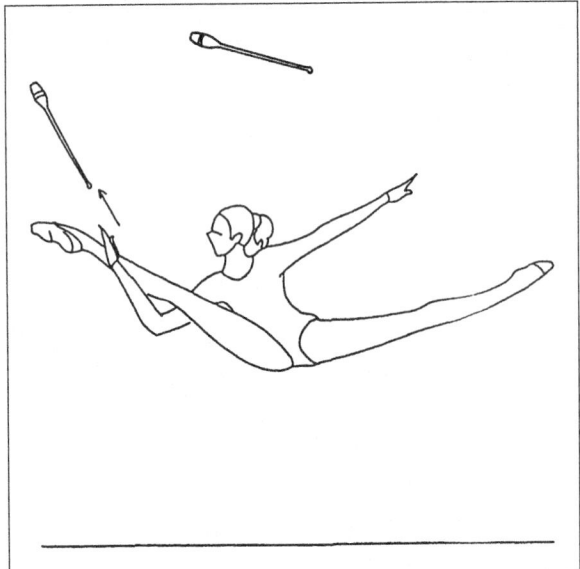

Figure 3.13 Split leap with a throw of the clubs under the leg.

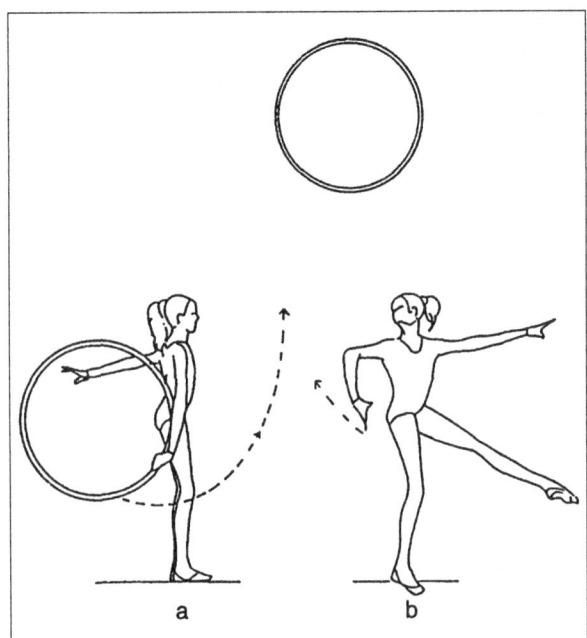

Figure 3.14 One-handed throws of the hoop with a preparatory swing and a semisquat: (a) forward, (b) under the shoulder.

able to maintain a given direction. Common errors seen in this throw are vibration of the hoop in flight and intersection of a rotation plane and a given trajectory of a flight, all of which are caused by insufficient rotation of the hoop. To eliminate such errors, the gymnast must simply rotate the hoop faster in the preparatory phase. A coach should have a gymnast who has this problem focus on the release phase at the point at which the hand begins actively to throw outward. Finally, to release the hoop accurately, the gymnast must learn to choose the correct angles α between the shoulder and the forearm as well as between the forearm and the hand.

The gymnast may also throw the hoop using atypical grips. In figure 3.15, the gymnast performs the split leap while throwing the hoop with her leg. She throws the hoop by swinging with her leg after a preliminary rotation on her leg.

To throw correctly with rotation around a vertical axis in flight, the gymnast must give the hoop a rotary moment M in the preparatory phase. Next she should give the hoop an active upward swing and then release it. Figure 3.16 shows that a rotary moment M may be achieved by uncrossing crossed arms.

The gymnast throws after rolling the hoop on her body by lowering her arm slightly and then smoothly releasing the hoop from her hand.

Ball The most important aspect of throwing a ball from a main grip is holding it on the palm without grasping it with the fingers in the preparatory phase. Meanwhile, the gymnast swings her arm and bends her legs slightly at the knees to create a sort of spring. In the release phase, the gymnast straightens her legs with or without rising onto her toes (figure 3.11, page 72); she may also choose to transfer her body weight from one leg to the other. The accuracy, height, and range of a ball throw depend on the arm angle α in relation to the horizontal and the arm direction during the release phase (figure 3.17).

In high ball throws using one or both hands, the gymnast must focus on the following:

- Swinging from her shoulder during the preparatory phase.
- Keeping her arm tension-free.
- Directing the movement of her fingers during the release phase.

Figure 3.15 Hoop rotation on the legs, split leap with the right leg throwing the hoop and catching it in rotation.

Figure 3.16 Uncrossing crossed arms to create rotary moment M to throw a hoop around an axis in flight, then catching it in a static grip.

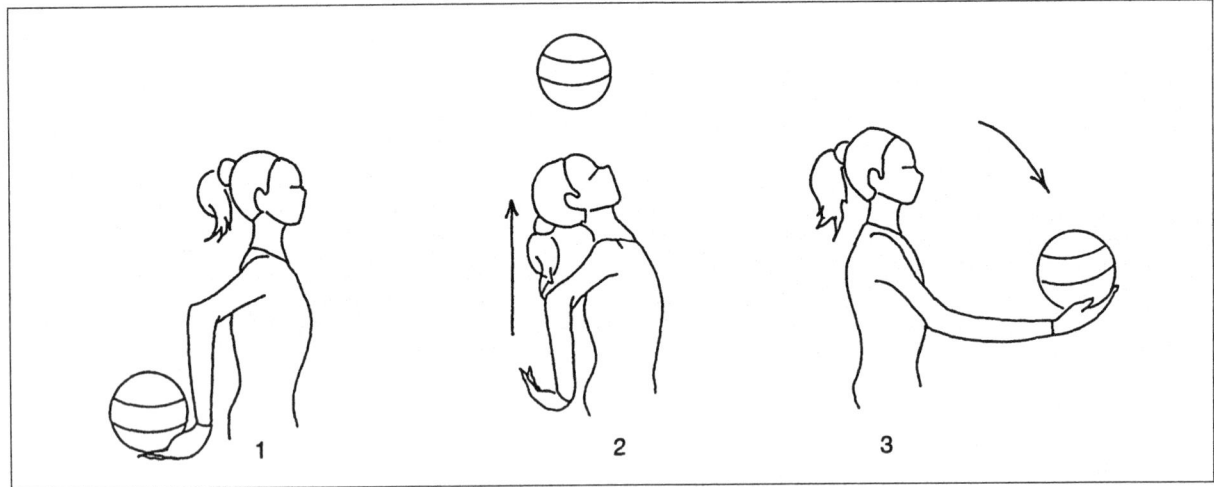

Figure 3.17 Throwing the ball under the shoulder.

- Gently placing her arm down during the finishing phase.

The procedure for throwing the ball after rolling it over the body is similar to the procedures for throwing the hoop.

A gymnast should strive to throw correctly, that is, she should connect her throws with her musical accompaniment.

Clubs The very nature of clubs makes throwing them unique. Specifically, as a twin apparatus, there are many different ways a gymnast can throw them. Club throws can:

- be held by similar or different grips by one or more parts of the body,
- be released with the same or different preparatory swings,

- be straight or bypass (under the arm, the leg, the shoulder),
- be in symmetrical or asymmetrical positions in relation to each other and the body when thrown,
- move in the same or other directions in the same or other heights and ranges, and
- rotate during the flight.

Throws of the clubs may be symmetrical and parallel (figure 3.18) or asymmetrical, created by consecutive throws by one or both hands. Moreover, the planes of the throws may be the same or different. Finally, the clubs can have the same or a different direction of flight.

To throw a club accurately, the gymnast must carefully direct the movement of her hand upon release. To be symmetrical, the clubs must fly in parallel positions without deviations. They may be released from a one- or a two-handed grip. While the two-handed grip is limited to between the forefinger and thumb or between the forefinger and third finger, the one-handed hold has three variations:

- One club between the forefinger and thumb and the second club between the forefinger and third finger.
- One club between the forefinger and third finger and the second club between the third and second fingers.
- One club between the third and second fingers and the second club between the second and little fingers.

Keep in mind that the center of gravity is in the body of each club, considerably far from the neck. In flight, the club rotates around its center of gravity in every possible plane. The clubs can rotate in parallel, or one club can rotate while the other does not (as in an asymmetrical throw). Furthermore, the clubs can rotate on different axes in flight. The gymnast may make small throws rotating the clubs in flight on either the vertical or horizontal plane. For such throws, the gymnast may choose either symmetrical or asymmetrical rotations. In the case of parallel rotation, the movements of each club should be synchronized. A one-handed parallel symmetrical throw should be performed without pressing the club head to the palm and fingers in conjunction with a non-tensive swing by the entire arm. It is very important to give the clubs equal acceleration.

The type of club throw depends on the zone of the grip. A rigid grip with the palm upward or downward facilitates a club throw. Less effort is needed to release the club after swinging it from a head grip than from a neck or body grip (figure 3.19). This is because the arm force e is greatest from the club's head to its center of gravity plus a straight line, formed by the gymnast's arm and club. In this case, the arm force e and rotary moment M are at their maximums, causing intensive rotation of the club during the flight. During a throw from a neck grip, it is more difficult to give the club a rotary movement M, because it depends on the arm force e of the club. In this case, the flight will be considerably shorter than from a head grip. Finally, it is more difficult for the club to rotate during flight after a

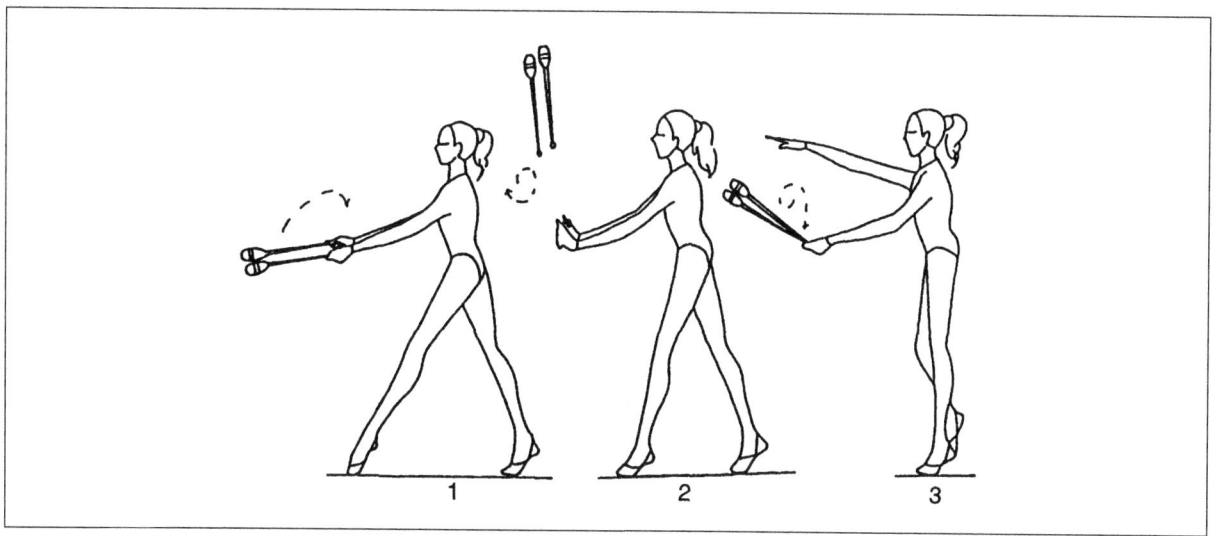

Figure 3.18 Throwing and catching both clubs.

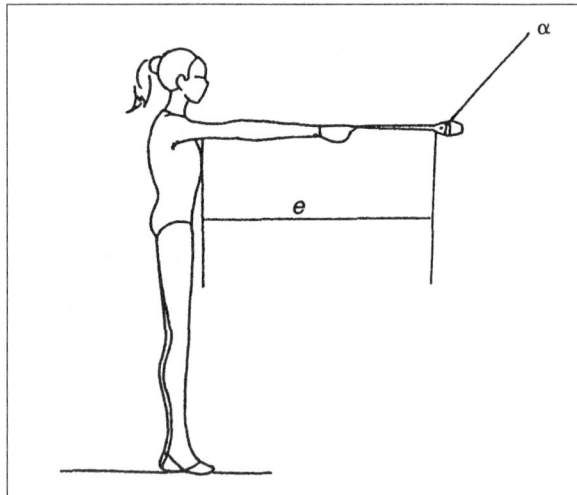

Figure 3.19 Biomechanics of a club throw from a head grip, where e is the maximum arm force and α is the center of the club's gravity.

body grip, because the arm force e is even less than in a neck grip.

Juggling the clubs involves low to medium-high throws, whether the gymnast uses one or both hands or does or does not pass the club or clubs from one hand to the other. Juggling is characterized by a high-tempo performance and rapid consecutive throws of the clubs. In this element, the next club throw is always performed during the flight of the other club (figure 3.20). Usually, the gymnast will juggle the clubs two or three times.

The gymnast may also opt to throw a club with her feet. To do so, she holds the body of the club with a static grip, and while rolling forward, throws the club upward by straightening her legs (figure 2.39, page 52).

Rope Throws are the most difficult rope elements performed. These exercises require the gymnast to have fine muscular sense, good orientation in time and space, and quick reactions.

To throw a rope folded in two from a main grip, it is necessary to circle and swing the rope to prepare to send it in the desired direction. In this preparatory phase, the arm swing should be arched and should accelerate. Immediately before releasing the rope, the gymnast should straighten her arm completely, extending it upward at an oblique angle. Then the hand and fingers actively participate in releasing the rope (figure 3.21). The direction of the flight depends on the final position of the arm, the hand, and the fingers. The height depends on the strength of the release.

The gymnast must especially focus on releasing the rope ends with equal acceleration, as the ends define the rope's shape during flight. If, however, upon release the gymnast give the ends of the rope different accelerations, the rope does not keep its shape during the flight, creating a technical fault. In throws with rotation, the gymnast should calculate the number of rotations of the rope during flight to help her subsequently catch the rope. To achieve stable rope flight, the elite gymnast can knot the rope ends together before the preparation phase. This technique requires excellent coordination abilities, because this action must be invisible to the judges and spectators.

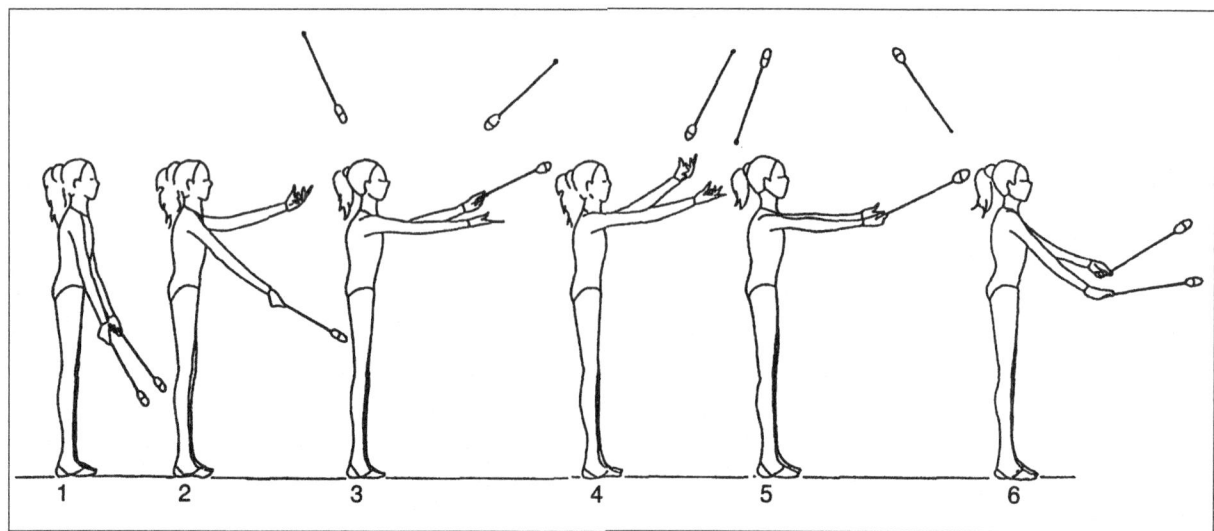

Figure 3.20 Juggling the clubs.

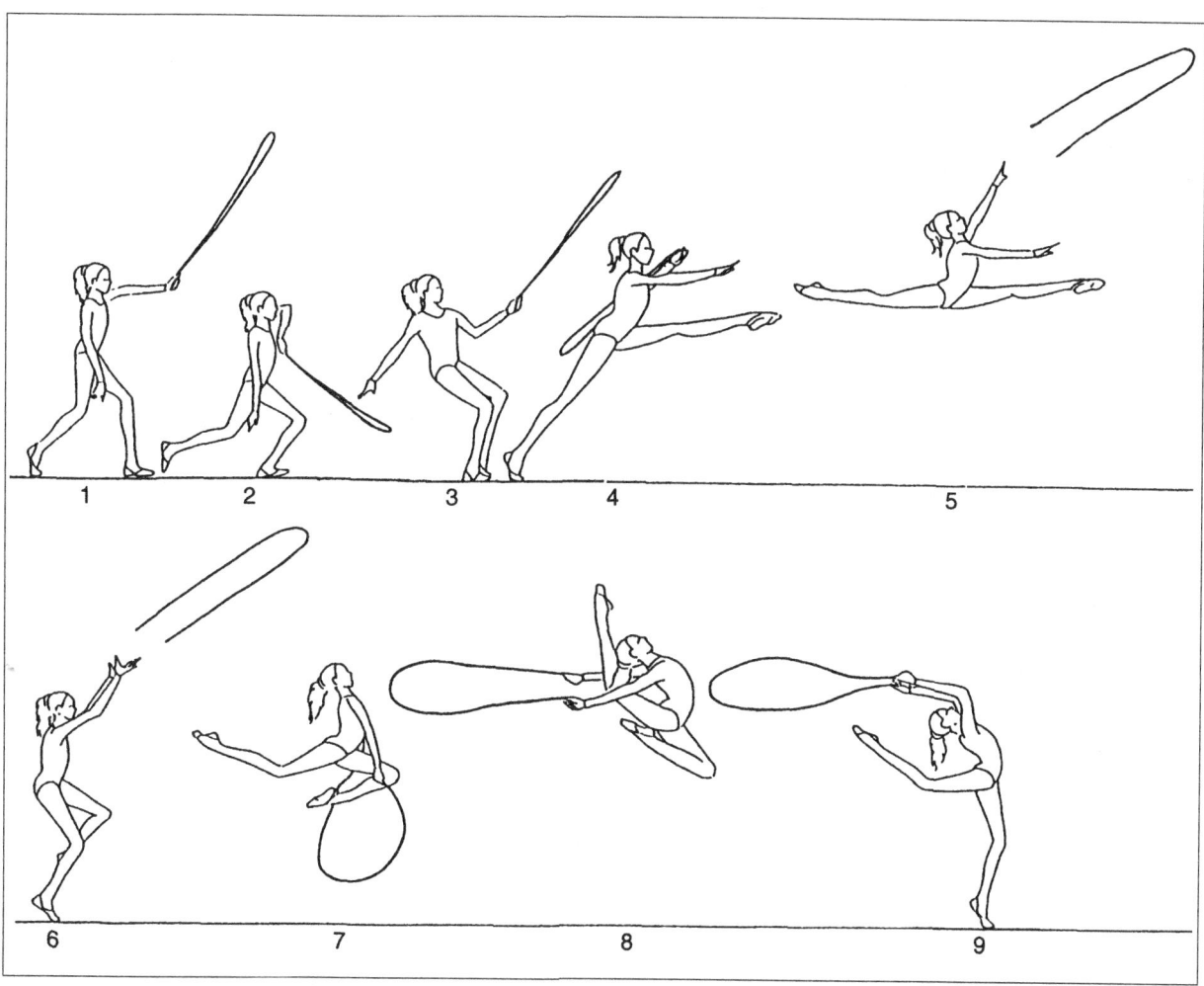

Figure 3.21 Split leap throwing the rope and catching it with a stag ring leap.

To perform a one-ended throw of the rope, or *échapper*, the gymnast should create a small preparatory swing, holding the rope (which is folded in two) by its ends. Then to release, she should pull one end down and send it upward at an oblique angle with a vigorous swing. Another variation is to throw one end of an open rope after a preliminary swing. It is possible to do arm rotations or figure eights, so that the rope moves on different trajectories. All preparatory movements should be active enough to avoid altering the rope's shape.

The gymnast can also throw the rope with her leg. Figure 3.22 shows a rope throw by swinging a leg during a forward roll. The gymnast throws the rope by straightening her knee.

Ribbon The unique aspect of ribbon throws is that less time is needed for the preparatory phase in comparison with other apparatus. Too much time in the preparatory phase would mean that the gymnast would not be able to maintain the pattern of the ribbon. Another problem is that in the release phase, the ribbon cannot be on the floor, but the extremity of the stick can voluntarily and momentarily touch the floor. Two main types of ribbon throws are possible, however: total throws and boomerang throws.

For total throws, the ribbon takes flight, and the shape of the pattern remains completely visible. Gymnasts may make a total throw using one of several methods, three of which are more typical:

- From the head: similar to the throw of a spear. The gymnast holds the stick forward by the bottom end. She throws quickly and strongly, making the ribbon fly in a gentle arch.

- From preliminary large circles: with or without rotating the stick around the hand, using a main grip. The gymnast must create circles at

Figure 3.22 Throwing the rope by swinging the leg, rolling forward, and catching it kneeling on the right knee.

a speed sufficient to keep the ribbon from knotting. Indeed, the shape of the loops or circles must be evident.

- From gripping the ribbon by both its stick and the ribbon material: the gymnast must grip the ribbon material near the attachment in a zone not more than 50 centimeters from the stick. After a preparatory swing, the gymnast releases the ribbon (figure 3.23, illustration 3). In the release phase, the end of the stick can voluntarily touch the floor momentarily. If the gymnast rolled the ribbon before the throw, it will spread in flight.

Boomerang, or returning, throws involve the gymnast throwing the stick end of the ribbon while holding onto the other end of the ribbon. During a boomerang throw, the ribbon straightens in flight, the gymnast jerks the hand that is holding the end of the ribbon, and the impulse is transmitted onto the stick, which changes trajectory and comes back to the gymnast's hand.

Depending on the flight's direction, there are three different types of boomerang throws (figure 3.24):

- Vertical candle—the stick flies upward or with a small deviation, and it must never touch the floor (figure 3.24a).
- Horizontal throw—the stick flies horizontally, either touching the floor or not. On the return, however, the stick must never touch the floor (figure 3.24b).
- Forward throw—the stick slides on the floor either during the throw or during the return, but the gymnast must catch the ribbon either with her hand or foot (figure 3.24c).

Gymnasts often toss the ribbon. Tosses are simply small throws of the stick without a large horizontal or vertical swing, with or without rotating the stick around the hand. Usually, gymnasts toss the ribbon to change their grip on the ribbon.

Bounces

Bounces as elements of a rhythmic sportive gymnastic program send the apparatus from one unsupported position to another unsupported position

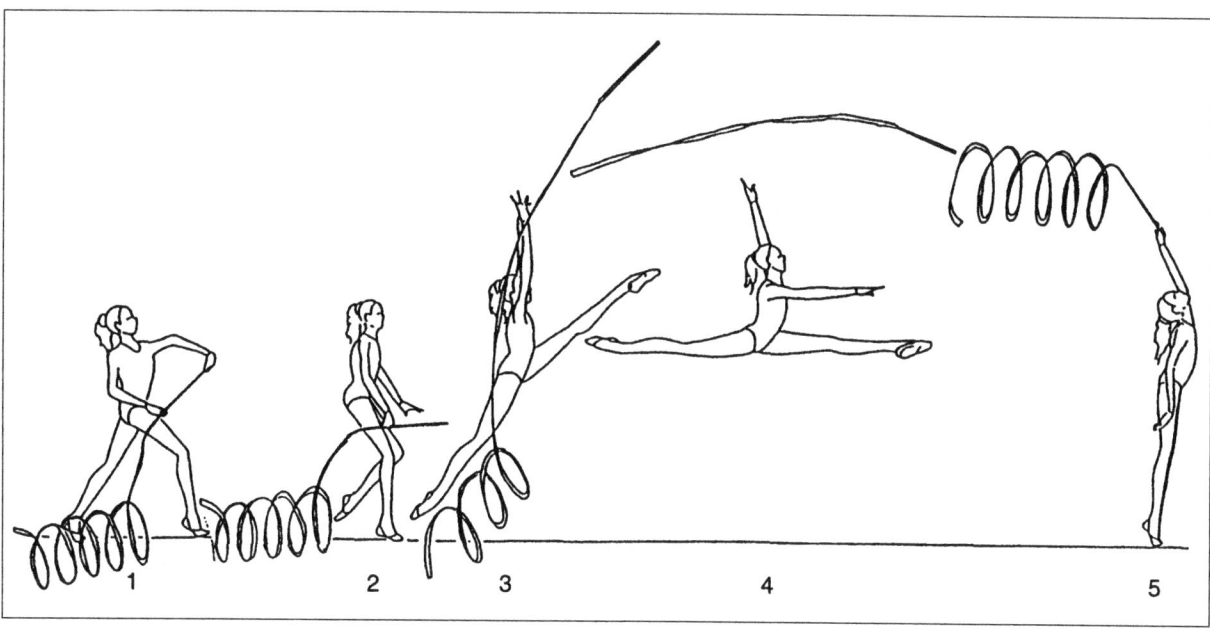

Figure 3.23 Split leap throwing the ribbon and catching in a stand on toes.

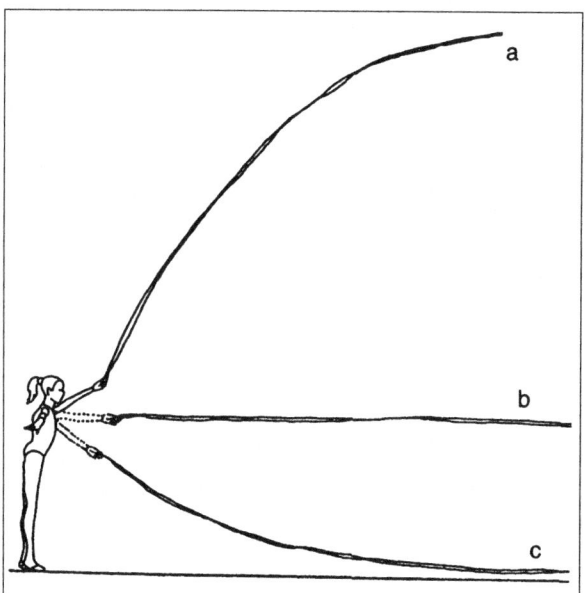

Figure 3.24 Boomerang throws of the ribbon: (a) vertical candle, (b) horizontal, (c) forward.

(flight-to-flight), simply due to the reaction of the apparatus with the floor.

Physics of Bounces

The force of the impact of the apparatus on the floor F_2 and the effect of the floor F_1 are equal and in opposite directions. The effect of the floor F_1 is a force, induced by the impact of the apparatus on the floor and forcing it to bounce in the opposite direction:

$$F_1 = -F_2$$

when F_1 is the effect from the floor and F_2 is the force applied by the apparatus.

The more force the apparatus applies to the floor, the greater the reaction of the floor. Thus, the greater the force, the greater the acceleration of the apparatus. The greater the acceleration of a bouncing apparatus, the greater the range and the height of the flight of the apparatus created by the bounce.

According to the force F_1 given to an apparatus, there are two types of bounces. The first type consists of those bounces actively performed by one or both hands or one or more other parts of the body. So, the force F_1 is given to the apparatus by the gymnast, and it receives force F_2 after contacting the floor. Usually these bounces are rhythmic bounces with the rope, hoop, or clubs. A second type of bounces are those that are passive in nature in which the gymnast throws the apparatus upward and allows it to fall down and then bounce from the floor again. The apparatus receives force F_1 when it falls down and force F_2 after contacting the floor. The gymnast uses passive bounces with the ball and hoop.

Phases of Bounces

We can describe the structure of bounces in three phases: the preparatory phase, the main phase, and the finishing phase. In the preparatory phase, the apparatus is flying downward. In passive bounces, this flight is after the throw, which is simply the preparatory phase. In active bounces, there are two subphases: the first subphase, in which the gymnast pushes off the apparatus, and the second subphase, in which the apparatus flies downward. In the main, or bounce, phase, the apparatus touches the floor and receives energy from it. In the finishing, or flight, phase, the apparatus returns to an unsupported position.

Techniques of Selected Bounces

The hoop and ball lend themselves most to bouncing. The clubs are too irregularly shaped to create good bounces. The elite gymnast can bounce a folded or open rope, but due to the soft nature of the ribbon, it is impossible to bounce. Thus, in the following sections, we will discuss techniques for effectively bouncing the hoop, ball, clubs, and rope.

Hoop As a rule, the gymnast bounces the hoop after large throws; thus, these are passive bounces. They are popular in group exercises.

Ball Of course, balls were made for bouncing! Because of the ball's elasticity, the gymnast can isolate bounces or create a series of rhythmic bounces. She can execute ball bounces perpendicular or at an angle to the floor, using one or both hands (figure 3.25).

To bounce the ball perpendicularly to the floor, the gymnast should make one or both of her hands accompany the ball downward through the push (figure 3.25a); this is, in effect, a small, gentle hand wave. During bouncing, the gymnast must avoid clapping her palm noisily against the ball or causing the ball to make a sound when it hits the floor. Then she must lift her hand (or hands) up together with the ball in preparation for the next push. Meanwhile, she must bend her legs so that the moment of the impact of the ball with the floor coincides with a semisquat. Remember, the height of the bounce depends on the force of the impact. The gymnast should use this fact to bounce the ball to different rhythms.

The gymnast may also bounce the ball at an angle to the floor (figure 3.25b).

Of course, the gymnast can bounce the ball with other parts of her body besides her hands. Figure 3.26 shows the ball bouncing from the gymnast's back.

Clubs Club bounces may be performed with one or both clubs. Direction of the club flight should be precise and well-oriented.

Rope A gymnast does not normally bounce this apparatus, but performances of these elements in a composition adorn it, demonstrating the gymnast's true mastery.

The elite gymnast can bounce a folded or open rope with one or both arms as long as the rope is taut. A preparatory swing is usually necessary so that the rope is not only stretched but also traveling at a certain momentum, enabling it to rebound from the floor. Figure 3.27 shows a rope bounced by the leg. The gymnast can bounce the rope using quick leg movements, straightening her trunk as necessary.

Rebounds

By "rebound" we mean an element in which the apparatus moves from an unsupported position to another unsupported position (flight-to-flight) due to interaction with the gymnast as opposed to interaction with the floor or other support.

Physics of Rebounds

Rebounds differ from bounces because the gymnast must quickly act on the apparatus, moving it in the direction she desires after the bounce. The gymnast can give the apparatus the necessary direction by turning, lowering, or lifting the body part that executes the rebound.

Usually, the gymnast rebounds with her hands or legs, but sometimes, she will use her trunk or shoulder. Of course, it can be quite difficult to intersect the complex trajectory of the apparatus with her body.

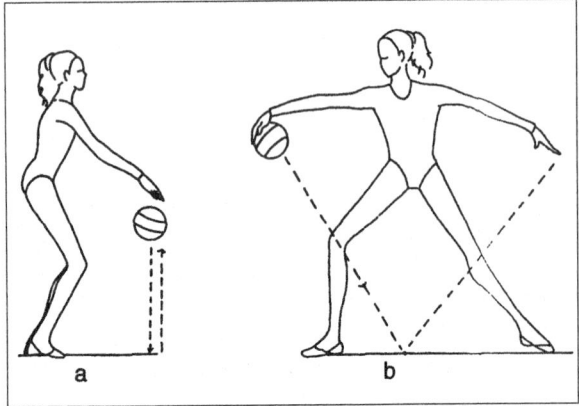

Figure 3.25 Bouncing the ball with one or both hands: (a) with both, perpendicular to the floor, (b) with one, at an angle to the floor.

Apparatus Handling Techniques 83

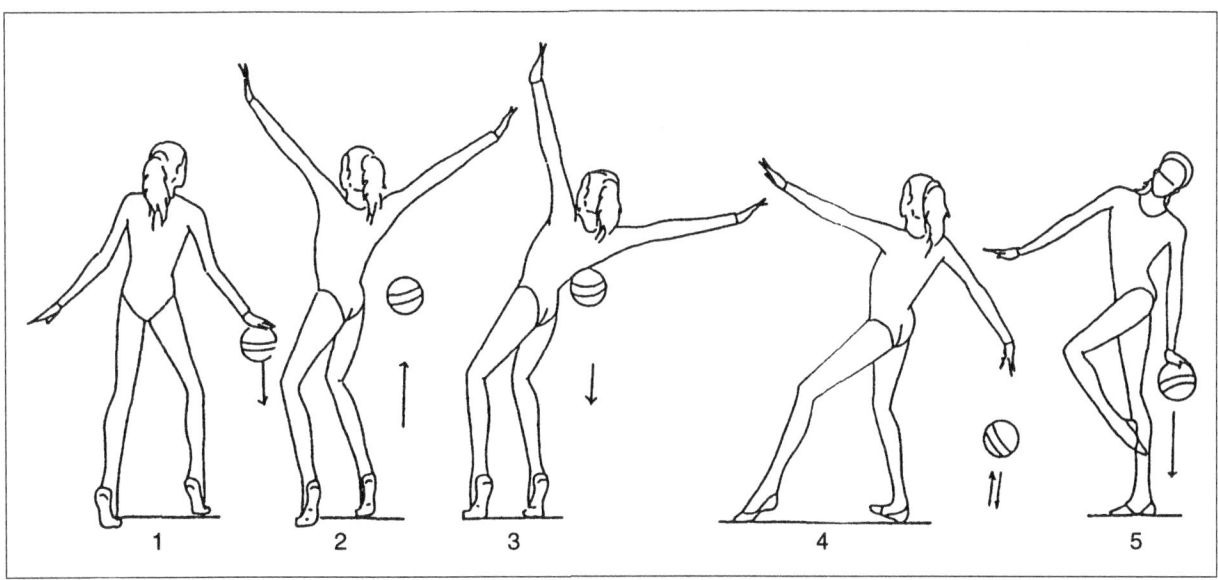

Figure 3.26 Bouncing the ball from the gymnast's back.

Figure 3.27 Bouncing the rope off the floor by swinging the leg.

Phases of Rebounds

As with bounces, the structure of rebounds divides into three phases: the preparatory, main, and finishing phases. In the preparatory phase, which is the flight of the apparatus after the throw, toss, or bounce, the gymnast guides the apparatus in time and space as she performs the movements necessary for rebounding. In the main, or rebound, phase, the apparatus touches one or more parts of the gymnast's body. In the finishing, or flight, phase, the apparatus has gained enough energy, and so it flies.

Techniques of Selected Rebounds

Naturally, the rigid apparatus have more rebounding potential than the soft apparatus. Indeed, even elite gymnasts rarely try to rebound a rope—and then only if it is folded two or four times. Gymnasts never rebound the ribbon; the material is simply too soft. They can rebound the stick only. In the following sections, we will describe the techniques for rebounding each apparatus—or not!

Hoop The gymnast usually makes the hoop rebound after throwing it with her leg or her arm (hand), or, sometimes, with her shoulder. Figure 3.28 shows a rebound of the hoop. After the toss downward, the gymnast swings with a straight leg before performing a split leap and rebounds the hoop upward with her shin.

Ball The gymnast can rebound the ball with her arm, her leg and arm, or with one or more other parts of the body. The novice, however, should start learning to rebound the ball using her hand (figure 3.29). The height and duration of the flight of the ball will be determined by the sharpness of the movements of the gymnast's hand.

As a rule, the gymnast uses her leg to rebound the ball during leaps (split, ring split, and the like). To create such an element, the gymnast should straighten and tighten her leg, then rebound the ball with her shin. By using different parts of her shin, the gymnast can direct the flight of the ball: if she wants the ball to fly forward, she should contact it near her foot; if she wants the ball to fly backward, she should contact it near her knee.

Clubs Due to the club's significant weight, its rebounds are limited, especially after high or far throws. But a gymnast can rebound one or both clubs. Certainly, to rebound a club, the direction of the flight must be precise and well-oriented in the direction and plane of the follow-through movement. Because of the club's displaced center of gravity, the gymnast should rebound it near its center of gravity, i.e., on the neck close to the body (figure 3.30). This will help her control the club's flight.

Ribbon Gymnasts seldom rebound the ribbon (stick). The softness of the ribbon's material causes two main problems: the risk of changing a definite shape or dropping the apparatus.

Rope The gymnast should rebound the rope only when it is folded two or four times.

Figure 3.28 Rebounding the hoop with the left leg with a split leap.

Figure 3.29 Split leap with a ball rebound using the hand.

Figure 3.30 Swinging the leg with a rebound of the club.

Catches

Catching is simply gripping the apparatus after it has experienced free movement, whether during flights or rolls. Thus, we can say that two kinds of catches exist: after flights and after rolls.

Physics of Catches

After flight, the apparatus has both potential and kinetic energy; after rolls, however, it only has kinetic energy. At the moment of catching the flying apparatus, the apparatus has gained great momentum because the potential energy has turned into kinetic energy. In contrast, an apparatus rolled over the floor or one or more parts of the body has less energy toward the end of its movement due to friction. Thus, the catch either extinguishes the energy of the movement of the apparatus or changes its direction to perform other elements.

The catches of rolling and flying apparatus differ because the amount of energy of the apparatus varies with the speed of the apparatus. The speed of a flying apparatus depends on two main factors: the height of the fall of the apparatus and the weight of the apparatus. The speed of a rolling apparatus depends on its initial speed, the weight of the apparatus, the angle of the surface (the part or parts of the body), and the range of the rolls.

The difficulty of catching a flying apparatus is determined by the trajectory of its flight, which depends on its slope, range, and height, and the particulars of the apparatus itself. Specifically, it is easier for a gymnast to catch the apparatus after high throws than low or medium-high throws. This is simply because the greater the duration of the flight phase, the simpler it is to determine the zone in which the apparatus will fall, making it easier for the gymnast to coordinate her actions to catch the apparatus. With the heavier apparatus (the ball, the clubs), the higher the flight, the more energy the apparatus acquires at the end of the flight. So, the difficulty in catching heavier apparatus lies in absorbing this energy or changing its direction.

The difficulty of catching the soft apparatus (the rope, the ribbon) lies in the difficulty of determining the zone in which it will fall due to fluctuations in its trajectory and in its small size (rope's end, ribbon's stick), which demands excellent coordination.

Thus, we can further divide all catches into two main groups according to the active interaction of the gymnast: static grip, similar to a stop (balancing), and dynamic grip, which immediately leads to another movement.

These grips can be main or atypical. In catching with a static main grip, encourage the gymnast to create a gentle, gradual transition from the flight of the apparatus to the catch with one hand (figure 3.31). A rigid grip without absorption (without a semisquat and bent arm) causes abrupt, angular movements, leading to two main faults: undesirable poses and stopping of the apparatus.

Figure 3.31 One-handed catch of the ball.

To catch with a static atypical grip by pressing the apparatus, in the main phase, a gymnast must press the apparatus a little bit to one or more parts of her body or to the floor; this is called a "pressing catch." A pressing catch stops the momentum of the apparatus. If a gymnast presses the apparatus with a large amount of force, it can receive enough energy from the movement and travel away from her. Figure 2.46 (page 56) shows a gymnast catching the hoop with a static grip using her legs. In illustration 4, she slightly presses the hoop to the floor with her shins to prevent the hoop from vibrating. Once she stops the hoop's movement, the gymnast straightens her legs (illustration 5). The same technique of catching is shown in figure 3.32, b and c, in which the gymnast demonstrates catching the club (b) and the folded rope (c) on her shoulders. To do so, she leans her head forward before touching the apparatus. After catching, she brings her head back to the erect position and slightly presses her neck and shoulders against the apparatus to stop its momentum.

When a gymnast catches an apparatus using a dynamic grip, she can follow the catch with a roll of the ball, the hoop, or the clubs, a wrap, various rotations and throws, and passing through the hoop or folded rope and ribbon. Figure 3.32a and figure 3.33 show a gymnast catching apparatus in dynamic atypical grips: catching the ball in rolls over the body and passing through the hoop with a lifted leg. These catches are more difficult for the gymnast than when using main grips. Why? Often they are performed without visual control.

All catches are divided into catches in front, to the side, from above, or from behind, relative to the gymnast's face. In the case of the latter, a gymnast usually catches with her hand using the reverse grip.

Naturally, catching the apparatus under or behind any other part of the body, called "bypass catches," can create difficulty for a gymnast. Specifically, bypass catches include catching the apparatus under the arm or leg and behind the back or head.

Phases of Catches

We can divide catching into three phases: the preparatory, main, and finishing phases. In the preparatory phase, the gymnast guides the apparatus in time and space and executes the movements necessary for catching the apparatus. In the main phase, which involves the actual catching of the apparatus, we can see two subphases: (1) contact with the apparatus and the gripping of it and (2) absorption of the movement through bending the arm or leg while catching, partially reducing the speed of the apparatus. In the finishing phase, active interaction takes place; in other words, the gymnast finishes stopping the apparatus and assumes the initial position for the next movement or actually executes the next movement.

Techniques of Selected Catches

Here, we will look closely at the techniques for selected catches. Notice how grips change technique and aesthetics.

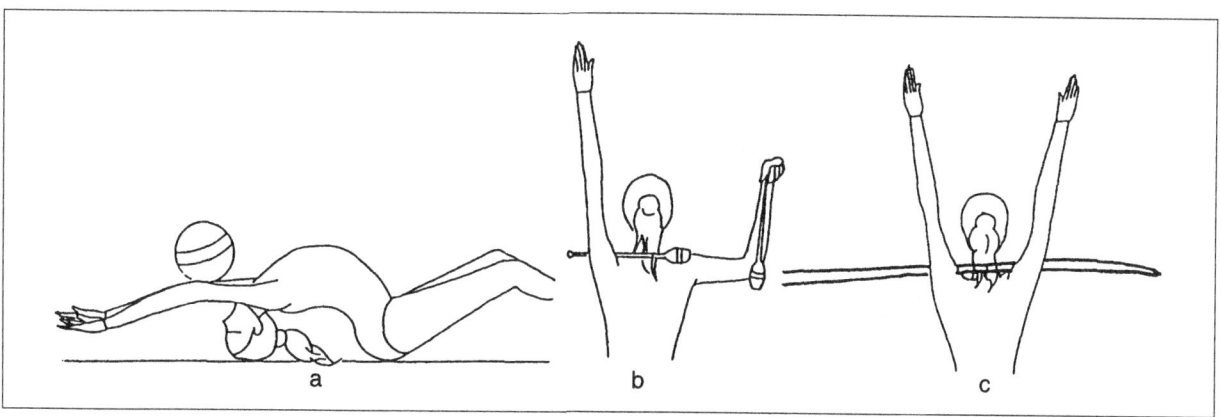

Figure 3.32 Catching the apparatus with atypical grips: (a) the ball into rolls, (b) the club with the shoulder, (c) the rope with the shoulders.

Figure 3.33 Catching the hoop with one leg lifted in a split, then passing through the hoop.

Hoop The most typical hoop catches are with one or both hands, gripping from inside or above. Very often the gymnast makes the hoop rotate or creates different movements, for example, swinging, jumping into or through the hoop, rolling through the hand or shoulder. The gymnast can catch the hoop over her head, behind her back, or in front of her body. Figure 3.15 (page 75) illustration 12 shows a gymnast catching a hoop with a static grip behind her back. The gymnast should avoid tightening her arm or stopping the hoop sharply. The coach should encourage the gymnast to focus on bending her arms and legs to absorb the kinetic energy when catching.

Review several of the drawings to see various catches:

- A main grip into rotation around the hand with ring split leap (figure 3.34) and behind the back (figure 3.15, page 75).
- An atypical grip with a leg (figure 2.46, page 56) and on a rising leg (figure 3.33).

It is possible to catch the hoop, then move directly into rolls over the arms (figure 3.35) or the spine or rotation around the waist or leg after the catch. Note, however, that the hoop cannot slide down the fore-

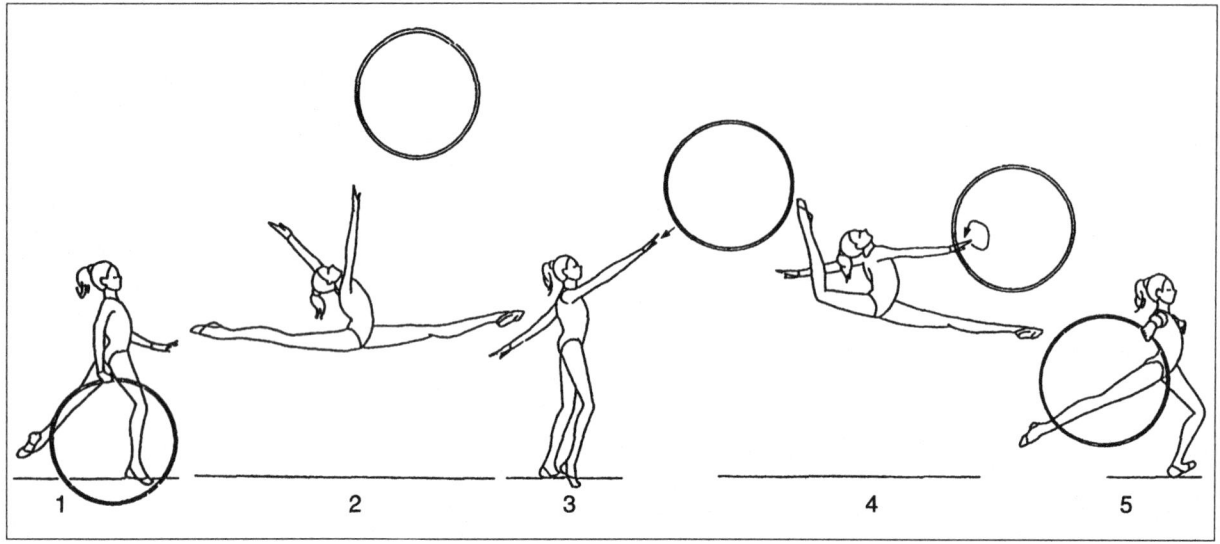

Figure 3.34 Split leap throwing the hoop and a split ring leap with catching the hoop in a rotation around the hand.

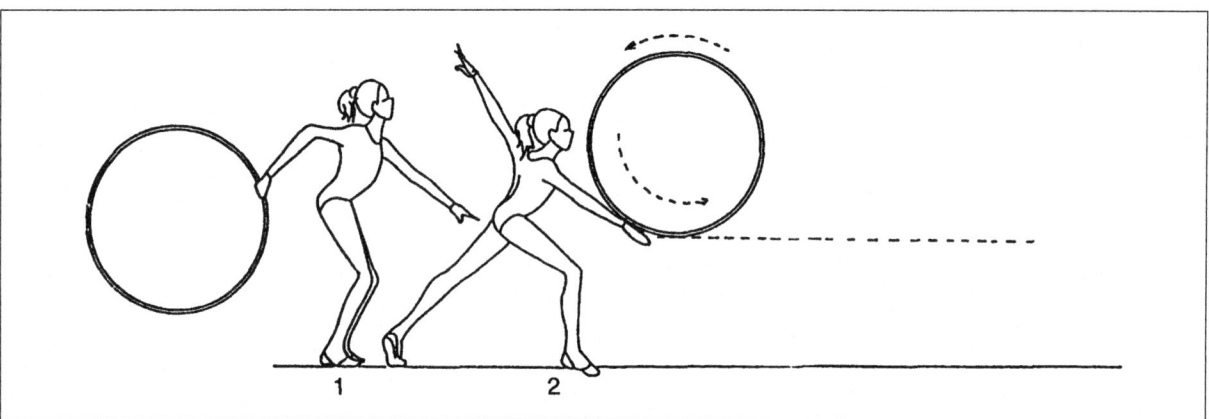

Figure 3.35 Creating a counterclockwise rotation with the hoop.

arm, over the arm, or over another body part when catching it into rolling. The hoop must only roll.

When catching the hoop after rolling it on the arm to chest to arm, the gymnast can grip the hoop with a static grip, then wrap or rotate it around her hand. Catching the rolling hoop without stopping it allows it to pass to the next movement gently and with good rhythm.

Ball Catching the ball with a main grip (figure 3.31) is the simplest. The gymnast should meet the ball with partly relaxed fingers. Then by rolling it from the tips of her fingers, the gymnast sends the ball to the middle of her palm. She should not clap the ball with her palm; indeed, the gymnast should create no sound when touching the ball. The ball should appear to glide to the fingers. Having made contact with the ball, the gymnast then gently lowers her partly relaxed arms, executes the swing movement freely, and smoothly reduces the speed of the fall to zero. Meanwhile, her legs should create a spring by semisquatting as she catches the ball. To prevent the ball from leaving her fingers and to reduce speed smoothly, the gymnast should make the ball move in spirals and circles while holding it.

During repetitive throws, the "give" of the hand during the catch should coincide with the push of the throw.

After low throws, the gymnast may choose to catch in unusual ways, such as on the back of one or both hands or in a reverse grip. She may catch the ball after various rolls, for example, over the arms, the chest, the spine, and the legs, using a variety of grips, such as on one or both palms, on the back of one or both hands, reverse, from one side, or from above. In every case, the gymnast catches the ball by rolling it from the tips of her fingers to her palm (figure 3.36). She should focus on creating continuity of movement between catching the ball and her next movement.

Clubs As there are many ways to throw the clubs, there are several ways to catch them. The difficulty of catching the clubs depends on the number of clubs, the trajectory of their flights, and the speed of their rotations. The gymnast may catch the clubs together or consecutively in one hand or two. Figure 3.37 shows two clubs caught in one hand.

The gymnast may catch a club by gripping any part of it, but catching the head of a club (figure 3.37) is the most typical. To be correct, a catch should not involve sharp stopping. The Code of Points requires that movements remain continuous in competitive compositions. The gymnast should reduce the speed of the club to zero by executing small circles when catching.

Repeated throws and catches of the clubs are possible, usually with rotation. In a series of throws, although the gymnast may grip the club by its body or neck, it is better to catch it by its head. This way, the gymnast can catch the club and immediately rotate it by its neck by wrapping it around her hand, or sliding it around her neck but she must finish the movement with the club's head in her palm. However, if she has caught the club by its body, she must change her grip to the club head. Gymnasts widely use bypass catches, either behind the spine or under the leg. Less common is a catch followed by rolling on one or both arms or on the spine. Of course, catches without visual control are the most difficult. Catching the clubs at the last moment of their fall, not far from the floor, is effective but requires good technique and accurate coordination of movements. When catching the clubs using main grips, the gymnast usually grips them without fixing her forefinger along the club. The gymnast can catch clubs in atypical grips, too. Figure 3.32b (page 87) shows a gymnast catching a club behind her head on her shoulders.

Ribbon A ribbon is usually caught by its stick, rather than by its material. The gymnast who catches the ribbon effectively *immediately* executes the next movement (e.g., circle, swing, spiral, snake) after gripping the stick. So, as a rule, she does not fix her forefinger on the stick. Common faults in this element are performing subsequent movements too slowly, which can alter the pattern and lower the end of the ribbon, or snapping the ribbon by beginning the next movement too sharply. To prevent these problems, the gymnast should avoid short-term acceleration and excessive tension in her arm. According to the Code of Points, the gymnast must catch the ribbon by the end of the stick, a maximum of 5 centimeters from the end. It is also possible to catch the apparatus by the ribbon material, near its site of attachment, in a 50-centimeter zone. When catching the ribbon, the gymnast must not allow it to stay on the floor.

Gymnasts often use bypass ribbon catches (figure 3.38) as well as catches followed by wrapping around the hand in compositions. Catches on the shoulders, under the arms, and between the knees or feet are very effective. Because of the softness of the ribbon, gymnasts rarely use atypical grips and then only at the end of a composition, in which case the grip may be static and the ribbon can remain on the floor.

Figure 3.36 Rolling the ball on the floor and catching it by rolling it from the fingertips to the palm.

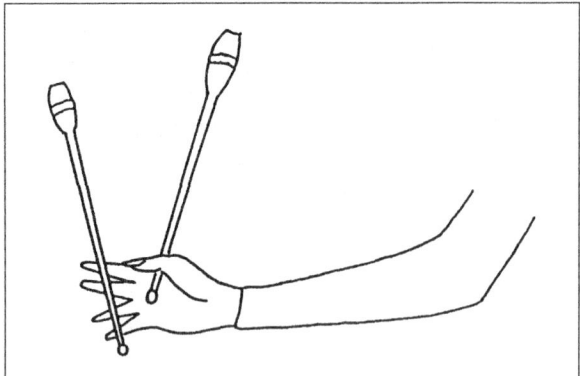

Figure 3.37 Catching the club by its head.

Figure 3.38 Split leap while catching the ribbon under a leg (bypass catch).

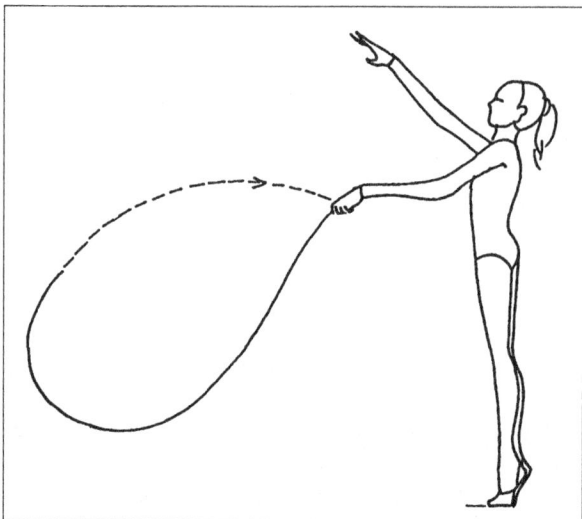

Figure 3.39 Catching one end of the rope.

Rope When catching the rope, it is important to maintain its pattern in flight. When catching using a main grip, the gymnast should quickly straighten her arm in the direction of the flying rope, and after catching the rope, her arm should be slightly bent. The Code of Points permits gymnasts to catch the rope 5 centimeters from one or both ends (figure 3.39).

But gymnasts may also catch the rope by its middle (figure 2.47, page 56) with one or two hands or with one hand in the middle and the other at one end. Because the rope is a soft apparatus, gymnasts should follow rope catches with circles, rotations, swings, or jumps into the rope. When catching the rope by jumping into it, gymnasts must separate their arms sideways after quickly gripping the ends, then begin to rotate it by their wrists (figure 3.21, page 79). Gymnasts frequently use bypass catches, either behind the spine or under the leg. They may catch the rope in dynamic grips, then rotate it, either wrapping around the hand, forearm, trunk, or leg. Gymnasts may catch the rope in atypical ways by wrapping it around any part of the body, such as the leg or the trunk.

Circular Elements

Circular elements refer to the movements of the apparatus in which all or part of the apparatus describes a circle. In the following sections, we will examine the physics and techniques of circular elements.

Physics of Circular Elements

The apparatus moves in a circle at a certain speed, which is influenced by three factors:

1. The centrifugal force F, directed onto the center of the radius of the circular movement R_I: the greater the force F, the greater the speed of rotation.

2. The apparatus mass m: the lower the mass of the apparatus, the greater the speed of rotation.

3. The radius of the rotation R_I: the smaller the radius, the greater the speed of rotation.

The centrifugal force F is calculated as follows:

$$F = \frac{m \cdot V^2}{R_I}$$

where F is the centrifugal force, m is the weight of the apparatus, V is the linear velocity, and R_I is the radius of rotation.

Thus, to change the speed of rotation of the apparatus it is necessary either to apply a different force F or change the radius of the rotation R_I. It is possible to increase the speed of the rope's rotation by applying a larger force F or by reducing the radius of rotation R_I (e.g., by folding the rope into halves or fourths).

The radius of the circular movement R_I can be either inside or outside the apparatus (figure 3.40). According to the radius of rotation, all circular movements with apparatus may be divided into five groups:

- Rolls—the apparatus rotates about its own axis at a certain distance on the given trajectory.
- Spins—the apparatus rotates about its own axis without displacement.
- Wrappings—the apparatus rotates around an axis, located outside of it on any part of the gymnast's body.
- Circles—the gymnast holds the apparatus with her hand in a static grip, and the apparatus rotates around an axis, located in the center of the gymnast's joint.
- Rotations—the gymnast holds the apparatus with any part of her body using a dynamic grip, and the apparatus moves around an axis, passed through the apparatus.

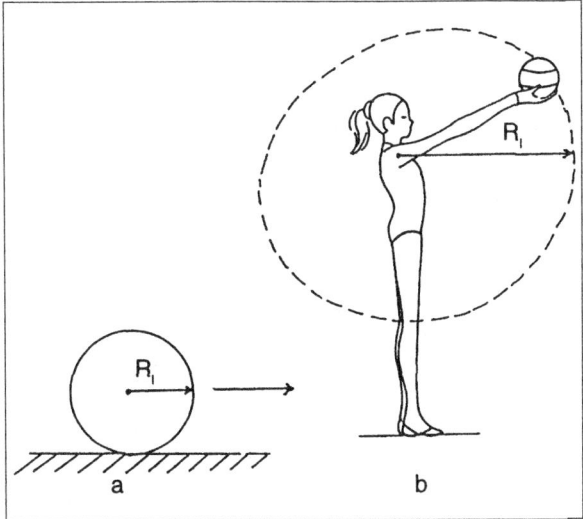

Figure 3.40 Rotational radii: (a) in the apparatus, (b) outside the apparatus, where R_I is the radius of the rotation.

In the following sections, we will discuss each of these circular elements in more detail.

Rolls

Rolls refer to the apparatus's circular movements about its axis with successive contact with the support (the floor or the gymnast's body). The gymnast, as a rule, performs rolls with the rigid apparatus (the hoop, ball, and clubs), but rolls with the stick of the ribbon and the folded rope on the gymnast's body are also possible.

Physics of Rolls

When the gymnast applies force F to an apparatus, she can perform two types of rolls: free rolls and assisted rolls. During free rolls, as the name implies, the aparatus moves freely by itself after receiving force F, without any help from the gymnast's hands or any other part of the body during the main phase. In assisted rolls, the gymnast assists the rolls with either one or both hands or another body part; assisted rolls, therefore, have additional energy during the main phase.

Rolls are useful in several situations: when the gymnast wishes to make the apparatus travel across the floor, after circular movement around one or both hands or one or more other body parts, and directly after catching the apparatus.

Rolls of the apparatus must be smooth. Specifically, rolls on the floor and over the gymnast's body must be fluid. Rolls over the body or floor must not vibrate or bounce.

The gymnast can roll an apparatus on the floor forward, backward, or sideways from her face and on various trajectories (e.g., straight, arched, and round). She can make the hoop perform return rolls.

If the gymnast rolls the apparatus on her arms and trunk, she must align these parts with her body: one arm—chest—other arm or the same arm—back—other arm. If she rolls the apparatus over her trunk and legs, she must also form a straight path. She can roll the apparatus over her body in two ways: over the straightened line without or with slope. Of course, with slope, the apparatus rises, because part of the body gives it greater acceleration. Furthermore, rolls over the body can be small or large. Small rolls are those on one part of the body, e.g., the arm, leg, or trunk. Large rolls are those on at least two parts of the body or on both arms stretched out horizontally.

Phases of Rolls

We can divide the structure of rolls into three phases: the preparatory, main, and finishing phases. In the preparatory phase, we can discern two subphases: (1) the gymnast places the apparatus in the initial position and (2) she prepares to apply the proper force to the apparatus. In the main phase (the actual rolling), the gymnast rolls the apparatus over the floor or her body. In this phase, a gymnast cannot manage the apparatus if she rolls it over the floor. But when she rolls it over her body, she can manage it by raising or lowering the involved part or parts of her body. In the finishing phase, the gymnast catches the apparatus or alters its direction in preparation for the next element.

Techniques of Selected Rolls of Apparatus

Of course, only the rigid apparatus can be rolled. The ribbon and rope are simply too soft and their shapes too hard to keep defined to roll. So here, we will discuss how a gymnast can effectively roll the hoop, ball, and clubs.

Hoop A gymnast can roll the hoop on the floor or over her body. Among the rolls on the floor are those performed straight or on an arch forward, backward, or sideways. The gymnast executes these smoothly by vigorously pushing the hoop with one or both hands. The movement of the gymnast's fingers will determine the direction of the hoop. Her arm, accompanying the hoop, keeps the movement smooth, without vibration or the slightest bounce. For example, a gymnast stands on one leg, the other leg is on pointed toes sideways to the hoop, which she is holding on the floor with an overgrip. With an easy push of her hands, she rolls the hoop to the side (figure 3.41). The hoop may roll in an arch if the gymnast places it at an angle to the floor.

Returned rolls, called "boomerang rolls," are technically more difficult. Figure 3.42 shows the boomerang roll forward. The gymnast's action is similar to the one she uses in the boomerang throw, making the hoop move forward, then backward. The hoop travels forward with simultaneous rotation in the opposite direction. Once the hoop loses kinetic energy from traveling forward, the hoop rotates in the opposite direction, slows, then stops its forward movement. Then it moves backward.

Hoop rolls over the gymnast's body are the most difficult (see figures 3.43 and 3.44). The gymnast rolls the hoop with the strength from her hand, one arm—chest—other arm, and then fixes it with a

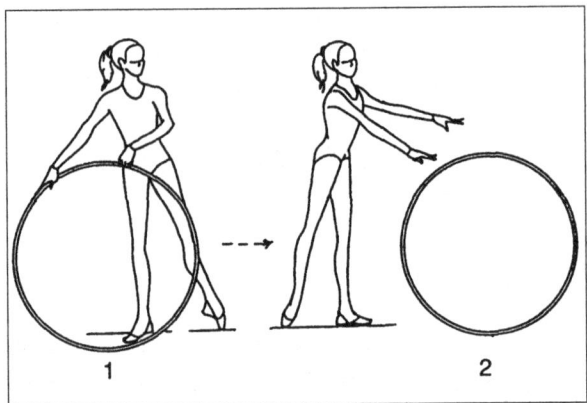

Figure 3.41 Rolling the hoop to the side.

static grip with her other hand (figure 3.43). The gymnast rolls the hoop on one arm—back—other arm (figure 3.44) in a similar fashion. When comparing both elements, it is evident that the gymnast slightly moves her head backward (figure 3.43) or forward, then immediately stands erect after the rolls. For the best technique, the gymnast's arms must remain straight, and she must perform the element without the hoop sliding, vibrating, or bouncing.

Ball The ball naturally lends itself to rolling, but the characteristics of the rolls differ depending upon the difficulty of the performance.

The most simple variations are rolls over the floor, which the gymnast performs with one or both hands or one or both legs. She can roll the ball straight or in an arch or circle, moving evenly without involuntary stopping or allowing the slightest bounce (see figure 3.36, page 89).

Rolls over any parts of the body are the most difficult. The gymnast must be skillful enough to maintain the movement of the ball. Fluid rolls depend on how well the gymnast sequences the movements, how smoothly she bends and extends her spine, and how effectively she provides continuity through the three phases of movement.

The most common are rolls over the arms and trunk. Ball rolls over the arms (figure 3.45) prepare a gymnast to perform more difficult rolls over various body parts by helping her feel if her muscles are the correct tension. Figure 3.46 shows rolls over the arms and back. The movement starts with a small toss of the ball, which sets the initial impulse of the movement (illustration 1). During the actual rolls, the gymnast takes the following pose: arms forward and upward forming a straight line with the trunk, looking at the apparatus (illustration 2). Then she

Apparatus Handling Techniques 93

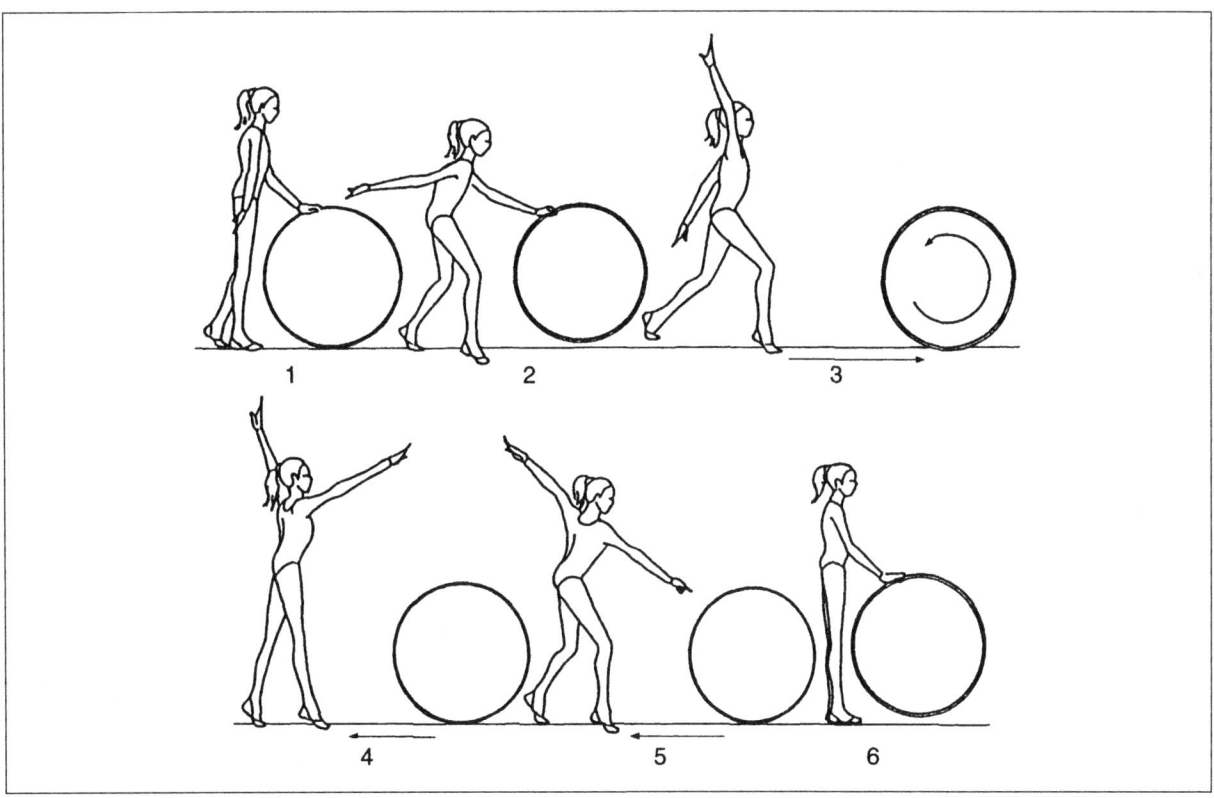

Figure 3.42 Boomerang rolls of the hoop.

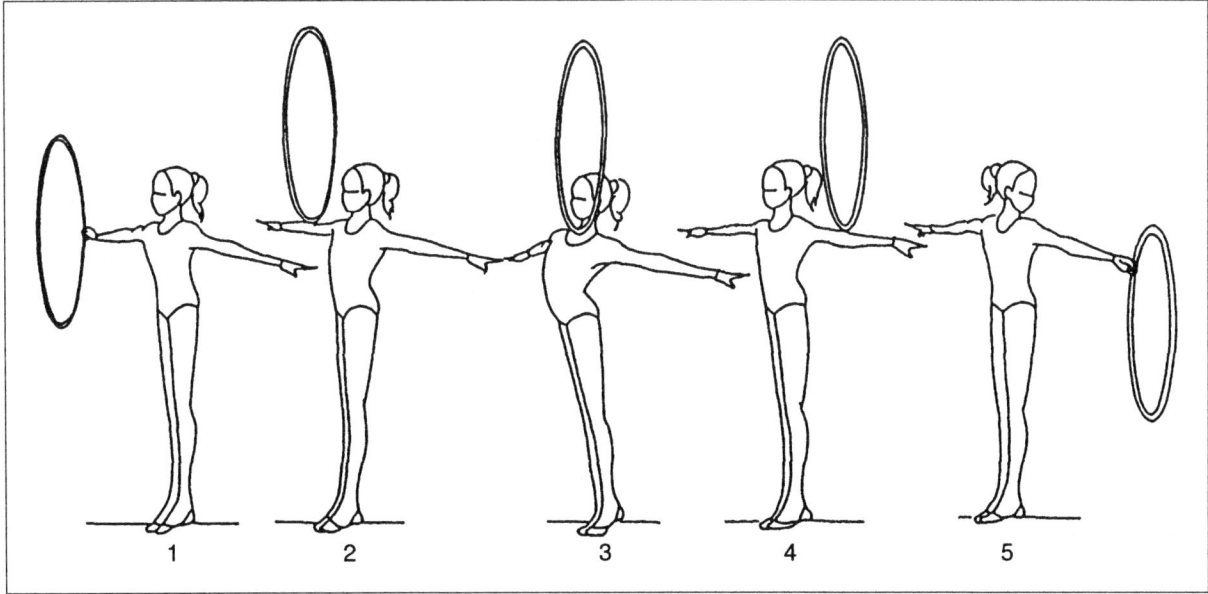

Figure 3.43 Rolling the hoop over one arm, then the chest, then the other arm.

lowers her head between her arms (illustration 3), and the ball moves freely over her forearms, shoulders, and back. By rounding her back (illustration 5), the gymnast reduces the speed of the ball, moves her arms backward, and prepares for the subsequent catch. To catch the ball more comfortably, the gymnast quickly arches her pelvis and abdomen instead of rounding her back.

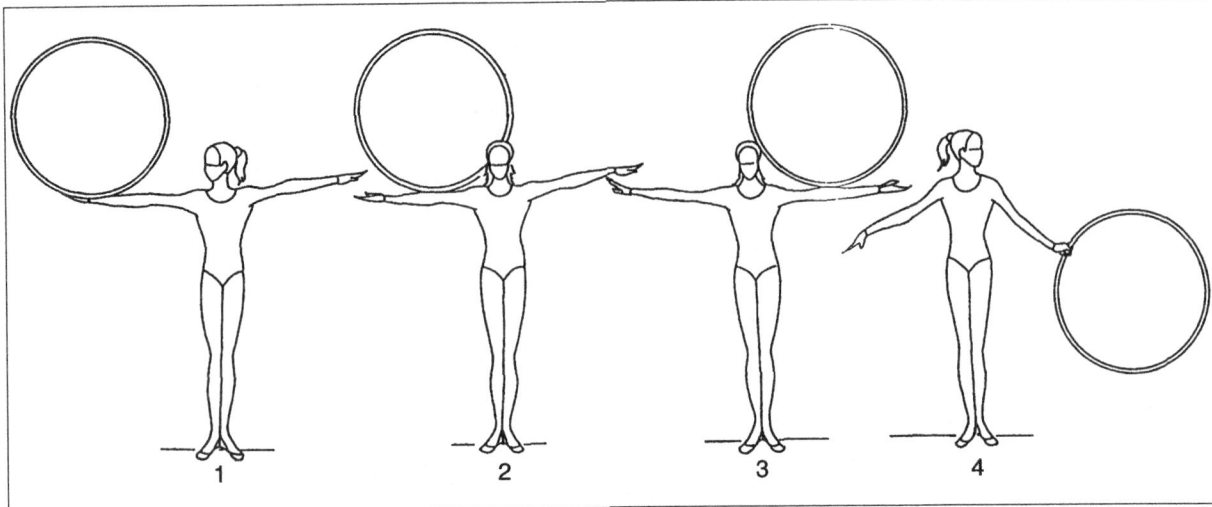

Figure 3.44 Rolling the hoop over one arm, then the back, then the other arm.

Figure 3.45 Rolling the ball over the arms.

Figure 3.47 shows a gymnast rolling the ball over one arm, then her chest, then her other arm. With a small push of her fingers, the gymnast gives an initial impulse to the ball. By moving her arm slightly to the side, the gymnast helps keep the ball moving at the necessary speed (illustration 1), and the ball rolls over the internal side of her arm. When the ball has rolled over her chest, the gymnast leans her head backward, then immediately brings it back to an erect position. Her left arm lifts horizontally (illustrations 4 and 5), rolling the ball over the arm where she catches it with her hand (illustration 6).

In competitive compositions, gymnasts often roll the ball over their backs. Figure 2.50 (page 57) shows a gymnast rolling the ball over her back while lying on the floor and moving her body with a wave-like motion. Figure 2.37 (page 49) shows a gymnast rising from kneeling to standing through the instep position while rolling the ball over her chest and arm.

Finally, the gymnast can use assisted rolls of the ball to prepare for free rolls over the body or to link free rolls.

Clubs While rolling along the floor, the club travels in an arch or circle because of the differing radii of its head and body. Thus, gymnasts rarely roll clubs in their compositions. In rolls over the arm, however, for which it is possible to support the clubs with the neck, the gymnast can maintain rectilinear movement of the club. When the gymnast does opt to roll the clubs, she must ensure that the clubs move without bouncing on the floor or over her body.

Spins

Spins refer to the circular movements of the apparatus around an axis, taking place through its diameter without traveling on the support (displacement). Gymnasts predominately spin the rigid apparatus (hoop, ball, and clubs), but sometimes they spin the rope.

Physics of Spins

The gymnast can spin apparatus either on her body (e.g., hands, chest, back, and legs) or on the floor independent of her body.

The exact initial impulse can create either of two types of spins: fading spins and nonfading spins. In fading spins, the apparatus receives an initial im-

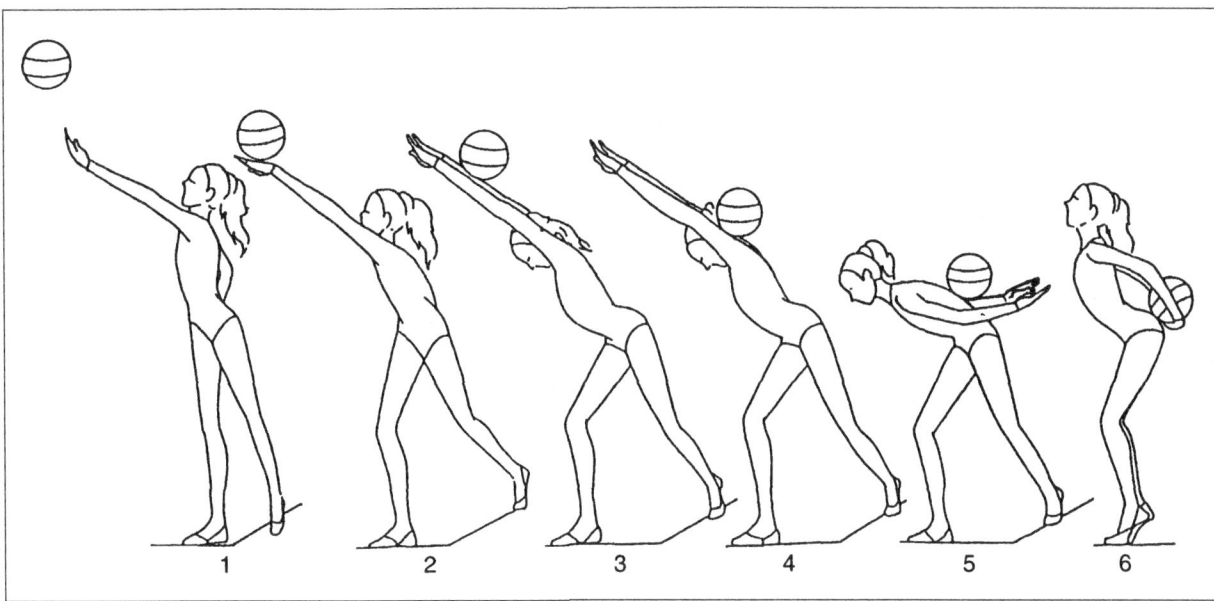

Figure 3.46 Rolling the ball over the arms and back.

Figure 3.47 Rolling the ball over one arm, then the chest, then the other arm.

pulse of force F, that is, the apparatus pushes off at a certain time. Then energy is reduced by friction when it rotates, unless it is stopped by the gymnast. In nonfading spins, the apparatus receives an initial impulse of force F_1, and then additional impulses of force F_2, enabling it to continue to make circular movements; these are nonfading spins. Of course, after the impulses stop, nonfading spins turn into fading spins.

Phases of Spins

Three phases comprise the structure of spins: the preparatory, main, and finishing phases. The preparatory phase has two subphases: the first preliminary subphase, in which the gymnast places the apparatus in the initial position for spinning, and the second momentum subphase, in which the gymnast gives the apparatus the impulse of force F to create the spins. In the main phase, the apparatus spins. For nonfading spins, the gymnast may give an additional impulse of force in this phase as well. In the finishing phase, the gymnast stops the apparatus or changes its direction to prepare for the following element.

While spinning, the movement of the apparatus must be fluid and precise. To make the apparatus spin longer and faster, the gymnast must provide a sufficient initial impulse of force. So she must make her fingers twist as powerfully as possible.

Techniques of Selected Spins of Apparatus

Spinning the hoop, ball, clubs, and rope gives a composition an added spark, often dazzling spectators. Of course, the ribbon does not lend itself to spinning. But the gymnast who can spin the rope is especially accomplished. In the following sections, we will look at specific techniques for spinning the hoop, ball, clubs, and rope.

Hoop The spinning of a hoop should be continuous, without vibrations or traveling. The hoop's rotating axis must be vertical. The gymnast may spin the hoop on the floor or her body, typically on her palm or chest. She should give the hoop the initial impulse I of force F sufficient to allow it to spin inward or outward. To actually make the hoop spin, the gymnast should rotate it by abruptly twisting her hand, which is gripping the hoop with three fingers from above (figure 3.48). The more abruptly the gymnast performs this movement, the longer the hoop will spin, maintaining its given axis of rotation. It is also possible to twist the hoop with both arms inward or outward. Whatever method the gymnast chooses, the hoop should rotate vigorously about its axis, fluidly and precisely.

More difficult types of spins are spins of the hoop with the legs, known as "Shougourova's spins," named after the first performer (see figure 3.49). The gymnast starts the element with a boomerang roll of the hoop, then she runs up, takes off, and cat jumps. During the cat jump, she twists the hoop with her feet. The difficulty is that the gymnast should execute the cat jump precisely over the rim above the hoop's vertical axis, thereby making the spins steady enough without traveling.

Ball Spinning the ball is similar to spinning the hoop as spins are created with an overgrip by one or both hands. A gymnast performs the simpler ball spins on the floor and the more difficult spins on her chest or palm, where she can, with practice, balance the ball correctly.

Clubs A gymnast typically spins clubs using an overgrip on the neck, close to or on the body of the club, on the floor, or on her palm or chest.

Rope Figure 2.47 (page 56) shows the atypical spin for this apparatus: spins of the rope on the gymnast's foot. The gymnast stretches the rope and gives the initial impulse of force (illustrations 4-6). The rope spins on the middle of her foot with the center of rotation at the point of contact.

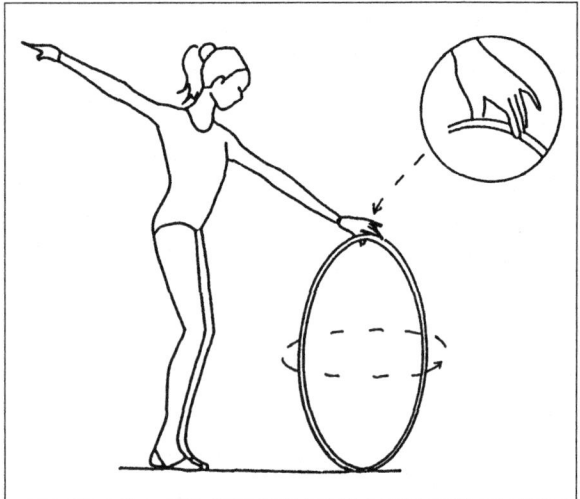

Figure 3.48 Spinning the hoop on the floor by twisting it with the fingers.

Figure 3.49 Spinning the hoop on the floor by twisting it with the legs (Shougourova's spins).

Wrapping

Wrapping refers to circular movements of the apparatus around one or more parts of the gymnast's body. The axis of rotation is around the gymnast's body (figure 3.50).

Physics of Wrapping

To wrap the apparatus around any part of her body, a gymnast must give it an initial impulse of movement I. Next, she must put the necessary part or parts of her body under the apparatus. Then, the apparatus travels around the expected part or parts of her body.

There are two types of wrappings: free wrapping, involving free circular movements of the apparatus around one or more parts of the body without help from any other body parts, and assisted wrapping, involving circular movements of the apparatus around one or more body parts with help by another body part. Gymnasts use assisted wrapping with rigid apparatus, mainly the ball.

Gymnasts wrap both rigid and soft apparatus, mainly around one or both hands or arms and sometimes around one or both legs or the trunk. Wrapping should be fluid without bounces and loss of contact with the apparatus. The uniqueness of each apparatus makes each wrapping unique.

Phases of Wrapping

The structure of wrapping divides into three phases: the preparatory, main, and finishing phases. The preparatory phase has two subphases: in the first preliminary subphase, the gymnast places apparatus in the initial position, preparing for the preparatory swing, and in the second momentum subphase, the gymnast gives the apparatus the impulse I of force F for wrapping the part or parts of her body. In the main phase, the apparatus actually wraps around the part or parts of her body. In the finishing phase, the gymnast stops the apparatus or changes its direction to prepare for the next element.

Techniques of Selected Wrappings of Apparatus

Here, we will discuss the specific techniques of wrapping the apparatus.

Hoop The gymnast can wrap the hoop along horizontal and vertical planes around any part of her body, without passing through it. The most common ways to wrap are around the hand, shoulder, forearm, neck, or trunk. Figure 3.51 shows a gymnast wrapping the hoop around her hand. The element starts with a preparatory swing in a static grip (illustration 1). Then the gymnast opens her hand and permits the hoop to move around it (illustrations 2-3). When she has completed the element, she holds the hoop once again in a static grip (illustration 4). It is possible to perform double wrappings, when the hoop rotates two times around the body part (usually the hand) after receiving the initial impulse.

Figure 3.50 Wrapping the rope around the gymnast's trunk.

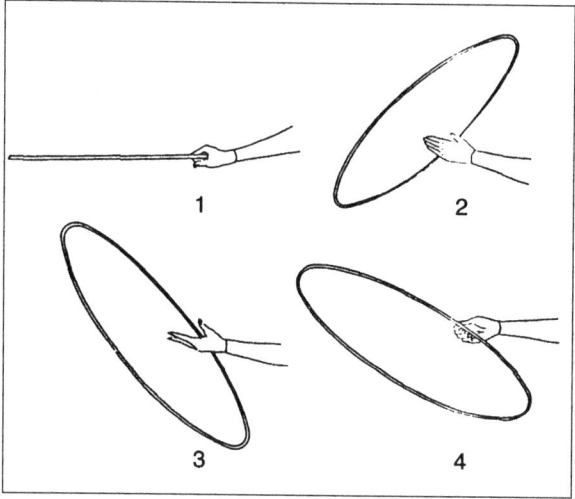

Figure 3.51 Wrapping the hoop around the hand.

Ball Wrapping the ball is possible around any part of the body: the arms, trunk, neck, and legs. The simplest type of wrapping is an assisted wrapping around one hand with help from the other hand. The elbow should be slightly bent and the palm should wrap the ball, slightly pressing and rotating it with support from the other hand (figure 3.52).

To execute a free wrapping of the ball around her hand, the gymnast makes the ball rotate by lifting her arm and turning her hand inward (figure 3.53). Then she lowers her arm slightly and forms a circle with her hand around the ball. At the last moment, the ball travels around her little finger, which is still in touch with the ball. She must hold her hand freely without tension.

Clubs The gymnast can wrap one or both clubs around any part of her body, but more typically, she uses her forearms and hands (figure 3.54). The technique of this wrapping is similar to free wrapping of the ball around the hand. The gymnast wraps her hand only from a main grip of the club's body or neck. To actually wrap a club, the gymnast must twist her fingers vertically or horizontally with a straightened elbow. If the gymnast uses two clubs, she may opt for symmetrical or asymmetrical elements.

Rope Wrapping a rope has its own features and challenges. First of all, the length of the rope is important. In addition, three other factors permit a gymnast to wrap the rope: (1) the initial impulse of rotary movement *I*, (2) slight movement of the wrapped part or parts of the body, and (3) sufficient tightening of the rope (it should be tight without room for undulation).

There are three types of wrapping of the rope: (1) proper wrapping, similar to other apparatus (figure 3.55), in which the gymnast holds one rope end in her hand while the other end wraps around the desired body part; (2) winding the rope with one or both hands around any part of the body; and (3) unwinding, the opposite of winding.

Gymnasts are more likely to wrap the rope around the arms and trunk, than around the legs. Figure 3.55 shows a gymnast wrapping the rope around one arm. She performs circular movements with the rope around her arm, aiming to maintain contact with it for as long as possible. Then she releases the end, which slides over her forearm. Finally, she grips it quickly.

Winding and unwinding the rope are unique elements for this apparatus. The rope is wound around any body part (figure 3.51), and it can be

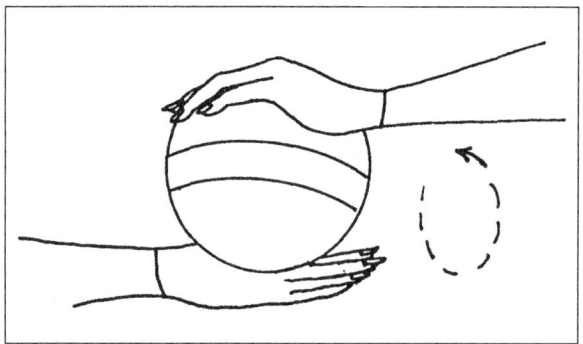

Figure 3.52 Wrapping the ball around the hand with the aid of the other hand.

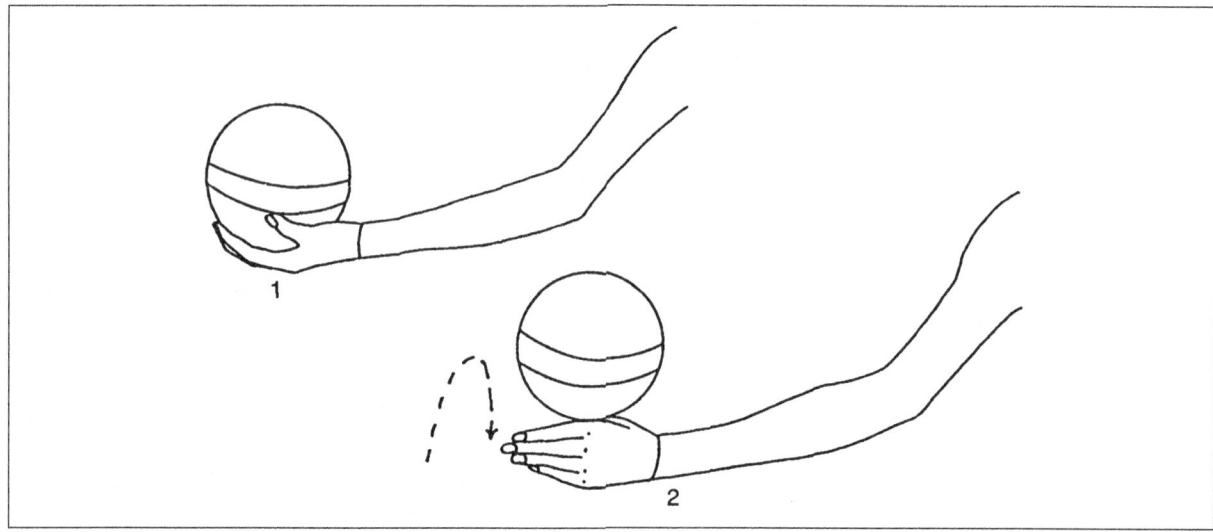

Figure 3.53 Free wrapping of the ball around the hand.

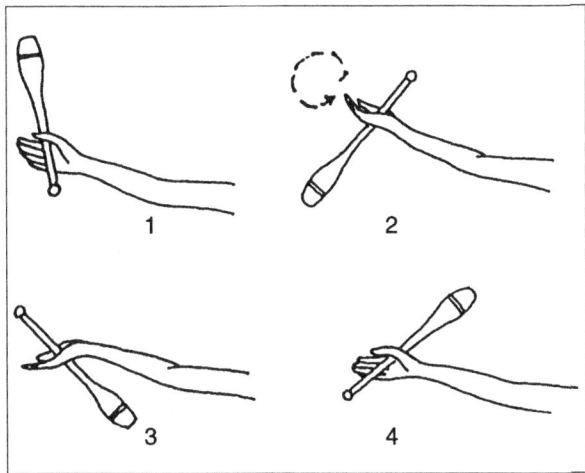

Figure 3.54 Wrapping the club around the hand.

open or folded. The gymnast must take care to wind the rope smoothly, avoiding any abrupt movement that infringes upon its shape. When performing these elements, the gymnast must focus on the rhythm of the movements and their coordination with the music.

Ribbon Typically, gymnasts wrap the stick around the hand to prepare to throw the ribbon backward.

Circles

Circles refer to movements of the apparatus with an axis of rotation in the joint of the body part circled around, aligning the apparatus with the arm.

Physics of Circles

Gymnasts create circles with all apparatus. There are three types of circles, each with its own center of the radius of rotation, R_r: large circles with their axes of rotation in the shoulder joint, medium circles with their axes of rotation in the elbow joint, and small circles with their axes of rotation in the wrist.

The tempos of the rotations also vary in connection with various weights of the arm rotated around joints with different radii, R_r. The gymnast can only achieve the higher speed of rotation around her wrist and the slower speed around her shoulder joint.

In relation to the gymnast's face, she may perform circles in front (in the facial plane), to the side (lateral), and to the back, in horizontal, vertical, and oblique planes. While making circles, the gymnast should concentrate on ensuring that the apparatus is aligned with, or a continuation of, her arm. Finally, she should only use a static grip.

Phases of Circles

We can describe the structure of circles in three phases: preparatory, main, and finishing phases. In the preparatory phase, the gymnast places the apparatus in the initial position needed to begin to circle. In the main phase, the gymnast uses her hand to make the apparatus circle the axis of rotation. In the finishing phase, the gymnast moves the apparatus to prepare for the next element.

Techniques of Selected Circles of Apparatus

Every apparatus can be circled, but each has its own unique features and challenges. In the following sections, we will describe the correct techniques for creating effective circles.

Hoop A gymnast uses a static grip with one or both hands to circle the hoop (figure 3.56). When circling, the hoop cannot alter its plane or vibrate. During large and medium circles, the gymnast should

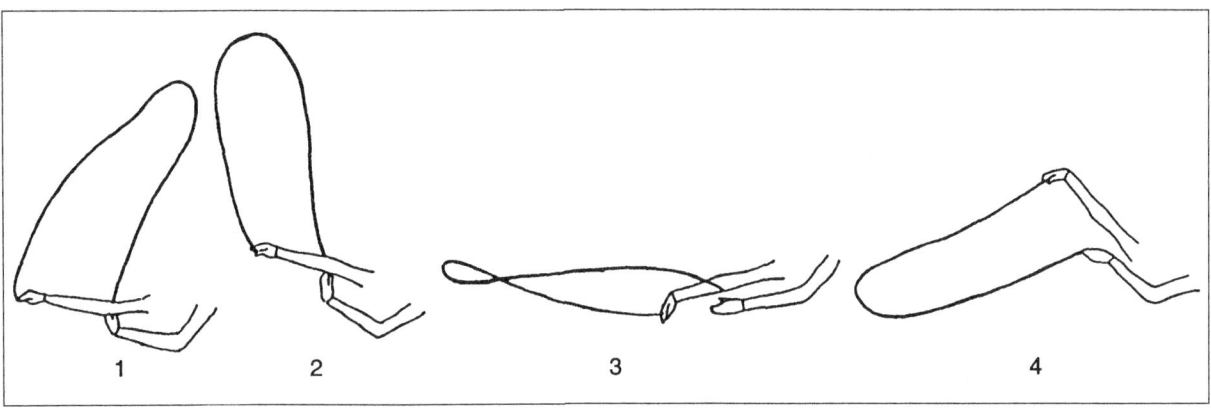

Figure 3.55 Proper wrapping of the rope around the arm.

avoid vibrating the hoop with her hand, as vibrations may lift or lower the hoop's far edge. During medium circles, the shoulder should be aligned with the collarbone and must not move forward or backward (figure 3.56b). The gymnast must ensure that her arm does not become too tense.

Ball To circle the ball, the gymnast must learn the technique of swinging in all planes. Large and small circles are natural for the ball, but medium circles are infrequently performed.

When circling the ball, it is difficult to maintain free movement of the arm. Simpler circles are those the gymnast makes with two arms and those she makes by passing the ball from one arm to the other. Large circles that include changing the grip of the ball at the highest point of the circle are more difficult. A gymnast can create horizontal circles by bending her arm slightly over her head, always keeping the ball on her palm. When making large vertical circles, she must straighten her arms and start the movement from her shoulder. She must guard against bending her arm abruptly to avoid infringing upon the line of the movement.

Connecting circles in various arm joints creates a specific ball element called a "reverse circle." To perform a reverse circle, the gymnast reverses her palm and allows the ball to lie on her palm; she should not grasp or press the ball to her body or arm. There are two types of reverse circles: vertical and horizontal. For the vertical reverse circle, the gymnast reverses her arm at the shoulder joint (360 degrees), moving it forward to the overgrip position. Her elbow should be slightly bent, and her hand should perform a small circle (figure 3.57a). Then, she returns the ball to the starting position by reversing her actions. The gymnast performs the horizontal reverse circle inward from the starting position, for which the arm with the ball is at the side or forward position. Then the gymnast bends her elbow slightly and makes her hand create a horizontal circle by moving her wrist inward while balancing the ball on her palm. She completes the reverse circle by straightening her arm to the side or forward position while holding the ball on her palm with a reverse grip (figure 3.57b). From this position, it is possible to perform the horizontal reverse circle outward, reversing the arm with the ball (360 degrees) to the starting position. The gymnast must strive to perform all reverse circles smoothly and continuously in combination while semisquatting, keeping her arm relaxed.

Clubs The gymnast can circle the clubs in various planes (figures 3.58 and 3.59), forming a straight line with each club and arm. The club must be held by the head while circling. When performing large circles, a gymnast needs to make pronounced circular movements in her shoulders while relaxing her shoulder muscles and feeling the sensation of the weight of the apparatus. The last factor is necessary because when the gymnast lowers the club, its weight pulls on her arm. While performing various circles in the facial plane, the gymnast should bend her arm slightly at the elbow. Figure 3.59 shows examples of medium circles with clubs.

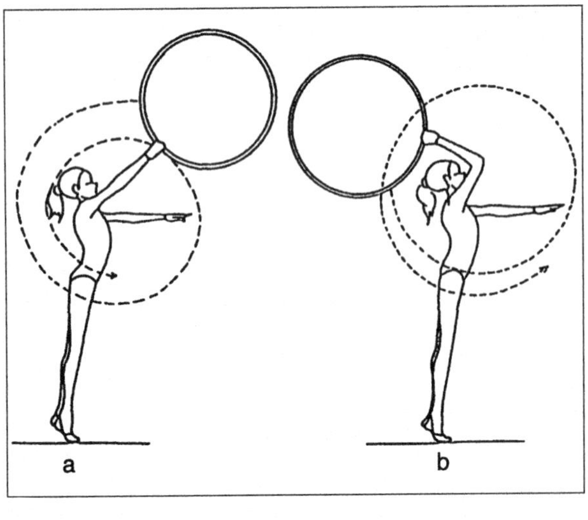

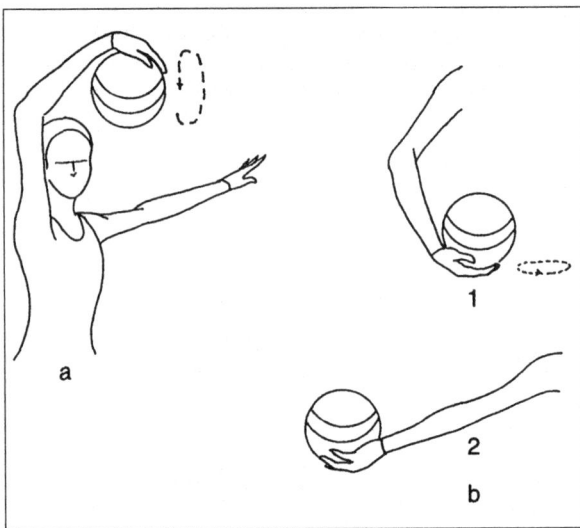

Figure 3.56 Circles of the hoop: (a) large in the lateral plane, (b) medium in the lateral plane.

Figure 3.57 Reverse circles of the ball: (a) vertical, (b) horizontal.

Apparatus Handling Techniques 101

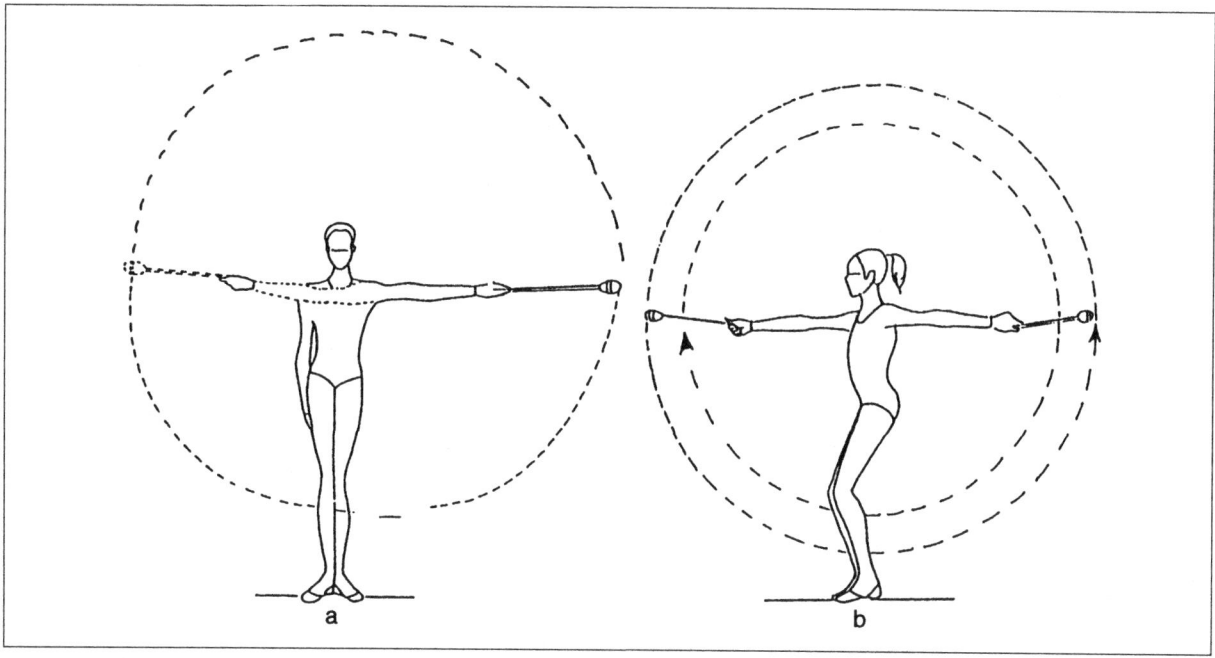

Figure 3.58 Large vertical circles of the clubs: (a) in the facial plane, (b) in the lateral plane.

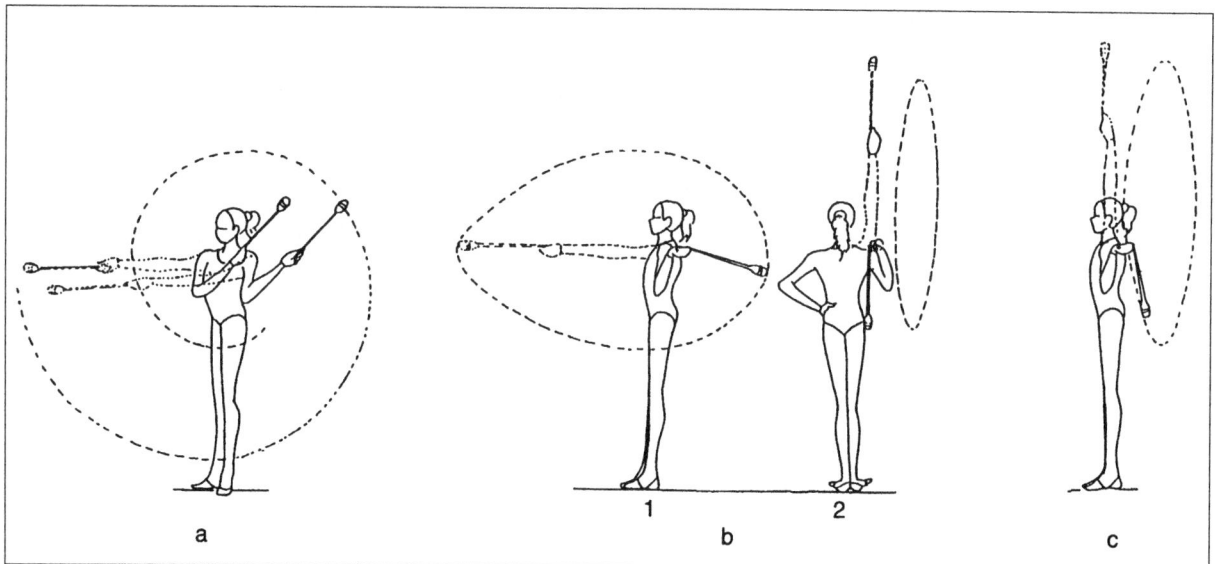

Figure 3.59 Medium vertical circles of the clubs: (a) in the facial plane, (b) in the lateral plane, (c) behind the head.

The order of difficulty for circles is large, small, and medium, from least to most difficult. Thus, the beginner should start with large circles. Then she should work on small circles; and finally, on medium circles. She should learn to make circles first with one arm, then with the other arm, and then, finally, with two arms moving simultaneously.

Ribbon As with other apparatus, the gymnast circles the ribbon by moving her shoulder, elbow, and wrist. The hand with the stick should be an extension of the forearm, forming a straight line.

The most obvious ribbon circle errors are snapping and whipping caused by abrupt acceleration and tension in the arm. The gymnast should perform large circles with strong and active movements of the arm, stressing upward movement. She should maintain the circular pattern of the ribbon during the entire element. Specifically, the whole ribbon must form the circle. So amplitude of motion in the shoulder should be at its maximum; indeed, its reduction infringes upon the ribbon's flight.

A gymnast performs large circles (figure 3.60a) in the facial plane upward or downward, passing the ribbon near her toes. Performing large circles in the lateral plane (figure 3.60b) requires flexible shoulders. Zigzagging the ribbon behind and over the shoulder indicates insufficient flexibility in the shoulders or an incorrect hand position. The gymnast performs circles in the lateral plane both forward and backward, and the ribbon should pass on the floor near her feet. The gymnast performs large horizontal circles over her head (figure 3.60c) by slightly bending her elbow over her head, holding the stick in a horizontal position. More than in any other plane, in the horizontal plane, a gymnast must make a great effort to maintain the inertia of the ribbon's motion. Therefore, we recommend that a gymnast learn how to circle the apparatus in the facial plane first, then in the lateral plane. A coach should save horizontal circles, the most difficult circles, for much later.

The gymnast performs medium facial circles strictly in the facial plane with her elbow bent. During medium lateral circles behind her facial plane, the hand with the stick is bent upward and outward, as for circling the hoop (figure 3.61).

Rope The gymnast can circle the rope in the following ways:

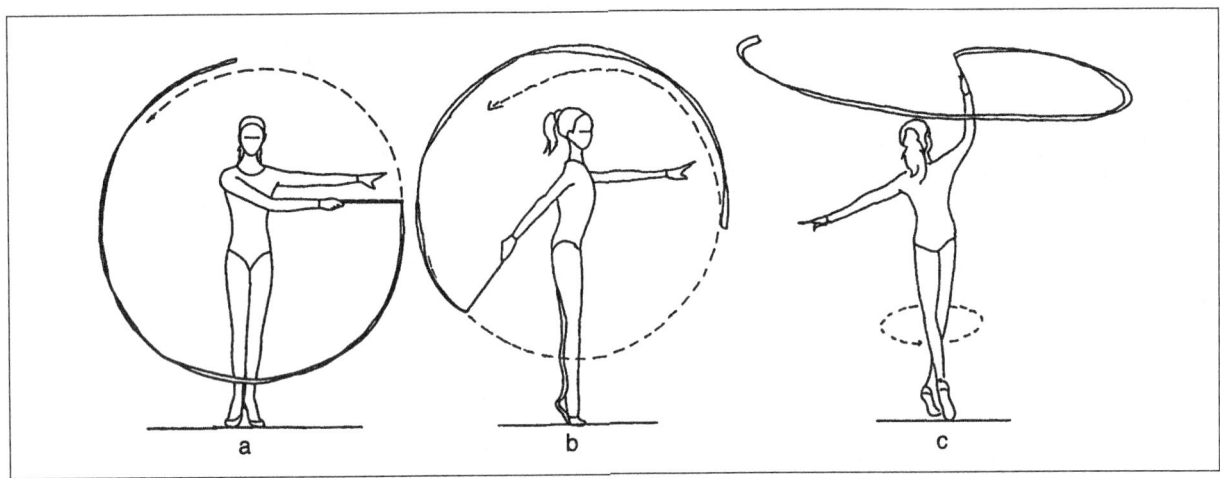

Figure 3.60 Large circles of the ribbon: (a) in the facial plane, (b) in the lateral plane, (c) horizontal above the head.

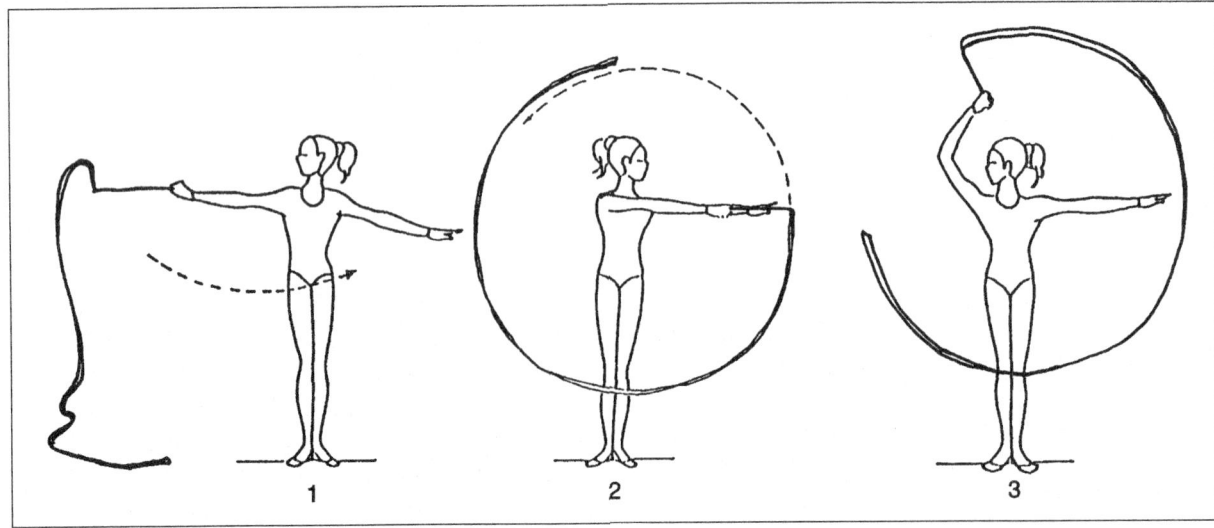

Figure 3.61 Medium circle of the ribbon in the facial plane and behind.

- In all planes, using her shoulders, elbows, and wrists.
- With an open or folded rope.
- With one or both arms.
- With single, double, or triple turns.

To perform acceptable circles, the gymnast must not allow the rope to undulate, alter its pattern, or touch her body. We recommend that the novice start learning circles in the facial and lateral planes. Later, she can work in the horizontal plane. She should learn to make large circles first, then, over time, learn how to make small circles, and, finally, medium circles.

Proper Rotations

By proper rotations, we are referring to circular movements of the apparatus around the axis passing through it.

Physics of Proper Rotations

The gymnast may properly rotate the apparatus using a dynamic (free) grip. We will look specifically at all rotations with the hoop around various parts of the body, small circles with clubs, and turns with the rope and hoop.

Each of the apparatus displays specific characteristics while rotating properly. For example, because of its rim, the gymnast can rotate the hoop by holding the inside of its rim in a dynamic grip by any body part. Such hoop rotations are considered simply "rotations" with the center of the radius in the rim (figure 3.62). There is a big difference between the diameters of the hoop and the part of the gymnast's body used. So, for the sake of convenience, when describing the hoop's rotation, we will not take the smaller diameter of the gymnast's body into consideration.

The club's round head enables the gymnast to fix it in her palm like a hinge. In fact, a dynamic grip gives the club a large degree of freedom to rotate (figure 3.7c-d, page 69). This is because the center of the radius of the rotations R_i is in the club's head. Small circles with clubs using a dynamic grip are proper rotations.

Rotational turns of the rope are proper rotations, too. When turning the rope, the gymnast should hold it using a dynamic grip. So the centers of radii of rotation R_i are in the ends that are held by the gymnast as long as the ends of the rope are in both hands. In this way, the gymnast can pass the force into the apparatus during the rotation of the rope. The size and speed of a rope's rotational turn depend in part on the rope's length and rigidity.

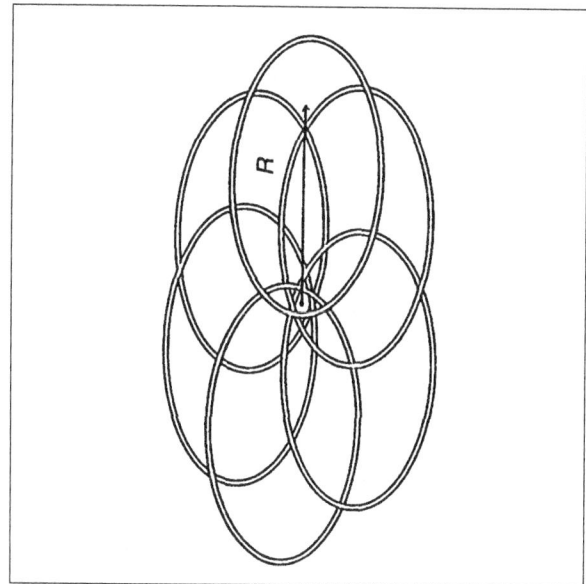

Figure 3.62 Center of radius of hoop rotations.

Phases of Proper Rotations

The structure of rotations lies in three phases: the preparatory, main, and finishing phases. The preparatory phase has two subphases: the first preliminary subphase, in which the gymnast places the apparatus in the necessary initial position, and the second momentum subphase, in which the gymnast gives the apparatus the impulse I of force F to start the rotation. In the main phase, the apparatus rotates. In the finishing phase, the gymnast stops the apparatus or changes its direction to prepare for the next element.

Techniques of Selected Proper Rotations of Apparatus

Proper rotations vary from apparatus to apparatus. In the following sections, we will outline the basic techniques involved with each apparatus.

Hoop Proper hoop rotations refer to circles around a part of the body, inside the rim. All hoop rotations must have continuous motion without vibration and without sliding over the next part of the body. The main ways the gymnast varies hoop rotations are to rotate around one or both hands vertically or horizontally. For these variations, the gymnast's arm can be slightly bent or straight at the elbow. She should avoid tensing her hand as she holds the hoop in a dynamic (free) grip between her thumb and forefinger.

Figure 3.63 shows a gymnast rotating the hoop vertically in front of herself. The starting position for this element is as follows: the gymnast holds the hoop forward and vertically, gripping it by its top edge from below. With a small preparatory swing of the hoop to the side, the gymnast opens her palm and rotates the hoop. The rim of the hoop describes a curve, close to a circle, as it rotates around her hand. To maintain the stability of the hoop, the gymnast must rotate the hoop fast enough to press it to her hand. To increase the stability, she must rotate the hoop even faster. With an increasing rotational speed, however, the danger of losing the hoop also increases. Moreover, horizontal rotations of the hoop are less stable than vertical rotations.

In addition, a gymnast will sometimes rotate the hoop on her forearm, neck, waist, knee, thigh, or foot (figure 3.63b). Figure 3.15 (page 75) shows rotations on a gymnast's legs (illustrations 1-7). No matter which body part the gymnast rotates the hoop around, she must focus on generating sufficient speed while maintaining the plane of the rotations.

To change hands while rotating the hoop (figure 3.64) in the vertical plane, the gymnast places her free hand near the hand around which the hoop is rotating, then quickly removes the "old" hand. She can change hands while rotating the hoop in a lateral plane in a similar manner.

A gymnast can perform rotational turns of the hoop by jumping or leaping into it as with the rope.

She holds the hoop with a dynamic (free) grip, enabling her to turn it in one or both hands. If she turns the hoop with both hands, the axis of rotation passes through a chord formed between the grips. If she turns the hoop with one hand, the axis of rotation is at the place of the grip. While jumping vertically, the gymnast turns the hoop mainly by moving it with her gripping palm (figure 3.65a). Leaps require the gymnast to move all the joints of her arm, beginning with her shoulder joint, as in, for example, the split ring leap into the hoop (figure 3.65b). The gymnast must rotate the hoop as soon as possible before completing the leap.

Clubs For small circles with a dynamic grip, the gymnast can rotate the club's head freely in her palm (see the section earlier in this chapter entitled "Grips"). Therefore, the center of radius of rotation R_l is in the club's head. The technique tips for rotating in small circles are as follows:

- The arm, holding the club with dynamic grip, should be straight and motionless.
- The club's head should rotate freely in the palm.
- To maintain sufficient rotating speed, the gymnast should make small twisting movements with her wrist, which controls the club's movement.
- The club's motion must be continuous, and use the inertia that comes from the weight of the club.

The gymnast can make small circles in horizontal and vertical planes in front of her face, to her side, and behind her back (figure 3.66). To make fast circles, the gymnast must have mastered the dynamic grip and must move her wrist intensely. When making small circles, the gymnast must work hard to maintain the plane of the club's rotation. When

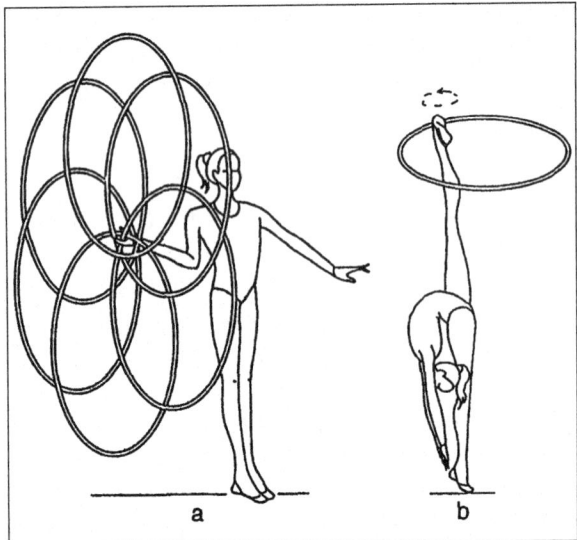

Figure 3.63 Hoop rotations: (a) vertical rotations with the hand in front, (b) horizontal rotations with the foot.

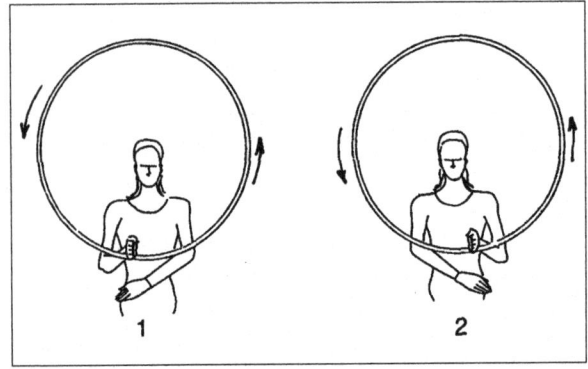

Figure 3.64 Changing hands while rotating the hoop.

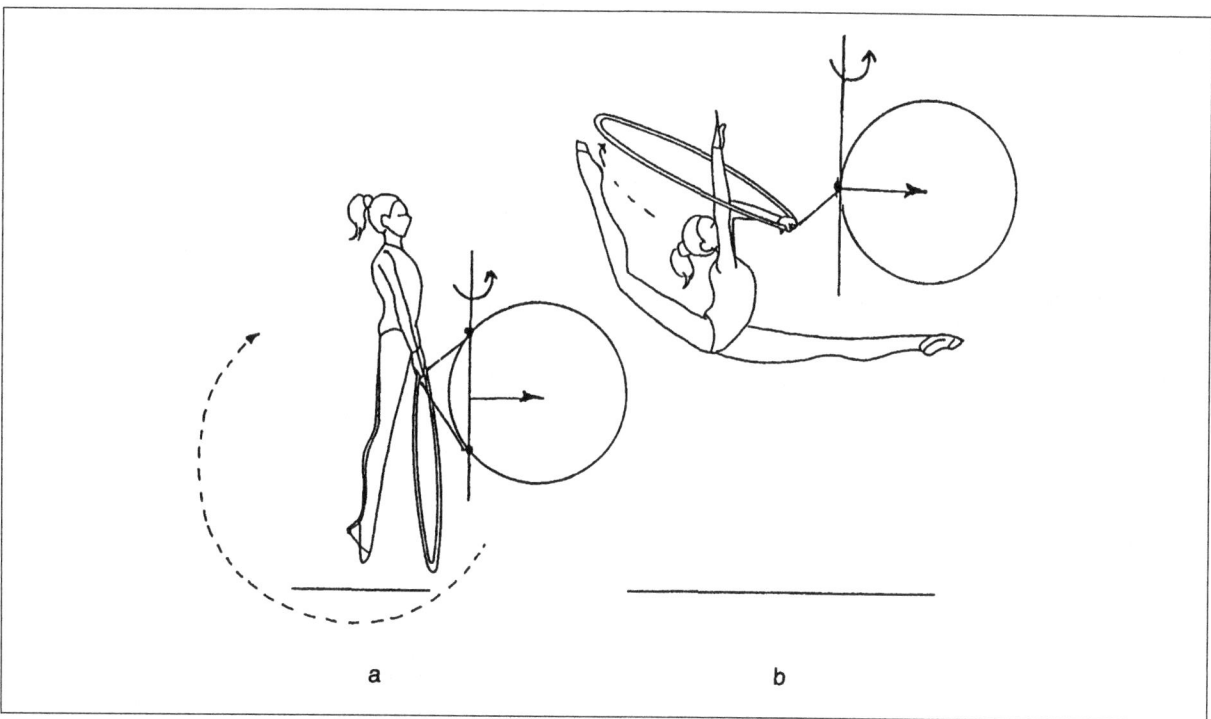

Figure 3.65 Jumping and leaping into the hoop, turning forward: (a) vertical jump, (b) split ring leap.

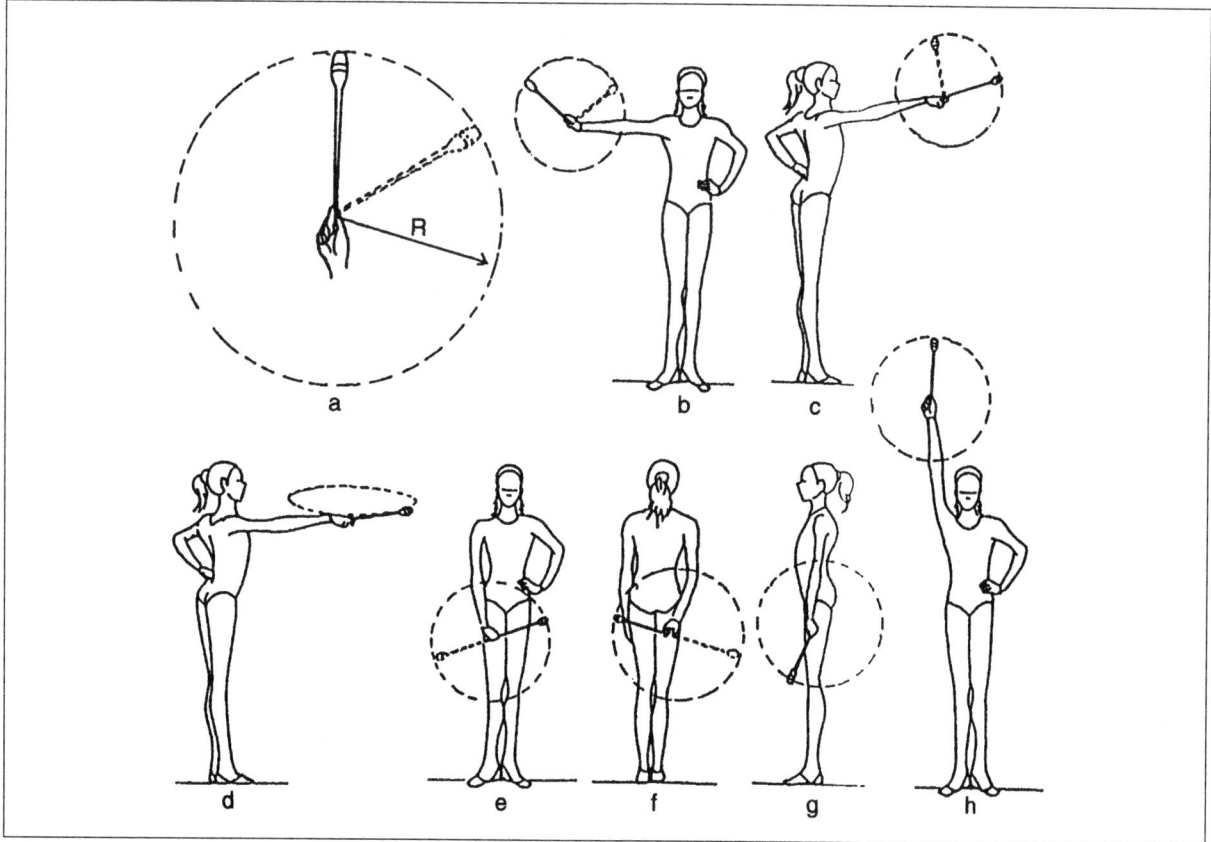

Figure 3.66 Small circles of the clubs: (a) rotating the club in the palm, (b) vertical with the arm to the side, (c) vertical with the arm in front, (d) horizontal with the arm in front, (e) vertical with the arm downward, (f) vertical with the arm downward and behind the back, (g) vertical with the arm downward and to the side, (h) vertical with the arm overhead.

changing plane or direction, the continuity of the club's motion cannot be interrupted.

Rope Rotational turns of the rope with the center of the radius within the rope are possible while making jumps and leaps into the rope (figure 3.67a) and small circles (when the gymnast grips one or both ends of a folded or open rope).

When jumping and leaping, the gymnast should hold the rope ends in her palm using a dynamic grip between her thumbs and forefingers, avoiding tension in her arms. Her wrist helps create rotational turns, and her elbows should be slightly bent. She should hold each shoulder and forearm at an angle. To perform the following jumps and leaps, the gymnast needs to engage the flexibility in her shoulders and elbows and extend them to their fullest in the split leap (figure 3.67b), vertical jump (figure 3.67c), and so on.

If the rope is folded into fourths, it cannot turn as an open rope because the gymnast must hold it with a static grip. In this case, the radius of rotation R_i is in the shoulder joint, making it a circle, not a proper rotation.

Jumps or leaps into the rope differ from similar jumps or leaps without apparatus. The preparatory phase should coincide with where the gymnast begins to turn the rope (figure 3.68). The gymnast's arms must be moving fast enough to make it easier to jump into the rope. Moreover, she must be able to take off with various degrees of power, depending on the form of the jump or leap, that is, she must be able to change the nature of the muscular tension to

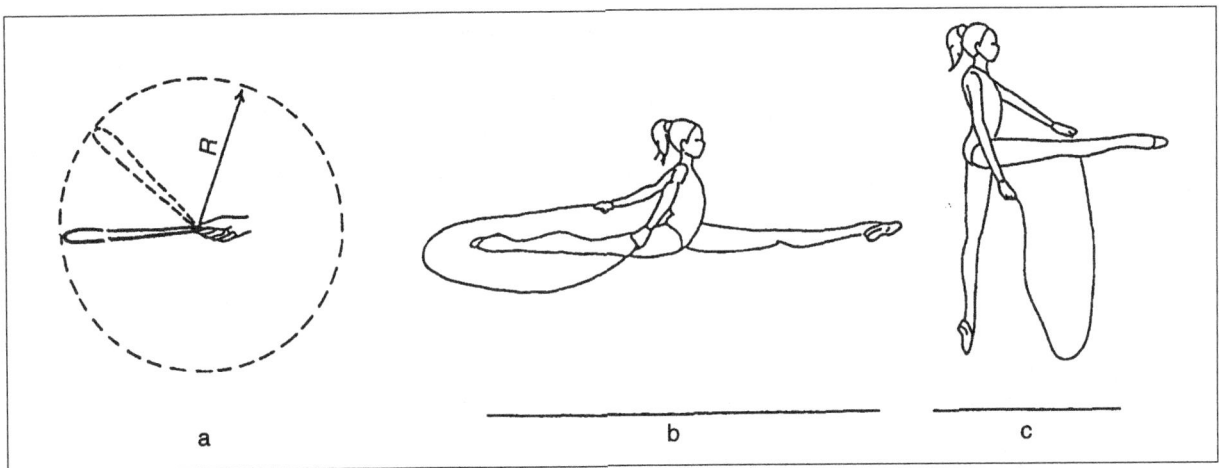

Figure 3.67 Jumps and leaps into the rope: (a) rotating the rope with the hand, (b) split leap, (c) vertical jump, one leg at horizontal.

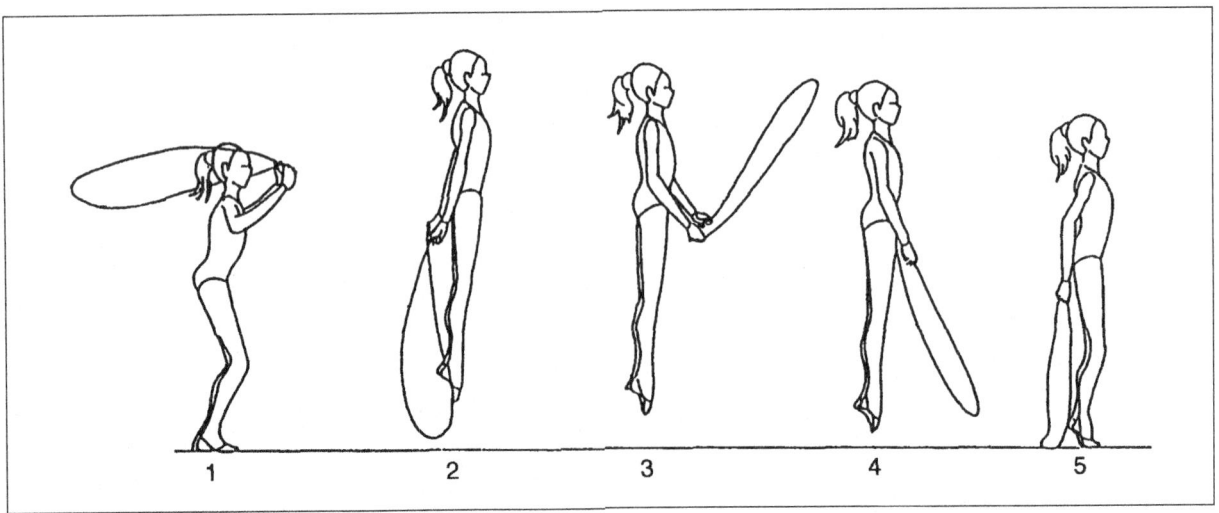

Figure 3.68 Vertical jump with a double turn of the rope.

control the jump or leap. For example, in simple jumps, skips, or hops with a single rotational turn, the takeoff should use less power but should be of sufficient power for the gymnast to pass over the turning rope. For jumps and leaps with a double turn, the takeoff should be vigorous, so that the gymnast can stay in flight while the rope passes twice under her legs. She should take off with maximum power to create the split and stag leaps into the rope, especially with a ring and body turn. In jumps and leaps into the rope, the gymnast must repeat the takeoff with various degrees of power. Therefore, she should try to distribute her use of power appropriately.

The degree of difficulty of jumps and leaps into the rope is determined by the speed of turns, which depends on the following factors:

- Shape of the jump or leap.
- Flexibility of the gymnast's wrist.
- Speed of the wrist movements.
- Radius of turns R_t.
- Height of the jump or leap.

Using these factors, the gymnast can give the rope the necessary rotational speed. It is possible to change the tempo of turns by changing the hand's movements or the radius of the turn by folding or opening the rope.

Reducing the radius of the rope's turns R_t increases the speed of rotational turns. Likewise, increasing the radius R_t decreases the speed of rotational turns. The speed of rotational turns also depends on the height of the flight of the jump or leap. The higher the flight, the slower the speed of the rope's turns. For a low flight, the speed of the rope's turns should be higher. For jumps or leaps with a single turn, the speed of rotation should be equal to the speed of the jump or leap. For jumps or leaps with double or triple turns, the speed of rotation should be higher than the speed of the jump or leap. In the last case, a gymnast doing only one jump or leap should have enough time to perform two or three turns of the rope. To create enough time, she must move her hands as abruptly and quickly as possible. Jumps or leaps with a double turn also differ from those with a single turn in that the gymnast semisquats less deeply and fixes her elbow rigidly, turning only at the wrist.

For jumps and leaps with a crossing rotational turn of the rope forward or backward, the gymnast should bend her arms slightly at the elbows while holding her arms wide apart. The loop should cross the middle of her body, not be displaced to the right or left (figure 3.69), and her elbows should almost touch one another. Then her hands move sideways to align with her body, barely higher than the level of the hips. To actually turn the rope, the gymnast moves her wrists, then completes each turn by vigorously moving her hands. Note that her arms must not be very bent, because bent arms shorten the rope and make it very difficult for her to pass into the loop. In crossing turns with the rope rotating backward, her arms should cross at waist level instead of over her head, a mistake made frequently by beginners.

For simple jumps, such as vertical jumps, the gymnast gives the rope the desired direction, whether forward, backward, or sideways, and then inertia turns the rope. For difficult jumps and leaps, the gymnast must make the rope move in various arches and directions. For example, in the split leap, the gymnast's arms turn the rope forward, then they move forward and downward, and, finally, downward and backward. The gymnast must ensure the rope moves in an arch, avoiding deforming its shape. If the rope alters its loop pattern ("breaks"), it is due to insufficient or abruptly decreasing rotational speed.

When skipping or hopping, elevation may not be high, but just enough for passing through the rope with pointed toes. If the body must be vertical while

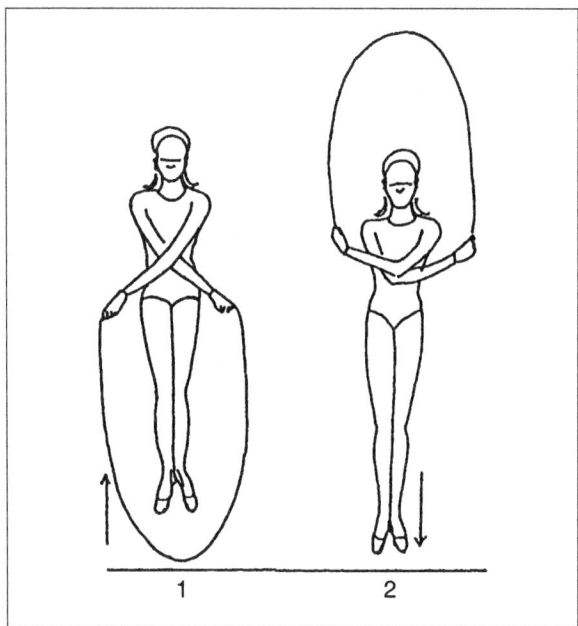

Figure 3.69 Vertical jump with a crossing turn of the rope.

jumping, the gymnast should avoid leaning, which would lead the body into a pike position. Jumps and leaps in sequence through the rope should be in good rhythm without interruption of the flow of movement.

Figure Elements

Figure elements refer to a group of elements in which the apparatus describes a certain figure pattern in space: figure eights, mills, snails, sails, snakes, swaying, and spirals. A gymnast can perform figure movements with all apparatus, but they are more natural with the ribbon. Before looking at the phases of figure elements, we will define the relevant terms.

- Figure eight means a solid performance of two opposite circles in the same or different planes: horizontal or vertical to the front or side or over the head. Depending on the center of rotation, figure eights can be large (in the shoulder), medium (in the elbow), or small (in the wrist).

- Swaying of the apparatus means executing sets of swings up and down or from side to side, and vice versa.

- A snake with the ribbon or rope means moving the wrist up and down or from side to side, so the ribbon or rope creates a snake-like pattern.

- A spiral with the ribbon or rope means consecutive circles in the wrist, so the ribbon or rope forms patterns like the spiral.

- Mills are consecutive small circles executed by the wrist with the clubs or small consecutive circles made by the rope.

- Snails with the clubs are successive half-circles made by the wrist and circles made with the elbow, with or without circular movement in the shoulder.

- Sails are the consecutive execution of large circles with the open rope, held in both hands in conjunction with trunk rotations.

Phases of Figure Movements

The structure of figure movements occurs in three phases: the preparatory, main, and finishing phases. The preparatory phase has two subphases: first, the gymnast places the apparatus in the necessary initial position, and second, the gymnast provides the impulse I of force F to start the apparatus moving. In the main phase, the apparatus performs the figure movement. In the finishing phase, the gymnast stops the apparatus or changes its direction to prepare for the next element.

Techniques of Selected Figure Movements With Apparatus

Figure movements can add grace and style to a competitive composition if performed correctly. Here we will describe the proper techniques for several figure movements with apparatus.

Hoop Among all figure movements, gymnasts perform figure eights and swaying most often with the hoop. Specifically, they may make large, medium, or small figure eights in all planes (vertical or horizontal, to the front, side, or over the head), keeping all hoop edges on one plane and using a static grip with a relaxed arm. Figure eights can be simple with one round in each half or complex with several (two or three) circles in each half.

Ball Gymnasts perform figure eights and swaying with the ball, holding it with one or both hands. Gymnasts can execute more difficult figure eights by passing the ball from one hand to the other one (figure 3.70). The designations "horizontal" and "vertical" are determined by the shape of the figure eight that results. But before learning to make figure eights with the ball, gymnasts should learn to move softly and smoothly in arches and catch the ball by gripping from it above without grasping and pressing with the fingers.

Clubs Of all figure movements with one or both clubs, the more natural ones are swaying, figure eights, mills, and snails. A gymnast can sway the clubs using a dynamic grip of both clubs together in one hand or separately, one in each hand. The clubs easily sway in the gymnast's closed palm from front to back, and vice versa, or from side to side. A gymnast can make large- and medium-sized figure eights in all planes using a static grip of the club's head. Small figure eights must be performed using a dynamic grip. She can make mills with the clubs on horizontal and vertical planes to the front, side, or over her head in an arch or a circle. Mills have the following characteristics:

- Dynamic grip of the club.
- Active rotation in the wrist.
- Crossed position of the forearms or hands.
- Parallel upper arms.

As for small circles, mill circles should rotate in the palm only as directed by the wrists; at the same time, the arms must not be too far apart. Mills can be in horizontal or vertical planes. Gymnasts use two types of one-turn vertical mills: double and triple. They only use double horizontal mills.

Double mills—whether vertical or horizontal—consist of two cycles of movements: successive small circles of one club and then of the other club for a total of four circles. Figure 3.71 shows double vertical mills over the gymnast's head. The gymnast must ensure that the clubs move slightly forward in front of her face and backward to behind her head without hitting herself. Figure 3.72 shows a gymnast performing double horizontal mills, consisting of two cycles of club movement above and under the lower arm.

Triple mills consist of six small circles, which a gymnast performs only on the vertical plane, usually in front of herself. She makes three small circles on one side and three on the other side, crossing and uncrossing her wrists. According to the Code of Points, a series of mills consists of a minimum of 12 circles.

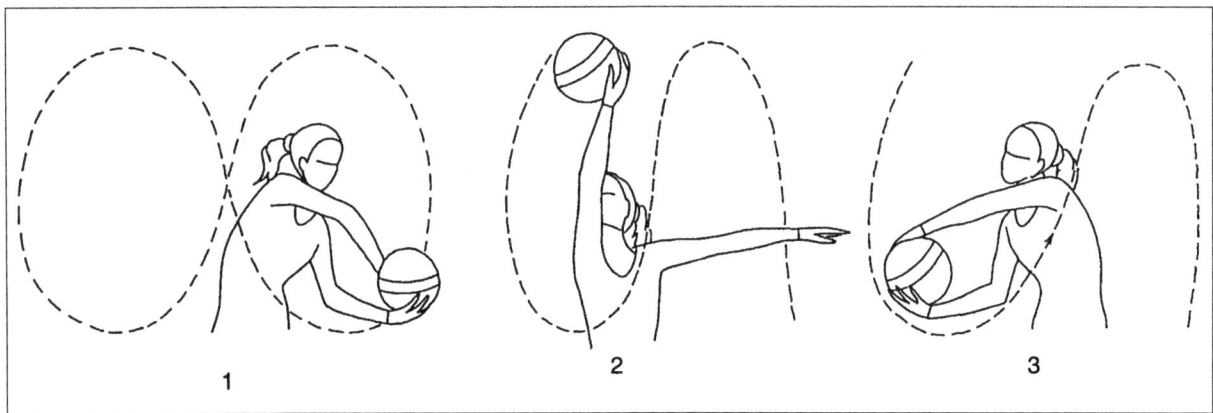

Figure 3.70 Figure eight with the ball in front.

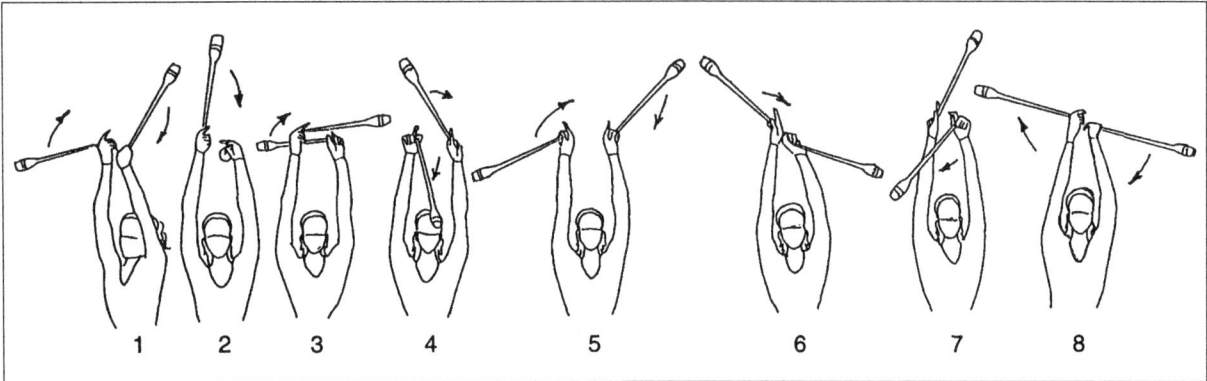

Figure 3.71 Double vertical mills.

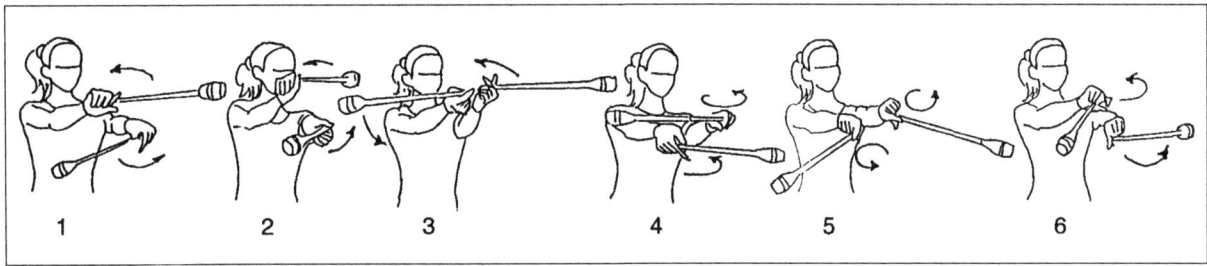

Figure 3.72 Double horizontal mills.

A gymnast performs a snail with clubs using two types of grips, which comprise the two phases of the snail (figure 3.73). To begin a snail, she uses a dynamic grip. This phase is called "packing," in which the gymnast turns the clubs in her palms, then moves them to her forearms. Then to finish a snail, she uses a static grip. To change from a dynamic to a static grip, she bends her elbows and grasps the clubs and moves them to her upper arms. At this point, the clubs should be at chest level. Then the second, or "unpacking," phase begins in which the gymnast straightens her elbows and moves the clubs in the desired direction using a static grip.

There are two types of snails: a simple snail, for which the gymnast unpacks the clubs in the initial direction, and the complex snail, for which the gymnast unpacks the club in different directions. A single complex snail involves unpacking the clubs toward another direction, for example, from the front to the side or from up above the gymnast's head to the front. A double complex snail involves unpacking the clubs toward another direction and back again, for example, from the front to the side and then from the side to the front.

When performing the snail, it is very important to maintain the plane that club moves in. A gymnast must not move the club involuntarily. No matter the plane, a gymnast may perform snails either symmetrically or asymmetrically.

Ribbon The more natural figure movements with the ribbon are figure eights, snakes, and spirals.

Large, medium, and small figure eights with the ribbon may be horizontal or vertical. The direction of the movement is determined by the motion of the stick. To create a figure eight with the ribbon, a gymnast turns her arm inward and then outward (figure 3.74). The outward movement must be especially active in medium and small figure eights. This is when the pattern comes close to forming two correct circles joining one another. Both loops should be joined to one another so that the pattern of the ribbon at the point of the crossing is not spread. When the loops cross, the gymnast must change the motion of the ribbon. The position of each circle is determined with respect to the gymnast's body. Figure eights should be performed energetically and continuously, so the entire ribbon is in motion.

A gymnast can perform a horizontal figure eight in the front by turning her shoulders to the side of the ribbon's movements (figure 3.74b). As in lateral circles, the ribbon passes directly beside her foot. When making horizontal figure eights on the side (medium and small), the gymnast bends her hand upward and outward strongly and in synchroniza-

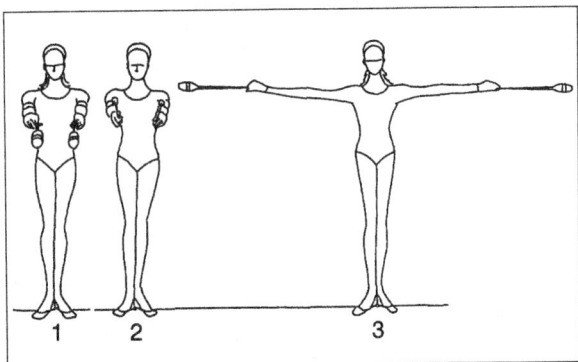

Figure 3.73 Single snail with the clubs from the front to the side.

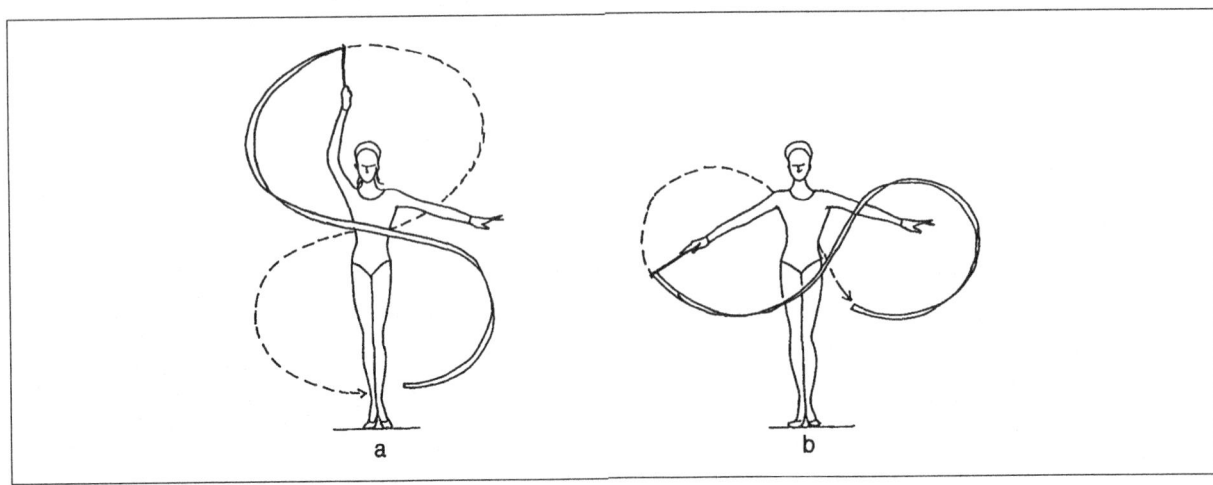

Figure 3.74 Figure eights of the ribbon in front: (a) vertical, (b) horizontal.

tion with the turn. When performing horizontal figure eights over her head, the gymnast moves her arm with her palm turned upward. For vertical figure eights in the front, the gymnast makes the top loop with her palm turned outward, and the bottom loop with her palm turned inward (figure 3.74a).

A gymnast should not attempt figure eights until she has learned to swing and circle the apparatus. Then she should practice large figure eights before attempting medium and small figure eights. When the gymnast is performing the first loop of a figure eight, the coach should check to make sure she is actively turning her hand outward to form a correct circle. When learning medium and small figure eights, a gymnast should do exercises to develop flexibility in her wrist and elbow.

There are two types of snakes with the ribbon: vertical, in which the loops are vertical to the floor, and horizontal, in which the loops are horizontal to the floor.

To snake the ribbon, the gymnast bends her elbow slightly and moves her wrist up and down or from side to side with maximum amplitude and tempo, quickly and freely without tension in the grip, creating at least four or five equal loops. In fact, loops of the ribbon should always be very close to one other, be of the same amplitude, and be spread throughout the whole length of the ribbon. To snake in the air, the length of the pattern increases a little, and the gymnast may decrease the quantity of loops to one or two.

The most commonly seen snaking errors include the following:

- A languid pattern, allowing the end of the ribbon to be passive, creating gentle loop "teeth," caused by hand movements that are too slow and weak, leading to insufficient tempo.
- Uneven spacing of loops and their various heights, caused by inconsistent speed and amplitude of the wrist movements.
- Large and wide loops caused by an extremely intense grip, which involves moving the forearm or even the whole arm instead of only the wrist and hand.

A gymnast can perform a vertical snake in front of herself and to her side by moving her wrist up and down, keeping her palm downward. When snaking the ribbon on the floor, the gymnast bends her hand up a little more (figure 3.75a), thereby moving the snake on the vertical plane. The loops of the ribbon should touch the floor slightly as they move vertically to the floor.

A gymnast may perform a horizontal snake in front of herself or to her side (upward, then downward, and vice versa) by moving her wrist side to side. For movements on the floor, all loops should lie on the floor. For movements in the air, the loops should maintain the horizontal plane at all times. A gymnast can create a horizontal snake on the floor by bending and extending her wrist. She can create a horizontal snake from down to up by moving her wrist from side to side. At this point, the forearm gradually passes from down to the upward vertical position. Meanwhile, the entire ribbon should be in the air (figure 3.75b).

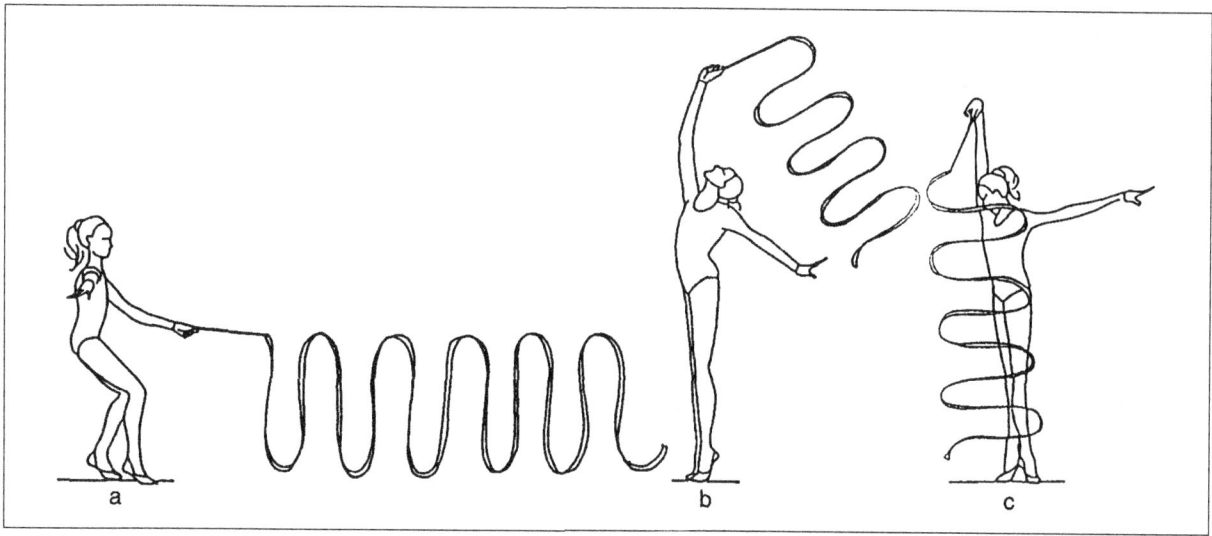

Figure 3.75 Snakes with the ribbon: (a) vertical in front, (b) horizontal overhead, (c) horizontal in front.

A gymnast can perform a horizontal snake over her head only by moving her arm forward with her hand bent backward and her palm turned up. Then she leads the ribbon with her hand to form a horizontal snake in front of her (figure 3.75c).

The novice should start by learning snakes on the floor, because this type of snake generally does not change because of contact with the floor. So she should be able to achieve fast, free, and even movements with her wrist. The coach should remind the gymnast to avoid excessive tension in her hand and to perform snakes using wrist movements only. Do not complicate other body movements before a gymnast learns how to tense her hand correctly. A gymnast should learn to do horizontal snakes over her head, which are the most difficult snakes, last.

A spiral with the ribbon is comprised of a series of circles created by small circular movements of the hand. It should have at least four or five circles of the same diameter, height, and length. Indeed, the circles must be very similar to one another in all lengths of the ribbon (figure 3.76).

There are two types of spirals: vertical and horizontal, that is, circles on the vertical or horizontal plane. A spiral's direction is determined in relation to the gymnast's face and may be clockwise or counterclockwise. The gymnast can perform vertical spirals in front of herself, to her side, and behind herself, either on the floor or in the air. Circles of spirals should not lose their correct pattern due to contacting the floor (figure 3.76a).

A gymnast needs much greater strength and speed in her wrist movements if she is performing vertical spirals in the air than she needs for downward spirals. When performing vertical spirals behind on the floor and over the head, the wrist is bent backward. The gymnast must maintain the horizontal position of the stick and the whole pattern of the spiral. As this is difficult, we recommend that the novice start learning how to spiral by practicing spirals that are connected to the floor. The inertia of a movement is easy to maintain in these spirals. A gymnast should note that vertical spirals ought to touch the floor with even cylinders and vertically standing circles. If the spiral has an elliptical shape, the coach needs to check and correct the gymnast's wrist movements. How? Have the gymnast try to make circular movements with her hand. Another widespread error is performing the spiral with an excessively tense and bent arm. In this case, help the gymnast relax her whole arm so that her wrist will move freely. Specifically, movement should start from the wrist then continue to the elbow, and end at the shoulder when performing gradually increasing vertical spirals in the front and side planes.

A horizontal spiral differs from a vertical spiral due to the position of the stick. When performing a horizontal spiral down and up, the stick and hand are vertical, and the gymnast lifts her arm a little higher than her shoulder and holds her forearm parallel to the floor (figure 3.76c). In the end, the gymnast should perform the spiral only with her hand turned vertically downward. During the spirals the entire ribbon is in the air, but the last circle touches the floor slightly. When performing a horizontal spiral around her body, the gymnast involves her shoulder and keeps the stick above her head (figure 3.76d).

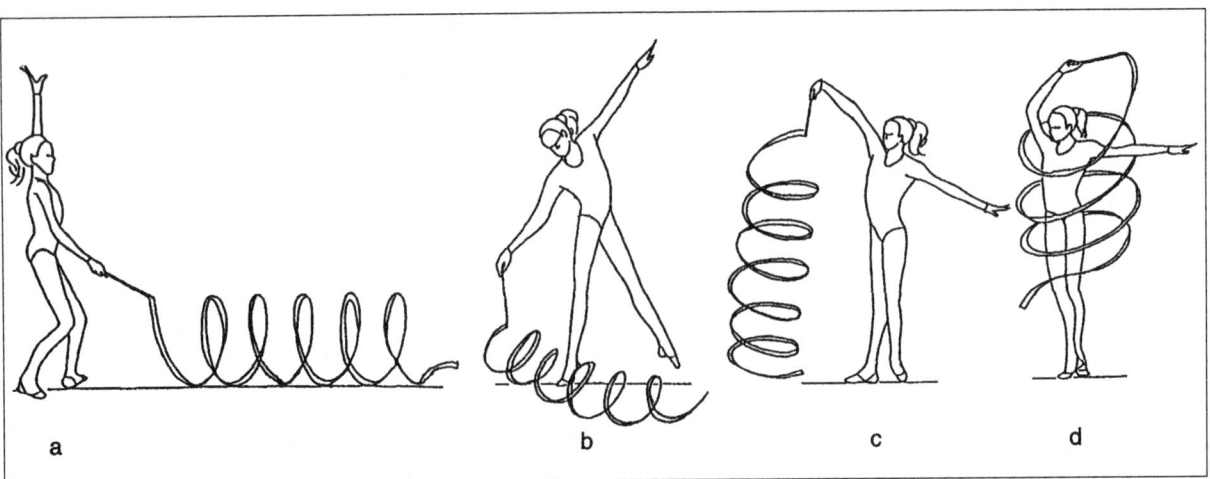

Figure 3.76 Spirals with the ribbon: (a) vertical in front on the floor, (b) vertical to the side on the floor, (c) horizontal in front, (d) horizontal around a gymnast.

Rope A gymnast may perform the following figure movements with the rope: swaying, figure eights, snakes, spirals, mills, and sails. The following list describes each element:

- Swaying is performed with the rope folded in two or open in front and side.
- Figure eights with the rope may be performed vertically or horizontally. They may be small, medium, or large.
- Snakes and spirals with the rope are atypical elements for this apparatus, but when used, they are performed by gripping one end.
- Mills can be performed either vertically or horizontally by gripping the middle of the rope. Figure 3.77 shows vertical double mills, which differ from similar mills with clubs because the gymnast bends her elbows slightly so that the rope does not touch her body.
- Sails may be performed in the frontal or lateral plane, in front and in back. Sails should be performed with a tight, unaltering rope. Large circles should be executed from the shoulder joints in sequence. The trunk should rotate with the rhythm of the rope: fast, moderate, or slow.

No matter the type of element, the rope cannot involuntarily touch the gymnast's body in figure movements.

Linking Elements

Linking, or work, elements refer to the following: regrips, tossing or passing, swings, passages through, transferring, and folding of the apparatus. As a rule, these elements do not have independent significance; gymnasts use them only for connecting other elements.

Physics of Linking Elements

To regrip simply means to change the way of holding the apparatus, accomplished in two main ways: by tossing, for which the apparatus has a small flight phase and the gymnast catches the apparatus with the same or other hand or part of the body, and by passing, for which the gymnast moves the apparatus from one hand or part (or parts) of the body to another body part without a flight phase. The gymnast can pass the apparatus in front of herself, behind herself, to her side, over her head, or under one or both legs or arms.

Swings with apparatus refer to the apparatus's free movement on a rotational axis in a circle, that is, up to 360 degrees. The gymnast must apply an angular acceleration to the apparatus to make it swing. The angular acceleration of an apparatus is higher (figure 3.78) if force F applied to it is higher, its mass is less, and if the distance from the apparatus's center of gravity to the rotational axis in the joint (for example, the radius of swing R_t) is also less. For example, a gymnast swings the ball and hoop at an angle α. She will keep her arms closer to her shoulders when dealing with the ball's center of gravity, than when dealing with the hoop's. Therefore, when swinging the ball, it is necessary to apply less force than for the same movement with the hoop. It is easier to grip the hoop more steadily than the ball,

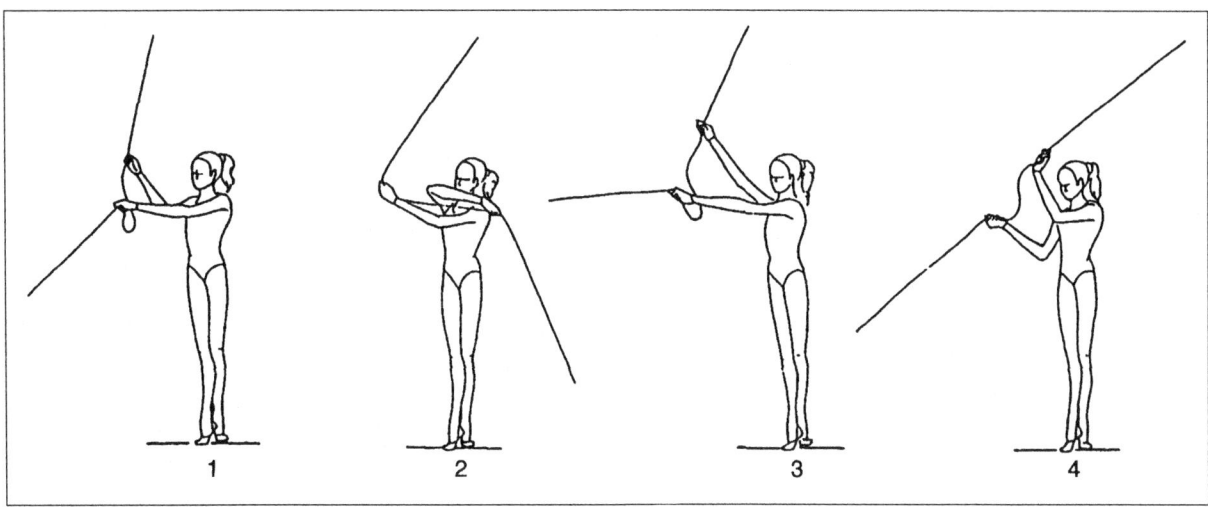

Figure 3.77 Double mills with the rope.

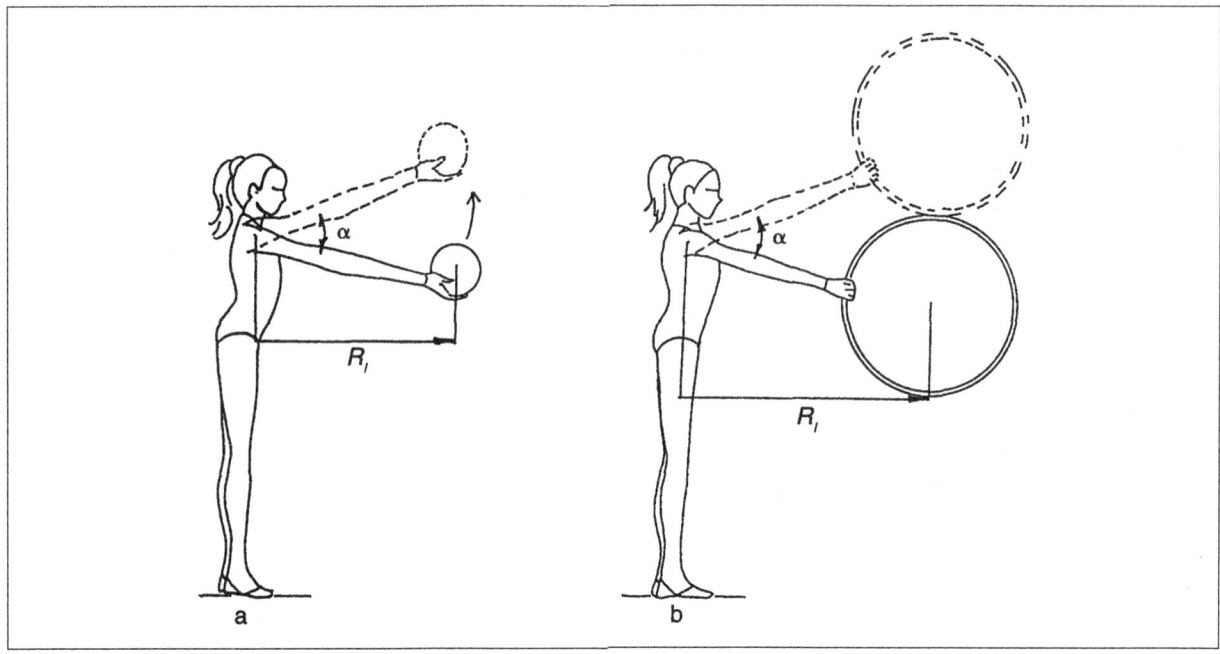

Figure 3.78 Dependence of a swing on the radius of rotation at the same acceleration: (a) the ball, (b) the hoop, where α is the angle of changing of apparatus position and R_l is radius of swing.

making a gymnast feel more confident when swinging the hoop than when swinging the ball.

When swinging soft apparatus, a gymnast should stretch it, then swing it with maximum angular acceleration, which is achieved with a maximum force F in a minimum time Δt. In other words, the movement should be abrupt enough, otherwise, the apparatus will sag.

A gymnast can swing the apparatus with one or both arms, vertically or horizontally in front of herself, to her side, or behind or over her head, clockwise or counterclockwise. Swings are divided depending on the radius of the swing: large swings from the shoulder, medium swings from the elbow, and small swings from the wrist.

Swings simply prepare for circles, figure eights, and throws. Specifically, they serve as connective and passing movements, allowing the gymnast to change the direction or plane of the action. But for beginners, swings are independent elements which play a greater role in compositions.

Now we will define three more terms that will help the reader better understand linking elements. Passage through the apparatus refers to when the gymnast puts the hoop, folded rope, or ribbon around her body or part of her body, encircling herself. Transferring refers to changing the position of the soft apparatus in motion, which gymnasts more often use to change the direction of a rotation.

Folding refers to changing the length of the soft apparatus. More often a gymnast will fold an apparatus in multiple numbers.

Techniques of Selected Linking Elements Using Apparatus

Linking elements can make an average competitive routine into an excellent one—provided the gymnast performs them smoothly, seamlessly. In the following sections, we will explain the techniques behind several commonly used linking elements.

Hoop Connections between various grips and an abundance of regrips make it possible to create a variety of compositions with the hoop. Of all the linking elements, however, the most difficult to learn are regrips. Therefore, beginners, when changing the hoop's position or plane, should know about the correct regripping variation that is most appropriate for the situation.

When teaching a regrip, a coach should demonstrate it slowly. The gymnast must work hard to maintain the correct plane with the hoop. Swinging in combination with springing movements of the legs helps beginners to reduce excessive tension in regripping the apparatus and to create a flowing motion. With the correct regrip, a gymnast does not stop the motion of the hoop; instead, she merges it smoothly with the movements of other parts of her body.

A gymnast passes the hoop from one or both arms or other body parts to another part after swings, rotations, circles, and rolls while standing or traveling. Passes create a variety of connections between elements.

As another connective element, a gymnast can swing the hoop with one or both arms, horizontally or vertically (figure 3.79). Swings create "flow" between movements and help the gymnast prepare for circles, figure eights, and throws. When swinging the hoop, the gymnast should maintain the plane of the hoop, which should be aligned with the arm or arms holding it. A gymnast should learn how to swing, regrip, and pass the hoop simultaneously.

Passage through the hoop is an element unique to this apparatus made possible by its rim. Most often, it connects with and prepares for rotations on the leg, arm, or waist. There are various types of passage, using any part of the body: the arm, leg, head, or the entire body (figure 3.80). Passage through the hoop with the entire body is possible from the side, above, or below. When passing through the hoop, the gymnast must concentrate on maintaining the chosen plane of the hoop.

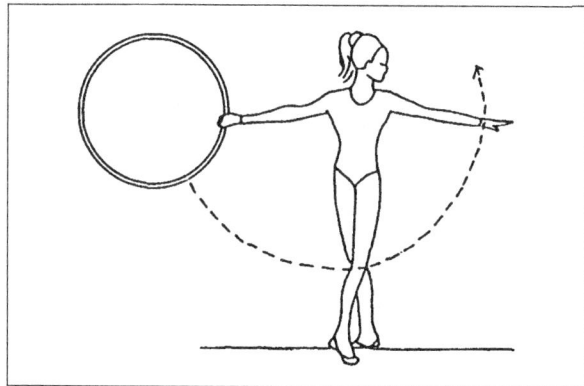

Figure 3.79 Large vertical swing of the hoop in front.

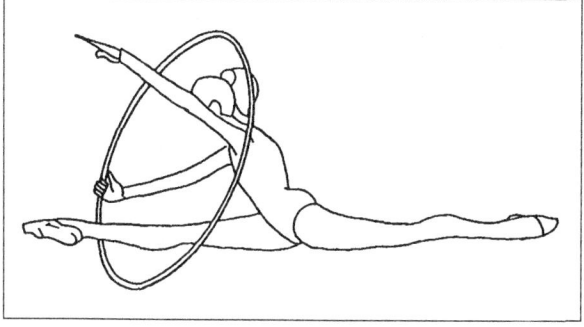

Figure 3.80 Split leap, passing through the hoop.

Ball A gymnast may regrip and swing the ball. In fact, regripping the ball is the main element that connects all other elements in a composition. It requires the same performance from the left hand and right hand. A gymnast may regrip from one palm to the other, from one leg to one arm or vice versa, from one part of the body to another one, and so on—all while either standing still or traveling. The plane may vary from in front of the gymnast, to her side, to behind or over her head. Regripping the ball from one arm to the other under one or both legs is possible with straightened or bent knees. A gymnast should learn how to pass the ball with flowing, continuous movement; the ball must not obviously appear to stop.

Ball swings are linking elements in a composition as well. A gymnast can swing the ball with one or both hands, vertically and horizontally, freely and rhythmically. To swing the ball correctly, the gymnast must hold her arms and hands freely without muscular tension and without grasping with her fingers. Instead, the ball should cling to her palm. Usually swings with the ball are connected to springing movements of the legs, giving each swing softness and integrity. A gymnast may also swing the ball to prepare for throws and to provide a linking element after the catch.

Clubs A gymnast may regrip and swing the clubs. To regrip the clubs, the gymnast may first toss them, rotating them outward or inward, following up by regripping or she may pass them from one hand to the other or from one part of her body to one hand, and vice versa.

Regripping, however, should not slow down the tempo of the main movements. Indeed, a gymnast should not interrupt the continuity of the movements when changing the plane or direction of the club's motion.

A gymnast may regrip one club during flights, rolls, or rotations of the other club. Again, the gymnast must be on the alert to maintain the tempo of the previous and subsequent movements. Then the gymnast may regrip both clubs simultaneously or consecutively.

A gymnast may swing one or both clubs vertically or horizontally, simultaneously or consecutively, asymmetrically or symmetrically. For large and medium swings, the club must be aligned with the forearm; it must not make an angle with the wrist or elbow. Thus, the gymnast must keep her arm straight but tension-free. The gymnast may swing to large and medium degrees using a static grip and to a small degree using a dynamic grip. She must learn to use the inertia of the movement of the clubs (figure 3.81). When learning swings, a gymnast must focus most on avoiding strong tension in her arm muscles.

Ribbon A gymnast may use the following linking elements with the ribbon: regrips, swings, folding, and transfers.

A gymnast may regrip the ribbon by tossing or passing it. She can pass the ribbon's stick simply by moving it from one hand to the other. She should execute this movement quickly, without interrupting the continuity of the ribbon's pattern. But this difficult element requires much training. To begin with, the gymnast should learn to pass at the last point of a slow tempo swing, then she should practice passing at medium and fast tempos at various points of the swing.

A gymnast can swing the ribbon vertically and horizontally by any of the joints of her arm. The stick and hand must be aligned with the forearm, however, during large and medium swings.

When teaching a swing with the ribbon, the coach should help the gymnast focus on using the whole ribbon for the swing, aligning the hand with the arm (during large and medium swings), having the hand smoothly overtake the forearm when changing the ribbon's direction, thereby creating even and free movements.

Several common problems may arise when swinging the ribbon. Do not allow the gymnast to snap the ribbon, which may be caused by the hand outdistancing the arm quickly and abruptly. The ribbon's point of attachment may touch the end of the ribbon and it may become tangled when changing directions. This is caused by insufficient hand movement and excessive tension when changing directions of the swing. The novice should begin learning ribbon exercises with swings by striving for even movements, continuity, accuracy of plane and pattern, and smooth connections with body movements.

A gymnast can create large swings with the ribbon by moving her arm energetically and evenly from her shoulder with a maximum radius R_r. For large swings, a gymnast cannot bend her elbow. When changing the direction of the large swing, the hand with the stick should come nearer to the last point of the swing and advance the arm by bending the wrist to the side of the swing. All of the material must finish the previous swing and the flight completely behind the arm. After this, the gymnast moves the stick in another direction at a tempo fast enough to keep the material from lowering during the change. For example, during a large lateral swing, the gymnast moves the stick upward in front of herself in a vertical motion, then flays the material over and completely behind her arm. Only when all the material is behind the stick does the gymnast make the stick change direction, moving it downward. The trajectory of the material's flight is steep, and the acceleration of the flight depends on the speed and degree of bending of the gymnast's wrist. Hand movements should be flowing but solid, involving the whole arm. This method keeps the end of the ribbon clear of the body when changing direction.

For large frontal swings upward, the arch of the trajectory is greater than 180 degrees, but the ribbon should never lie on the floor (figure 3.82a). It may only touch the floor very briefly as it passes the gymnast's feet. The gymnast should focus on keeping her elbow straight during frontal swings.

In horizontal swings, the ribbon should fly at shoulder level. In horizontal swings inward, the gymnast may bend her arm slightly at the elbow. To maintain the inertia of the flight in horizontal swings, the gymnast's arm must work harder than in vertical swings to create the speed the ribbon needs. But the swing should not turn into a jerk. Certainly, horizontal swings are the most difficult, so a gymnast should learn them last.

As with the rope, a gymnast may transfer the ribbon to either prepare for or follow jumps and

Figure 3.81 Large vertical swings of the clubs at the side.

leaps into the ribbon. So, not surprisingly, the gymnast transfers the ribbon in a manner similar to transferring the rope.

A gymnast sometimes folds or passes through the ribbon (as with the hoop). These elements require perfect coordination of movements, as an error can cause the ribbon to tangle, interrupting its pattern and destroying its tempo.

Rope Softness of the rope lends itself to creating linking elements, including transferring, regripping, swinging, and folding.

Transferring the rope from one plane to another allows a gymnast to change the direction of a rotating rope, thereby varying a composition. To change directions, the gymnast must transfer the rope with one or both hands from its position in front of herself to behind (or vice versa) or from one side to the other (figure 3.83). The gymnast must avoid stopping the rope when transferring it. Any element may immediately follow a rope transfer.

A gymnast may regrip a folded or open rope by passing and tossing it. She may pass the rope in various directions by swinging or circling it. Specifically, she can pass the rope from one hand to the other when moving in an arch or under any part or parts of her body (bypassing). The actual pass occurs in the last point of the swing or circle, when the force of inertia is at its greatest. A gymnast should try not to touch her body or floor with the rope. The requirements for regripping the rope are similar to those for swings.

A gymnast may swing the rope vertically or horizontally with one or both arms as follows:

- Holding the ends open or folded rope with one or both hands.

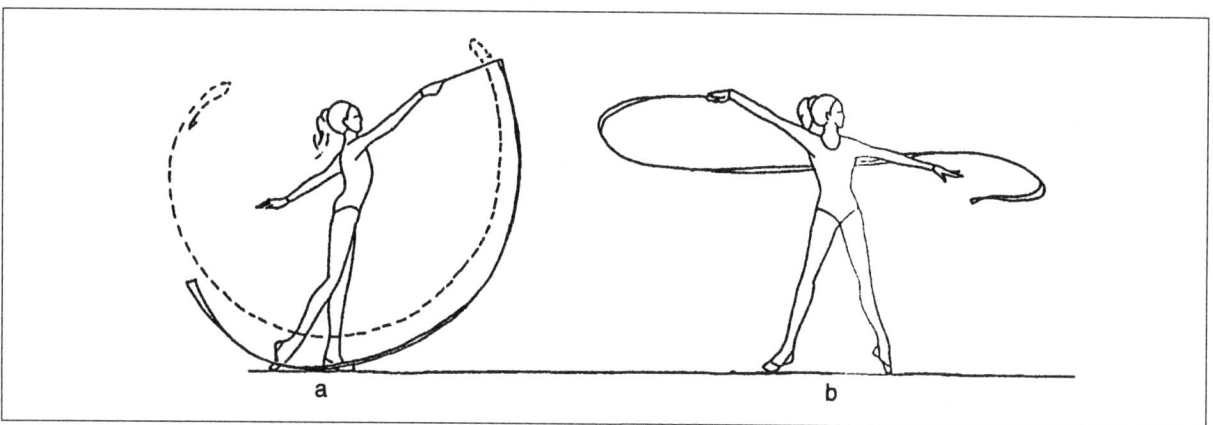

Figure 3.82 Large swings with the ribbon: (a) vertical swing with the ribbon at the side, (b) horizontal swing with the ribbon in back.

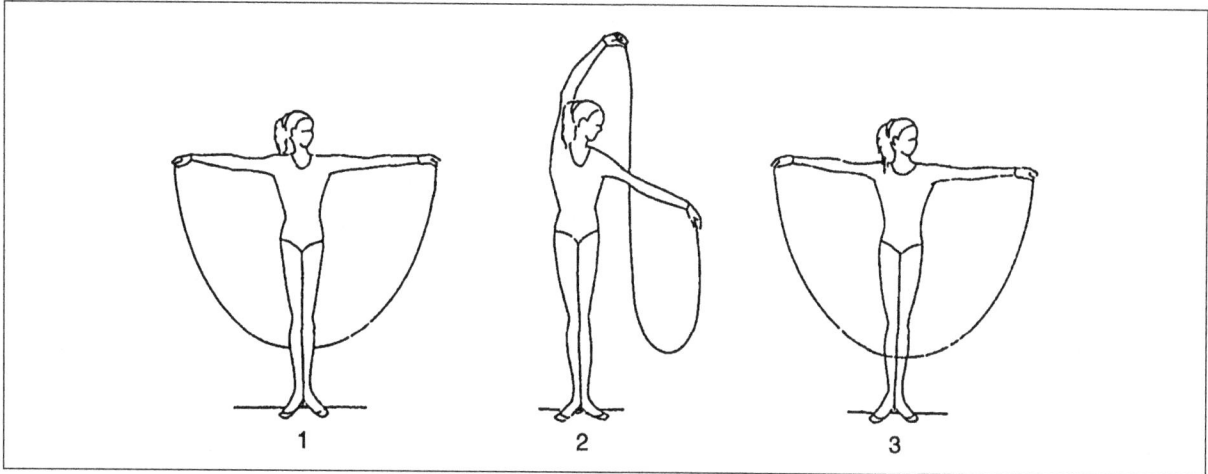

Figure 3.83 Transferring the rope.

- Holding one end of the rope with one hand and its middle with the other hand, allowing one part of the rope to hang down freely.
- Holding tightly to the middle of the rope, allowing the ends to hang freely.

Swings of the rope should arch through tension that creates a definite shape. The specific technique of a swing depends on the speed and amplitude of the movements following it. All the while, a gymnast should maintain the plane and direction of each swing. But if the plane and direction of a swing are distorted, it is difficult to continue with the next rope movement. So take into account when a turn, pivot, jump, or leap is followed by a swing of the rope so that a preparatory swing can create the correct position for the rope.

Folding the rope is a common linking element. It is easier, however, for a gymnast to use the rope folded in halves than in fourths. When the rope is folded, a coach should help the gymnast focus on holding the rope securely and on maintaining the tempo necessary for performing the following element.

Summary

In this chapter, we have described the basic elements using apparatus. We have discussed the characteristics of each apparatus, the physics behind moving each apparatus in various ways, and specific techniques to lead the gymnast toward mastery.

As we have shown, the apparatus share many features in common. For example, the rigid apparatus—the hoop, ball, and clubs—react in many of the same ways to the same actions due to their structure. Likewise, the soft apparatus—the rope and ribbon—share similarities in their reactions to a gymnast's actions. But, of course, each apparatus is unique, presenting its own strengths and challenges. For example, only the clubs have such irregular shapes that they cannot be rolled or bounced easily, but, of course, the ball was made for rolling and bouncing.

Moreover, each type of movement presents its own strengths and challenges. Flights, circular elements, figure elements, and linking elements are all unique for each apparatus. Together, each type of apparatus and each type of movement form a vast pool of elements from which both the novice and elite gymnast may choose to create a successful competitive composition.

In the next chapter, we will discuss how a gymnast can take the information we have laid out in chapters 2 and 3 toward true mastery.

Chapter 4

Mastering Technique

A gymnast's technical mastery is determined by what she is capable of performing and whether she conforms to the standard (or model) for each technique. Technical mastery may be evaluated according to the following criteria:

- Volume.
- Versatility and ambidexterity.
- Stability.
- Variety.
- Rationality.

In this chapter, we will describe how to evaluate a gymnast's technical mastery and discuss how acquisition of technique fits into the overall training framework.

Evaluating a Gymnast's Technical Mastery

A coach must be able to evaluate each gymnast's technical mastery in order to tailor training to each individual's needs. In the following sections, we will examine each aspect of technique and discuss how a coach can help to develop each in a gymnast.

Volume

Acquired elements are those performed without errors. Volume is the general number of acquired elements that a gymnast performs in lessons and competitions. Each gymnast has two different volumes of technique: competitive volume and training volume. Competitive volume consists of the acquired elements she includes in her competitive compositions, including difficult elements, and apparatus handling. Training volume includes all elements acquired by a gymnast. Naturally, the training volume of technique is much greater than the competitive one. It forms the basis for skills and habits to include in future compositions. A gymnast should therefore constantly work to expand her training volume, not exclusively her competitive volume.

A gymnast cannot control her volume of techniques without her coach's supervision and analysis, however. The coach must accurately analyze each gymnast's training volume of techniques according to the Code of Points. This analysis must include a list of acquired elements within each difficulty group, and the requirements for compositions with each apparatus.

We recommend that a coach record the list of acquired elements on a separate card for each gymnast. Monitoring the volume of techniques will allow a coach to create an effective plan for technical preparation.

Versatility and Ambidexterity

Versatility means that, using each apparatus, a gymnast can perform a variety of elements in a variety of combinations, including the use of different body parts. Ambidexterity means that a gymnast can use both her right and left hands and can move from both the left to the right and the right to the left with equal skill. The judges will look for the ratio of left- and right-handed and left- and right-sided elements to be about one-to-one.

A coach must ensure that a gymnast acquires elements from the various levels of difficulty; is able to handle the apparatus with both hands equally well, no matter the level of difficulty; and can perform each element equally well on both the right and left sides.

It is especially important to monitor the last parameter during the preliminary steps of preparation and sport specialization. For example, a gymnast first learns to do a split leap while holding an apparatus. Later she learns this leap while rotating the hoop and throwing the ball, clubs, and rope. After this, she could include the split leap in a combination move, starting with the split leap while throwing the ball or hoop, progressing to a forward roll, then arching her back while kneeling and catching the apparatus. This progression demonstrates versatile technique with the split leap, because every apparatus requires specific variations while performing it.

We can classify a versatile technique as in table 4.1. It is possible to use the same scheme to monitor handling of the apparatus.

The coach can monitor a gymnast's acquisition of elements on the right and left sides using the form in table 4.2. When a gymnast has learned to perform an element, the coach marks a plus sign next to the element learned, noting on which side the gymnast can perform the element. The coach marks a minus sign next to the elements that have not been learned. In the sample form, the gymnast has learned to perform both a 720 degree pivot in *passé* and a balance in *attitude* on the right side, but has not learned to perform either element on the left.

TABLE 4.1

Sample Analysis of Versatile Technique

Gymnast's name:						
	Handling of apparatus					
Body movements	Hoop	Ball	Clubs	Ribbon	Rope	Connections
Split leap	Rotate with right hand	One-hand throw	One-hand parallel throw	Swing with right arm	Into the open rope	With stag ring leap
Back balance	Swing with left arm	Swing with right arm	Swing both clubs	Swing with left arm	Rope folded in half, swing with left hand	With vertical balance, right leg in front

TABLE 4.2

Sample Form for Acquisition of Elements on the Right and Left Sides

Gymnast's name:		
	Side of acquisition	
Element	To the right	To the left
Pivot, 720°, in *passé*	+	−
Balance in *attitude*	+	−

A coach can calculate the coefficient of asymmetry of a gymnast's acquired elements. To do so, he or she has the gymnast perform elements of body movements or elements with apparatus on both sides. The coach evaluates her performance on each side under the Code of Points, reducing the score accordingly from a perfect score of 1.0. The coefficient of asymmetry is then calculated as follows:

$$A_S = \frac{R_{right} - R_{left}}{R_{right}} \cdot 100$$

where A_S is the coefficient of asymmetry of the acquired element, R_{right} is the result of the performance using the right (or dominant) arm or leg, and R_{left} is the result of the performance using the left (nondominant) arm or leg.

The coach can also calculate a coefficient of asymmetry for a number (N) of acquired elements, $A_{S(N)}$:

$$A_{S(N)} = \frac{\sum_{1}^{N} A_S}{N}$$

where $A_{S(N)}$ is the coefficient of asymmetry of acquired elements, N is the number of acquired elements, and A_S is the coefficient of asymmetry of a specific acquired element.

The coefficient of asymmetry increases with the difficulty of the element. Different apparatus may also affect the coefficient of asymmetry. Elements with the ribbon, hoop, and ball should have a coefficient of 41 percent or less. Elements with the clubs and rope should have a coefficient of 18 to 21 percent or less. Once the coach determines a gymnast's asymmetry of performance, he or she should assist her in increasing the number of acquired elements on both sides. At the same time, it is necessary to take into account the need for the gymnast to perform original and very difficult elements on her "best" side.

Stability

Stability of technique is an important measure of technical preparation. The ability to perform any element or composition depends on many different factors. The stability of a technique is independent of the gymnast's training and performance conditions. The gymnast's ability to perform an element or composition in an adverse and unusual environment is the foundation of this aspect of technique. It defines the gymnast's overall level of technical development and mastery.

Training stability is not the same as competitive stability, however. The former depends on the gymnast's acquisition of elements, while the latter depends on the gymnast's ability to perform a composition under stressful conditions. In either case, we evaluate stability based on the gymnast's ability to perform an element or composition without errors or loss of the apparatus. Tables 4.3 and 4.4 define stability by helping the coach evaluate a gymnast's performance reliability for certain elements and connections in all compositions for competitions, testing, and lessons.

In practical work, the coach should systematically collect and analyze information regarding the main parameters of competitive compositions. When a gymnast is performing a composition, the coach or other gymnasts should record all the elements she performs. The coach should consider an element or connection as not acquired if the gymnast commits an error; the coach should mark a minus sign on the form (table 4.3). Of course, each coach can use his or her own system of noting errors; simply having a system is the key.

At the end of the lesson, testing, or competition, the coach should record all the data obtained on the form. The coach should then analyze the perfor-

TABLE 4.3

Sample Analysis of a Composition to Determine Stability of Performance

Gymnast's name: _____

Year of birth: _____

Annual training cycle: _____

Sequence of elements	Name of element	Performance of composition, type of performance, date					Stability of performance		
		TP Sept 9	CTP Nov 1	CTP Dec 3	CP Jan 8	CP Feb 6	Total possible	Stable performances	%
1	Balance in *attitude* with ball rolls	+	+	+	+	+	5	5	100
2	Pivot, 720°, in *passé* with ball swing	–	–	–	+	+	5	2	40
Heart rate (for 10 seconds)		30	30	29	28	29	Average 70%		

TP: training performance; CTP: control training performance; CP: competitive performance

TABLE 4.4

Sample Analysis of Performance Stability of All-Around Compositions

Gymnast's name: _____

Year of birth: _____

Annual training cycle: _____

Date	Total number of elements	Good elements	%	Performance stability (%)				
				Hoop	Ball	Clubs	Ribbon	Rope
Sept 9	42	33	78.5	70	65	60	80	70
Nov 1	42	30	71.0	60	63	58	75	65
Average	42	31.5	78.4	75	64	59	77.5	67.5

mance by determining the number of elements performed and calculating the stability of the performed elements. Such an analysis by the coach and gymnast helps them to do the following:

- Evaluate the gymnast's level of specific technical development.
- Determine which parameters need further technical development.
- Compare the performance of each gymnast in a group to a selected (most qualified) gymnast.
- Evaluate the ratio of jumps and leaps, balances, and other elements in competitive compositions and determine their conformity to the requirements of the Code of Points and compositions of leading gymnasts.

When a gymnast is learning any new element, the coach should monitor technique and correct errors. One way to effectively supervise the development of technique is to test the gymnast once a month or at the end of a mesocycle (a subcycle of the yearly training cycle; see chapter 8). For the test, each gymnast should perform from 5 to 10 trials of each element that she is learning. The coach evaluates each element, calculates the average score (with a perfect score equal to 1.0), and notes it on the gymnast's individual card. The coach should also note errors on this card.

The coach can summarize the stability of a gymnast's acquired elements in a composition by evaluating each difficult element and then adding them up as follows:

$$K_A = K_1 + K_2 + \ldots K_N$$

where K_A is the parameter of acquisition of elements in a composition in points and K_N is the evaluation of element N in points. By constantly updating K_A, the coach gathers reliable information about the technical preparation of a gymnast and how to go about correcting errors.

Rationality

Rationality of technique results from the rational use of the gymnast's strength in competitive compositions. If all other conditions are equal, the best performance of a composition involves the least tension and expenditure of energy. A gymnast can conserve her energy by constructing a composition in which she alternates energy-demanding elements (jumps and leaps) with various poses, steps, or balances and with original manipulation of an apparatus. While performing easier elements, a gymnast "rests" psychologically, which is why such an alternating construction of a composition makes her technique more economical. An uneven distribution of energy-intensive elements may cause the gymnast to commit gross faults due to fatigue at the end of a composition.

Rationality of technique is closely connected to specific endurance. One way to judge a gymnast's rationality of technique is to measure her pulse at the end of the composition. A lower pulse is an indication of an improving rationality of technique.

Framework of Technical Preparation

The technical development of a gymnast is a process. She must learn the techniques of RSG exercises in a systematic, gradual way to be able to peak in competitive compositions. The goal of a gymnast's technical development is to form skills and habits that will allow her to obtain better results in competitive compositions.

We have developed a complex framework (figure 4.1) to provide a method by which a rhythmic gymnast can obtain maximum sport results through technical development. Competitive compositions reveal a gymnast's technical mastery. There are two types of technical development: specific and general.

To compete at her best, a gymnast must develop a fixed style of performing every element and connection in her composition. The specific technical development of a gymnast concerns the process of teaching and perfecting every aspect of her competitive composition. The general technical preparation of a gymnast is the process of forming good element and connection skills and habits to choose from when creating a composition.

General technical preparation includes elements that are part of previously performed competitive compositions, new elements for future competitive compositions, and elements and connections to further develop the coordination and technical abilities of a gymnast. Thus, the gymnast's acquired reserve of elements and connections is constantly changing and expanding.

RSG is unique in that it requires mastery of two motor tasks at the same time: using the body and handling the apparatus. Therefore, general technical development occurs on two levels. The first level concerns performing one motor task, either a body movement exercise or an apparatus exercise. The body movement exercises are the basic groundwork of RSG. This kind of preparation must take the lead, even though only a few countries have competitions in freehand (without any apparatus) at this writing. The second level is the simultaneous performance of two motor tasks: the reserve exercises performed by the body and apparatus in tandem. These elements and connections are from both old and new compositions. They develop coordination and technical abilities.

Summary

In this chapter, we described how a coach may evaluate a gymnast's level of technical mastery and how to organize the training framework to enable a gymnast to reach her full potential. Specifically, we discussed the various aspects of technique, including volume, versatility and ambidexterity, stability, and rationality. We encouraged the coach to balance work on each of these aspects in each gymnast's long- and short-term plans. For example, volume is not very helpful if a gymnast cannot perform the elements with stability. Moreover, knowledge of versatility and dexterity can help a coach guide a gymnast in deciding when to perform the most difficult elements.

The exercises with apparatus are a distinctive feature of RSG. As skill and technique with the apparatus develop, they play a larger role in the success of a gymnast. In turn, the development of apparatus techniques naturally leads a gymnast to increase the number and variety in her competitive composition as she combines movements and elements in new and exciting ways.

Emphasizing a gymnast's general technical preparation will increase her reserve of skills and habits, forming a firmer foundation of technical mastery. In this way, general technical preparation leads to a greater positive transfer of habits between elements.

In the next chapter, we will examine the components of fitness that will help a gymnast have the strength, stamina, and flexibility to master every aspect of technique.

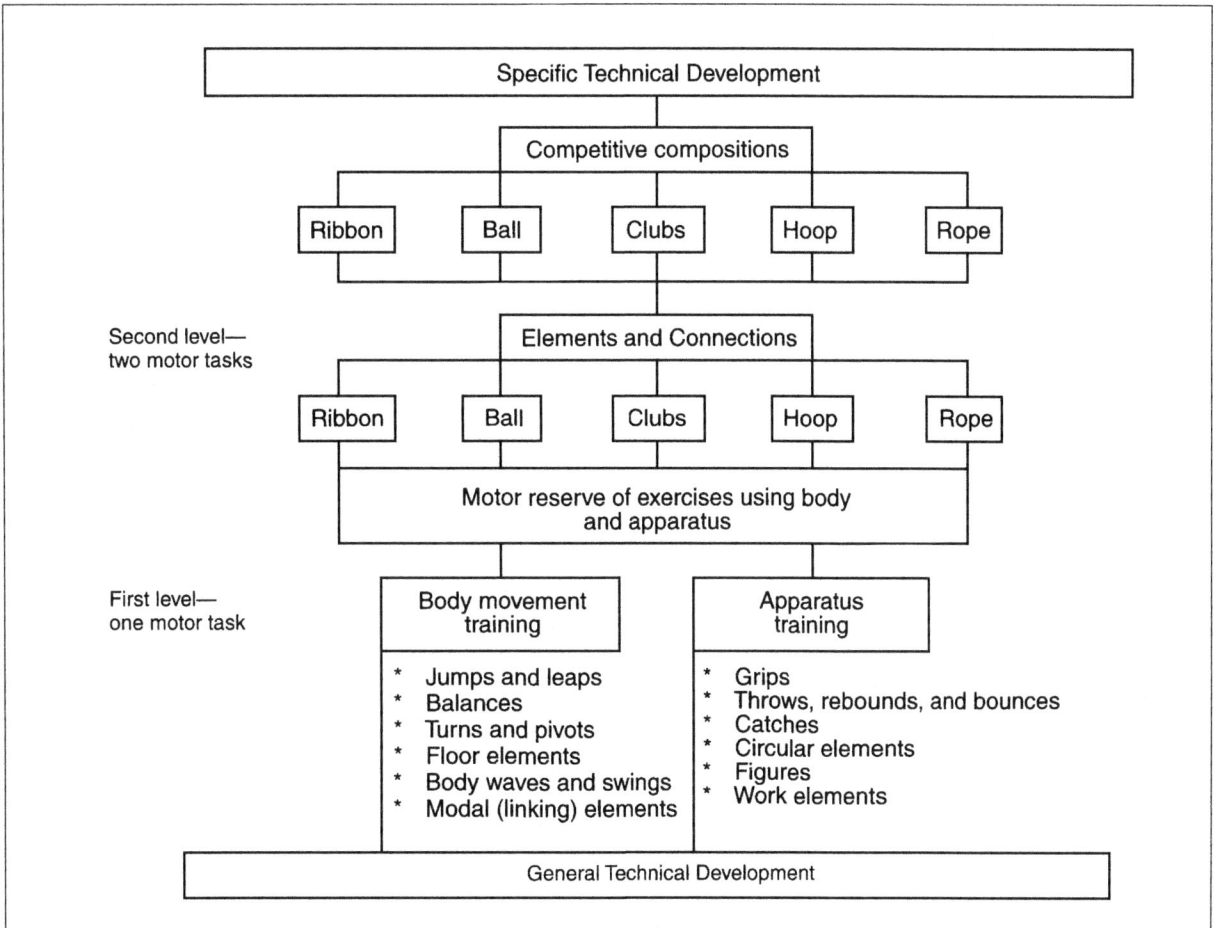

Figure 4.1 Framework of a gymnast's technical development in RSG.

Part II
Training

RSG skills are very complex. Although they include techniques of body movements and apparatus, they also include fitness and graceful and artistic presentation. Thus, no coach should limit RSG training to teaching technique only; fitness and dance training are compulsory activities for the rhythmic sportive gymnast.

Not only is RSG a complex sport, it also involves a large number of difficult skills. Most of the skills necessary for successful competitive compositions take a gymnast a long time to learn and master. Indeed, it is impossible for a beginner to start with difficult elements. Nor will the beginner earn high scores from the judges after only a few months of training. Only systematic, well-planned training can produce high results. Through the many steps of RSG training, a gymnast will both learn and then master all the necessary elements as she also improves her fitness level and dance abilities. In addition, as RSG is an artistic sport, a gymnast's body shape must be aesthetic, making it very important to maintain an attractive body weight.

In this part of the book, we will discuss how to develop flexibility and coordination (chapter 5), how to develop speed, strength, and endurance (chapter 6), how to structure workouts (chapter 7), how to create a comprehensive training program (chapter 8), and the aspects of dance important to RSG (chapter 9).

Chapter 5

Developing Flexibility and Coordination

Researchers and coaches alike have studied the many aspects of physical fitness. They have asked many questions including the following:

- How much of an individual's physical fitness is due to inborn ability and how much is due to learning technique and consistent training?
- How can an individual best be physically prepared for a particular sport?
- What are the components of physical fitness?
- How can the training of an elite athlete be advanced further?

In this chapter, we will answer these and other questions regarding physical fitness and RSG. We will look at how both inborn qualities and pedagogy influence an individual's performance and the elite gymnast. Then, we will examine the important components of physical fitness. Finally, we will discuss the details of each component of physical fitness as it relates to RSG.

Physical Fitness and Abilities

Physical (motor) fitness refers to the levels of biological and mental properties of a person that permit her to execute locomotion. Specifically, physical fitness concerns coordination, flexibility, strength, endurance, and speed. All of these make up the basis of physical abilities. Physical ability refers to the inborn and acquired capabilities of a person to perform concrete motor actions in line with her physical fitness. Inborn qualities are anatomical-physiological characteristics, such as a high energy level, body composition, and so on. Acquired qualities are a result of RSG training.

Inborn Qualities and Pedagogic Influence

What is the ratio between inborn qualities and pedagogic influence in forming physical abilities? This is a difficult question. It is known that the development of physical abilities is to a certain degree programmed by genotype. A genotype is the genetic constitution of a person, in other words, all the genes that a person has received from her parents. The children of elite athletes often display a high degree of physical ability. Some research shows that simple movements of coordination are pre-determined by inborn qualities. The development of flexibility in joints may be influenced considerably by hereditary factors, especially in females (Volkov and Filin 1983). At the same time, the influence of genetic factors on the development of flexibility can be decreased when goal-directed pedagogical influence is involved. In other words, the systematic influence of a coach can overcome genetic deficiencies (Balsevich 1977).

Certainly, by admitting the important role of genetic factors, we do not mean to belittle the role of pedagogical influence. Indeed, inborn qualities may only be completely realized if they come under pedagogical influence at the appropriate age. This would establish that pedagogical influence is not equal at all stages of development. There are critical (sensitive) periods when there is an intensive increase in physical fitness. For motor function, as a whole, this period is at 7 to 17 years old. During this period, the combination of genetic and pedagogic factors has the greatest effect. A coach must use his or her expertise to uncover the inborn qualities of a gymnast by using an optimum amount of pedagogical influence (exercise and number of repetitions) and to offer it to a gymnast during sensitive periods of development of certain physical abilities (Volkov and Filin 1983).

Table 5.1 will help a coach define the limits of sensitive periods in the development of physical abilities. A coach, however, should take into account that the sensitive period for each girl depends on her biological age, or her tempo of biological maturation. Pedagogical effects on motor talented children may be stronger at an earlier age than those shown in table 5.1 (Matveev 1990). For children not possessing the necessary inborn qualities, however, pedagogical effects have the most influence at a later age.

Important Physical Fitness Aspects

RSG requires uneven development of certain physical abilities. Flexibility, strength, and coordination must be at their maximum levels for the gymnast to be successful. But other physical fitness aspects, such as strength, speed, and endurance, need only be at optimum levels—those that will allow a gymnast to perform successfully.

TABLE 5.1

Sensitive Periods of Development of Physical Abilities for Girls

Physical fitness	Physical abilities	7-8	8-9	9-10	10-11	11-12	12-13	13-14	14-15	15-16	16-17
Strength	Proper strength abilities			✔	✔			✔			✔
	Power abilities			✔			✔	✔			
Speed	Rate of movements			✔	✔	✔					
	Speed of single movement			✔	✔	✔	✔				
	Speed of reaction time	✔	✔	✔	✔	✔					
Endurance	Static regime	✔						✔	✔	✔	
	Dynamic regime			✔	✔	✔					
	Heavy intensity			✔	✔	✔		✔			
	Average intensity		✔								
Coordination	Simple coordination	✔	✔			✔					
	Difficult coordination		✔			✔					
	Stability	✔	✔	✔		✔					
	Precision of movements		✔			✔					
Flexibility	Flexibility	✔	✔	✔	✔	✔	✔				

Physical Preparation

Physical preparation is a pedagogical process aimed at developing the following physical fitness components through the development of physical abilities: strength, speed, coordination, and flexibility. Thus, physical preparation of gymnasts should enable them to acquire the necessary RSG elements, creating a broad base for developing technical skills and taking into account features of the development of physical abilities and features that display physical abilities in elements.

Physical preparation is closely connected to other preparations of a gymnast, mainly technical development (Fomin and Vavilov 1991). Therefore, one of the main aims of physical preparation is to increase the quality of the technique of elements, connections, and compositions. We can look at physical preparation pertaining to physical abilities in concrete elements as both general and specific in nature.

General Physical Preparation

General physical preparation greatly influences all parts and systems of the body, providing the basis for effective motor activity. A coach should use exercises that replicate the features of competitive compositions in general physical preparation but that will have a positive transfer of benefits to performing in RSG. For example, running, especially cross-country races, will help develop general endurance and improve the cardiovascular and respiratory systems. Sport games will develop speed, reaction times, and coordination (orientation in space and precision of movements). Moreover, general exercise is a way of reducing the mental stress caused by daily specific training.

Specific Physical Preparation

The specific physical preparation of a gymnast should develop her physical fitness and abilities to a degree that will enable her to master RSG exercises. These specific preparatory exercises must have dynamic and kinematic characteristics similar to RSG elements.

A gymnast's physical preparation should consist of both the general and specific. At different stages of preparation, various combinations of general and specific physical preparations are appropriate. For example, in the general preparatory phase, a gymnast should concentrate on general physical preparation exercises. Then in the specific preparatory phase, she should get less general exercise and more specific exercise.

Developing Flexibility

Flexibility as a component of physical fitness is displayed in the ability of a person to perform motor actions that require some amplitude in the joints. Specifically, flexibility is reflected in the degrees to which the joints can move and the condition of the muscular system, which is connected to the mechanical properties of the muscular fibers (Sobina and Farfel 1979), that is, their resistance to stretching as well as to regulating muscle tension while moving. Insufficient flexibility hinders the performance of certain elements, for example, split leaps, balances with splits, and the like.

Types of Flexibility

We can classify flexibility as passive or active and general or specific. Passive flexibility involves an amplitude of movements caused by external forces such as a partner's weight or the gymnast's weight as in passive stretching. Active flexibility involves an amplitude of movements caused by stretching the muscles that are located around the joint only. Passive flexibility has more amplitude than active. In addition, fatigue will decrease active flexibility by reducing the muscle's ability to relax after total contraction. In contrast, passive flexibility will actually increase with fatigue, because the muscle's resistance to the effects of stretching will be lower.

General flexibility is characterized by a maximum amplitude of movements in the largest joints, including the hips, shoulders, and vertebral column. Specific flexibility is the amplitude of movements in concrete elements, such as balances, leaps, pivots, and so on.

Sensitive Periods in the Development of Flexibility

Girls' flexibility increases drastically between 7 and 10 years of age, and is maximized between 11 and 13 years of age (Fomin and Vavilov, 1991). Indeed, development of flexibility in the joints seems twice as effective between 9 and 13 years than in any other period of growth. After 13, however, flexibility stops increasing abruptly if no steps are taken to develop it. After the sensitive period, the difference between the active and passive types of flexibility is decreased, making it hard to discern.

At the same time, flexibility in the various joints develops unevenly. For example, flexibility in the vertebral column increases for girls between 7 and 12 years. For shoulder joints, flexibility increases between 12 and 13 years. In the hips, growth of flexibility peaks between 7 and 10 years, subsequently slowing down and getting closer to the adult parameter at age 13 or 14.

Methods of Developing Flexibility

The main methods used to develop flexibility are stretching exercises, including dynamic exercises, which involve spring and swing movements, and static exercises, which involve holding a maximum amplitude in various poses.

A gymnast can do the stretching exercises with or without weights. If using weights, they should not reduce the speed of the swinging or springing movements. Therefore, the weights should not weigh more than two to three percent of the gymnast's body weight.

To develop flexibility, a coach should have the gymnast use the repetition method in which the gymnast performs the stretching exercises in sets of 10 to 12 repetitions. The amplitude of a movement must increase gradually from set to set, not be reached all at once. It is very important to control the number of sets and the number of exercises in each set with this in mind. Girls 7 to 10 years old will usually achieve maximum amplitude after 20 to 30 repetitions of bending and extending the hips. For 11- to 14-year-olds, it usually takes 30 to 40 repetitions, and a 15-year-old usually needs 45 repetitions. But if the number of repetitions is increased more than the optimum for each age, the amplitude of the movements will actually decrease. So more than the appropriate number is definitely not better!

Bear in mind that once the exercises have been completed, the flexibility in developed joints will drop. In fact, on average, a significant increase in the amplitude of the joints occurs—about 27.4 to 40 percent—after 15 minutes of stretching. Then it starts to decrease quickly. After 3 minutes, it falls to 18 percent and after 6 minutes it falls by another 7 percent (Sobina and Farfel 1979). This information should help the coach decide the optimal time between the end of stretching exercises and the start of a competitive performance.

We recommend that a coach use the following methods to develop flexibility:

- Develop flexibility from the first RSG lesson and during every lesson if a girl does not have maximum amplitude in her joints.
- Always keep in mind the significant role flexibility plays in developing good technique in the elements.
- Give the gymnast concrete tasks to perform while stretching, such as touching a certain apparatus or part of her body (e.g., side swing with the leg to touch the ear).
- Insist that the gymnast warm up enough to induce sweating before starting the stretching exercises. This could avoid injuries.
- Conduct flexibility exercises at the end of the warm-up session *and* at the end of the main part of the lesson.
- Have the gymnast increase the amplitude of the stretching movements gradually, avoiding abrupt or jerky movements.
- Have the gymnast do relaxation exercises between the sets of stretching exercises. For example, after swings, have the gymnast do squats. Moving other groups of muscles enables the muscles that are being developed to rest and stretch in an easier, passive regime.
- Combine flexibility exercises with exercises that strengthen the appropriate joints.

Develop active and passive flexibility at the same time. It has been shown that using only dynamic exercises during a certain time causes active flexibility to increase by an average of 20 percent and passive flexibility by an average of 10 percent. Likewise, using only passive exercises increases active flexibility by up to 13 percent and passive flexibility by up to 20 percent (Matveev 1990). Avoid these imbalances. Instead, flexibility improves the most when the gymnast combines an active regime with forcible, passive stretching, carried out with a partner. This combination will enable the gymnast to achieve maximum flexibility in her joints.

Specifically, it is very important to use a correct ratio between passive and active development of flexibility. It is most effective to develop flexibility by using dynamic exercises to develop active and passive flexibility two-thirds of the allowed time and static exercises one-third of the time. For example, in a lesson, the coach may spend 15 minutes on developing flexibility. She or he should use 10 minutes for swings, bends, and passive exercises with a partner and 5 minutes for balances that require high flexibility in the joints, such as split balances.

The level of development of flexibility should be a little higher than the amplitude the gymnast needs to master the element, creating a reserve, or excess, flexibility. The gymnast should then maintain the appropriate level of flexibility through repetitions of the movements in future lessons.

Monitoring the Development of Flexibility

A coach can evaluate the level of flexibility based on the amplitude of movements as measured either in angular degrees or centimeters. In practice, various tests may be used to define the level of flexibility in joints. This section will discuss some of these tests. Table 5.2 lists some standards by which a coach can judge a gymnast's flexibility.

TABLE 5.2

Flexibility Rating Scale for Gymnasts at the Stage of Realization of Sport Possibilities

Tests	Rating scale			
	Excellent	Good	Fair	Poor
Circling the stick, cm	0-5	6-15	16-25	26 and above
Bridge, cm	0-5	6-15	16-30	31 and above
Stand and reach, cm	25 and above	15-24	5-14	Less than 5
Trunk lateral bending, cm	5 and below	6-10	11-20	21 and above
Split, scores	The shin and hip touch the floor; the body is straight with arms at the sides	The shin and thigh touch the floor; arms at the sides	The shin and thigh touch the floor; the body leans forward slightly	Only the shin touches the floor; the body leans forward; fingers touch the floor

Test: Circling the Stick

Objective
To determine the degree of flexibility in the shoulders.

Equipment
A meter stick (with calibrations in centimeters).

Procedure
Starting position—straddle stand. The gymnast holds the stick forward with both hands. She raises the stick upward and then brings it over her back. She must not bend her elbows; instead, she should stretch her arms at all times.

Scoring and Trials
Allow each gymnast a warm-up trial and two test trials. Note the best result. To be measured, the gymnast must fix the position of her hands holding the stick over her back. The tester then looks at the units on the stick and notes the distance between the nearest parts of the gymnast's hands. The tester should ensure that the gymnast's knees are straight. The test must be repeated if her elbows are bent.

The coach can measure the flexibility of the vertebral column using the three tests that follow, all of which involve extending and bending the vertebral column.

Test: Bridge

Objective
To determine the degree of flexibility in the spine.

Equipment
Measuring tape.

Note: this test requires two testers.

Procedure
Starting position—straddle stand, arms held upward, the tester facing the gymnast with his or

her hands on the gymnast's waist. With the tester's support at the waist, the girl arches backward, keeping her knees straight and her arms stretched.

Scoring and Trials

Allow each gymnast a warm-up trial and one test trial. The first tester should support the girl while a second tester measures the distance from the tip of her third finger to her heel. The testers should ensure that the gymnast's knees and elbows are straight.

Test Modifications

The girl should be able to touch her heels with her fingers without bending her knees. She can do this test without support from the tester as long as she can manage without bending her knees.

Test: Stand and Reach

Objective

To determine the degree of flexibility in the spine while bending forward.

Equipment

Gym bench and ruler.

Note: a partner is needed for this test.

Procedure

Starting position—the gymnast stands on a gym bench, her toes at the edge of the bench. Her legs should be straight (fully extended) and one hand should be placed on top of the other (overlapped). Then the tester should instruct the gymnast to place her hands lower and slowly reach as far as possible. She should reach her maximum level and be able to hold that position for two full seconds. A partner should ensure that the gymnast's legs remain straight throughout the test by lightly holding back the knees.

Scoring and Trials

Allow each gymnast a warm-up trial and two test trials. Note the best result. The tester should ensure that the gymnast's toes are in line with the edge of the bench and her knees are straight. The tester measures the distance between the tip of the gymnast's third finger and the upper border of the bench.

Test: Trunk Lateral Bending

Objective

To determine the degree of flexibility of the spine while bending sideways.

Equipment

Ruler.

Note: a partner is needed for this test.

Procedure

Starting position—straddle stand with feet parallel and arms sideways. The gymnast's legs should be straight (fully extended). The tester instructs the gymnast to place her hands lower, slowly reaching as far as possible. When she achieves her maximum level, she should be able to hold that position for two full seconds. A partner should ensure that the gymnast's legs remain straight throughout the test by lightly holding back the gymnast's knees.

Scoring and Trials

Allow each gymnast a warm-up trial and two test trials. Note the best result. The tester should ensure that the gymnast's knees are straight and her buttocks are above her heels. The tester measures the distance from the top of the third finger to the floor. The tester should obtain data on one side and then on the other.

Test: Split

Objective

To determine the degree of flexibility in the hips.

Equipment

Gym bench.

Procedure

Starting position—the gymnast faces the gym bench with one leg on it. She then "sits" in a split position with one leg on the bench. When performing the split on the right or left leg, the gymnast must not bend her knees, or turn her body and shoulders to the side (the body and shoulders must be facing the bench). She should not lower her heel from the bench (it must be on the bench at all times), or lie on her body with her leg stretched forward.

For the straddle split test, the gymnast must keep her legs and hips in a straight line; the body and shoulders must be in a vertical line above her hips, and her arms must be straight at her sides.

If the gymnast is not able to do the split position within these parameters, then she can touch the floor with the tips of her fingers. The gymnast must maintain the "split sit" position for two seconds.

Scoring and Trials

Allow each gymnast a warm-up trial and one test trial. The tester should ensure that the gymnast's performance is correct, then measure the quality of performance.

Developing Coordination

Coordination as an aspect of physical fitness allows a person to use the neuromuscular and kinesthetic senses of the body parts to perform exercises successfully and accurately. In the following sections, we will look at several components of good coordination. In a performance, coordination depends on the following factors:

- Adequate reaction to the appearance of an irritant.
- Ability to judge a situation quickly.
- Ability to make the right motor decision.
- Evidence of precise movements.

A gymnast has the opportunity to display the highest degree of coordination in unforeseen complex situations. Indeed, coordination itself is a complex entity. Certainly, among all aspects of physical fitness, coordination plays a very specific role, as it is connected with other areas of fitness. Coordination is based on a variety of motor habits, a highly developed "feeling" for the body and apparatus, and the ability to control the body. The higher the gymnast's perception of her own movements and its sensations, the faster she will learn new elements.

Coordination abilities are connected to the gymnast's management of movements in space and time, including space orientation, precision of repetitive movements with the necessary strength in space and time, and static and dynamic balances.

Space orientation refers to the skill needed to reconstruct movements in line with changes of external conditions (situations). But it is not easy to react to external situations. The gymnast has to take into account the possible effects of the changes to predict subsequent events, and based on this information, decide what further action will bring about positive results.

A gymnast who can consistently repeat space, strength, and time movement parameters displays precision. But this kind of control depends on how well the gymnast's sensory mechanism regulates her movements.

Vestibular stability is characterized by the ability to maintain a pose or direction of a movement after the irritation of the vestibular analyzer has passed. To this end, we can differentiate all balances as either static or dynamic balances. A gymnast displays a static balance when she maintains a certain pose for a long time in a gymnastic balance. She creates a dynamic balance by maintaining the direction of a movement in a pose as in a turn or pivot.

We can further differentiate coordination abilities as being either general or specific. General coordination abilities (or simply "general coordination") are those involved with any motor task. Specific coordination abilities (or "specific coordination") are those relating to the specific motor tasks of RSG. Therefore, specific coordination is a vital part of technical preparation. Indeed, precise muscular efforts as well as the space and time parameters of movements are especially important in RSG exercises. To this end, although there are intermediate abilities, we can consider the following to be the main specific coordination abilities:

- Holding dynamic and static stability in various poses.
- Holding various apparatus in various poses.
- Performing movements with precision in a given time frame.
- Moving while using an apparatus.
- Coordinating movements in different directions, involving one or both arms or legs.
- Coordinating movements between the body and apparatus.
- Learning and coordinating multistep movements.
- Relaxing the muscles at will ("rational" muscular relaxation).

In RSG, specific coordination abilities play an important role in creating the preconditions necessary to allow the gymnast to learn the many RSG techniques.

Sensitive Periods for Developing Coordination

Research has established that 6 to 12 years (see table 5.1, page 131) is a sensitive period for developing coordination. Then from the age of 12 to 14 or 15, this process stabilizes. After that, it will increase a little up to 17 or 18 years (Matveev 1990). This does not mean, however, that these are the only times in which a gymnast may develop coordination abilities; quite the contrary—a gymnast can develop coordination whenever she practices RSG. Still, a gymnast will be better off in the future if she develops her coordination during a sensitive period. Her chances are average from 14 to 16 or 17 years and below average from 12 to 14 years. So take advantage of the scientific data and ensure that each gymnast develops her coordination abilities during the prime time of ages 6 to 12.

The coordination abilities that are most sensitive to development from 6 to 12 years and their prime periods are as follows:

- Precision of space orientation—from 7 or 8 years to 10 years; stabilized until 13 years, then will increase again from 13 years.
- Precision of muscular efforts—from 8 to 12 years.
- Ability to reconstruct movements—from 7 or 8 years to 11 or 12 years.
- Ability to transfer movements from one body part to another—from 8 to 9 years only.

A coach must be sure to take advantage of these sensitive times whenever possible.

Methods of Developing Coordination

When developing coordination abilities, remember that the more motor habits a gymnast has, the more RSG experience she will have had, and, consequently, her coordination abilities will be greater. A coach can see that a gymnast is able to coordinate movements better when she learns and acquires more new and difficult elements. In spite of this large reserve of RSG skills and habits, however, it is in the gymnast's best interest to regularly update and perfect her coordination abilities. If she only possesses a few abilities, she will suffer a "coordination barrier," which will limit her potential as a gymnast.

The main way to develop the ability to coordinate movements is to introduce unfamiliar factors into actions the gymnast is accustomed to. Thus, a coach should take the following general methods into account:

- Modify certain parameters of elements by, for example, changing starting or final positions or customary movement speed or tempo or by performing an element with the other leg or arm or in a different direction.
- Change the way of performing an element, for example, the way of catching or throwing an apparatus.
- Complicate a familiar element by adding movements, for example, adding a reverse circle with a ball to a 720 degree pivot in *passé*.
- Combine a familiar element in unfamiliar ways with other elements.
- Change the external conditions of a performance, for example, performing an element with two apparatus or with an apparatus that is heavier.

When developing stability abilities alongside the general methods for increasing coordination, the coach should:

- lengthen the time the gymnast maintains a steady pose,
- exclude or restrict visual control temporarily,
- reduce the support area,
- increase the height of the support area by using, for example, a gym beam or bench,
- use an unstable support, for example, a skateboard,
- include preliminary movements that hinder maintaining balance, for example, balancing after jumping or leaping,
- include accompanying movements that hinder maintaining balance, for example, balancing while juggling tennis balls, or
- introduce unhelpful movements from a partner, for example, pulling by a partner while in a relatively unstable stand.

When developing the ability to orient in space, the following special methods are helpful when used in tandem with the general methods:

- Reproducing tasks with precise repetitions by using marking, for example, the consecutive bounces of a ball from 50 to 100 centimeters from the floor, according to marks on a wall.
- Performing the tasks to precise specified deviations, for example, throwing an apparatus to 50 percent of the height of the previous throw, then 75 percent and so on.
- Combining contrasting and similar tasks, for example, combining contrasting throws in pairs from six meters and then from three meters, followed by similar throws from six, five, four (and so on) meters.
- Evaluating the angles of movements as seen in any illustration.

We recommend the following methods be used with the general methods when developing the ability to orient in time, to form a "feel" for time:

- Performing exercises on signals, for example, to a metronome or count or cue from the coach.
- Performing some elements or their phases at intervals of 1.0 to 1.5 seconds on cue at the starting and finishing points of the movement and, for connections, in 2.5 to 5.0 seconds.
- Performing connections at temporary intervals, which are necessary for competitive composition cues at the starting and finishing points of the movement.
- Measuring the temporary intervals from 1.0 to 10.0 seconds on a stopwatch without looking at the stopwatch.
- Performing exercises at fast and slow tempos, for example, swinging with four repetitions for 8 seconds under the count, then twice as fast without counting, and then checking.

When developing the ability to differentiate the strength of a movement, use two methods. Measure the strength of the hand during various tasks: maximum, 50 percent of the maximum, 75 percent, 25 percent, and so on. Have the gymnast adjust the length and height of jumps during various tasks: maximum, 50 percent of the maximum, 75 percent, 25 percent, and so on.

There are efficient methods of using apparatus with weights asymmetrically. Weights as plates should not change the form of an apparatus. They are fixed as follows (Biriuk and Vlasova, 1985):

- For a ribbon, the weights may be 1 by 4.5 centimeters at a distance of 20 centimeters from the end of the material.
- For the clubs and hoop, the length of the weights may be up to 12 centimeters.
- For a ball, the size of the weights may be up to 5 centimeters square.

Weighted apparatus allows the gymnast to improve her specific coordination abilities by altering her efforts (the force she applies in manipulating the apparatus), and it also enables her to consistently control the movements of the apparatus. Then, in turn, the gymnast can learn to vary the height of the flight and the rhythm and tempo of movements and their amplitude, ultimately leading to technical mastery. Weighted apparatus (the hoop, ribbon, and clubs) should not exceed 20 percent of the original weight of that apparatus, and for the ball, 15 percent of the original weight of the ball.

We recommend that a gymnast warm up with heavy apparatus during a special session for about 15 minutes. She should use heavy apparatus at intervals between competitive compositions and after practice sessions with the same apparatus. It is ideal to perform these exercises at each lesson during the preparatory phase and two or three times per week during the competitive phase. The exercises consist of up to 10 repetitions with four to six sets with or without changing conditions, such as, with open or closed eyes, at various tempos, and with the right or left hand. The exercises are made up of elements from all structural groups: throws, catches, figure movements, and so on. When a gymnast starts to perform these exercises, she will exhibit a minor lack of coordination and decreased height of flight, but previously imperceptible errors in technique will be evident. All of these aspects may be upsetting to the gymnast. Simply explain that the changes are due to the fact that asymmetrically heavy apparatus does not travel on the usual trajectories. Reassure the gymnast that once the weights have been removed, she will be able to perform the elements precisely and with finesse.

So that the gymnast will be able to sense the position of her arms and legs while jumping or leaping, turning or pivoting, and balancing, we recommend that she wear weights on one or both wrists and (or) ankles. The total weight can be from 200 to 500 grams, but should not exceed two percent of the weight of the gymnast and should not change the shape of the elements.

When planning training loads to develop the coordination abilities, we recommend that the coach apply the following methods: (1) the volume should not result in lack of coordination of movements; if the error occurs in the technique of the element, the gymnast should repeat the exercise, and (2) the gymnast should develop coordination abilities at the start of the main phase of a lesson; if the gymnast has mastered the exercise, she should be able to perform it at the end of the main phase.

Monitoring the Development of Coordination

The following are tests for monitoring the degree of specific coordination abilities. Table 5.3 lists the control standards.

Test: Balance on Toes

Objective

To determine the ability to maintain body stability.

Equipment

Stopwatch.

Procedure

Starting position—an *arabesque* balance with hands to the sides. A gymnast rises onto her toes and maintains this position for as long as possible.

Scoring and Trials

Allow the gymnast one warm-up trial and one test trial. Once the gymnast has fixed the balance on her toes, the tester should start the stopwatch. When the gymnast is no longer able to remain stable, the tester must stop the stopwatch. The gymnast must perform the vertical balance according to the Code of Points. If not, the trial is not valid, and the test is over. Test both the right and left legs.

Test: Balance on One Leg

Objective

To determine the ability to maintain body stability without visual control.

Equipment

Stopwatch.

Procedure

Starting position—the gymnast stands erect on her right or left leg with the left or right leg flexed at the knee and foot pressed at the knee of the supporting leg, toes pointed and arms forward (balance in turned-in *passé*). On the tester's cue, the gymnast closes her eyes and tries to maintain this position for as long as possible.

Scoring and Trials

Allow the gymnast one warm-up trial and one test trial. The tester starts the stopwatch after cueing the gymnast and stops it when the gymnast is unable to maintain her stability. Test both the right and left legs.

Test: Turns While Leaning Forward

Objective

To determine the ability to maintain vestibular stability.

Equipment

Markings on the floor (see figure 5.1).

Procedure

Starting position—the gymnast stands erect in the center of the circle and leans forward. She makes ten 360-degree turns in 20 seconds (2 seconds for each turn). Then the gymnast stands erect and walks forward toward a "corridor," trying to travel in the center. The tester evaluates this by the marks. At the end of the corridor, the gymnast stands in a square and tries to jump five times vertically.

Scoring and Trials

Allow the gymnast a test trial only. The tester evaluates the gymnast's ability to travel in the corridor and perform the jumps without moving out of the square. For example, the gymnast walking in the corridor earns five marks. If she steps out of the center corridor to either side, her score is reduced to four. If she does not move out of the square while jumping, she earns five more points. The average of the two marks is the final score.

Test: Double Pivot in *Passé*

Objective

To determine the ability to maintain dynamic stability of the body.

TABLE 5.3

Coordination Rating Scale for Gymnasts at the Stage of Realization of Sport Possibilities

Tests	Rating scale			
	Excellent	Good	Fair	Poor
Balance on toes (sec)	20 and above	15-19	7-14	1-6
Balance on one leg (sec)	30 and above	20-29	10-19	1-9
Turns while leaning forward (scores)	4.5-5.0	4.0-4.4	3.0-3.9	1.0-2.9
Double pivot in *passé* (times)	5 and above	3-4	2	1
Rolling a ball over the arms (times)	9 and above	5-8	3-4	1-2
Throwing and catching a rope (times)	9 and above	5-8	3-4	1-2
Three cross turns, throwing and catching a hoop (times)	9 and above	5-8	3-4	1-2
Throwing a ball, rolling forward, and catching it (times)	9 and above	5-8	3-4	1-2
Jumps into a hoop (times)	25 and above	18-24	11-17	10 and below
Juggling the clubs (times)	9 and above	5-8	3-4	1-2
Vertical and horizontal throws of both clubs followed by catching (times)	9 and above	5-8	3-4	1-2
Throwing one club while making small circles with the other club (times)	9 and above	5-8	3-4	1-2
Small circles with the clubs (times)	20 and above	15-19	10-14	10 and below
Stride jumps with a double turn of a rope (times)	7 and above	5-6	3-4	1-2
Learning exercise (scores)	5	4	3	1-2

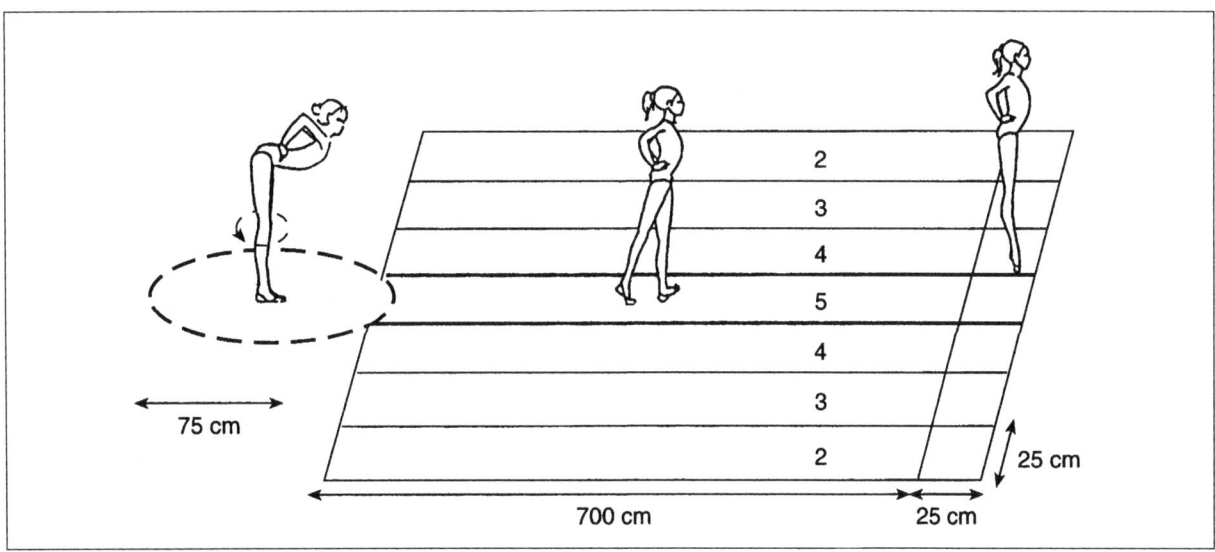

Figure 5.1 Marking on the gym floor for test to determine vestibular stability (test "Turns While Leaning Forward").
From "Methodology of Pedagogical Control and Perfection of Fitness Preparation of RSG Gymnasts" by I.Firiljeva, 1981, Pedagogical Gertsen's Institute, Leningrad.

Equipment
None.

Procedure
Starting position—the gymnast lunges on the right (or left) leg with the right (left) hand forward and left (right) hand to the side. The gymnast pivots 720 degrees, keeping her free leg in *passé* with voluntary arm positions. She does as many pivots as she can using the correct technique.

Scoring and Trials
Allow the gymnast one test trial only. The tester only allows pivots that are correct according to the Code of Points. If a gymnast performs a pivot with an error, the test ends.

Test: Rolling a Ball Over the Arms

Objective
To determine the ability to maintain dynamic stability of apparatus.

Equipment
One ball.

Procedure
Starting position—the gymnast stands erect with the ball on the right (or left) palm and hands to the sides. On the tester's cue, the gymnast starts to roll the ball over one arm, then across her shoulders, and finally over her other arm. A variation of this test involves rolling the ball over one arm, then across the chest, then over the other arm.

Scoring and Trials
Allow one test trial only. The tester evaluates only correct rolls according to the Code of Points. If the ball falls, the test ends.

Test: Throwing and Catching a Rope

Objective
To determine the ability to evaluate the trajectory of the rope's flight.

Equipment
One rope.

Procedure
Starting position—the gymnast stands erect with the rope in her right (left) hand, arms to the sides. The tester cues the gymnast to begin. The gymnast performs two circles with the rope on the lateral plane and throws the rope to a height of no less than four meters, catches it with both hands, and jumps into it. She repeats this test as many times as she can.

Scoring and Trials

Allow the gymnast a test trial only. The tester evaluates only correct performances according to the Code of Points. If the gymnast loses or tangles the rope, the test ends.

Test: Three Cross Turns, Throwing and Catching a Hoop

Objective

To determine the ability to evaluate the trajectory of the flight of the apparatus after vestibular loading.

Equipment

One hoop.

Procedure

Starting position—the gymnast stands erect with the hoop in her left hand. She performs three cross turns from the right leg. While turning, she should pass the hoop at waist level from the left hand to the right one, and vice versa. Immediately after the turns, she throws the hoop with her left hand as high as she can. She should catch it while standing still on her toes. The gymnast repeats this test as many times as she can.

Scoring and Trials

Allow the gymnast a test trial only. The tester only notes correct performances, according to the Code of Points. If the hoop falls, the test ends.

Test: Throwing a Ball, Rolling Forward, and Catching It

Objective

To determine the ability to evaluate the trajectory of the flight of the apparatus after vestibular loading.

Equipment

One ball.

Procedure

Starting position—the gymnast stands erect on her toes with the ball in her right (left) hand. She throws the ball forward and up, rolls forward, kneels, arches her back, and catches the ball. The gymnast performs this test as many times as possible.

Scoring and Trials

Allow the gymnast one test trial only. The tester only evaluates correct performances, according to the Code of Points. If the ball falls, the test ends.

Test: Jumps Into a Hoop

Objective

To determine the ability to perform movements quickly and with precision in a given time frame.

Equipment

One hoop and one stopwatch.

Procedure

Starting position—the gymnast stands erect, holding the hoop in an undergrip vertically in front of herself. On the tester's cue, the gymnast skips in and out of the rotating hoop for 15 seconds.

Scoring and Trials

Allow the gymnast one test trial only. The tester only notes correct performances, according to the Code of Points.

Test: Juggling the Clubs

Objective

To determine the ability to perform movements quickly and with precision in a given time frame.

Equipment

Two clubs and one stopwatch.

Procedure

Starting position—the gymnast stands erect, holding the clubs forward. On the tester's cue, the gymnast juggles the clubs at a slight height for 10 seconds.

Scoring and Trials

Allow the gymnast one test trial only. The tester only notes correct performances, according to the Code of Points. The test ends if the gymnast drops one or both clubs before the 10-second time limit.

Test: Vertical and Horizontal Throws of Both Clubs Followed by Catching

Objective
To determine the ability to perform movements in different directions.

Equipment
Two clubs.

Procedure
Starting position—the gymnast stands erect, holding the clubs downward. On the tester's cue, the gymnast throws the clubs in different directions: one club upward and horizontally and the other one vertically. Then she catches both clubs. The gymnast performs the test as many times as she can.

Scoring and Trials
Allow the gymnast one test trial only. The tester only notes correct performances, according to the Code of Points until the gymnast loses one or both clubs.

Test: Throwing One Club While Making Small Circles With the Other Club

Objective
To determine the ability to coordinate movements of the legs and arms in different directions.

Equipment
Two clubs.

Procedure
Starting position—the gymnast stands erect, holding the clubs downward. On the tester's cue, the gymnast walks with sliding steps, beginning with either leg. She should make small circles with one club; with the other hand she should throw the second club under her arm and catch it in front. The gymnast performs the test as many times as possible without breaking the original tempo.

Scoring and Trials
Allow the gymnast one test trial only. The tester only notes correct performances, according to the Code of Points until the gymnast breaks the tempo of the performance.

Test: Small Circles With the Clubs

Objective
To determine the ability to coordinate arm movements in different directions.

Equipment
Two clubs.

Procedure
Starting position—the gymnast stands erect, holding the clubs forward. On the tester's cue, the gymnast simultaneously creates small outer circles with one club and small inner circles with the other. The gymnast performs this test as many times as she can while maintaining the same tempo as when she started.

Scoring and Trials
Allow the gymnast one test trial only. The tester only notes correct performances, according to the Code of Points before the gymnast loses the tempo of the performance.

Test: Stride Jumps With a Double Turn of a Rope

Objective
To determine the ability to coordinate the body movements with the rope.

Equipment
The rope.

Procedure
Starting position—the gymnast stands on her toes, holding the rope behind her. On the tester's cue, the gymnast takes off with both legs and performs a front split jump (stride jump) with a double turn of the rope. The gymnast performs the test as many times as she can.

Scoring and Trials
Allow the gymnast one test trial only. The tester notes only correct performances, according to the Code of Points. If the gymnast loses or tangles the rope, the test ends.

Test: Learning Exercise

Objective
To determine the ability to learn difficult coordination movements.

Equipment
One stopwatch.

Procedure
Teach the gymnast how to perform an exercise with four to eight counts with different movements of one or both legs and one or both arms and turns of the head (vestibular loading) for two to five minutes. Then she must repeat this exercise four times on the tester's cue. To start, the gymnast stands erect. Then we recommend she do the following exercises:

1. Position the right leg to the back on the toes, right arm bent with right hand on the left shoulder, left arm upward and head to the right.
2. Bring the right leg forward, move the arms downward, and nod the head.
3. Place the left leg to the back on the toes, the left arm bent with left hand on the right shoulder, right arm upward, and head to the left.
4. Return the left leg to its position next to the right leg, arms downward, and head forward.
5. Make a full turn to the left, clap hands above the head, and look at the hands.
6. Stand erect and clap hands on thighs.

Scoring and Trials
Allow the gymnast one test trial only. The tester cues the gymnast and starts the stopwatch, stopping it once the gymnast has completed the fourth repetition. The tester evaluates the quality of the performance based on a scale of five marks: without errors and one error scores five marks, two errors scores four marks, three errors scores three marks, four errors scores two marks, and more than four errors scores one mark.

Nutrition: Protein, Fat, and Carbohydrates

Nutrition plays an important role in RSG. The main purpose of food is to supply the body with the necessary energy and nutrients (vitamins and minerals) to ensure that the body functions well. Good nutrition requires a balance between energy requirements and food intake. For some gymnasts, the amount of energy needed may range from 3000 to 3500 calories (60-62 calories per kilogram of body weight). The gymnast's energy needs and her age should determine her food consumption. An ideal RSG competitor's diet should be varied in order to ensure the necessary intake of vitamins and minerals, and should compliment her training or competitive regimen.

Protein is the major substance that ensures proper growth. Some gymnasts may need up to 2.2 grams of protein for each kilogram of body weight every day. The following food sources are high in protein: meat, seafood, eggs, and milk products. Plant proteins are less complete than animal proteins. However, combining plant proteins wisely can create high quality complete proteins. For example, serving red or black beans with rice forms a high quality complete protein. Inadequate protein intake may result in lower energy, endurance, and coordination. Excess protein, however, does not provide any real benefits.

Fats in the diet are high-calorie "fuel" for the body. Fat contains more energy per gram than do carbohydrates or proteins. A gymnast should consume 1.7 to 1.9 grams of fat for each kilogram of body weight each day. While fat is an important part of the daily diet, excess fat often causes digestive problems and reduces appetite, in addition to increasing the amount of fat stored by the body and increasing the potential risk of artherosclerosis.

Carbohydrates can provide the energy needed for short periods of intensive exercise. Foods of plant origin, such as bread, cereals, potatoes, vegetables, and fruits, are good sources of carbohydrates. Carbohydrates are the foundation of the daily diet; a gymnast

> might consume from seven to nine grams of carbohydrates per kilogram of body weight each day. However, because the body easily changes excess carbohydrates to body fat, over-indulging in carbohydrates can result in increased body weight if more calories are consumed than demanded by the body's energy needs.

Summary

In this chapter, we have examined the roles of flexibility and coordination in relation to RSG. We have looked at general fitness parameters and training guidelines, and at two individual components of physical fitness, coordination and flexibility. Each aspect depends both on inborn abilities and pedagogical influences. Naturally, a coach must bring to bear appropriate pedagogical influences to maximize a gymnast's development. Thus, we outlined the optimal times during youth for developing each aspect of physical fitness and provided specific tests to help the coach monitor a gymnast's progress.

In the next chapter, we will explore the keys to developing strength, speed, and endurance.

Chapter 6

Developing Speed, Strength, and Endurance

As noted in the previous chapter, flexibility and coordination must be at their maximum levels for the gymnast to be successful. Other physical fitness aspects, strength, speed, and endurance, need only be at optimum levels—those that will allow a gymnast to perform successfully. In this chapter, the aspects of building speed, strength, and endurance are discussed. Finally, we will look at the complex development of physical fitness.

Developing Speed Abilities

Speed allows a person to move her body in a short span of time. A gymnast can demonstrate speed through the following speed abilities:

- Speed of simple and complex motor reactions.
- Speed of a single movement without external resistance.
- Movement rate (tempo of movements).

Many abilities that describe speed include other aspects of physical fitness, especially coordination.

The speed of motor reaction as a sensory reaction is the minimum time needed to start a movement from the time a signal (cue) is given. Motor reactions can be classified as simple or complex. Simple motor reactions (selective reactions) are certain movements that appear once a signal is given. For example, the gymnast performs vertical jumps with a double turn of the rope on cue.

Complex reactions are divided into selective reactions and reactions to a moving object. For example, while performing a group exercise, two gymnasts lose their apparatus and run to catch them. But, a third gymnast decides to quickly catch one of the apparatus, resulting in a complex reaction.

Because motor reactions are sensory reactions, they are components of coordination abilities. These reactions play a significant role in space orientation and the ability to reproduce movements within given parameters of time.

The speed of a single movement is the minimum time taken by a part of the body or the whole body to move a given distance. In actuality, single movements are united in cyclic or noncyclic exercises as, for example, in consecutive jumps into the rope.

The quantity of movements in a unit of time, that is, the movement rate, depends on the maximum quantity of movements in a certain time period, for example, the quantity of raising the trunk for 20 seconds. This action depends on the speed of a single movement, the strength of the trunk muscles, and the gymnast's endurance.

Speed abilities are sometimes not connected with one another. In fact, the time of a motor reaction is not connected to the speed of a single movement. It is possible to react well to an external signal, but at the same time, be able to produce only a small number (quantity) of movements in a unit of time, and vice versa. The psycho-physiology mechanisms create different speed abilities. So, different mechanisms hinder their transfer from one to the other, requiring different means and methods to influence them.

Speed abilities can be general or specific. General speed ability refers to the ability to perform any movements or actions as general motor reactions to various irritants at the necessary speed. Specific speed abilities are the abilities to perform parts of a competitive composition, the whole composition, certain elements, or connections with the necessary speed—without destroying the technique.

In RSG, a gymnast demonstrates speed by making quick changes in the rhythm and tempo of her movements, by alternately tightening and relaxing her muscles, and by performing movements at maximum speed. She may also show speed by regulating the speed of the movements of various body parts to match the tempo and rhythm of the music.

Sensitive Periods in the Development of Speed

Speed abilities improve as a girl grows. Yet, as they are relatively independent of one another, their sensitive periods do not always coincide. Overall, however, the best period to perfect the functions that ensure quick reactions occurs from 7 or 8 years old to 11 or 12 years old. Once the gymnast is 14 or 15 years old, the intense period for perfecting speed abilities seems to lessen, but still continues until the gymnast is 17 years old.

Under the influence of RSG lessons, 9 to 12 years old is the best time to improve speed abilities; this, for example, is when the maximum increase in the movement rate occurs in girls. From 13 to 14 years old, the speeds of single movements are close to that of adults, making the most effective period for the development of speed from 9 to 13 years old.

Speed is developed through practicing motor tasks. The coach can determine progress in developing speed by measuring the amount of time a gymnast spends on a performance; the less time, the better—as long as the gymnast does not sacrifice technique. Therefore, a coach should not encourage speed until an exercise has been mastered by a gymnast.

To develop the speed of simple motor reactions, a gymnast should repeat exercises with the purpose of reacting quickly to any signal, that is, she should practice exercises simply for speed of reaction. For this a coach may use the following methods:

- Have the gymnast concentrate on the movement, not on waiting for the signal (cue), because if she focuses on waiting, the reaction time, as a rule, will be greater.
- Ensure that the gymnast can perform the required movement; for example, if she is not able to jump into the rope, her reaction time will be greater.
- Have the gymnast perform speed of reaction exercises in sets.

Remember, complex motor reactions are more difficult to develop than simple reactions. A gymnast needs to have acquired certain skills before a coach has her work on them. Preconditions for developing complex motor reaction speed include the following:

- The gymnast should possess a wide reserve of skills and habits connected with displaying complex motor reactions; first and foremost, she should have mastered various ways of catching the apparatus.
- The time it takes the gymnast to make simple motor reactions should be decreased.
- The gymnast should have developed specific coordination abilities.

A coach can help a gymnast perfect her complex motor reactions. One way is to make sure the gymnast develops the skill of keeping the apparatus in her field of vision, including peripheral. Another way is to encourage the ability to anticipate the movements of the apparatus. How? Make the movements of the apparatus more complicated by varying the speed, requiring the gymnast to perform movements with the help of a partner, or increasing or decreasing the tempo.

When developing the speed of single movements, a coach should have the gymnast perform the exercises at maximum speed (her individual best) or close to it. Such an approach should have the following characteristics:

- It should focus on realizing individual speed possibilities.
- It should cover a short time; as a rule, not more than 20 to 22 seconds before the gymnast allows the speed to decrease.
- It should occur without additional weights, as the speed of movements and weights are inversely connected.
- The technique of the exercise should have already been truly mastered by the gymnast.

The main method for developing the movement rate is simply to repeat exercises stressing speed. Using different exercises with a constant increase or decrease in tempo is, indeed, effective. In RSG, a coach can have a gymnast jump at various tempos, including maximum tempo, to improve movement rate.

When developing speed abilities, rest intervals between repetitions should be not less than 95 percent of the time needed for full recovery after the previous exercise. This is because the nature of rest must be active. Thus, a coach should schedule speed development exercises in the main part of a lesson.

Monitoring the Development of Speed Abilities

A coach can monitor the development of speed abilities by measuring the time a gymnast takes to make a simple motor reaction, the single movement speed, and the movement rate. Table 6.1 lists the standards.

Test: Tapping

Objective
To determine the degree of ability for maximum movement rate of the wrists.

Equipment
Chair, table, paper, and pencil.

Procedure
Starting position—the gymnast sits on a chair, her forearm lying on the table. On the tester's cue, she starts to tap points on the paper using the

TABLE 6.1

Speed Abilities Rating Scale for Gymnasts at the Stage of Realization of Sport Possibilities

Tests	Rating scale			
	Excellent	Good	Fair	Poor
Tapping (scores)	38 and above	34-37	29-33	28 and below
Reaction time (cm)	10 and below	11-12	13-14	15 and higher
Jumping into the rope with double turns (times)	20 and above	16-19	14-15	13 and below

pencil. She must do this for five seconds as fast as she possibly can.

Scoring and Trials

Allow the gymnast two test trials, using the right or left hand. The tester counts the number of points for each trial and notes the best.

Test: Reaction Time

Objective

To determine simple reaction time.

Equipment

Reaction time ruler or regular ruler.

Procedure

Starting position—the gymnast stands erect, extending one arm forward, palm and thumb held vertically upward. The tester holds the ruler vertically one to two centimeters from the gymnast's palm. Zero centimeters and the gymnast's palm should be aligned. The tester signals the gymnast that she or he is going to drop the ruler after not more than five seconds. The gymnast must catch the ruler between her thumb and fingers as fast as she possibly can.

Scoring and Trials

Allow the gymnast three test trials, using either hand. The tester notes the best trial, based on the lowest number the gymnast touches when she catches the ruler.

Test: Jumping Into the Rope With Double Turns

Objective

To determine maximum movement rate.

Equipment

One rope and one stopwatch.

Procedure

Starting position—the gymnast stands erect, holding the rope behind her. On the tester's cue, the gymnast jumps vertically into the rope and makes double turns, according to the demands of the Code of Points. She must do this as fast as possible for 10 seconds.

Scoring and Trials

Allow the gymnast one warm-up and one test trial only. The tester counts only correct jumps.

Developing Strength Abilities

Strength is characterized by the degree of tension in the muscles. Specifically, strength is the ability of a person to overcome or counteract external resistance, using his or her muscles. There is a difference between proper strength and speed strength (power). Proper strength is the most typical for static and slow movements, which demonstrate the maximum muscular contraction, for example, when maintaining the free leg in balance. Power is the ability to overcome external resistance at a high speed of muscular contractions as found in fast movements, for example, while taking off to jump.

Jumps as a physical exercise are ballistic, that is, a throwing action, in which the gymnast uses her body like an apparatus. In this connection, springiness is the complex ability to combine strength and speed in muscular contractions. The power is determined by the speed of the muscular contractions. In the first place, the result of a jump depends on the speed of the muscular contractions of the sole of the foot. So the gymnast can take off at a high speed by using a small number of muscles.

To compare the strength of people of various weights, we must apply the concept of relative strength, which is the amount of strength in one kilogram of body weight. The strength displayed in any movement regardless of the weight of a person is called absolute strength. We can calculate relative strength in respect to the absolute strength of the body.

The strength of the muscle is proportional to its diameter. A coach must take this into account when developing strength in RSG. Unfortunately, however, increasing the diameters of the muscles—especially in the legs—is undesirable for a gymnast. Thus, gymnasts should develop power instead of proper strength, especially in the muscles of the abdomen, spine, legs, and arms.

As for all other areas of fitness, we can divide the abilities of strength into two categories: general and specific. General strength abilities are maximum strength or power of movements, not connected with RSG exercises. Specific strength abilities form the necessary (optimum) level of strength or power in RSG exercises.

Sensitive Periods in the Development of Strength Abilities

The strength of a gymnast is closely connected to her age. Absolute strength of the main muscular groups increases from birth to 20 or 30 years old. By 17 to 18 years old, it achieves the level of adult strength. The relative strength reaches a maximum level at 13 to 14 years old and becomes established at this maximum level by 17 years old. Researchers have revealed three sensitive periods for accelerated development of absolute strength (Kuramshin 1981).

The first period is from 9 to 11 years old, the second from 13 to 14 years old, and the third from 16 to 18 years old (see table 5.1, page 131). Power abilities, especially "springiness," reach the highest level from 9 to 10 years old and from 12 to 14 years old.

Methods for Developing Strength Abilities

In RSG, some muscular groups must have the strength to produce quality performances. For example, the muscles that move the leg forward, backward, and sideways must be at optimum strength levels. But we do not recommend that the rhythmic sportive gymnast make a maximum effort to build strength, such as doing exercises with large and average weights. Instead, RSG coaches generally use average repetitions with low weights (dynamic efforts) and isometrics (static tension) to develop strength.

Dynamic efforts involve repeating exercises six to eight times in a set with intervals of active rest of three to five minutes between each set. Dynamic efforts develop muscular strength in the abdomen and spine, for example, by raising the trunk from a supine position (to work the abdomen) or from a prone position (to work the back muscles), and holding it for 20 seconds. This method helps develop springiness, too.

There was a time when experts thought that gymnasts should develop the springiness only through doing RSG jumps and leaps. Research and coaching experience, however, have proven that although this method does develop springiness, it does not bring the gymnast to the level suitable for performing difficult leaps (Jastrjembskaia, 1989). Therefore, using special jumps and leaps to prepare the muscles for fast takeoffs is justified. Moreover, scientific research has proven the effectiveness of using classical ballet drills, especially *plié* and *battement*, for strengthening leg muscles and developing springiness.

To develop a strong takeoff, we recommend the following exercises:

- Jumping on a support (for example, gym bench or steps).
- Deep jumping from a support, 40 to 100 centimeters high.
- Jumping over a gym bench.
- Jumping rope, using two or three turns.
- Jumping high and long.

Combining these jumps produces good results. The following combinations are effective:

- A deep jump followed by a jump onto or over a gym bench.
- A jump onto a gym bench, followed by a deep jump.
- Repeated jumps over low gym benches, spaced 50 to 60 centimeters apart.

The gymnast should perform all of the jumps we have listed in sets of five to eight jumps with an interval of active rest of three to five minutes. No matter what jump the gymnast performs, however, we recommend that she use a fast, elastic takeoff from a support. The movements should be continuous, rebounding from one jump to the next without hesitation.

To develop specific springiness, or power of the leg, we recommend that the gymnast use new jump connections by combining the jumps we have already described with gymnastic jumps, for example, a deep jump followed by a gymnastic jump or leap, jumps over two or three benches parallel to each other, followed by a gymnastic jump or leap. The gymnast may execute connecting jumps, that is, those immediately before jumping or leaping, by using a gymnastic springboard.

When developing springiness, the gymnast should focus on perfecting her landings after jumps (especially for deep jumps) and leaps. Landing is simply the breaking of a free fall of the body as it makes contact with a support. The braking force when landing (absorption of force) depends on the speed of the fall, created by the height from which the gymnast makes the deep jump, and the size of the absorbing arch. The absorbing arch includes the amount of "give" in the floor or mat and the degree to which the gymnast bends her legs during the landing.

The lower the absorbing arch, the higher the braking force. That is why it is necessary to bend the legs in time, that is, to squat down to soften the landing. For deep jumps on the floor, the braking force needs to be increased. So, the gymnast can bend her legs less when landing on a gym mat. The ideal is to bend the knees less than 90 degrees. Moreover, it is possible to soften the landing considerably by lowering the arms after the legs contact the floor.

If a gymnast learns to land softly only by bending her legs, then it will be very difficult later for her to increase the speed of her takeoff after the first landing in repeated jumps. Therefore, a gymnast should also learn the more rigid landing that is followed by a fast takeoff. For repeated deep jumps on the floor, the height of support should be only one-half or one-third of that for ordinary deep jumps. In addition, initially, the gymnast should only perform deep jumps on the gym mat, not on the floor.

In RSG, to have a specific effect on certain muscle groups, static (isometric) tension is widely used as this does not change the length of the muscle. For each exercise, a gymnast should hold her muscles at maximum tension for four to six seconds, three to five times, with six to eight seconds of rest between. Rest between sets must be two to four minutes. A gymnast should perform isometric exercises in positions that are similar to certain phases of elements, for example, in positions for which she raises a leg or an arm. Usually, each isometric exercise set consists of six to nine exercises. A coach should set aside 10 to 15 minutes per lesson for isometrics, two or three times per week, for 8 to 10 weeks, gradually increasing the static tension and number of repetitions. Finally, a gymnast should do dynamic exercises before and after static exercises.

When using static tension exercises, remember that a large number in a lesson allows the gymnast to adapt to static work.

Monitoring the Development of Strength Abilities

Table 6.2 lists the standards for strength abilities.

Test: Jump Upward

Objective

To determine the degree of power ability of the legs (springiness).

Equipment

Ruler fixed vertically on a wall and chalk.

Procedure

Starting position—the gymnast stands erect, one shoulder near the wall, stretching her arms upward with chalked fingers. A tester notes the point the gymnast can reach in centimeters. The gymnast takes a few steps back, to about 20 to 30 centimeters from the wall, and without stepping, jumps as high as she can and touches the

TABLE 6.2

Rating Scale for Strength Abilities of Gymnasts at the Stage of Realization of Sport Possibilities

Tests	Rating scale			
	Excellent	Good	Fair	Poor
Jump upward (cm)	45 and above	39-44	31-38	30 and below
Triple jump (cm)	600 and above	520-599	440-519	439 and below
Lifting legs (times)	10 and above	8-9	5-7	4 and below
Bending and extending the arms (times)	10 and above	8-9	5-7	4 and below
Time of 10 bends (sec)	10.0 and below	10.1-10.6	10.7-11.2	11.3 and above
Angled hang (sec)	10 and above	8-9	6-7	5 and below

ruler with her fingers. The tester notes the height of the jump in centimeters. The gymnast must land on the takeoff place.

Scoring and Trials

Allow the gymnast one warm-up and three test trials. A tester must calculate the difference between the starting point and the height of the jump, calculating the real height of the jump. The tester records the highest real height.

Test: Triple Jump

Objective

To determine the power ability of the legs (springiness).

Equipment

Tape measure.

Procedure

Starting position—the gymnast stands erect near the starting line. She jumps as follows:

1. First jump—she takes off from both legs and lands onto the right (left) leg.
2. Second jump—she takes off from the right (left) leg and swings the left (right) one, then lands onto the left (right) leg.
3. Third jump—she takes off from the left (right) leg and swings the right (left) one, then lands onto both legs.

The gymnast should swing her arms when jumping.

Scoring and Trials

Allow the gymnast one warm-up and three test trials. The tester measures the distance each test trial covers and notes the best result.

Test: Lifting Legs

Objective

To determine the power ability of the abdominal muscles and front-of-thigh muscles.

Equipment

Gym wall and stopwatch.

Procedure

Starting position—the gymnast hangs on the gym wall bars. On the tester's cue, the gymnast lifts her extended legs up at an angle of 135 degrees for 10 seconds, then lowers them, and immediately brings them back up to 135 degrees. The gymnast must point her toes and must not bend her arms or legs.

Scoring and Trials

Allow the gymnast one test trial only. The tester counts the number of consecutive times the gymnast can lift her legs at 135 degrees for 10 seconds.

Test: Bending and Extending the Arms

Objective
To determine arm power.

Equipment
Stopwatch.

Procedure
Starting position—the gymnast gets into a push-up position with her legs on a block, so that when her arms are extended, her legs and spine are in alignment. On the tester's cue, the gymnast bends and extends her arms as fast as possible for 10 seconds. She must keep her buttocks down, and her legs and spine in alignment.

Scoring and Trials
Allow the gymnast one test trial only. The tester counts the number of times the gymnast bends and extends her arms correctly (buttocks down, legs and spine aligned).

Test: Time of 10 Bends

Objective
To determine the power ability of the abdominal and spine muscles.

Equipment
Ruler and stopwatch.

Procedure
Starting position—the gymnast stands erect, hands up and palms forward, touching the ruler held by the tester with her fingers. On the tester's cue, the gymnast starts to bend forward 10 times, touching the floor and then standing erect and touching the ruler. She must not bend her arms or knees.

Scoring and Trials
Allow the gymnast one test trial only. The tester counts the bends and stops the stopwatch when the gymnast stands erect after the 10th repetition.

Test: Angled Hang

Objective
To determine the power ability of the abdominal and front-of-thigh muscles.

Equipment
Stopwatch and gym wall.

Procedure
Starting position—the gymnast should be hanging with her spine to the gym wall bars. On the tester's cue, the gymnast lifts her legs horizontally and maintains this position for as long as possible. She must keep her legs straight and level (parallel to the floor) and point her toes.

Scoring and Trials
Allow the gymnast one test trial only. The tester must stop the stopwatch if the gymnast's legs fall below horizontal.

Developing Endurance

A gymnast demonstrates endurance as a component of physical fitness through her ability to resist fatigue in any activity. Fatigue is a protective function in an organism. It causes a temporary reduction in the gymnast's ability to do work before the working parts and systems are truly exhausted.

The entire human body is involved in any activity. Depending on the activity, however, one part of the body may have to do a large part of the work. For example, when mental work is involved, the person becomes fatigued mainly in the cortex; and when intensive muscular activity is involved, the muscles become the most fatigued. Furthermore, the number of muscles involved in the movement influences the degree of fatigue.

Work involving only certain parts of the body causes fatigue in only those particular parts of the neuromuscular system. In movements in which two-thirds of all of the body's muscles are involved, fatigue is caused by the respiratory and cardiovascular systems, in which case a gymnast is able to overcome the fatigue. In other words, if the fatigue is specific, the endurance demonstrated by a gymnast is also always specific.

Therefore, the development of endurance should proceed from the physiological mechanism of fatigue, or neuromuscular fatigue, caused by physical activity.

The degree of endurance is determined by the following complex factors:

- Amount of the reserve energy in the body.
- Functional capacities of organs and systems, both hereditary and acquired.
- Technical mastery.
- A gymnast's willpower.

The first factor that decides the endurance of a person is the amount of energy mechanism of the muscular activity.

There are three types of endurance:

1. Aerobic, from the Greek word *aer*, meaning air.
2. Anaerobic, from the Greek words *an*, meaning negative particle, and *aer*, creating a word meaning "not air."
3. Mixed, aerobic and anaerobic.

Varying with the duration of physical loads, the maximum energy of a muscular activity depends on the anaerobic and aerobic processes or their combinations (see table 6.3).

Physiologically, aerobic endurance is linked to the absorption, circulation, and use of oxygen in the body. Aerobic endurance depends only slightly on the acquisition of technique. Therefore, the gymnast may transfer it from one type of exercise to another. So we may also think of aerobic endurance as general endurance.

Anaerobic endurance determines a number of functional properties of the body that allows it to perform physical exercises when oxygen is lacking. Because of its specialized application, anaerobic endurance is also called specific endurance. Most importantly, in RSG, specific endurance is defined by its useful role in the techniques necessary to create competitive compositions. The transfer of this type of endurance is very specific and limited.

Strength endurance can be found in either static or dynamic movements when the gymnast is overcoming tension, mainly during various combinations of anaerobic and aerobic routines. Specifically, static strength endurance is defined by the amount of time a gymnast maintains a pose. Dynamic endurance is determined by the number of

TABLE 6.3

Relative Contents of Anaerobic and Aerobic Processes During Heavy Training Loads

Duration of heavy training loads	Relative contribution in %	
	Anaerobic process	Aerobic process
10 seconds	83	17
1 minute	60	40
2 minutes	40	60
5 minutes	20	80
10 minutes	9	91
30 minutes	3	97
60 minutes	1	99

From "The Bases of Theory and Methodology of Physical Culture" by A. Gudjalovsky (editor), 1986, Physical Culture and Sports, Moscow.

repetitions of any exercise or movement the gymnast can perform within a certain period of time.

In RSG, endurance is expressed by the gymnast's ability to perform a competitive composition without making any errors in technique. The degree of specific endurance depends on many factors, including general endurance, power, technical mastery, and willpower.

Sensitive Periods for Developing Endurance

Endurance for heavy training loads is increased intensively for girls from the age of 9 up to 12 (table 5.1, page 131), whereas for average loading it is from the age of 8 to 9. The highest increase in endurance of isometric strength is observed from 13 to 16 years old, that is, when the gymnast sexually matures.

Methods of Developing Endurance

Coaches widely use continuous exercises or interval training to increase aerobic endurance. In continuous training, the gymnast can train almost continuously 10 to 30 minutes at HRmax (maximum heart rate) of 150 to 175 bpm (beats per minute). Note, however, that an extremely long workout beyond the gymnast's capabilities decreases the level of oxygen consumption and therefore lessens the desired training effect.

In interval training, each interval must be 1 to 3 minutes long, at the end of which the HR should be 170 to 180 bpm. Rest, which should lower HR to 120 to 130 bpm, is usually 45 to 90 seconds long, depending on the duration of the entire workout and the gymnast's level of fitness. Not only does such training produce a high heart rate, it also induces a high rate of oxygen consumption and increases cardiovascular endurance. Thus, a coach should use this method during the early stages of endurance development.

When developing endurance for static tension (isometrics), we recommend the following methods:

- Static endurance is increased faster when the gymnast alternates static with dynamic work.
- Additional weights are not recommended.
- The gymnast should also alternate static exercises with stretching and relaxation exercises.

- An increase in static training loads (isometric intervals) should be accompanied by an increase in rest.
- The gymnast should do static exercises at the end of the main part of a lesson, so the cooldown can be longer and active.

A coach can develop a gymnast's specific endurance mainly by gradually increasing the volume and intensity of interval training loads. Specifically, a gymnast needs to:

- increase the number of performed compositions,
- perform each composition without pausing to rest,
- increase the motor density (amount of physical activity) in a lesson, and
- increase the number of lessons per week.

The gymnast's heart rate should only decrease to 90 to 108 bpm before she repeats her composition. This is high enough to maintain the quality of repeated trials, thereby developing specific endurance.

Monitoring Endurance Development

A coach can measure a gymnast's endurance in several ways. For example, the duration and number of times a gymnast can correctly perform the technical elements of her composition before having to stop is a good indication of endurance. Another way to tell the level of endurance a gymnast possesses is to monitor the number of times she can repeat a set of exercises with strictly limited rest; for example, how many times in a row can she jump vertically into the rope at a maximum tempo for 45 seconds with 45 seconds of rest, three repetitions per set, and three minutes of rest between sets. In addition, the coach can check how well the gymnast performs a task at maximum work capacity within a certain period of time. Finally, the most objective way to measure endurance is to evaluate heart rate and respiratory rate both during work and in the recovery phase. The lower these are for the same effort, the higher the gymnast's endurance. Table 6.4 lists the standards for endurance.

TABLE 6.4

Rating Scale for Endurance of Gymnasts at the Stage of Realization of Sport Possibilities

Tests	Rating scale			
	Excellent	Good	Fair	Poor
30 seconds jumping into the rope (times)	60 and above	57-59	51-56	50 and below
Raising the trunk (times)	25 and above	22-24	18-23	17 and below
Snakes of the ribbon (sec)	25 and above	21-24	17-20	16 and below
Mills (times)	10 and above	5-9	3-4	1-2

Test: 30 Seconds Jumping Into the Rope

Objective

To determine the endurance of the legs.

Equipment

A rope and a stopwatch.

Procedure

Starting position—the gymnast stands erect, holding the rope in both hands behind her back. On the tester's cue, the gymnast jumps vertically with a double turn of the rope for 30 seconds, according to the Code of Points.

Scoring and Trials

Allow the gymnast one test trial only. The tester counts the number of jumps performed correctly.

Test: Raising the Trunk

Objective

To determine the endurance of the muscles along the spine.

Equipment

High support (vaulting horse) and a stopwatch.
  Note: this test requires the help of a partner.

Procedure

Starting position—the gymnast lies prone, legs resting horizontally on a high support like a vaulting horse, with her trunk hanging off the end. Her hands should touch her shoulders, while her partner securely holds her legs. On the tester's cue, the gymnast lifts her trunk into a vertical position as many times as possible in 30 seconds.

Scoring and Trials

Allow the gymnast one test trial only. The tester counts and records the number of repetitions.

Test: Snakes of the Ribbon

Objective

To determine the endurance to perform movements with fine coordination.

Equipment

A ribbon and a stopwatch.

Procedure

Starting position—the gymnast stands erect, holding the ribbon in her hand. On the tester's cue, the gymnast performs vertical snakes with the ribbon in front of her chest, then returns it with a swing to the starting position. The gymnast must perform the exercise according to the Code of Points.

Scoring and Trials

Allow the gymnast one test trial only. The tester notes how long it takes until the gymnast starts to make errors. The test may be performed with either hand.

Test: Mills

Objective

To determine the endurance to perform movements with fine coordination.

Equipment

Two clubs and a stopwatch.

Procedure

Starting position—the gymnast stands erect, holding the clubs forward. On the tester's cue, the gymnast performs double mills, according to the Code of Points.

Scoring and Trials

Allow the gymnast one test trial only. The tester notes how long it takes until the gymnast starts to make errors.

Complex Development of Physical Fitness

In RSG, circuit training is the way to develop the complex aspects of physical fitness. Circuit training encourages the gymnast to simultaneously develop her general physical abilities while perfecting complex abilities, for example, power or static endurance.

In circuit training, the gymnast repeats gymnastic exercises, which are arranged as stations located sequentially in a circle. The entire circuit is repeated a few times. The coach should select exercises for each station so that they influence certain muscular groups, such as the legs, arms, or another body part.

After warming up the main muscle groups to prepare the body for exercise, the gymnasts can go in either direction around the circuit exercises, starting from any station. Figure 6.1 shows a set of exercises for circuit training.

The important feature of circuit training is the exact rate of training loads for a group of gymnasts and particularly for each individual. A coach can determine individual training loads with the help of the maximum test (MT). This test determines the maximum number of repetitions for each exercise on the training circuit.

There are three methods a coach may use for conventional circuit training. The first is called the continuous-flow method in which the gymnast exercises at one station after another with short rest intervals. This method calls for a gradual increase in the individual loading by increasing the work capacity to 60 percent of the MT and increasing the number of exercises in one or a few circles. The time for this method is reduced by 15 to 20 seconds while the duration of rest is increased by 30 to 40 seconds. This method promotes the complex development of physical abilities.

The second method of using conventional circuit training is the low-interval method. This method consists of exercises of simple techniques for 20 to 40 seconds, at 50 percent of MT for each station with minimal rest. This method will promote the development of general and power endurance and condition the respiratory and cardiovascular systems.

The third method of using conventional circuit training is the intensity-interval method, used for well-conditioned gymnasts. These gymnasts exercise at 75 percent of MT at a high intensity for 10 to 20 seconds followed by 30 to 40 seconds of rest. This method primarily promotes the development of power abilities.

In circuit training, a coach should always record the weightloads and number of repetitions a gymnast can perform. Then the coach should systematically evaluate the gymnast's achievements, based on the volume of work performed, the heart rate before and after completing the circuit, and the systematic definition of MT.

Gym benches, sticks, wall bars, apparatus, medicine balls (0.5 to 1 kg), and elastic bands are helpful circuit training equipment. A coach should be as creative as possible. For example, practicing outdoors or at a stadium, forest, or beach, the coach should use every possible means: pebbles for juggling, sand to jump on, water for running, and so on. With a creative approach, the gymnasts will never be bored with circuit training; in fact, they'll be emotionally renewed, not merely physically strengthened.

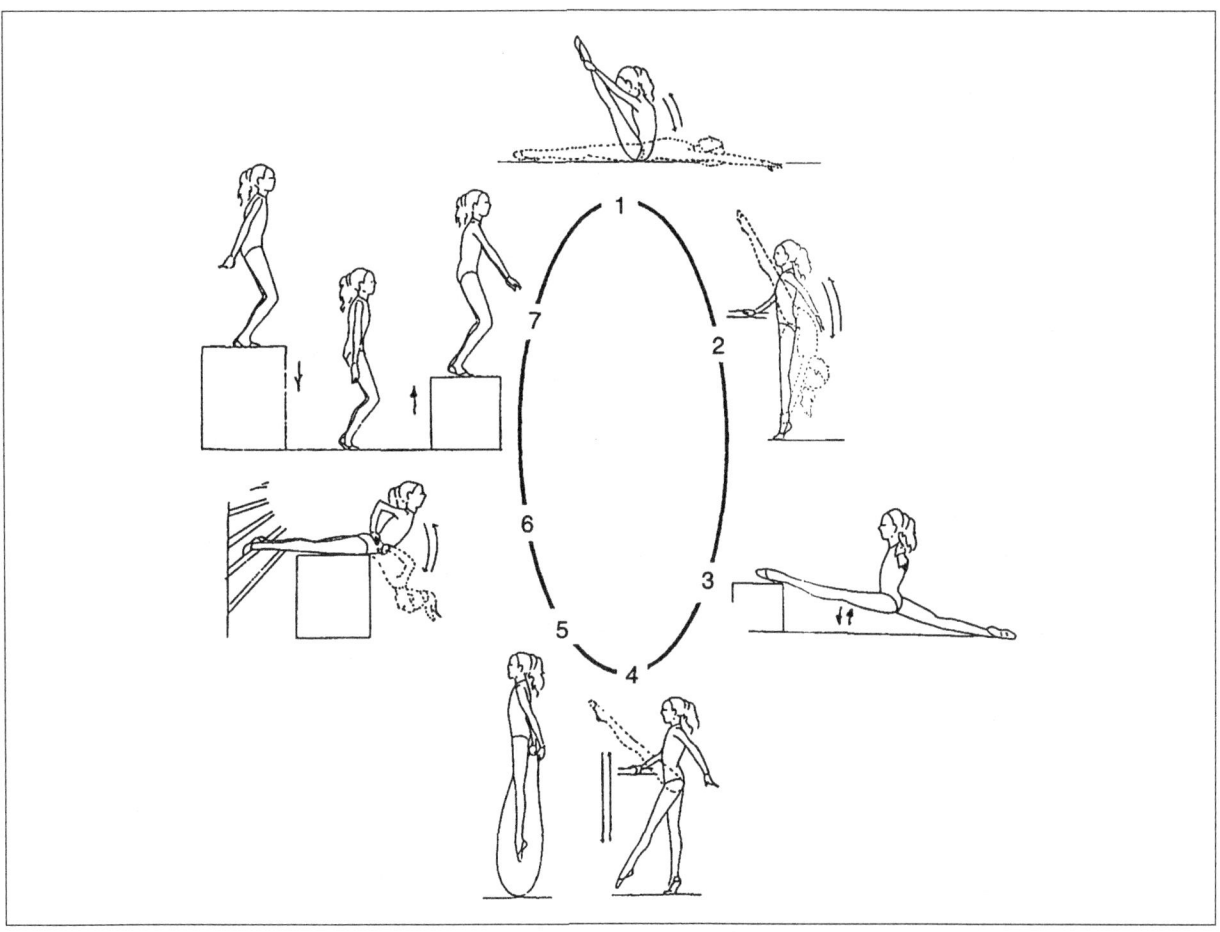

Figure 6.1 Exercises for circuit training to develop power and flexibility abilities. Training load for each station: (1) 20 seconds, repeat 3 times; (2) 20 seconds each leg, 1 time; (3) 3 minutes for each leg; (4) 10 swings forward then keep the leg at the maximum height for 10 seconds, repeat 2 times for each leg; (5) vertical with double turn for 20 seconds, repeat 3 times; (6) 20 seconds, repeat 3 times; (7) jump 10 times.

Summary

In this chapter, we have described the aspects of speed, strength, and endurance as they relate to RSG. Each of these three aspects depend both on inborn abilities and pedagogical influences. Again, a coach must bring to bear appropriate pedagogical influences to maximize a gymnast's development. Finally, we discussed complex physical fitness, in which the gymnast experiences circuit training to further develop her physical fitness. In the next chapter, we will look at how to take this information and develop specific workouts.

Elena Vitrichenko

Born November 25, 1976, in Odessa, USSR, Elena Vitrichenko began training as a rhythmic gymnast at the age of four. She trains 35 hours a week under the tutelage of her mother and trainer Nina Vitrichenko.

At the 1996 Olympics in Atlanta, Elena placed third in the all-around competition with a score of 39.331. Her score of 39.749 in the all-around competition at the 1997 European Championships in Patras, Greece, vaulted her to first place. At those same championships, she placed first in the hoop competition and tied with Ekaterina Serebrianskaya, Eva Serrano, and Maria Pagalou for second in the ribbon.

At the 21st World Championships in Berlin in 1997, Elena scored two perfect 10s, one in rope, one in clubs, en route to sweeping the championships. Elena came in first in both the ribbon and the clubs, tied with Yana Batyrchina for first in the rope, and was crowned the all-around champion.

Elena resides in Odessa, Ukraine. Her other sport interests include synchronized swimming and figure skating.

Chapter 7

Structuring Workouts

Although each lesson in RSG is a relatively independent unit in a gymnast's overall program, it is closely related to the previous and subsequent lessons; it is one step in a sequence. Each lesson consists of physical exercises (training tasks) that a gymnast performs in order to achieve the objective of the lesson. To prepare a gymnast, a coach plays a leading role in a lesson by directly organizing and explaining training tasks. The coach then observes, analyzes, and evaluates the gymnast's performance compared to the objective. In this chapter, we will examine several aspects of designing effective workouts and lessons, including primary goals (main, additional, selective, and complex), type (educational, training, learning-training, recovery, modeling, controlling), and intensity (heavy, average, light).

Primary Goals

All lessons in RSG are divided into two categories: core and additional. To create core lessons, a coach chooses essential RSG tasks and uses the most effective means and methods of preparing a gymnast. The gymnast spends most of her time and energy on these tasks. But a coach may organize special additional lessons for the gymnast who is having problems. These lessons usually consist of a lighter training load, volume, and intensity, and fewer physically and mentally difficult exercises.

For lessons that consist of a number of tasks that will accomplish a major objective, we can divide the means and methods into selective and complex, based on how they are organized.

Selective Lessons

Selective lessons proceed in one direction, based on one task, such as perfecting an element of a technique or physical ability, like flexibility or special endurance. Therefore, when a coach selects exercises he or she may seek to reach the one main objective by using the same exercise or composition throughout the lesson or various exercises.

The most powerful influence on a gymnast is the selective lesson. This is because, in a selective lesson, she concentrates on achieving one pedagogic task. Therefore, coaches tend to use such lessons to train top level gymnasts whose bodies and minds have already adapted to various training effects.

Unfortunately, however, using the same exercises repeatedly in a lesson is monotonous. Monotony causes the gymnast to lose interest and motivation and, concurrently, training effects. But that is not to say repetitious training does not have its place. It can increase psychological stability, which promotes better competitive compositions.

Complex Lessons

Complex lessons are directed toward achieving two or more objectives. In consecutive complex lessons, a gymnast achieves one objective, then works on the next. In parallel complex lessons, the gymnast works on the objectives simultaneously.

In constructing consecutive lessons, the coach needs to pay attention to two problems: how to connect one objective with the next and how to divide the number of exercises in the lesson between the objectives, asking "Are the exercises evenly divided between the objectives?"

As a rule, an effective coach divides a complex lesson into two or three relatively independent parts, working on new exercises when the girls are fresh at the beginning of the main part of the lesson. After the girls have worked on perfecting these new techniques, they then work on their competitive compositions at the end of the main part of the lesson. At this point in the lesson, repeatedly performing their compositions with short rest intervals when they are tired develops specific competitive endurance.

But a coach should decide how exactly to divide the number of exercises in a lesson case by case. His or her decision should depend on the pedagogical sequence he or she is following and the gymnast's personality, health, physical fitness level, individual composition features, and level of mastery.

In complex lessons, gymnasts do multiple tasks in parallel, for example, developing specific endurance for executing a competitive composition while developing the mental strength to overcome fatigue. In combining exercises (quantity, sequence) in complex lessons, the impact of the training load on a gymnast's body can be quite significant, having either a positive, neutral, or negative effect. When the effect is positive, the training load strengthens the effects of the previous training load. In other words, the current lesson builds on the last lesson. When the effect is neutral, the lesson has no influence: the training load of the lesson does not really change the character and degree of the gymnast's responses. When the effect of the lesson is negative, the training load decreases the strengths gained in the previous lesson. Of course, a coach never consciously chooses to create a negative effect, but it does happen.

Therefore, it is important to understand which parameters should guide the training tasks and which exercises should be included in each part of a complex lesson. In practice, a coach may apply different variables to construct lessons, depending on the timing and the lesson's position in the weekly, monthly, and yearly cycles of preparation; the gymnast's qualifications and level of physical fitness; and on the lesson's goals and objectives (see chapter 8).

If a coach plans a complex lesson, he or she should strive for consecutive achievement of objectives for gymnasts at the earlier stages of long-term preparation. In this way, the complex lesson is really a series of selective minilessons and is therefore more effective. Moreover, the more variety there is in the exercises and the more mentally and emotionally stimulating they are, the more effective the lesson will be in training young gymnasts. Finally, exhaustion and overtraining injuries can occur if selective lessons are used with beginners. Therefore, a coach should change exercises frequently—about every 15 to 30 minutes.

Preparing top level gymnasts with complex lessons, however, can proceed more aggressively. One way, most expediently used during the competitive period, is to maintain the level of training the gymnasts have already achieved. The second way is to use complex lessons for active rest, necessary after selective lessons with heavy training loads.

In summary, qualified gymnasts should take part in mostly selective lessons, and less-qualified gymnasts should take part in mostly complex lessons.

Lesson Types

We can distinguish the types of lessons, depending on the objectives: learning, training, learning-training, recovery, modeling, and control. Each type of lesson has its place in an overall training program.

Learning lessons develop new elements, connections, and compositions. Training lessons repeat mastered exercises and compositions to increase skills and reinforce habits. Learning-training lessons are intermediate in nature: the gymnast studies new elements, connections, and compositions as well as practices mastered elements and compositions.

Recovery lessons differ from the first three types of lessons in that they involve a lighter training load, more emotional exercises such as games and dances, and more play, all of which help revitalize a gymnast. A coach should plan these lessons to provide active rest for gymnasts after competitions and heavy training load lessons.

Modeling lessons prepare the gymnast for upcoming competitions. These lessons focus on building concentration, dealing appropriately with other gymnasts, and developing composure and other correct behaviors. Control lessons test the gymnast's level of fitness (technical, physical, mental), determining her overall level of preparation.

Lesson Components

Each lesson—no matter its type—consists of three main phases: warm-up, main, and cool-down. No lesson is complete without all three parts.

Warm-Up Phase

The warm-up phase helps the gymnast by providing both information and the chance to prepare for the lesson both psychologically and physically. In this phase, the coach outlines the goal and objectives of a lesson and prepares the gymnast for the main part of the lesson. Specifically, this phase disciplines the gymnast to concentrate on the training objectives. It also works on warming up and conditioning the physiological systems (cardiovascular, nervous, and so on). To this end, the gymnast should perform a set of special exercises to prepare her body for the main phase of the lesson.

An effective coach divides the warm-up into general and specific components. As its name implies, the general component consists of general development exercises, such as running and active games. The specific component consists of preparatory exercises specific to RSG: dance steps, drills using the bar, jumps and leaps, balances, turns and pivots, leans, flexibility exercises, and a set of preparatory exercises with the apparatus.

The selection of exercises in a warm-up should follow a logical sequence, starting at the ankles and working upward. First the gymnast exercises her ankles, then her knees, legs, hips, vertebral column, and arms, gradually increasing the amplitude of the movements. The preparatory phase can last anywhere from 15 to 60 minutes, depending upon the particular gymnast, the nature of the upcoming work, and the external conditions in which the lesson is taking place.

Main Phase

The main phase consists of exercises with or without apparatus, competitive compositions, and exercises to prepare the gymnast physically, and so on. It lasts from 20 to 30 minutes for beginners, up to 90 to 150 minutes for advanced gymnasts. Here, the coach covers the core tasks of the lesson. Therefore, the duration depends on the nature, means, and methods of the exercises involved and the training load planned. The actual selection and number of exercises determine the lesson's direction and training load.

Cool-Down Phase

In the cool-down phase of a lesson, which lasts 3 to 10 minutes, the gymnast should gradually reduce the intensity at which she is working at or near the pre-lesson state, allowing her to recover. Walking, relaxation exercises, musical games, and expressive exercises (for beginners) in which the gymnast emulates birds, waves, and so on, all help the gymnast cool down after intense activity.

Understanding Intensity

In sport, training load refers to the degree of impact that the physical stimuli have on the organism (the gymnast's body) and the reaction of her internal systems to the physical stimuli. We can characterize the size, or quantity and quality, of the training load both internally and externally. The external size of a training load is characterized by volume and intensity. The volume is concerned with the duration of the training, and the intensity involves the strength of physiological effect on the body (see table 7.1). Since training loads of different volumes and intensities can elicit varying reactions from a gymnast, they are divided into heavy, average, and light.

We can determine the internal size of the training load based on a gymnast's heart rate, which is one of the most accessible and informative parameters reflecting the reaction of the cardiovascular system to a training load. To measure heart rate, the gymnast presses her fingers on the temporal, carotid (neck), or femoral (thigh) arteries, on the wrist, or above the heart for 10 to 15 seconds (see figure 7.1). After counting the heartbeats, they should be multiplied by an appropriate factor to define the number of beats per minute (bpm). If, for example, the heartbeats were counted for 10 seconds, multiply by six; if the heartbeats were counted for 15 seconds, multiply by four.

The gymnast or the coach should check the heart rate immediately—within the first 10 seconds after the end of an exercise. Immediate checking is nec-

TABLE 7.1

Training Loads in RSG Lessons

Parameters of volume	Parameters of intensity
Time spent on performance of exercises Duration of lesson General number of training hours per week, month, and year	Speed and tempo of a movement
Time spent on elements, connections, and compositions with different apparatus in a lesson, week, month, and year	The percentage of difficult elements to total elements in a lesson
The pure training time, excluding breaks and rest time, in a lesson, week, month, and year	The quantity of elements, executed in a minute, for a particular lesson
The general quantity of elements, connections, and compositions in a lesson, week, month, and year	The ratio of elements of different structural groups (jumps and leaps or throws) to the total number of elements

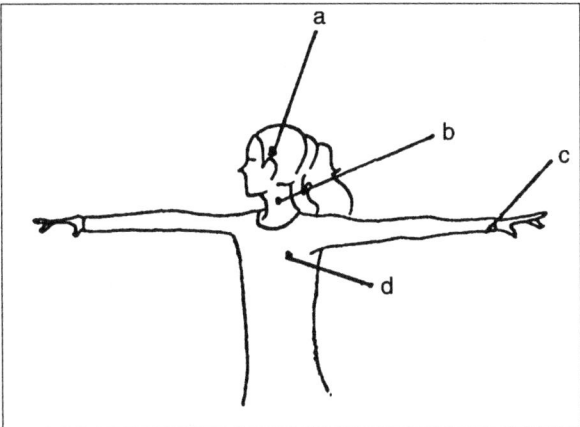

Figure 7.1 Pressure points for determining heart rate: (a) on the temporal artery, (b) on the carotid artery, (c) on the wrist (inside part of the forearm), (d) above the heart (approximate point is between the fourth and fifth ribs from the collarbone).

essary since the first few minutes after the end of an exercise a significant reduction in heart rate occurs as the gymnast rests. Then upon the start of a new exercise, the heart rate changes in the first few seconds. During strenuous training loads, the gymnast achieves the optimum rhythm in the first 30 seconds and the maximum at the end of the first few minutes of work.

To determine a heart rate that reflects a training effect, a coach must take a gymnast's working heart rate into account. This is the maximal heart rate, which is calculated by subtracting the gymnast's age from 220 (for beginners from 200). The working heart rate is determined by subtracting the resting heart rate from the maximal heart rate:

maximal heart rate − resting heart rate = working heart rate

Hence for a 20-year-old gymnast with a resting heart rate of 70 beats per minute, the pulse reserve will be 130 beats per minute. This is the working heart rate at which the training effect of a lesson will occur. Therefore, the training load should be strenuous enough to increase the heart rate to 130 beats per minute.

Training at a high intensity is, of course, accompanied by an increase in heart rate significantly above 170 bpm. Training at average intensity increases the heart rate from 140 up to 170 bpm, and training at a low intensity increases the rate from the initial rate up to 140 bpm. In each lesson, we recommend the coach include two or three short intensity "peaks" of up to two minutes at a heart rate that is close to 170 bpm, making the heart rate go up and down during a lesson (see figure 7.2).

During the course of childhood, the heart rate at rest decreases until puberty when the heart rate is the same as for an adult. It is 85 to 90 bpm at 7 years of age. By 14 to 15 years, it decreases to 70 to 76 bpm. Then it drops to 65 to 75 bpm by 16 or 17 years, which is practically the same as the resting heart rate of an adult.

When the training load is increased, the change in the heart rate depends on the gymnast's age. Specifically, any training load increase for children or adolescents is accompanied by a greater increase in heart rate than in adults. The recovery rate after physical exercise also depends on the size of the training load and the gymnast's age. For average and heavy training loads in girls of 11 to 14 years of age, the resting heart rate is restored faster than in adults.

Lesson Organization

A coach can organize a lesson as an individualized or a group experience. In an individualized lesson, the coach gives the gymnast a particular task she needs to work on, creating the optimum conditions for training the individual appropriately. But if the coach gives the same task to all the gymnasts, it is a group lesson. In a group lesson, the girls can either execute the task all together or in two or more subgroups. The main problem with group lessons is that it is difficult to guide and control each gymnast's

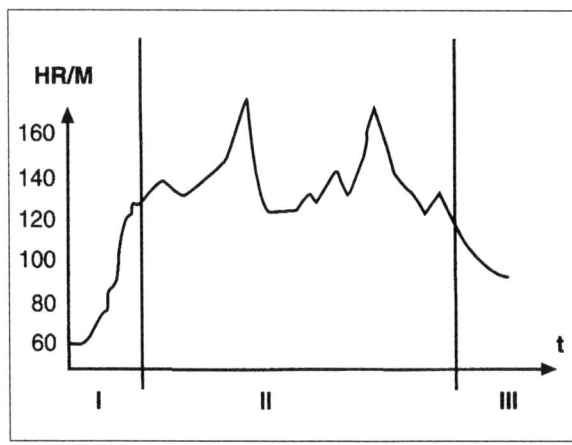

Figure 7.2 Graph of the change in heart rate during a lesson, where *HR/M* is heart rate per minute, *t* is time of a lesson, and I, II, and III are the parts of the lesson (warm-up, main, and cool-down).

execution of the task. Still, group lessons can be helpful in certain circumstances, such as when introducing a new task. A coach can tailor a group lesson in three main ways to make such a lesson more effective, depending on the circumstances. For example, the coach may have all the gymnasts perform the task simultaneously. Or she may have subgroups of four to six gymnasts take turns performing the task. Or she may have the entire group line up and have one to three gymnasts execute the task down the line until all have finished.

Lesson Effectiveness

Training load is the main factor that determines the training effect a lesson has on a gymnast. The parameter for effectiveness in a lesson is its density, which consists of how much the coach puts into a lesson. Two kinds of density exist: general (pedagogic) and motor. General density involves the amount of time the gymnast actually spends working on lesson objectives and how much time she loses during a lesson to explanations, demonstrations, and trying to mentally understand the exercise. These are the only uses of lesson time that are pedagogically justified other than actually physically working on a lesson. Personal or other matters should wait until after a lesson.

Motor density is concerned with how much time the gymnast spends on physical activity instead of on instructions. We can express both kinds of density as percentages. Table 7.2 shows a sample form for defining the density of a lesson. The form will help coaches monitor lesson activity.

Depending on how the coach conducts a lesson, all actions of a gymnast can be either efficient or inefficient. For example, after the group executes an exercise, the coach corrects an error in the movement of one gymnast while the rest of the group stands around without attention or direction. This pause is inefficient for the group. Inefficient actions and idleness reduce the gymnast's interest in the lessons, harm the working atmosphere, and can lead to injuries. An effective coach will avoid such times!

To create more effective lessons, we recommend that the coach accommodate the gymnasts in the most rational way. The coach should strive to exclude unjustified movements from the lesson plan. In addition, attracting quality assistants, perhaps by enlisting more seasoned gymnasts, can provide more one-on-one assistance to less experienced gymnasts. Another way to make lessons more efficient is to offer gymnasts waiting their turns the opportunity to analyze the execution of elements by other gymnasts in their class or on video or giving them the space to perform individual elements, connections, and so on. Circuit training, in which stations focused on one element of a competitive composition are set up around the gym, will keep all gymnasts involved and therefore learning for most of the lesson.

Use the column labeled "Types of activity" to list the contents of the lesson. These might include, for example, explaining directions, correcting mistakes, and practice time. Use the column labeled "Time" to record the beginning and ending times.

Calculate general density by dividing the efficient time by the total training time and multiplying by 100. This will give you the percent of time spent on learning-related activities. For example, if 75 minutes of a 90-minute lesson were rated efficient, we would find the general density of the lesson as follows:

$$75 \div 90 = 0.83$$
$$0.83 \times 100 = 83\%$$

We would not consider this example lesson to be very efficient as the general density of a lesson should be close to 100 percent.

We can calculate motor density by dividing the time of performance by the total training time and then multiplying by 100 to find the percentage.

The motor density of a lesson depends on its tasks, the amount of rest versus activity, training state of a gymnast, and conditions of the venue. Therefore this parameter fluctuates widely. For example, when perfecting techniques and qualities of elements, motor density may be only 70 to 80 percent. In lessons spent on learning elements that require the coach to spend a lot of time explaining and allowing the gymnast to think, motor density may fall to as low as 50 percent.

We can draw a training load curve using heart rate data collected during training (figure 7.2). Then we can use the height of the curve to judge the intensity of a training load. The size of the area under the curve, from the initial heart rate to the final heart rate, indicates the volume (duration of effect).

The classical physiological curve of a lesson's training load is represented following the "wave":

- rising fast in the beginning,
- fluctuating in the main phase (120 to 160 bpm),

TABLE 7.2

Sample Protocol for Defining the Density of an RSG Lesson

Date: _____   Group: _____

Goals and objectives of the lesson: _____

_____

_____

Types of activity	Time (start-finish)	Explanation and demonstration of the lesson (in minutes) Plus	Minus	Exercise performance (in minutes) Plus	Minus	Rest and pauses (in minutes) Plus	Minus	Notes
Gathering of gymnasts and announcement of goals and objectives	2:57-3:03	2	4	N/A	N/A	N/A	N/A	Explanation dragged
Dance steps	3:03-3:20	2	3	10	2	N/A	N/A	Coach could not get gymnasts in the gym
Ballet exercises at the barre	3:20-3:50	5	3	18	4	N/A	N/A	Coach spent too much time explaining
Stretching	3:50-4:10	N/A	N/A	15	N/A	N/A	5	
Apparatus drills	4:10-6:17	21	5	87	9	5	N/A	
Total	200 min	30	15	130	15	5	5	

Positive (plus) time: 30 + 130 + 5 = 165 min

General density: $\frac{165 \times 100\%}{200} = 82.5\%$

Not good enough; coach wasted some time.

Performance time: 130 + 15 = 145

Motor density: $\frac{145 \times 100\%}{200} = 72.5\%$

Not too bad for this type of lesson, but there was not enough rest during apparatus drills.

- reaching the high point in the main phase (170 to 180 bpm), and
- gradually decreasing in the finishing phase.

Such a curve is desirable for an RSG lesson. An actual physiological curve, however, is jagged in character, although a curve can be drawn along the top of its peaks. The jagged character of the physiological curve is explained by the alternation of exercises with different intensity and rest intervals. Therefore, the heart rate varies widely during the different components of a lesson. For example, it can reach 130 to 160 bpm at the end of a warm-up. After a lesson, the heart rate should not exceed the normal rate plus 10 to 15 bpm.

Nutrition: Vitamins

Simply taking in the correct amount of energy in calories does not necessarily result in good nutrition for a gymnast. The body also needs specific nutrients, which can be obtained from the diet and from supplements.

Vitamins play an important role in metabolism and growth, especially vitamins A (carotene), B1 (thiamine), B6 (pyridoxine), B12 (niacin), C (ascorbic acid), and E (tocopherol). Vitamin A is found in many fruits, carrots, green onions, and sorrels (members of the buckwheat family). Liver, beans, and cereal grains contain vitamin B1. Vitamin B6 can be found in chicken, fish, potatoes, brown rice, and green peas, and Vitamin B12 is found in chicken, fish, milk, and eggs. Vitamin C is found primarily in citrus fruits, although some vegetables, such as bell peppers, broccoli, and tomatoes contain some vitamin C. Vitamin E is obtained from vegetable oils, cereal grains, butter, and eggs.

Summary

In this chapter, we have examined aspects of designing effective workouts and both selective and complex lessons, including primary goals, lesson type, and intensity. We have also discussed lesson organization and effectiveness, along with providing information about calculating the efficiency of a training program based on the gymnast's heart rate at different stages.

In the next chapter, we will examine how to develop an effective training program, one which prepares the gymnast for competition through planning and goal-oriented training.

Chapter 8

Creating a Training Program

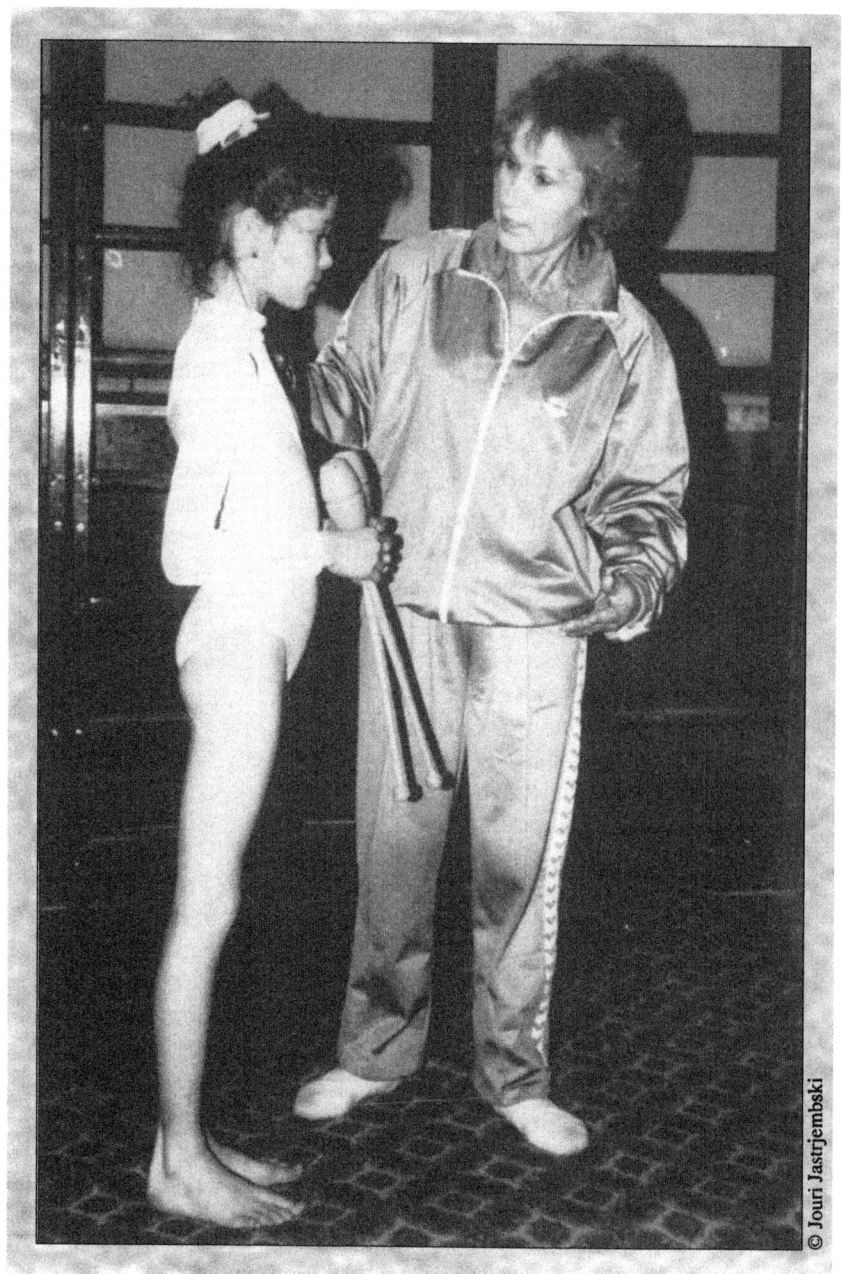

An effective coach does not magically produce top gymnasts. He or she must plan for success. An effective plan outlines a developmental sequence of training that will prepare a gymnast for competition. In turn, the main goal of planning is to systematically control a gymnast's program over time. In this chapter, we will examine and discuss the components of developing an effective training program.

Essential Principles of Planning

Since planning is determined by the particular training program, we can say that the act of planning helps coaches narrow down and formulate objectives. Then, coaches should base their decisions regarding training and loading methods on these objectives. Effective planning also takes into account specific aspects, such as lessons, competitions, and supplementary factors. Proper planning will also consider a gymnast's individual needs and economic situation. When coaches take all these factors into consideration, a highly effective program will result.

Specifically, for effective planning, a coach should include the following factors:

- Goals—planning to reach a level that has been set for the gymnast.
- Systematic development—mapping out various intervals of time, for instance, one lesson, one week, one month, one year, and so on, to ensure continuity in the training process.
- Comprehensiveness—working toward objectives for the different aspects of a gymnast's development, including technical, physical, dance, and so on. Objectives must conform to the final goal, and coaches should choose training methods accordingly.
- Concrete components—mapping out detailed objectives and methods in relation to the gymnast's needs and economic situation.
- Reality—making an objective evaluation of a gymnast's potential, training state, and quality of lessons.
- Number of students—planning for either an individual or a group or team of gymnasts.
- Planning period—taking into account the duration of the plan (long-term, annual, monthly, weekly, and daily).

All lesson plans—no matter their duration—need to include several very specific components:

- Information about each gymnast, including the time she has spent in RSG and her level of mastery.
- Ultimate goal for each gymnast and specific objectives for the various aspects of training.
- Means and methods of achieving the objectives, including the exercises, training loads, number of competitions, and so on.
- Specific systematic instructions regarding correction techniques, training loads, exercise performance, and lesson organization.
- Terms of competitions, testing, and medical examinations (for weekly, monthly, and longer-term plans).

When choosing specific activities for any type of lesson plan, a coach should be sure to choose exercises based on the objectives of a gymnast's training program and her abilities, so that the gymnast will be able to achieve the objectives in the planned term. But the right exercises used with the wrong methods and training loads will ruin the best-laid plans, so after choosing the appropriate exercise, the coach must make sure the methods and training loads are appropriate as well. Next, the coach must double-check to ensure that his or her choices are sequentially organized and that he or she has allocated enough time to perfect elements, connections, and compositions before progressing on to the next stage. Then, the coach must work out a systematic sequence and set aside enough time for technical, physical, dance, and other aspects. Finally, the coach must define how he or she will monitor medical issues and test for mastery.

Long-Term Planning

To be successful in sports, including RSG, long-term training is essential. Therefore, coaches should work out long-term plans so that they may gain perspective. An effective long-term plan gradually increases what it requires of a gymnast while taking her individual needs into consideration. Indeed, a coach can only create a rational plan if he or she bases the plan on the proper stages of development taking training factors into account (see figure 8.1).

Long-term planning is a process that occurs in three stages: basic training, realizing sport possibili-

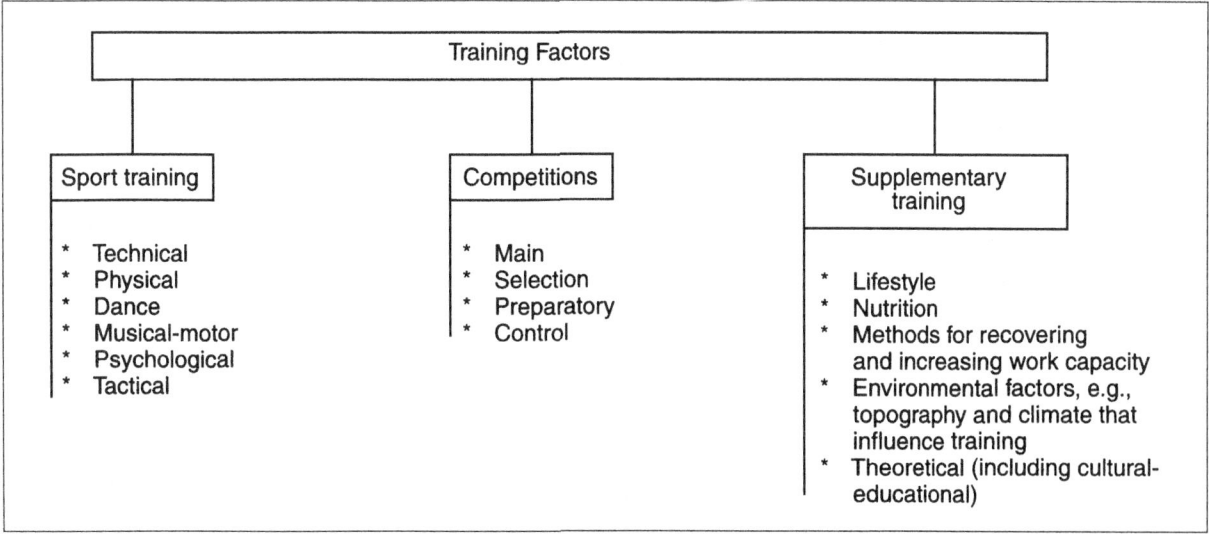

Figure 8.1 Training factors to consider while developing gymnastic mastery through long-term planning.

ties, and encouraging sport longevity. Each of these stages consists of large steps, or components, perhaps as large as 12 to 36 months. But the stages and steps of training do not have strictly fixed limits. Their starting and completion points depend on the calendar and biological age of a gymnast, the sport talents and individual needs of a gymnast, the gymnast's ability to adapt to training, her training experience in RSG, and the organization of the training process. Table 8.1 outlines the objectives of training at various stages.

We will turn, now, to describing each stage of long-term planning in RSG in more detail.

Building a Base

It takes four to six years to complete the basic training a gymnast needs to progress to the next stage. Of course, different gymnasts will progress at different rates, based on talent. Nevertheless, the goal at this stage is to master the basic skills necessary for earning top results in RSG in the future.

Although it would be ideal, attaining good to excellent sport results in children's competitions is not important at this stage. Thus, competitive success should not be the sole goal of coaches.

In the following two sections, we will discuss the two parts of the basic training stage: preliminary sport preparation and sport specialization.

Preliminary Sport Preparation

Preliminary sport preparation usually begins at the kindergarten age (five or six years) and finishes when sport specialization begins, usually in two to three years. Because of the breadth and depth of the subject, we will only outline the specific features of the training process here. Lessons at this stage involve classical drill, dances, mobile games, musical-motor education, physical and technical development, including studying the basics of body movements in conjunction with apparatus.

Five- and six-year-old girls are usually ready to begin training in RSG. The problem that arises is that by aiming for sport success too soon, coaches may move their gymnasts into sport specialization prematurely, possibly leading to adverse consequences. Spending adequate time on preliminary training, using all kinds of methods and covering all aspects of the basics, however, can ensure many victories in the long run. Still, coaches can gradually introduce specialized exercises by slowly replacing games with more difficult exercises and basic RSG elements.

When gymnasts are learning the techniques of elements, a coach's choices should be guided by the need to master the various preparatory exercises. But at this stage, a coach should not expect technical mastery. Instead, a coach should help the gymnasts build an "arsenal" of RSG skills and habits, thereby developing a "motor reserve." Ample exercises involving body movements and apparatus will form the basis for subsequent technical perfection.

Typically, lessons at this step are conducted two or three times a week for 60 to 90 minutes each. The annual volume of training hours should be relatively low—150 to 200 hours. It depends on how long the girl needs to be at this step, which is in turn connected

TABLE 8.1
Objectives of RSG Training at Various Stages

Stage	Steps	Duration	Training objectives
Basic training	Preliminary sport training	2-3 years	1. To create interest in practicing RSG 2. To master basic elements of body movements and apparatus 3. To create artistic impression and gymnastic style 4. To master basic dance and musical-motor skills 5. To develop coordination abilities and flexibility 6. To prepare for competitions and participation in mass performances
	Sport specialization	2-3 years	1. To motivate practice in RSG 2. To create a reserve of basic skills of body movements and apparatus 3. To master basic compositions 4. To create a reserve of basic skills for group exercises 5. To develop artistic impression 6. To acquire gymnastic style 7. To master a reserve of dance and musical-motor skills 8. To develop flexibility, coordination, strength, and speed abilities 9. To compete in classification, club, and regional competitions 10. To participate in mass performances 11. To master basic tactical skills for competitions
Realization of sport possibilities	Training for the elite level	2-3 years	1. To motivate to achieve top results and success in RSG 2. To participate in competitions at the national and international levels 3. To create a reserve of difficult elements of body movements and apparatus 4. To choose individual or group exercises 5. To master perspective competitive compositions 6. To polish artistic impression and gymnastic style 7. To acquire advanced dance and musical-motor skills 8. To search for an individual performance style 9. To optimize all physical abilities of flexibility and coordination 10. To master psychological training for competitions 11. To polish tactical skills for competitions
	Actual top results	Personal pace	1. To achieve high results 2. To perfect competitive compositions of suitable difficulty 3. To add a reserve of difficult elements of body movements and apparatus

Stage	Steps	Duration	Training objectives
			4. To perfect expression and individual style
			5. To maintain fitness abilities at the necessary level and develop ones that are low
			6. To perfect psychological training for competitions
			7. To perfect tactical skills for competitions
Sport longevity	Maintaining top results	Personal pace	1. To stabilize high results
			2. To perfect competitive compositions
			3. To add a reserve of difficult elements of body movements and apparatus
			4. To perfect individual style
			5. To maintain fitness abilities at an optimum level and develop ones that are low
			6. To perfect psychological training for competitions
			7. To perfect tactical skills for competitions
	Maintaining the training state	Personal pace	1. To enjoy RSG at the recreational level

with her starting age in RSG. If, for example, the girl started to practice at the age of five, the duration of this step will be about three years. If she started to practice late, say at the age of seven or eight years, this step may be reduced to 12 to 18 months.

Sport Specialization

The step of sport specialization can also be called specialized basic training. As with preliminary sport preparation, this step may take two to three years. Because this step will have a strong influence on the gymnast's future, it should be organized well. The coach must pay special attention, for example, to building the young gymnast's interest in long-term sport training.

The main emphasis of this step is on technical development. The gymnast should master a large number of apparatus and body movement elements, incorporating the basic elements into basic compositions. She should perform in club or classification competitions. As a rule at this stage, competitive results improve at a rate that is usually not proportionate to the volume of training. In other words, the appropriate training load is not high in comparison to subsequent stages. This is primarily due to the fact that the body's sensitivity to training loads increases concurrently to natural development and, secondly, to the transfer of training effects among different exercises.

At this step in the basic training stage, volume should increase without an equivalent increase in intensity. The intensity certainly grows a little bit, but at a considerably lesser degree than the volume. Thus, it is necessary to carefully standardize the intensity of lessons, taking into consideration that the gymnast's body is maturing at a fast pace which in itself is actually a training load for her to deal with.

Many coaches use this step to physically prepare gymnasts, bringing their physical abilities up to the optimum level. Focusing on coordination abilities and flexibility are especially important at this time. But a coach should save high-intensity lessons with heavy training loads for when physical abilities are at their peak.

During the sport specialization step, the preparatory period dominates, and the competitive period is shorter. Remember, as the gymnast grows physically, mentally, and emotionally, she will naturally increase her mastery of basic RSG techniques, enabling her to achieve top results in RSG.

Realization of Sport Possibilities Stage

Gymnasts at this stage in RSG are generally 12 to 14 years old up to 20 to 22 years old. We can divide this stage into two steps: training for top results and actual top results.

A gymnast usually spends 5 to 10 years at this stage. This is the time for actively practicing RSG skills, blossoming of sport abilities, and, finally, mastering of sport skills.

Training for Top Results

This step sees the introduction of classical features. In addition, a gymnast should choose her specialty—either group or individual exercises. This step has some advantages. For example, from 12 to 15 years of age, it is easier for the gymnast to form motor habits than when she is 16 to 20 years old. This is because of biological changes in the female body. Therefore, an effective coach plans the gymnast's training so that she will acquire the necessary difficult elements before she attains sexual maturity.

In this step, the volume of technical and specific physical training is increased tremendously compared to all other stages of training. Total volume and intensity are increased more than in the previous stage as well. A coach should, however, set the parameters of volume, duration (total training time), and frequency (number of lessons per week) according to the individual's capacity for work and level of talent. Concurrently, the number of competitions will also gradually increase and, subsequently, their influence on the contents of training will increase as well.

A coach must, at this point, individualize a gymnast's road to mastery. He or she should plan each gymnast's program according to the category of achievement she falls into, gearing it toward helping the individual attain maximum results—as far as the abilities and fitness of the gymnast permit. But the gymnast has to want to succeed. If a coach can create the conditions that allow the gymnast to experience feelings of accomplishment, confidence, and success, RSG mastery may become the main goal in the gymnast's life. To create this environment, the coach must give the gymnast the chance to improve by incorporating all aspects of training and placing her in numerous competitions. Such a method works well for talented gymnasts.

Actual Top Results

This step, as a rule, coincides with the age that is most favorable for achievement of top sport results—15 to 20 years. Here, planning needs to be in line with the Olympic four-year cycle. Typically, such a cycle proceeds as follows:

- Years 1 and 2. The first two years involve training cycles with extended preparatory periods. The goal is to lay the base needed for significant achievement in the Olympic year.
- Year 3. In this year, the program should be a "dress rehearsal" of the Olympic year in terms of training and the schedule of competitions. This year, it is very important to finalize a gymnast's competitive composition so that she will be prepared for the Olympics.
- Year 4. This is the year of true realization. The gymnast should repeat the training she received in the third year with any necessary changes. But this year, she must use all her energy and abilities to achieve the desired results she has worked for over the years.

This is certainly not a unique variation of the Olympic cycle. The precise cycle should depend on the gymnast's training and competitive experience. If a gymnast starts young, the start of the Olympic cycle will differ because it will already consist of a high level of training. Gymnasts who have a great deal of experience in competitions may benefit from a different plan. Specifically, their training in the first year of the Olympic cycle should be a progressive program with a significant volume of work, but with a lower intensity and fewer competitions.

Sport Longevity Stage

This is the final stage in a long-term career. Sooner or later, the results a gymnast achieves in competitions will begin to stabilize. At this point, her body will be less able to perform old skills or learn new skills. This change in the gymnast's body will begin to limit her RSG achievements. The precise point at which this takes place may differ from one individual to another and may depend on many factors. In most cases, however, it happens after 13 or

14 years of practicing RSG, perhaps for two reasons. First, the body's abilities naturally decrease with age. Second, defective long-term training methods can accelerate a gymnast's decline. But a coach can organize the training process to help lengthen the time during which a gymnast may achieve a high level of success.

The sport longevity stage consists of two steps: maintaining top results and maintaining the training state. We will look, now, at each step in more detail.

Maintaining Top Results

In the beginning of this step, the coach should stabilize the gymnast's total volume of training. Nevertheless, there will be times when the gymnast will need to increase the volume for certain kinds of preparation. But many less strenuous ways (an inexhaustible list, in fact!) of maintaining RSG achievements exist. How? A seasoned gymnast should, for example, seek to perfect her competitive compositions, look for new expressive means, and otherwise enrich her competitive composition. To encourage the veteran to improve her training state, a coach should be sure to vary the means and methods of training.

Maintaining the Training State

From the stage of maintaining top results, a gymnast comes to a point at which the best she can do is maintain a high level of fitness. Here, RSG must, unfortunately, become a recreational activity. The coach can reconstruct the original training process so that the gymnast maintains a high capacity for RSG involvement, perhaps as a coach. Group competitions are another possibility for the older gymnast.

Long-Term Planning: A Closer Look

As we have discussed, effective planning for a long-term RSG program can increase the longevity of a gymnast's participation. Moreover, an effective planner should be able to foresee the difficulties each stage of training presents, then organize the overall program accordingly. Only then will it be possible for the gymnast to reach her targeted technical and physical levels. Specifically, the intensity of the training process should include the following factors:

- Planned increases in the total volume of training loads from one stage to another.

- Gradual specialization of individual or group exercises.
- Gradual increases in the number of lessons in a week and, concurrently, gradual increases in the number of lessons with heavy training loads.
- Planned increases in the number of lessons that concentrate on only a few skills or elements.
- Increases in the number of major competitions.

During the few years that girls can succeed in RSG, coaches should slowly guide their gymnasts toward the intense training work needed to reach top results. Unfortunately in practice, many coaches ignore this rule. Instead, they aim for top results for young gymnasts, any way possible—no matter the long-term costs. In effect, this means that 11- and 12-year-old gymnasts take part in competitions for which extensive specific training is required. Therefore, the gymnast fails to master new difficult elements at this critical point, interfering with her developing her motor reserve—the very basis for future successes! Thus, a young gymnast and her coach will begin to copy the methods and means used to prepare top level gymnasts. True, the result of such high-speed training is a rapid increase of achievements during adolescence. The talented girl is, indeed, successful in competitions for a short time. Unfortunately, the fast-paced, intense training required forces her body to adapt to these means too quickly, ultimately exhausting her capacity to adapt. Then, if she achieves top results too early, her training will cease to be so effective. Ironically, her body does not even rebound with a lighter training load, which could have been effective if the coach had not worked her so hard. Therefore, we strongly recommend that the wise coach refrain from pushing a gymnast too fast, too soon. The end results will be much more satisfying!

Individualizing Long-Term Planning

An effective coach strives to use any means available to improve a gymnast's training without harming her longevity in the sport. But each gymnast must have her own program, tailor-made to her needs. To this end, the initial data a coach needs to construct a long-term plan includes the following:

- Projected duration of training to achieve top results.
- Rate of the gymnast's development from grade to grade.
- Projected optimum age for achieving top results.
- Individual needs and talents of the gymnast.
- Training conditions.

Use these data to estimate the long-term plan a gymnast needs to achieve top results. Then go from there to create a detailed, individualized plan.

Indeed, the secret of successful planning lies in appropriately choosing the final goal of long-term training. Next, working backward from the final goal, the coach can determine the main objectives. The coach then needs to define the number and content of the stages of training, their duration, and the main competitions associated with each stage. Of course, all these factors depend on the age of the beginner.

Typically, a gymnast's individual plan should include the following sections:

- Brief notes on the gymnast's age, state of health, sport qualifications, levels of all aspects of development, main defects in her development, and body structure data.
- Goal and main objectives of long-term training.
- Steps and stages of training and their duration.
- Objectives of each kind of training at each stage.
- Main means of reaching the goal and objectives for volumes of training loads at each stage as well as the balance of the various kinds of training that will be used (technical, physical, and so on).
- Main competitions to aim for at each stage, with the exception of the stage of preliminary sport preparation.
- Projected results of major competitions.
- Terms of the medical and pedagogic monitoring.
- Test standards, relating to the various aspects of the gymnast's training.

In turn, the long-term plan for a young gymnast forms the basis for planning her annual preparation cycle.

Planning Training Cycles

Cycle comes to English from the Greek word *kyklos*, meaning circle. It is a set of processes carried out within a certain time. Cycles should work together to prepare a gymnast. In RSG, cycles include:

- exercises in each lesson,
- lessons in one week (microcycle),
- microcycles in a three- to four-week cycle (mesocycle),
- mesocycles in a half- or full-year cycle (macrocycle), and
- macrocycles in the stage of the long-term plan.

When planning any one of these cycles, the coach should consider other cycles in this process. Therefore, when the coach determines the contents of a microcycle, he or she should take the macrocycle and mesocycle plans into consideration. And the contents of a microcycle help the coach set the contents of the individual lessons. Likewise, the contents of a mesocycle are related to microcycles and macrocycles, and the macrocycle is related to the mesocycles and the stage of the long-term plan. It is important to bear in mind that each subsequent cycle should not be an exact copy of the previous one; it should change according to the set objectives.

Macrocycles

A macrocycle is, as its name implies, a large cycle. It outlines the "big picture" for the year, half-year, or season (in other sports). In each macrocycle of a gymnast's career, we can divide the training process into three main phases:

1. Preparatory—the main preparation phase.
2. Competitive—the main competition phase.
3. Transition or transitive-preparatory—the transition from one cycle to the next.

To plan a macrocycle, the coach must set the overall objectives for acquiring and preserving skills and for recovery.

Aiming for top results in the main competitions of the year requires a coach to plan a macrocycle first. From this, he or she can create the best conditions for gradually increasing the fitness and skill levels of each gymnast so she will peak at the right time. Figure 8.2 shows a nine-month-long macrocycle for the USSR RSG national group exercise team. Note the ratio of difficult elements to competitive compositions.

The chart in figure 8.3 represents the appropriate intervals for macrocycles for gymnasts at all levels. Of course, different ratios of intervals are appropriate for some phases, depending on the level of mastery.

A coach should base the macrocycle goals on what is appropriate at this stage on the way to the ultimate goal, the results of pedagogic and medical testing, and his or her analysis of the previous macrocycle. At the same time, the goals of the macrocycle may help refine the goals of the long-term plan. In particular, new goals that were not stated earlier can now be stated. In such a way, the planning becomes realistic and individualized. Thus, the first step in planning a macrocycle is simply to state the goals of the macrocycle. Then the coach can list the objectives for each phase in view of the gymnast's specific needs and strengths.

To summarize, we recommend that the following be part of a macrocycle plan:

- Calendar of competitions, listing main goals and planned results.
- Ratio of different kinds of training to each other.
- Equal number of competitions in different phases of the macrocycle.
- Notes regarding expected results of competitions.
- Approximate distribution of load volume and intensity across the different phases of the macrocycle.
- System for monitoring the training state (technical, physical, dance, and so on).

We will turn, now, to describing the specific contents of each macrocycle phase. Coaches can use this information to help them refine their general macrocycle plans for each gymnast.

Preparatory Phase

When planning macrocycles, bear in mind that how a coach divides the periods depends on the long-term goal and objectives for each gymnast. In the preparatory phase of a macrocycle, a gymnast should

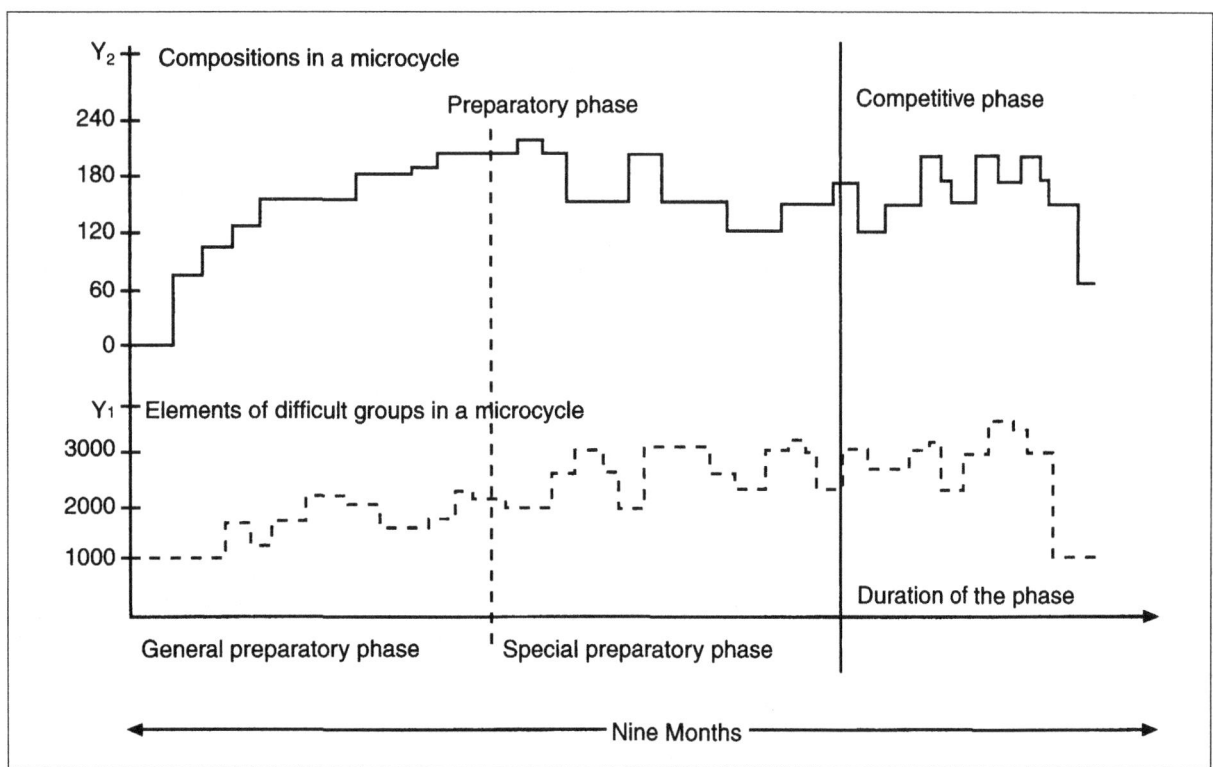

Figure 8.2 Nine month macrocycle with training loads appropriate to elite gymnasts.
From "Using the Conjugate Method of Physical Preparation in RSG Group Exercises" by Nochevnaya, N. (1990). Ph.D. diss., Moscow.

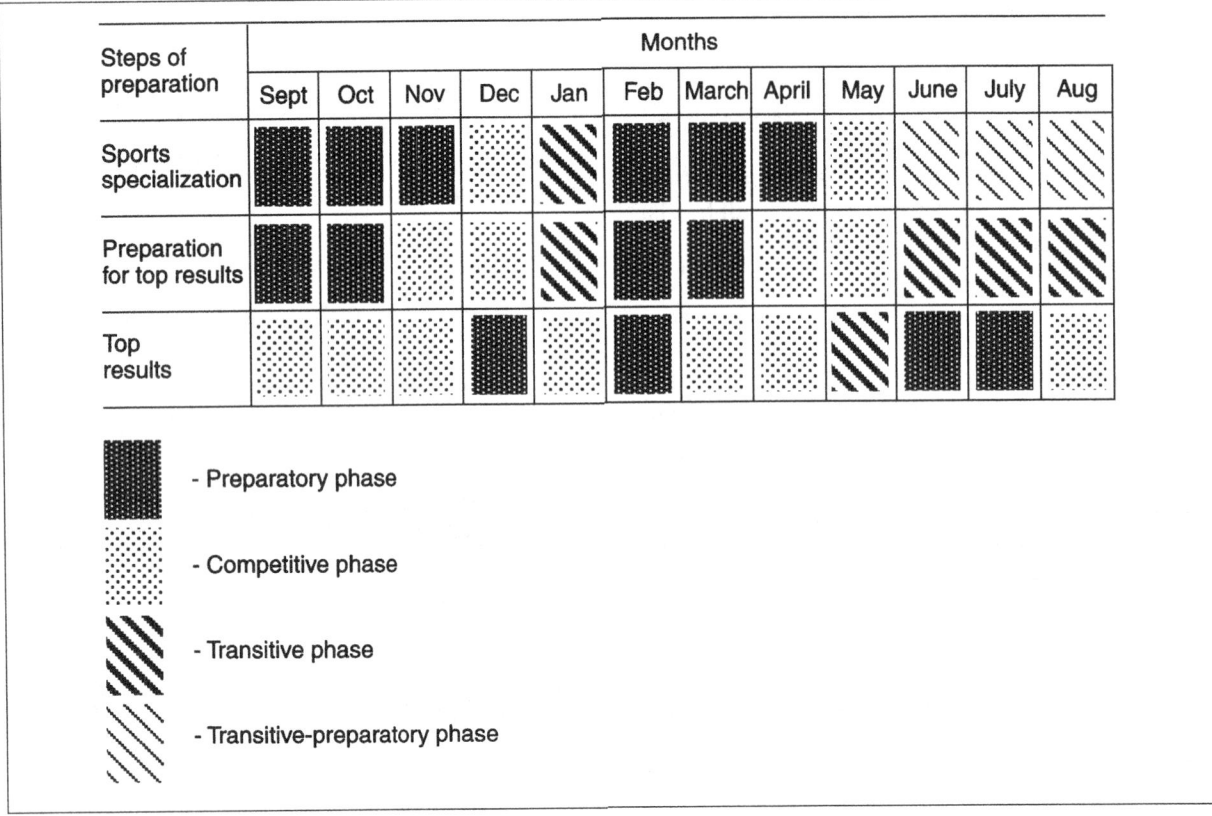

Figure 8.3 One year macrocycle appropriate for gymnasts at various levels.

work on—among other things—general physical and psychological conditioning, RSG techniques, and choreography. Naturally, beginners need a longer preparatory phase than more qualified gymnasts. But no matter the gymnast's experience level, a solid base of training here will enable her performances to peak at the right time, guaranteeing she will achieve her goal. We can further divide this phase into two subphases: general preparatory and specific preparatory.

General Preparatory Subphase Here a gymnast should work primarily on creating, expanding, and perfecting the following in order to peak later in the macrocycle:

- Increasing her level of flexibility and coordination.
- Adding to her reserves of difficult elements and handling of apparatus.
- Choreographing her competitive composition.
- Perfecting her dance skills.
- Developing her strength and endurance.

In this phase, coaches seldom have gymnasts actually perform their competitive compositions. First, the gymnasts must go through the necessary physical and technical training. To keep the gymnast's interest, it is necessary to be creative to achieve the objectives of this phase, which often includes the more tedious exercises like flexibility drills and strength conditioning. Coaches should set objectives based on her individual needs, personality, and level of training. For example, a gymnast may need to focus mainly on both physical fitness and mastering body movement elements.

The general dynamics of training loads in this subphase are characterized by an increase in volume and intensity. Such loads are essential because a stable peak depends on the total volume and duration of this phase. Typical mesocycles for the preparatory phase are the leading and basic types. The total number of mesocycles depends on the initial level of the gymnast's training state and the total duration of the preparatory phase. (See further discussion of mesocycles later in this chapter.)

Specific Preparatory Subphase Here the training process must be specially constructed to move toward the macrocycle's peak. Therefore, all lessons must focus predominantly on developing the specific training state needed for competitions and on truly mastering the competitive composition. Concurrently, a gymnast must prepare herself psychologically for competition.

This subphase must be somewhat of a mirror of the competitive phase. Because peaking involves performing competitive compositions, elements, and connections, so too must the focus of the specific preparatory phase. Therefore, general preparation activities decrease in this subphase. Instead, near the end of this subphase, it is helpful for a gymnast to participate in friendly or sport club competitions. These competitions will help her perfect her psychological discipline, gain experience, and check and evaluate her potential. Indeed, it is very useful to test how well she can execute difficult elements and connections, thereby completing her specific physical training.

It is necessary to plan ahead if a gymnast's calendar mandates that she participate in a number of respectable (but not main) competitions while she is in the preparatory phase of a macrocycle. A coach can handle this situation effectively in one of three ways:

- The gymnast can participate in competitions without changing the training process, reducing training loads on precompetitive days only. This is appropriate for a gymnast who is not aiming for victory in these competitions, but who instead considers participation in such competitions as a kind of training.
- The gymnast can participate in the most important competitions after going through precompetitive training for two to four weeks.
- The coach can revise the macrocycle plan, that is, interrupt the preparatory phase, call it a new competitive phase, and then prepare in the usual manner.

No matter what the circumstances, however, we do not recommend that a gymnast participate in competitions during the preparatory phase if she has not conquered the elements, connections, and composition she needs to learn—at least to the level of mastery appropriate for her stage of training. This is because prematurely participating in competitions reinforces poor techniques, and poor performance can negatively affect the gymnast psychologically. Physical injuries are more likely as well. Consequently, various problems may arise, for example, the fear of performing certain elements and connections and a hatred for certain apparatus. Finally, preparatory competitions should never interfere with training for main competitions.

A coach should increase the intensity of lessons in the specific preparatory subphase. Concurrently, the coach should stabilize total volume, then slowly increase it before finally reducing it. This is accomplished by reducing, first of all, dance and fitness exercises, then by reducing elements and connections that are not included in the gymnast's composition. Meanwhile, the gymnast practices her competitive compositions more and more. Next, this should level off, then partially decrease when intensity is increased.

Competitive Phase

The objectives of the training process in this phase are to maintain peaking throughout the main competitions and to create conditions for maximum achievement. Therefore, a coach must adapt lessons to bring them in line with the competitive activity. Specifically, the training should be direct preparation for intense competitive loads. This maintains the gymnast's high level of fitness during the competitive phase. Meanwhile, the technical training must be able to bring the gymnast's competitive composition up to the highest possible level of perfection, enabling her to master her composition—no matter the conditions under which she competes. To achieve this, a gymnast must improve the coordination of her movements in her composition, smoothing out rough spots to polish her performance. Therefore, lessons should focus on performing competitive compositions and perfecting the connections between the elements that comprise the composition. To fine-tune her psychological approach, a gymnast should develop her will to succeed. Moreover, she should learn to control her emotions during competitions.

Training loads should continue to increase during the whole competitive period until they reach the highest point two to three weeks before each main competition of the macrocycle. After this, the coach should gradually reduce the volume while gradually increasing the intensity until no closer than a week before the main competition (or competitions). Then the coach must gradually reduce intensity during the precompetition week (leading microcycle), allowing the gymnast to fully recover, thereby creating the best possible circumstances under which to compete.

Competitions solidify the necessary specific emotional and physiological development, increasing the effect of training exercises and helping a gymnast display her full potential in a way that training lessons alone cannot elicit. Thus, we can safely claim that competitions play an irreplaceable role in increasing a gymnast's technical mastery, level of experience, specific competitive endurance, and psychological maturity. Therefore, competition itself becomes the major means and method of perfecting performances.

A coach should establish the intervals between competitions by taking into account the gymnast's capacity for total recovery from work and her ability to prepare for decisive starts. The number of main competitions is usually three to five in one macrocycle. Again, this depends on how qualified and experienced the gymnast is. Competitions used to prepare a gymnast require shorter recovery intervals between them than between main competitions. Naturally, preparatory competitions should precede main competitions. Likewise, less important main competitions should precede more important ones. This is, indeed, the best way to obtain top results, based on the experiences of outstanding gymnasts in the past.

The order of mesocycles in the competitive phase of a macrocycle depends on the duration of this phase and the distribution of competitions within it. The following are variations in which the mesocycles are alternated in the competitive phase (see "Mesocycles" section for details about types of mesocycles):

- First variation: competitive I, competitive II, recovery-supporting, competitive III.
- Second variation: competitive I, competitive II, recovery-supporting, competitive III, recovery-preparatory, competitive IV.
- Third variation: competitive I, competitive II, recovery-supporting, competitive III, pre-competitive, competitive IV.

Remember, main competitions should take place near the end of the competitive phase of a macrocycle.

Transition Phase

The transition phase, a part of year-round training macrocycles, differs from the other two phases. Instead of building a gymnast to peak performance, its objective is to prevent overtraining by allowing the gymnast to recover her strength through resting. At the same time, however, this does not mean that there should be a break in the training process. Instead, a coach should still create conditions for maintaining a certain level of fitness and skill. Typically, a "classic" type of transition phase is used in the preliminary sport preparation steps and in sport specialization.

In other steps, this stage may actually be transitive-preparatory. Here, the training state of a gymnast is maintained for a certain time after the main competitions of a year, and the gymnast stays at the maximum level of control of her body movements and apparatus. Therefore, this phase is a good time for learning new difficult elements, perfecting mastered elements and connections, and choreographing new competitive compositions. The main content of lessons in the transitive-preparatory phase involves general physical preparation in a regime of active rest as well as correction of errors in the techniques of difficult elements.

Normally by the end of the season, however, gymnasts suffer from mental rather than physical fatigue. Thus, during this phase, we do not recommend very monotonous loads. Here especially, variety in the choice of exercises and conditions of lessons is important. For example, a lesson in the forest or mountains is sure to elicit new enthusiasm for training as it refreshes the gymnast's mental state.

Usually a transition phase does not include more than one or two mesocycles, which are usually recovery-supporting or recovery-preparatory (see the next section). How does a coach know exactly when a particular gymnast has recovered enough to start a new macrocycle? A coach should base the answer to this important question on how determined the gymnast seems to be to start working on new and much more difficult objectives and the results of the medical and pedagogic testing. Thus, the job of the transition (or transitive-preparatory) phase should be to prepare a gymnast for the start of the next cycle. An effective transition phase will bring the gymnast to a healthy and well-rested state for the next level of technical, physical, and other development.

Sometimes instead of the transition phase, however, a coach may opt to plan a relatively short-term unloading phase of recovery, using only one mesocycle or even only one microcycle. This may be appropriate when the gymnast, for some reason or other, did not train at high enough loads in the preparatory phase. If a coach chooses this course, a dual microcycle phase, consisting of a competitive phase and then a second preparatory phase will be appropriate. This should then be followed by a second competitive phase and only then comes the transition phase.

Mesocycles

As mentioned earlier in the chapter, a macrocycle is made up of mesocycles and a mesocycle is made up of microcycles. How many mesocycles make up a macrocycle and how many microcycles make up a mesocycle depends on the needs of the gymnast and her long- and short-term goals and objectives. One mesocycle includes a minimum of two microcycles, but more typically, mesocycles consist of three to six microcycles and last about a month. The overall macrocycle plan dictates the content of the mesocycles; the mesocycle plan controls the content of the microcycles within it. Working from the big picture to the smaller pictures helps the coach optimally manage a gymnast's training program because the ultimate goal of the macrocycle is never forgotten.

Planning Mesocycles

All types of mesocycles can be repeated throughout the year. In a mesocycle, the training loads gradually increase and decrease; therefore, microcycles should alternate between heavier and lighter loads. For example, one microcycle may be characterized by an increase in the load volume, but another may be characterized by a decrease in volume and an increase in load intensity, and the next microcycle may be characterized by increased volume and decreased intensity, and so on.

As mentioned, a coach should base the plans for mesocycles on the objectives of the gymnast's program in the macrocycle. We recommend that each mesocycle plan include the following:

- Type and duration of the mesocycle.
- Total volume of the training load.
- Dominant focus of microcycles—technical, physical, or other kinds of training.
- Dynamics of loads from one microcycle to another.
- Monitoring of the training state—when, which parameters to apply, which tests, planned standards, and so on.

Types of Mesocycles

Different types of mesocycles have evolved based on the goals and objectives needed to meet the macrocycle goal: leading, basic, control-preparatory, precompetitive, competitive, recovery-preparatory, and recovery-supporting. In the following sections, we will describe the content of each of these types of mesocycles.

Leading Macrocycles should always begin with a leading mesocycle, which usually starts with two or three ordinary preparatory microcycles and ends with a recovery microcycle. As a whole, the load intensity is not very high, but the load volume can be. Normally, skill development is the main focus, including technical, physical, and dance aspects. If a gymnast is fit and well, it is possible to limit the macrocycle to one leading mesocycle. But if she is ill or injured, it is wise to incorporate a second leading mesocycle.

Basic This type of mesocycle is also used in the preparatory phase of the training process. The gymnast achieves the main objectives by mastering elements, connections, and compositions. There are two kinds of basic mesocycles, divided according to the training loads involved: developing and stabilizing. The basic developing mesocycle is used by the gymnast to reach a peak. Therefore, the parameters of the training load differ significantly from that of a basic stabilizing mesocycle. In a basic stabilizing mesocycle, the coach temporarily suspends increasing the training load when the gymnast reaches a certain level. The emphasis is on maintaining that level.

In all variations of the basic mesocycle, the main types are proper training microcycles, but they appear in different combinations. In one variation, the basic mesocycle is made up of different versions of these microcycles: three ordinary and one strike or two ordinary and two strike ones, alternated. In other cases the recovery microcycle may be inserted as an addition; for example, one ordinary, two strike, and one recovery microcycle.

The number of basic mesocycles depends on the time a gymnast has for training and her individual needs.

Control-Preparatory This is a transition mesocycle between the basic mesocycle stage and the competitive mesocycle stage. Here, a coach combines proper training work with participation in less important competitions that help him or her monitor the gymnast's training. For example, this type of mesocycle can consist of two proper training microcycles and two competitive microcycles. The inclusion of competition allows the contents of training lessons to be different if necessary. In certain cases, for example, it is necessary to intensify the training process, in others, the load has to be stabilized or reduced.

Precompetitive This type of mesocycle is essential to a successful competitive phase. It is modeled on the upcoming competition, creating training conditions that will help the gymnast achieve her goal. The main microcycles are the proper training and leading ones. The total volume of the training load is decreased when the gymnast is ready to peak.

Competitive Of course, this is the type of mesocycle to use while the gymnast is participating in the main competitions of the macrocycle. More often than not, this mesocycle includes one training and one competitive microcycle or one training, one competitive, and one recovery microcycle. Naturally, the structure of competitive mesocycles is dictated by the need to preserve a gymnast's peak training state. Table 8.2 outlines an example of the competitive mesocycle for elite gymnasts.

Recovery-Preparatory and Recovery-Supporting In a long competitive phase (three, four, or more months long), the structure is more complicated. Therefore, intermediate mesocycles are necessary. These are recovery-preparatory and recovery-supporting mesocycles that should help develop and maintain the training state. The former is similar to the basic mesocycle, except that it includes an additional number of recovery microcycles, for example, two recovery and two ordinary preparatory ones. The latter is characterized by a lighter training load and more diverse means of recovery.

Microcycles

Once a coach has planned the macrocycle and its mesocycles, he or she is ready to plan the microcycles that will meet the goals and objectives of each mesocycle. A microcycle is a series of lessons, conducted over several days, ensuring that the gymnast achieves the macrocycle objectives.

Microcycles generally last three or four days to two weeks, depending on the number of lessons

TABLE 8.2

Example of a Competitive Mesocycle for Elite Gymnasts

Microcycle	Objectives	Trend of training loads
Ordinary specific-preparatory	To perfect difficult elements To polish performance To increase specific endurance	Adding more compositions and difficult elements Average training load
Strike specific-preparatory	To create the functional reserve of stability	Adding more compositions Heavy training load
Leading	To increase the quality of performance To mentally prepare for competition To model the regime and conditions of competition To devise tactical training for competition	Decreasing the duration and volume of training lessons Average training load
Competitive	To compete To continue psychological training for competition To continue tactical training for competition	Decreasing the duration and volume of lessons Light training load

needed to accomplish the microcycle's objectives, the types of lessons needed, the training state of the gymnast, the current need for alternating training loads and rest, individual reactions to training loads, the lifestyle of the gymnast, and the microcycle's place in the larger cycles. A seven-day microcycle is the most popular because it meshes best with a gymnast's lifestyle.

Planning a Microcycle

How a coach plans a microcycle depends on the processes of fatigue and recovery after lessons, the effects of having several lessons a day, and the fluctuation of the workload during a day (when planning two or three lessons daily).

The system of alternating loads in a microcycle is the basis for the concept of decreasing training loads in the super recovery phase after the first load, when the training effect is the best. If the gymnast goes through the next load after the effects of the first load have worn off, the effect of the subsequent load will be less. However, repeatedly maintaining or increasing training loads without allowing for recovery will lead to fatigue, overtraining, and, possibly, injury. But the microcycle scheme can prevent these problems, as the processes of recovery after physical work vary in the time they take. In other words, different body systems recover and super recover at different rates. In practice, a coach can alternate training loads with rest in a microcycle by carefully alternating training means and methods, thereby alternating which muscles each lesson fatigues. Thus, the effective planning of several subsequent lessons will lead to super recovery of the work capacity.

Specifically, alternating training loads with rest in a microcycle may cause the gymnast's body to maximally increase its training state, experience little or no training effect, or suffer from extreme fatigue. Microcycles will maximize the gymnast's training state when there are an optimum number of lessons with heavy and average loads at rational intervals alternated with lighter loads. But if none of the lessons include heavy and average training loads, a gymnast may experience little or no training effects. Finally, too many lessons with heavy loads or irrational alternation with rest may lead to extreme fatigue. Thus, a coach must strive to strike a balance among heavy, average, and light training loads and various means and methods to produce the desired training effects. The proper balance, however, will vary from individual to individual, depending on each gymnast's needs, strengths, and training state.

While it is tempting to overload a gymnast in the hopes of accelerating her development, a coach should plan only two consecutive lessons with heavy loads that work on the same aspect of training for elite gymnasts. Here such a plan will be successful if cautiously applied and rationally combined with lessons of differing loads and rest in the remainder of the microcycle. Of course, general preparatory and recovery microcycles include fewer lessons and lighter loads.

Typically, a coach includes a heavy training load once or twice per week and lighter loads once or twice a week (but in some cases, active rest once per week is enough in heavier training load microcycles). The following is an example of the typical training loads in an RSG microcycle:

- First day—average.
- Second day—heavy.
- Third day—light.
- Fourth day—average.
- Fifth day—heavy.
- Sixth day—light (or average).
- Seventh day—active rest.

Thus, the week cycle consists of two waves of heavy training loads, occurring on the second and fifth days of the week (see table 8.3).

When planning microcycles, a coach must not lose sight of the big picture—the long-term plan and the macrocycle plan. A coach must always be especially aware of the phase of the macrocycle a gymnast is in. For example, during preliminary sport preparation, lessons with heavy training loads are not appropriate. But heavy loads are appropriate one to three times per week when the gymnast is training for the top results stage and four to six times per week in the actual top results stage (with 10 to 12 lessons per week). Finally, the gymnast's stage in the long-term plan cannot be forgotten. For example, microcycles with average training loads help increase the training capabilities of young, inexperienced gymnasts who have not adapted to intense training.

As mentioned, an elite gymnast has a greater need to increase training loads more quickly. But a few problems may arise when planning two or more lessons in one day, including:

- establishing the optimum time of training lessons,

TABLE 8.3

Sample Plan for Training Loads in a Week-Long Strike Microcycle (Special Preparatory Phase)

Day of week, training load	Warm-up	Rope exercises	Hoop exercises	Ball exercises	Club exercises	Ribbon exercises	SPT*
Mon., average	With clubs	N/A	1st** P2×4*** C×5****	N/A	N/A	2nd P1,2×3 C×3	Leg power
Tues., heavy	Ballet drill, jumps, leaps	3rd P1,3×3 C×4	N/A	2nd P1,2,3×2 C×4	1st P1×3 C×4	N/A	Flexibility
Wed., light	Aerobics	N/A	N/A	2nd P2×3 C×3	N/A	1st P2,3×4 C×2	Coordination
Thurs., average	Ballet drill, balances	1st P2,3×3 C×4	N/A	N/A	2nd P1,2,3×4 C×4	N/A	Leg power
Fri., heavy	With ribbon, turns, pivots	3rd P1,2×3 C×4	1st P1,3×4 C×5	2nd P3,4×3 C×4	N/A	N/A	Flexibility
Sat., light	Ballet drill, waves	N/A	N/A	1st P1,2,3×3 C×3	N/A	2nd P3×3 C×3	Coordination
Sun., rest	Aqua-aerobics						

SPT* - Specific physical training, trend in developing physical abilities.
1st** - Sequence of performance exercises with this apparatus in main part of lesson.
P2×4*** - Part of composition and number of repetitions (second part, performed four times).
C×5**** - Composition and number of repetitions (composition, performed five times).

- defining the focus, volume, and intensity of the training loads, and
- deciding how to alternate the focus and training loads of the day's lessons.

In special situations, such as a gymnastics camp, a gymnast may have three or four lessons per day. But too much training, can, of course, lead to injury or discouragement. Thus, most elite gymnasts practice twice a day. Table 8.4 presents four variations of this pattern.

The variations shown in table 8.4 are distinguished by the number of elements the gymnast focuses on, the particular compositions, and the special features of morning and evening training. The lessons vary as other lesson's vary: according to the gymnast's training stage, her health and level of fitness, the volume and intensity of

TABLE 8.4

Variations of Two RSG Lessons per Day

Variation	1st lesson	2nd lesson	Recommendations
1st	Main: 50-70% of daily elements, 100% of compositions, 4-5 apparatus	Additional: 30-50% of daily elements, ballet drill, fitness	For transition phase and beginning of preparatory phase
2nd	Main: 60-70% of daily elements, 70-80% of compositions with 2-3 apparatus	Additional: 30-40% of daily elements, 20-30% of compositions with 1-2 apparatus, ballet drill	For the end of preparatory phase or beginning of competitive phase
3rd	Main: 40-60% of daily elements, 50-60% of compositions with 2 apparatus	Main: 40-60% of daily elements, 40-50% of compositions with 2 apparatus	For competitive phase (not more than 1 or 2 per week)
4th	Main: 50-60% of daily elements, 50-60% of compositions with 4-5 apparatus	Main: 40-50% of daily elements, 40-50% of compositions with 4-5 apparatus	For competitive phase before starting competition

the training load, and the purpose of the microcycle.

A coach can have a gymnast repeat a microcycle as many times as necessary to achieve the objectives. While the coach should keep the same focus in repeated cycles, she or he should change the volume and intensity, the means and methods, and the training conditions. Then, once the gymnast has reached the objectives of the microcycle, the coach should move on to a new microcycle to meet a new set of objectives.

If a gymnast misses a lesson, we recommend that the microcycle remain the same, not be shifted to other days. A missed lesson is simply a defect of a microcycle. It should not be allowed to disrupt the customary rhythm of the training process. Still, a coach should not be too rigid when it comes to planned training loads. He or she must alter a microcycle and the content of its lessons if the gymnast's capacity for training changes due to injury, illness, or another problem.

To summarize, the following should be components of every microcycle plan:

- Total volume of training loads.
- Focus and alternation of lessons of differing training loads.
- Means and methods of training.
- Particular exercises of the various kinds of training (technical, physical, dance, and so on).
- Combination of training and competitive loads and means of recovery and stimulating the work capacity.
- Means and timing of testing of the gymnast's training state.

When planning a microcycle, we recommend that a coach compose a form. First, a coach should distribute the lessons throughout the day. Then, keeping the objectives of the microcycle in mind, the coach should list the contents of the lessons, taking into account the optimum combinations of different exercises. Then, the coach should specify the apparatus (the hoop, ball, and so on) and the number of elements and compositions in each lesson.

Types of Microcycles

The types of microcycles relate to the objectives set in the microcycle and are divided into the following categories: proper training, leading, competitive, and recovery. In the following sections, we will take a closer look at each type of microcycle to help the coach refine his or her plans.

Preparatory Microcycles Proper training microcycles can be general-preparatory (involved) or specific-preparatory, depending on the stage in the macrocycle and the individual needs of the gymnast.

General-preparatory microcycles are geared toward preparing a gymnast's body to handle intense training loads. Their objectives include improving the gymnast's motor reserve of technical skills, fitness, and dance abilities. As a rule, they belong in the first period of the preparatory phase at the beginning of a mesocycle. They form the basis for developing the training state.

Specific-preparatory microcycles play an especially important role in the preparation of a gymnast. They help the gymnast achieve an adequate training state while increasing her level of technical, physical, and other kinds of development.

Finally, whether a specific- or a general-preparatory microcycle, the training loads can be ordinary or "strike." The lessons within an ordinary preparatory microcycle proceed according to a standard increase in the training loads from one lesson to another and a significant increase in volume, but at a low intensity in the majority of lessons. Strike preparatory microcycles are characterized by a heavy load and high intensity.

Leading Microcycles Leading microcycles guide gymnasts toward competitions, modeling their content and its sequence. The precise contents, however, depend on the precompetitive state of the gymnast and the planned tactics for the competition.

Competitive Microcycles Competitive microcycles assume that a gymnast will participate in competitions, therefore, the structure and duration of a cycle are determined by the number of competitions and the pauses between them. Specifically, these microcycles include lessons that prepare a gymnast for competition, actual participation in competitions, lessons that offer specific training to correct errors the gymnast made in competition, and recovery activities.

Recovery Microcycles The recovery microcycles usually conclude a series of strike or preparatory microcycles. And of course, they are also appropriate after intensive competitive activity. Their main objectives are to allow the gymnast to recover and adapt both in body and in spirit. Therefore, light training loads and active rest comprise recovery microcycles.

Dividing the phases only helps a coach plan training lessons. Achieving the objectives of a lesson depends a lot on good planning. That is why the coach should carefully plan the contents of each lesson. At the same time, it is not possible to predict all the situations that might develop during sessions with gymnasts. Therefore, a coach is wise to divide his or her planning book into spaces for planned contents and spaces to record the actual contents of the lessons. To be able to evaluate and respond to the actual situation a lesson presents requires a knowledgeable and experienced coach as well as a broad base of pedagogic and sport skills.

It is ideal for a coach to prepare all tasks for a lesson ahead of time so that he or she is sure to take into account the biological principles of the gymnast's work capacity, the logic of the training process, and the step and phase of a gymnast's preparation. The planning of a lesson can be written as a general scheme or as a detailed plan. The scheme for an RSG lesson is a brief account of its contents, but a more detailed plan lists the individual steps of the lesson. A coach should list either or both types of plans in the microcycle plan. At the same time, however, a coach must daily take into consideration whether or not the objectives of the previous lessons have been met, the training state of the gymnast, and her performance in previous lessons.

Setting Objectives

In each lesson, a coach should teach a gymnast new skills and habits as well as how to perfect old skills. The latter helps a gymnast see her level of mastery improving, encouraging her greatly. This is possible only through striving for the concrete objectives of each lesson. Ill-defined objectives will hinder the smooth flow of the training process. A concrete objective is one for which the descriptive words reflect the final desired result of the lesson, for example, "To learn (or master, establish, improve, perfect) any element (or connection or composition)."

Once a coach defines a lesson's objectives, it is necessary to choose exercises that will help the gymnast reach the objectives. We recommend that a coach follow these steps in the order given:

1. Define the means and methods of achieving each skill objective.
2. Define the means and methods to achieve the objectives of different kinds of training, including physical, dance, and other areas.
3. Assign tasks in view of the work capacity of the individual gymnast.
4. Define the training loads for particular exercises and parts of lessons, including the number of repetitions, sets, and duration of rest intervals.
5. If the lesson is conducted with musical accompaniment, indicate the musical time signature (3/4, 4/4, or the like).
6. Define the criteria for and types of evaluation of the gymnast's activity (execution of elements and the mark it deserves).

Remembering the Details

Working out a detailed lesson plan is rather laborious, but it will help a new coach understand the training process in a lesson better. Experienced coaches use less detailed lesson plans and more often compile more long-term plans.

Each lesson plan should consist of the following (see table 8.5): the title, the lesson number, date of execution, and group name or surname of a gymnast if a private lesson. Then the coach should list the

TABLE 8.5

Sample Lesson

Lesson plan: number 15 **Date: February 18**
Group: A—beginners
Objective: To teach gymnasts how to throw the hoop upward and catch it (at advanced lesson)

Concrete objectives	Exercises	Dosage (repetitions × sets)	Teacher's points
1.1. Teach how to throw the hoop with one arm after performing different body movements	Perform throws with one arm a) After polka steps b) After 4 vertical jumps c) After 2 vertical jumps and 180° cross turn	8 × 3 8 × 3 6 × 3	The following sequence must be used: 1st set—by left arm; 2nd—right arm; 3rd—left arm
1.2. Teach how to catch the hoop after performing different body movements	Perform catches: a) After clapping palms b) After 360° cross turn c) After vertical jumps	10 × 3 6 × 3 8 × 3	Perform in the same sequence as objective 1.1
1.3. Teach how to throw and catch the hoop in conjunction with body movements	a) Throw the hoop with one arm after polka steps and 360° cross turn and catch it with the other arm b) Four vertical jumps with a half turn, throw the hoop with one arm, clap palms four times, and catch the hoop with the other arm	4 × 4 4 × 4	Perform alternatively with right and left arm: left-right-left-right

main objectives of the lesson. If necessary, the coach should indicate the following: the equipment (apparatus, weights, and so on), illustrations, videotapes for viewing, videocamera for recording, and so on.

Table 8.5 lists the objectives in the first column. Note the difference between general and specific objectives. For example, the general objective is to learn how to throw the hoop, and the specific objective is to learn how to throw the hoop after performing body movements. The specific objectives are written in the manner in which they will be achieved. The second column lists the means (exercises) to reach each objective. The column entitled "Dosage" lists the number of repetitions, intensity, and duration of the exercises. Once a coach has mapped out the main parts and details of a lesson, he or she can plan the appropriate warm-up and cool-down.

Although it may be very difficult to choose the appropriate training load for a gymnast, it is extremely important that a coach not require a gymnast to do more than is suitable for her. This is where actual lessons may differ from planned lessons. A coach must be willing to be flexible and adjust the training load if it proves to be too much for the gymnast. Then when a coach does increase the training load, this action should be pedagogically justified and in line with the lesson's objectives.

Other difficulties a coach might face include choosing the correct amount of time for each lesson and the amount of time for each exercise. We recommend that a coach mark the amount of time needed for each exercise alongside the lesson plans. Such notes will help a coach plan new lessons.

In the following sections, we will explore the three major components of each lesson plan in more detail.

Warm-Up

The warm-up should proceed methodically from a general warm-up of the cardiovascular and musculoskeletal systems to a specific warm-up for particular exercises. During the warm-up, the gymnast should wear sweats. Later, she should change into more comfortable clothes, such as a gym leotard, sport shorts, or the like. Each general warm-up:

- should give the gymnast a feeling of warmth,
- must include classical drills at the barre,
- should be easy to perform with little concentration,
- should increase intensity gradually but steadily,
- should not be too long or too short, and
- should include music to evoke the emotions of the gymnasts.

A specific warm-up with apparatus starts with repetitions of four or five truly mastered elements, enabling the gymnast to restore her muscular sense for the apparatus. Then she can practice the leading exercises for learning elements and connections. She should repeat similar specific warm-ups before practicing with other apparatus in the main part of a lesson. Thus, specific warm-ups may occur at appropriate times throughout a lesson, not only at its beginning.

In the competitive phase, coaches sometimes allow gymnasts to warm-up by themselves. Independent warm-up sessions do not promote positive emotions, however, and gymnasts tend to stray away from the gymnastic style. For instance, they do not point their toes, bend their knees, or the like. A coach should take these disadvantages into account when planning the lesson. Finally, remember, in the competitive phase, gymnasts should only perform truly mastered elements as part of their warm-ups.

The warm-up for beginners plays an especially important role. Its objectives are to form motor culture, body posture, and to teach simple elements. Therefore, the warm-up session must be longer for them than for elite gymnasts. Thus, a coach should pay more attention to the planning of exercises in the warm-up session as they play a vital role in preparing young gymnasts. Individual independent warm-ups are definitely not advisable at this stage.

Main Phase

The coach, as a rule, should be guided by the following principles when planning the main part of a lesson.

Technical Development

Work on meeting the objectives of technical development at the start of the main part of a lesson, when the gymnast's body is at optimum training readiness to learn new elements and to polish mastered elements.

Join Interconnected Objectives

If there are several interconnected objectives, follow this sequence. First, have the gymnast perfect techniques of elements, connections, and compositions and develop her speed abilities. Then concentrate on developing coordination abilities. Third, the gymnast should work to develop strength and power abilities. Finally, she should train to develop her endurance abilities.

The heavy training loads in a lesson should be in the middle of the main part of a lesson and gradually lessen toward the end.

Depending on the objectives set and the training state of the gymnast in the main part of a lesson, a coach may schedule a large number of exercises with a few apparatus. There are different ways to alternate apparatus exercises. For example:

- One or two apparatus—practice elements, connections, and compositions or practice the composition only.
- Two or three apparatus—practice elements, connections, and compositions.
- Two to four apparatus—practice elements and connections only or practice connections and compositions only or practice compositions only.
- Four apparatus—practice compositions and selected elements, especially in the competitive phase.

There are different ways to alter the apparatus and the related dynamics:

- Rope, ball, hoop—the training load has inconsistent dynamics, as usually compositions with the rope are more dynamic, the ball is much slower, and the hoop has an average tempo.
- Clubs, hoop, rope—the training load gradually increases dynamics.
- Ball, ribbon, hoop—the training load increases dynamics very little.

How does a coach choose which order will work best? It is best to have the gymnast practice with the apparatus that is most difficult for her first. Moreover, she should practice with the apparatus first for several lessons while learning new elements, connections, and compositions at a rapid pace. Then how a coach alternates exercises when planning precompetitive lessons should depend on the program of competitions.

A coach should plan lessons in such a way that a gymnast is constantly acquiring new elements. It will allow her to renew her motor reserves and replace less difficult elements with more difficult ones in future competitive compositions. It will also help improve the quality of the elements she has already mastered. Continuous acquisition of new difficult elements allows the gymnast to perfect old ones.

It is true that only by repeating a composition many times can a gymnast perform it easily and elegantly. In a preparatory phase, other than acquiring elements and connections, the gymnast should execute a competitive composition solely to develop specific endurance. Gymnasts who do not repeat competitive compositions will lose or fail to gain specific endurance. Therefore, we recommend that a gymnast gradually increase the number of compositions she performs in training. This will ensure that she will have the necessary specific endurance in the competitive phase. An analysis of training loads of the RSG Russian national team in the competitive phase has shown that gymnasts repeated compositions 16 to 30 times per lesson with two or four apparatus.

If the main part of a lesson includes a heavy training load, gymnasts may suffer from various problems, such as pain in the muscles, liver (right side), spleen (left side), and Achilles tendon. In such cases, the coach should reduce the intensity, extend the rest intervals, and move on to the cool-down.

Cool-Down

After a heavy training load, a lesson should not end abruptly with passive rest. Instead, a gymnast should experience active rest, which is exercising for relaxation. This is a good time to work on flexibility when the muscles are already warm. Working on flexibility also allows the cardiovascular and musculoskeletal systems to recover. At this time, it is very important to analyze the results of the lesson. The coaches should discuss the positive and negative sides of the lesson and outline the objectives for upcoming lessons.

Summary

Planning is essential for successful coaching of RSG. Plans should be goal-oriented, and should include short- and long-term planning, upcoming competitions, and warm-up and cool-down phases. Periods of rest and non-sport specific training should be included as part of the gymnast's training to keep the gymnast interested and motivated.

In the next chapter, we will look at the influence dance has on RSG, and how mastery of dance skills can help a gymnast reach the elite level of her sport.

Eva Serrano

Eva Serrano, a member of the SM Orléans rhythmic gymnastics club, began training when she was eight years old. Guided by her coaches Atanassova Kostadinka and Mladenova el Snéjana, Eva trains 25 hours a week.

After a sixth place finish in the all-around competition at the 1996 Olympics in Atlanta, Georgia, USA, Eva made an impressive showing at the 1997 European Championships. She tied for second in both the rope and the ribbon, tied for fourth in the hoop, tied for fifth in the clubs, and placed fourth in the all-around with a final score of 39.623. At the 1997 21st World Championships in Berlin, Eva placed third in both hoop and ribbon, fifth in rope, and seventh in the all-around.

Born April 22, 1978, in Nimes, France, Eva lives and trains in Orléans, France.

© Steve Lange

Chapter 9

Dance

A successful gymnast must be able to pull the audience into her performance, involving them in the beauty and poetry of her composition. Dance elements link the technical aspects of a performance to the music, allowing the gymnast to reach out to the audience with the full effect of her personality.

In this chapter, we will examine the technical and artistic elements of dance, discuss the importance of classical ballet drills and their methods, and review common dance steps borrowed from classical ballet, traditional folk dances, and modern dances.

Artistic Impression

The ability to make a good artistic impression is one of the important attributes a gymnast must acquire. Aesthetics, in this case, perfect movements, help her elicit the desired emotions from spectator and judge alike. Aesthetics encompasses the "school" of her body movements (gymnastic style: pointed toes, straightened knees, clean body lines; see discussion in chapter 2), her ability to maintain static and dynamic balances, and the relationship between her movements and the music.

Perfect aesthetics colors compositions with emotion, making them expressive. Specifically, its role is crucial to interpreting the musical accompaniment—not only to emphasize its rhythm but also to project its emotional character and reflect its subtle nuances.

Technical Mastery

How closely related are aesthetics to technical mastery? This question is difficult. Some RSG experts believe that aesthetics are a component of technical mastery. Others believe that aesthetics and technical mastery are equal components of sport mastery. Indeed, it is possible for the gymnast who possesses a lower degree of technical mastery to make a good artistic impression. Likewise, many gymnasts possess a high degree of technical mastery especially in handling apparatus, but are very short on artistic impression.

A gymnast makes a good artistic impression by executing the detailed, sometimes almost imperceptible, technique of an element, "adorning" its performance. For example, a slight change in the angle of the elbow produces a much softer line. Light movements of the hands or the head slightly turned with the chin raised change the impression of the element. Thus, artistic impression determines the aesthetics of the composition.

Certainly, aesthetics depend on technical mastery. If a gymnast must concentrate on performing difficult elements, she cannot think about the details of technique. She must possess technical mastery to go beyond the basics to create a good artistic impression. Naturally, aesthetics is of prime importance for elite gymnasts.

In practice, however, coaches tend to focus too much on aesthetics, thereby limiting the perfection of technical mastery. Still, coaches should build lessons developing aesthetics into every gymnast's program, because insufficiently developed aesthetics hinders the growth of sport mastery. There are three reasons for this: the more elite a gymnast, the greater the demands on aesthetics; the details of element technique are indirectly influenced by aesthetics, including correct body posture, straightened knees, and pointed toes, which all help to stabilize the execution of an element; and graceful movements mean good muscular coordination, meaning "unnecessary" muscles are not used involuntarily.

Dance Preparation

Dance preparation in RSG refers to a system of exercises and methods for using dance, directed toward forming the gymnast's artistic impression as she increases her range of expressive techniques. Dance preparation is a part of the process of a gymnast's overall preparation and should be linked to other kinds of preparation. Dance lessons cover not only classical movements but also elements of free expressive dance (waves and swaying), exercises to develop flexibility, and practice doing balances, turns and pivots, and jumps and leaps.

To ensure that movements are beautiful, light, graceful, and expressive, it is necessary to borrow many exercises from classical dance. From the very first steps, these exercises teach a gymnast to coordinate her movements as well as develop her feeling of harmony and sense of shape. The gymnast should remember, however, that although she can handle the apparatus faultlessly, ugly poses and poor body posture will spoil the total impression. Only excellent technique and a high degree of aesthetics expertly meshed with the musical accompaniment will make a harmonious composition, indeed, a composition that will reflect the epitome of gymnastic mastery.

Dance lessons are an important means of developing aesthetics and creativity. In fact, during dance lessons a gymnast learns the meaning of art. She learns to understand the beauty of movement and appreciate the ability to express emotions and moods through movement.

The springboard of dance development is classical dance, which teaches a gymnast to produce clean movements and correct body and leg positions. Still, experts disagree on the precise content of dance preparation appropriate for RSG. Dance lessons can be based on classical, folk, historical, and modern dances and expressive movements. Moreover, it is possible to base the lessons on jazz, modern, rock 'n' roll, or other dances. The actual selection by the ballet master in consultation with the coach depends on the level of development of the gymnast and the goals of the lessons.

Still, because the basic requirements of RSG body movements depend on the principles of classical dance, they should be the primary foundation for dance development in RSG. Mastering the basics of classical dance helps a gymnast progress to elements of folk, historical, and modern dances. Moreover, mixing elements of classical and other dances at the barre does not produce good results. The exercises at the barre should carefully respect and preserve all positions of the arms and the legs. For example, the most efficient positioning of the arms and legs during a warm-up is with the feet and thighs turned out.

At the same time, it is impossible to shift canons of classical dance to gymnastics. In RSG, interpretation of the positions of the arms and the legs in the center can be more free than at the barre. Thus, dance lessons should acquaint gymnasts with the classical positions of the arms, but rigidly imposing these habits upon RSG movements is not necessary because they stiffen the shoulders. Yet, because of its importance to RSG, we will look at classical dance in more detail before examining other types of dance.

Classical Dance

The poise and discipline that classical dance training brings to RSG are invaluable. The most important aspects of classical dance are the drills used to teach the components of ballet. A classical drill consists of exercises from classical dance at and away from the barre.

Rationale for Using Classical Drills in RSG

The following are the primary reasons to use classical drills to help train a gymnast:

- To form habits that relate to the gymnastic style, including pointed toes and extended knees.
- To teach the gymnast to turn out her legs.
- To instill the correct body posture, that is, a straight trunk.
- To encourage expressiveness through fluidity and coordination of movements.
- To master practical dance habits.

By systematically practicing classical drills, gymnasts will be able to gain specific classical aesthetics.

When performing elements of body movements in RSG, a gymnast should turn out her legs in a certain way (figure 2.2a, page 13). Specifically, originating with the thighs (not the toes), the inner sides of her feet, shins, and thighs must be turned outward for both aesthetic and functional reasons. Indeed, this position will create the impression of completeness in a movement or pose. Moreover, this position encourages the gymnast to move with a greater amplitude, increases the support area, and assists body stability. In addition, this position distributes the weight of the body evenly on both legs and feet. Meanwhile, the gymnast presses her fingers firmly toward the floor and keeps her knees extremely straight.

A gymnast must work on turning out her legs before she turns 12, which is when development of the shins and feet finishes. What, then, affects turn-out? It depends on three main factors: construction of the hips, elasticity of the ligaments fixing the femur in the socket in the pelvis, and construction of the legs. Depth and placement of the sockets are the most important aspects of the construction of the hips. The turning out of the head of the femur is better if the depth of the socket is smaller. It is also better if the sockets are placed more toward the sides of the pelvis than toward its front. Moreover, if the ligaments that fix the femur in the socket have good flexibility, the turn-out possibilities are also better.

The ligaments of the knees influence leg turn-out as well. If these ligaments are more elastic the turn-out position will be good. In RSG, many gymnasts can turn out their hips well but not their knees and feet. But if a gymnast's hips turn out well, it is possible to help her turn out her legs better if her knees and feet will not turn out well. How? Classical drills are the best means.

Classical Drills

When performing any classical drill, the gymnast should stand with her body tightened, her buttock and leg muscles braced, her shoulders lowered and moved a little backward, her head erect, and her neck muscles relaxed.

Leg and Arm Positions

According to the Russian school of ballet, leg positions for classical drills include the following (figure 9.1):

- First position: the heels are together, the toes are turned outward, and the feet form a straight line.
- Second position: the heels are apart by about the length of one of the gymnast's feet and body weight is distributed equally between both feet.
- Third position: one foot is in front of the other with the heel of the front foot against the instep of the back foot.
- Fourth position: the foot at the back is now parallel to the other foot and further behind.
- Fifth position: one foot is in front of the other, and the heel of the front foot is aligned with and touches the toes of the back foot, and vice versa.

It is better for a beginner not to turn out her leg to a full first position. Thus, we recommend that a gymnast start learning leg positions with a first half-turned-out position. This means that the gymnast places her feet as far as apart as she can to create good stability. To do so, first she faces the barre and places her left leg in the first half-turning out position, her feet forming more of a V rather than a straight line. Then she places her hands on the barre and turns out her left leg halfway, keeping her trunk vertical. She turns out her shoulders and lowers her shoulder blades, keeping her head erect. Meanwhile she braces her thigh, shin, buttock, and back muscles. She places her feet lightly on the floor, pressing down her heels and little and big toes. The gymnast must remember how her muscles feel in this pose.

Once a gymnast has acquired the first half-turning out position, she is ready to learn the first position. To do so, she stands in the half-turning out position, facing the barre. Next, she turns out her left leg to the first position and then her right leg.

Remember, when a gymnast stands in any leg position, she must turn out her thighs and shins as far as possible. Her body weight should be distributed over the support area.

Figure 9.2 shows the arm positions from classical drills according to the Russian school of ballet. All arm positions are variations of these three main arm positions and the one preparatory arm position.

In every arm position, the gymnast must hold her fingers loosely, without tension. She should bend her elbows slightly, and her middle fingers should be near her thumbs (figure 2.2e, page 13). She should bend her wrist slightly, forming a

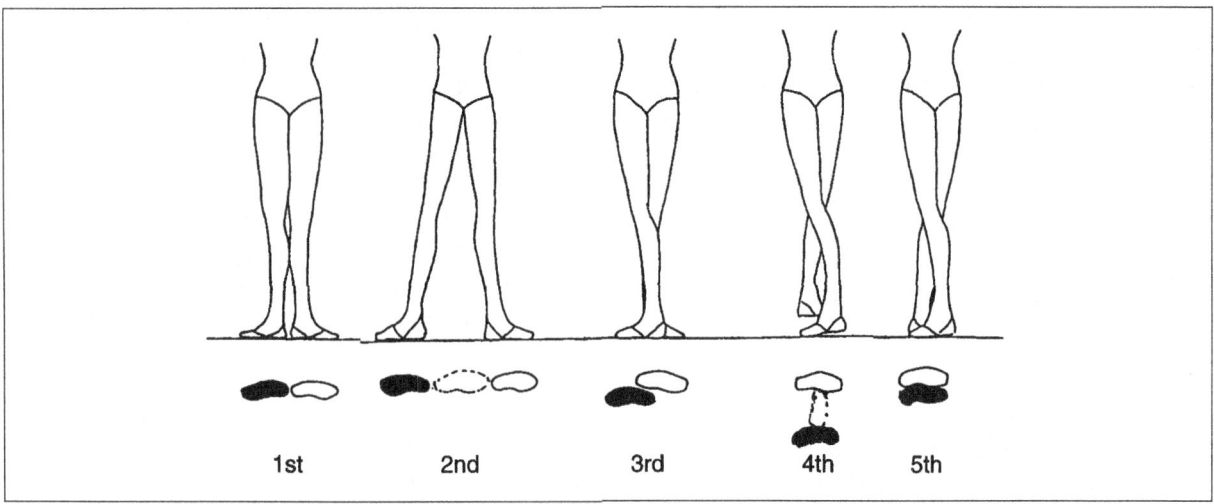

Figure 9.1 Classical drill leg positions according to the Russian ballet school.

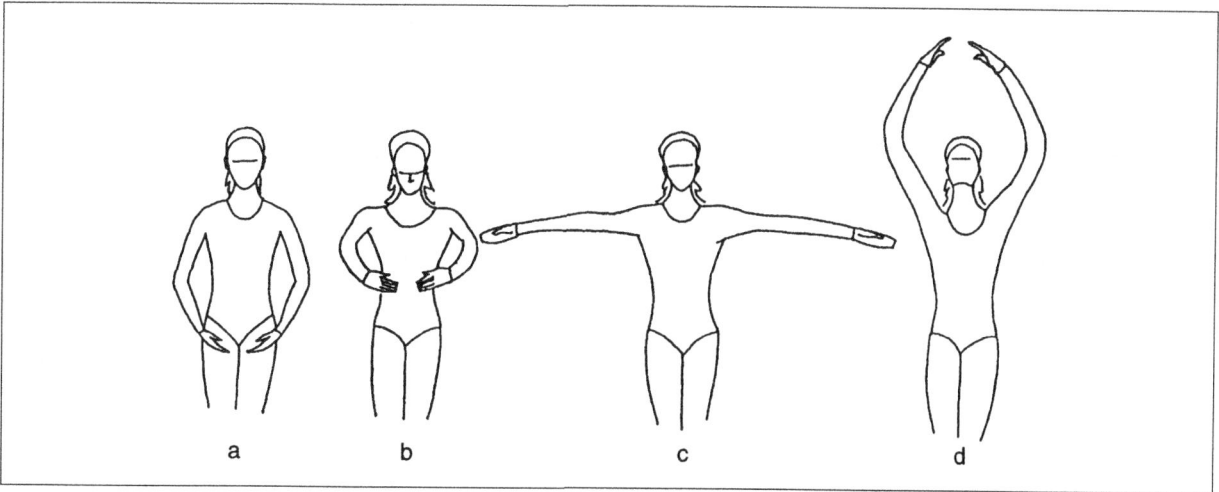

Figure 9.2 Classical drill arm positions: (a) preparatory, (b) first, (c) second, (d) third, according to Russian ballet school.

rounded line from her shoulders to her fingertips. In each of the following paragraphs, we will describe what a gymnast's arms should be doing for each position.

Preparatory Position The arms are lowered and rounded into an oval. The elbows are bent slightly and held at the side, and the palms are turned upward to continue the oval shape. The palms do not touch each other. The arms should not touch the trunk except where joined at the armpit (see figure 9.2a).

First Position The arms are slightly rounded into an oval and raised in front of the body up to the diaphragm. The elbows and hands are slightly raised. The fingertips of the hands are three to five centimeters apart. The shoulders are lowered, not forward or upward. The muscles of the upper arms should be braced. The fingers are poised and rounded (see figure 9.2b).

Second Position Slightly rounded arms are extended to the sides with a soft line beginning from the shoulders and ending at the fingers. The muscles of the upper arms should be braced. The fingers are a little below the shoulders, slightly away from the trunk, and the palms face each other. The shoulders should not be moved forward or upward. The shoulder blades must be lowered (see figure 9.2c).

Third Position Rounded arms are raised upward, and the hands are slightly apart, but the fingers are not joined. The palms are turned downward and the arms are bent forward, and the gymnast should be able to see them without raising her head. The elbows should be directly above the shoulders, a little bit higher than the ears (see figure 9.2d).

Another important aspect of arm positions involves properly moving the arms from one position to another. For example, to move the arms from the preparatory position to the first position, the gymnast assumes the starting position by standing in the first half-turned-out leg position with her arms straightened downward without touching her trunk. She first performs the preparatory arm position and then lifts her arms to the first position. She should raise her hands and elbows simultaneously, keeping her shoulders motionless. In the first position, her elbows should be rounded more than in the preparatory position, placed in front of the diaphragm. Her trunk should be relaxed and her shoulders lowered. Then she should lower her arms back to the starting position without tension. The coach should check to ensure that the gymnast's arms and hands are not tense and that her elbows and wrists are not lowered.

We recommend that the gymnast learn arm positions in the following sequence: preparatory, then first, third, second, and, finally, moving from one to another and lowering to the starting position.

Exercises at the Barre

A gymnast must perform classical ballet exercises at the barre according to a systematic plan. For example, the exercises move progressively from the simple to the difficult. In addition, each exercise is repeated several times. Furthermore, the exercises are designed so that each leg performs the exercises progressively. First, the gymnast uses her right leg to perform the exercise in three directions: forward, sideways, and backward, and then sideways again. This is called *crossing*. Then the gymnast repeats the process with her left leg. This is done so that the gymnast learns to coordinate her movements with the musical accompaniment, that is, to finish it on 4, 8, or 16 bars. For example, if the gymnast executes the movement four times each forward, sideways, backward, and sideways, the total is 16 movements, which the gymnast can perform in 32 counts. Therefore the coach needs 8 bars in 4/4 time. The movements should start and end with the music. Thus, we recommend that the gymnast always perform the classical drill exercises with musical accompaniment in the order shown in table 9.1.

The appendix (page 245) includes additional exercises at the barre of various levels of difficulty for beginners and more experienced gymnasts. A similar combination of simple and difficult exercises is ideal as a warm-up session for gymnasts before they move on to difficult RSG elements. Therefore, coaches should set aside 20 to 30 minutes at the start of each training lesson for this purpose.

Almost all classical ballet movements or combinations of such movements are preceded by preparatory exercises. "Preparation" is done on two beats during two bars of 2/4 time. At this point, the gymnast lifts her free arm forward and sideways and moves her supporting leg in a sideways arch with pointed toes.

In this section, we will describe in detail several drills performed at the barre. Then, in the next section, we will discuss drills performed without a barre.

The support (the ballet barre) consists of two special bars that the gymnast uses to support herself with her arms. The lath should be round and 5 to 6 centimeters in diameter. The lower bar is 65 centimeters high and the upper bar is 85 centimeters high. In the absence of a ballet barre, the following exercises can be performed at gymnasium wall bars or old artistic gymnastics bars.

A gymnast should begin exercises at the barre in the following manner (figure 9.3): She faces the barre, supporting herself with both hands or sideways with only one hand on the barre. In either case, it is not necessary to rely totally on the barre for support. Instead, the gymnast should distribute her body weight equally on both feet. When facing the barre, the gymnast should bend both arms slightly at the elbows; her hands should be on the barre, shoulder-width apart, slightly higher than her waist.

When standing sideways to the barre, one arm (the "support arm") is bent slightly at the elbow and supported on the barre at a level slightly higher than the waist and away from the body. The other arm (the "free arm") may be in any arm position. Before

TABLE 9.1

Performance Order of Classical Drill Exercises at the Barre

Exercise order	Purpose
1. *Relevé* and *plié*	Helps prepare the foot and knee muscles for practicing other movements
2. *Battement tendu* (various versions)	Uses small and large muscles of the legs
3. *Battement tendu jeté*	Uses small and large muscles of the legs
4. *Rond de jambe par terre* (often in conjunction with *port de bras*)	Improves hip flexibility
5. *Battement fondu*	Muscles switch from smooth to abrupt movement
6. *Battement frappé*	Muscles switch from smooth to abrupt movement
7. Stretching exercises	Develops hip and knee flexibility
8. *Rond de jambe en l'air*	Develops hip and knee flexibility
9. *Battement développé, relevé lent*	Develops hip flexibility, improves thigh muscle strength, and stabilizes balance
10. *Grand battement jeté*	Develops hip flexibility
11. Jumps and leaps	Develops springiness

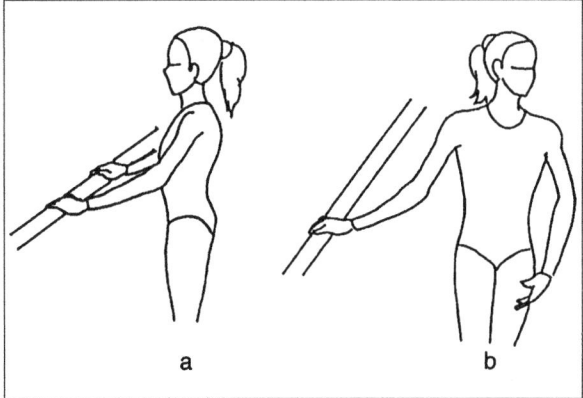

Figure 9.3 Position at the barre: (a) facing the barre, (b) sideways.

starting an exercise, the gymnast should bring her free arm to the necessary position, usually the second position. Next, she moves her arm from the preparatory position to the first position, then returns it to the second position.

The leg nearest the barre is called the "supporting leg" while the other leg is the "working (or free) leg." During classical drills the gymnast must shift her body weight onto her supporting leg while her working leg moves. If her left hand is on the barre, she mostly moves her right leg, and vice versa. Always keeping one side to the barre, the gymnast alternates using her right and left legs.

In addition, for some exercises, it is possible for a gymnast to stand with her back to the barre while raising her working leg forward, for example, *battement fondu*, *battement frappé*, *battement développé*, *battement relevé lent*, and the like. With her back to the barre, the gymnast places her hands on the barre with her elbows slightly bent.

In each of the following sections, we will describe specific exercises performed at the barre. All exercises at the barre are divided into rises (*relevés*), squats (*pliés*), removal and return of the working leg (*battement*), and arched movements of the working leg either on the floor or in the air (*rond de jambe*).

Relevé *Relevé* means rising on the toes (the high stand on toes; see chapter 2). The gymnast must stand on her toes, pressing the floor equally with her big, second, and third toes when facing the barre. She must distribute her body weight equally between both legs. The projection of her center of gravity must pass between her heels, placing it on the middle of the support area. She must turn out her legs, keeping her knees straight. She must tighten her buttock and trunk muscles. Meanwhile, she must keep her trunk vertical and her hands lying relaxed on the barre. After touching her knees to each other, she should lower her heels quietly.

We recommend that the novice start by learning the low stand on toes in first position, facing the barre, then move on to the high stand. In this way, the gymnast will learn to hold her legs in the turned-out position.

Pliés **(Squats)** These exercises involve the bending of one or both knees. There are two kinds of *pliés*, the *demi-plié*, or half-bending of the knees, and the *grand plié*, or full bending of the knees. In *pliés* the body weight must be evenly distributed on both feet. *Pliés* are important to the gymnast because she must use them before and after all jumps and leaps. *Pliés* enable her to reach greater heights in her jumps and leaps.

Demi-pliés (figure 9.4) are performed by half-bending the knees, hips, and ankles without lifting the heels from the floor. The gymnast distributes her weight equally between both feet without fully supporting herself on her large toes. She keeps her knees and feet in the turn-out position and her spine straight at all times. The knees must be above the middle of the feet. The shoulders and knees are in one vertical line. The back muscles must be braced. All leg positions require *demi-plié*. The gymnast has to focus on executing this exercise softly, with no jerky movements, and nonstop. We recommend that the gymnast study the *grand plié* only after she can perform the *demi-plié* perfectly.

A *grand plié* (figure 9.5) consists of two parts: a *demi-plié*, for which a gymnast presses her heels to the floor, and total bending, for which the gymnast raises her heels off the floor gradually and smoothly, keeping her heels on the floor as long as possible. Then she returns her legs to the starting position. However, when a gymnast performs a *grand plié* in second position, her heels stay pressed to the floor. In the second position the gymnast does not raise her heels from the floor because she can bend her knees with her heels remaining where they are. So, she raises her heels off the floor in the first, third, fourth, and fifth positions. It is necessary to keep the heels on the floor for as long as possible. Meanwhile, the gymnast must turn her thighs and knees out to the sides maximally and always maintain this position. When she is straightening her legs, she must place her heels on the floor as early as possible. In addition, she must ensure that her body weight is evenly distributed, not placed on her large toes. Finally, she must brace her back muscles, especially her lower

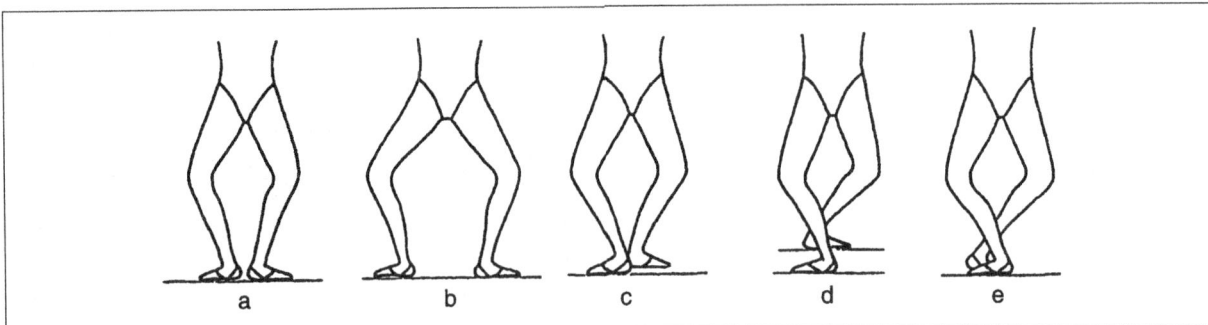

Figure 9.4 *Demi-pliés*: (a) first, (b) second, (c) third, (d) fourth, (e) fifth.

Figure 9.5 *Grand plié* in (a) first and (b) second positions.

back. We recommend starting to teach the *plié* from the *demi-plié*, then the *grand-plié* in third position, then the fifth, then the fourth and second positions.

Gymnasts may have trouble with their buttocks moving backward when executing the *grand plié*. This is because of insufficient turn-out in the coxofemoral joints of the hips. The coach should focus on the tension of the buttock and thigh muscles. At the same time, the coach should also check that the position of the buttocks is directly above the heels and the knees are above the toes. The mistake occurs when the heels are raised off the floor when executing the second position. This is due to insufficient flexibility of the ligaments and muscles in the back of the calf. Therefore, it is advisable to fix the heels on the floor at the lowest point of the movement. The gymnast should work to develop flexibility in her ankle and calf and concentrate on keeping her body weight equally on her toes and her heels. If this is a problem, we recommend that the coach exclude, for the time being, exercises in the second, fourth, and fifth position. Instead, the gymnast should perform the *grand plié* in the first and third positions, for which she must turn out her legs as far as possible.

Battement This type of exercise involves moving and returning the working leg. These core movements will train the gymnast to turn out her legs. Specifically, *battement* assists in developing flexibility in the ankle, strengthening the Achilles tendons as well as the calf and the foot muscles, developing insteps (points and arches), and improving strength and springiness of the legs. There are many types of *battement*, each having a shape and particular name.

Battement tendu simple (figure 9.6) is the most fundamental *battement* (*tendu* means stretched). In this movement, the gymnast moves her working leg forward, sideways, and backward while pointing her toes. When practicing the *battement tendu* starting in first, third, and fifth positions, the working leg moves smoothly with a sliding movement and then closes back to the starting position. At first, a gymnast should slide her leg on her entire foot, but gradually she should learn to lift her heel from the floor. Then, she should use a similar sliding movement to move her leg back into the starting position. She must concentrate on maintaining the turn-out position from the groin of the working leg and keeping her knees straight. The gymnast should shift her body weight onto her supporting leg while simultaneously moving her working leg. Meanwhile, her trunk should be vertical, not turned toward her working leg, and her shoulders should be lowered and her abdomen drawn in.

We recommend that a gymnast start by learning *battement tendu* sideways from the first position, facing the barre. Then, the coach should teach the gymnast the exercise forward, sideways, and backward from the third position and later from the first position, forward and backward, facing the barre. After learning to perform the *battement tendu* perfectly, a gymnast may learn to perform it from the fifth position sideways to the barre.

At the last point of movement, the gymnast should raise off her heel as high as possible, turning it forward, when practicing the *battement tendu* sideways. She tightens her working leg, which is turned

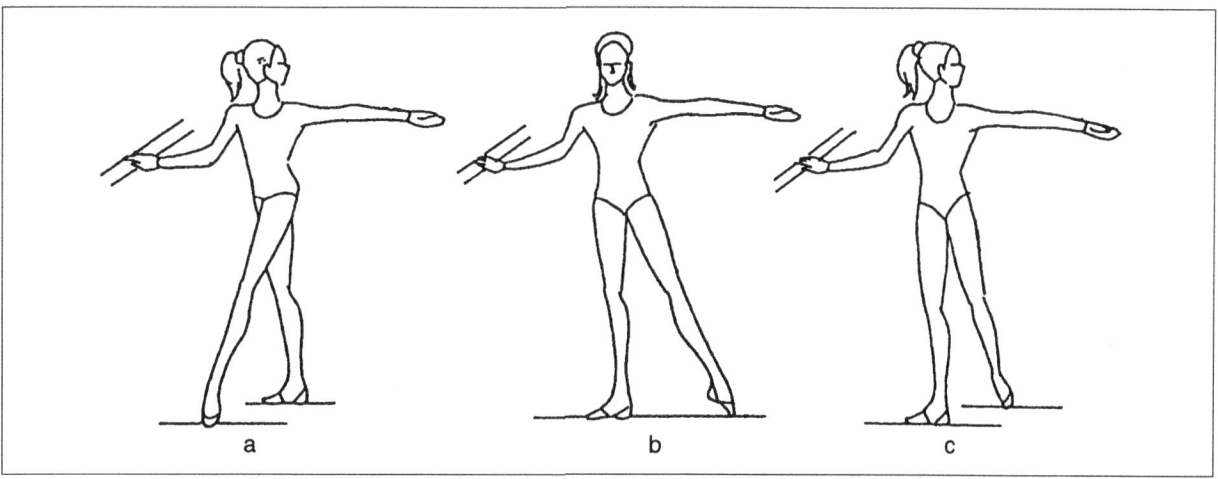

Figure 9.6 *Battement tendu simple*: (a) forward, (b) sideways, and (c) backward.

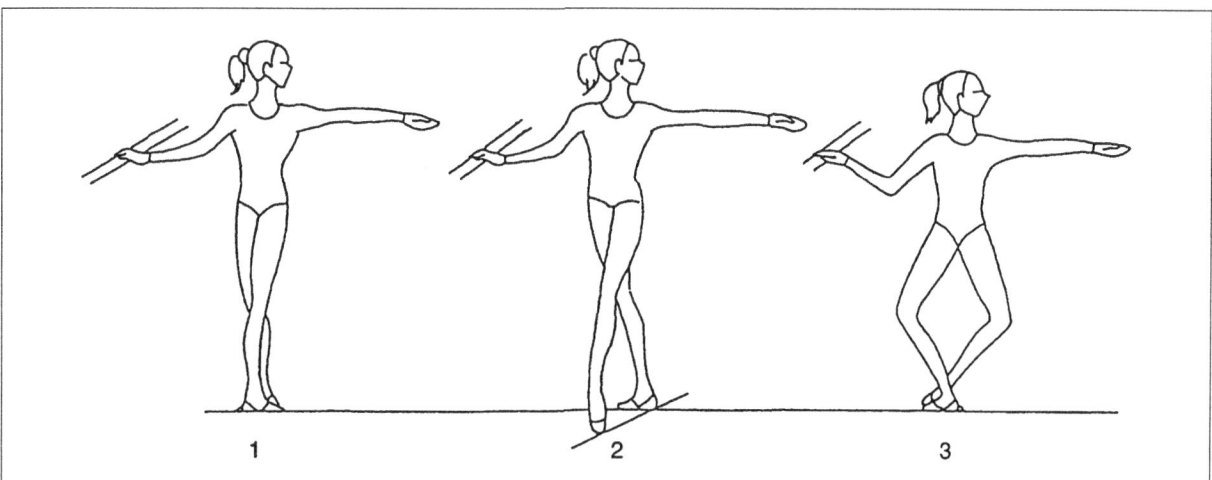

Figure 9.7 *Battement tendu demi-plié*: (1) starting position, (2) *battement tendu* forward, (3) fifth position, *demi-plié*.

out from her groin, with her knee drawn in. The coach should check to see that the gymnast does not press her toes on the floor and does not bend her leg.

When practicing the *battement tendu* forward, the gymnast slides the heel of her working leg first and then slowly lifts it upward. At the last point of the movement, she must place her pointed toes opposite the heel of her supporting leg.

The difficulties in performing the *battement tendu simple* include transferring the body weight onto the working leg, flexing the knee and raising it off the floor without a sliding movement, and moving the point of the working leg sideways while performing a movement forward and backward. To solve this problem, we recommend that in the final part of the movement the gymnast lift her leg from the floor a little with her toes pointed. In this case, it is best for the coach to slow the tempo of the movement and start the gymnast facing the barre from the third position. To help the gymnast understand, the coach should draw lines on the floor for the gymnast to follow.

Battement tendu demi-plié (see figure 9.7) is a smooth combination of the *battement tendu simple* and the *demi-plié*. The bending of the knees in *demi-plié* begins slightly before the working leg is closed back into the starting position. The working leg is slid on pointed toes as in the *battement tendu*. Then the heel is lowered and pressed to the floor, aligning it with the toes. If she moves her working leg forward or backward, the gymnast can perform the *demi-plié* in fourth position. She can practice a *demi-plié* in second position if she moves her working leg sideways. In any case, the gymnast must shift her body weight onto both legs first, and after finishing the *demi-plié*, she must shift her body weight back to her supporting leg.

Double battement tendu (figure 9.8) is another version of the *battement tendu simple*. This movement is executed by lowering the heel of the working leg on the floor after moving onto pointed toes. While lowering her heel, the gymnast keeps her body weight on her supporting leg. She must lower her heel with an "accent" and immediately straighten her working leg and point her toes. After she performs this *battement tendu simple*, she closes her working leg to the starting position.

Battement frappé (figure 9.9) involves bending and extending the working leg to a 45-degree angle. This movement consists of bending the knee of the working leg to make quick contact with the front or back of the ankle of the supporting leg and then immediately extending the working leg.

Battement frappé is executed abruptly and strongly. It begins with a starting position where the working leg is positioned at the side, on or above the floor. So, before the start of this movement, the gymnast opens her working leg from the starting position to the side with pointed toes. She lifts her free arm from the preparatory position into the second through the first positions.

We recommended that a gymnast begin to learn the *battement frappé* at a slow tempo from the first, then the third, and, finally, the fifth position. The coach should check that the working leg makes contact with the supporting leg energetically without stopping, then immediately extends to the starting position. Both legs must be turned out from the groin. The trunk and supporting leg should be straight, tight, and motionless.

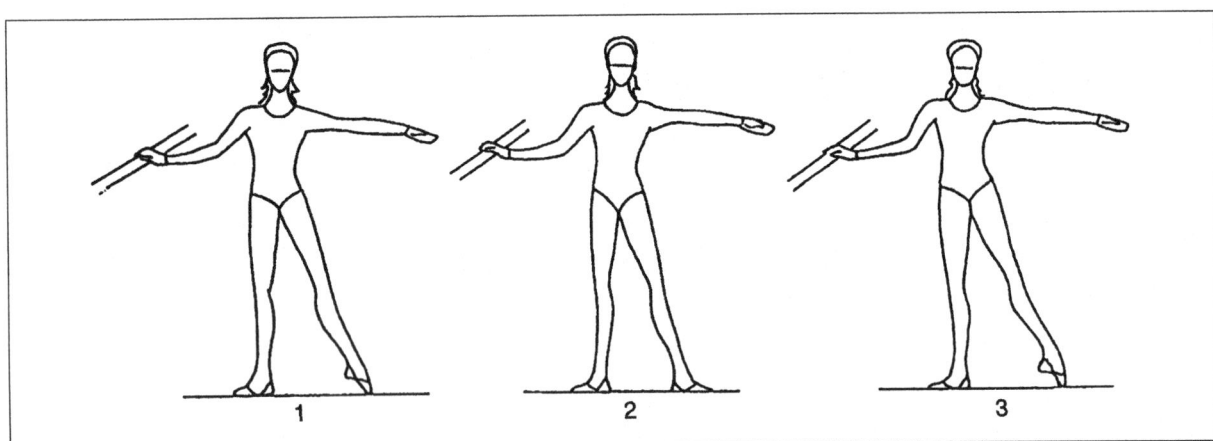

Figure 9.8 *Double battement tendu*: (1) *battement tendu*, (2) second position, (3) *battement tendu*.

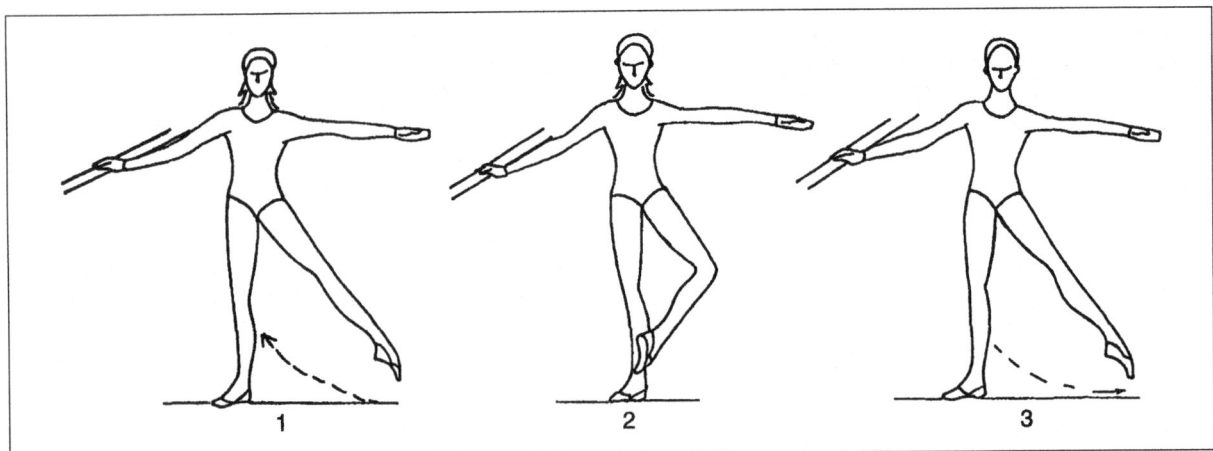

Figure 9.9 *Battement frappé* sideways: (1) moving the working leg sideways and downward, (2) *sur le cou-de-pied* in front, (3) straightening the working leg sideways and downward.

A related position for which the working leg is bent at the ankle of the supporting leg is called the *sur le cou-de-pied* (figure 9.10).

There are two kinds of *sur le cou-de-pied*: to the front, for which the toes are in front of the support ankle (figure 9.10a), and to the back, for which the toes are behind the support ankle (figure 9.10b). In both cases, the thigh and the knee of the working leg should be turned out.

We recommend that the gymnast start learning the *battement fondu* after mastering the *sur le cou-de-pied* position.

Battement fondu (figure 9.11), which means smooth *battement*, is a combination of half-bending the supporting leg while simultaneously bending the working leg into a *sur le cou-de-pied* position to the front or back. Then the gymnast extends her working leg and straightens her supporting leg. *Battement fondu* may be practiced forward, sideways, or backward with the toes pointed on the floor or with the working leg at a raised angle of 45 or 90 degrees. When the working leg is bent into the *sur le cou-de-pied* position, the gymnast first flexes her knee but keeps her thigh at an angle of 45 degrees. She then gradually lowers her working thigh together with the shin into the final position. When her supporting leg is half-bent, her knee must be above the middle part of her foot. Meanwhile, she must keep her trunk vertical and tight. When practicing this movement at 90 degrees, the gymnast should first lower her working leg to 45 degrees, next bend her knees, then straighten her working leg and lift it to an angle of 90 degrees.

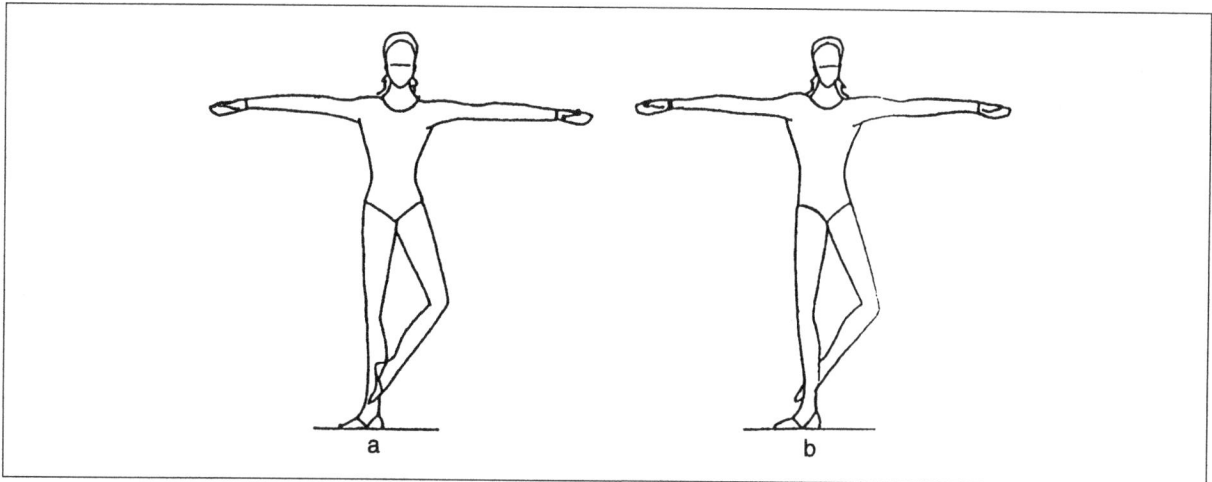

Figure 9.10 *Sur le cou-de-pied*: (a) in front, (b) at the back.

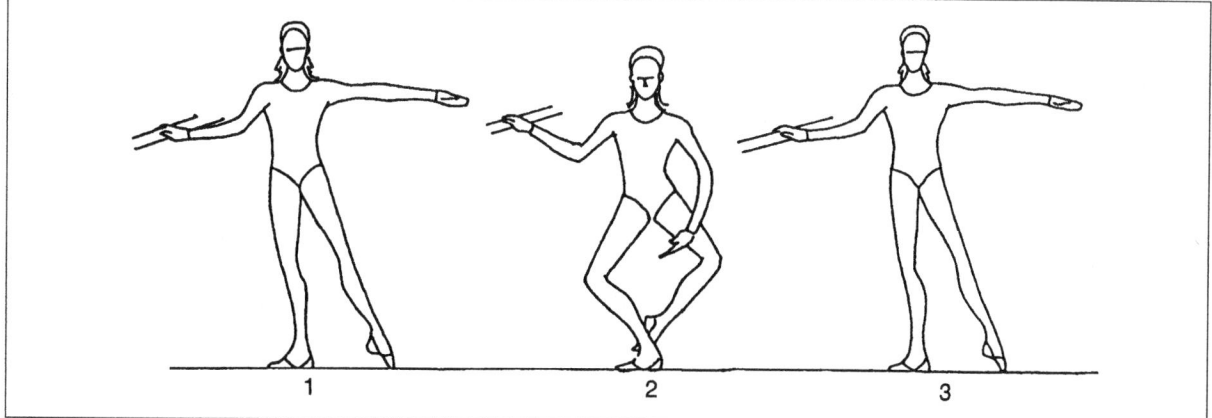

Figure 9.11 *Battement fondu* sideways with pointed toes: (1) moving the working leg sideways into the point, (2) *demi-plié* in *sur le cou-de-pied* at the back, (3) straightening the working leg sideways into the point.

The novice should learn this movement from the first position, facing the barre sideways, forward, and backward. The coach should ensure that the gymnast half-bends her supporting leg and bends her working leg simultaneously, then straightens both legs simultaneously. Finally, the gymnast should focus on turning out her legs as far as possible.

Battement tendu jeté (figure 9.12) involves "throwing" the working leg. This exercise is actually the basis for all swinging exercises. Unlike other *battements*, however, this one is executed by moving the working toes from the floor with a 25- to 45-degree swing. The gymnast may raise her working leg forward, backward, or sideways, using easy sliding movements. The toes of the stretched working leg, which is in the air, should be opposite the heel of the supporting leg. Then the gymnast must place her working leg at the starting position without delay by using her stretched leg to touch the floor vigorously and not relaxing the instep at this point. She must maintain her legs in the turn-out position and support her body weight on the supporting leg.

We recommend that the gymnast start by learning the *battement tendu jeté* beginning from the third and first position, then learn beginning from the fifth position. For each position, the gymnast should learn sideways, then forward, and, finally, backward. This movement should be practiced at a slow tempo, fixing the position of the working leg at the highest point in the air first. The coach should ensure that the working leg moves in the desired direction.

The principle difficulty with the *battement tendu jeté* is the absence of a sliding movement of the working leg in the first part of the exercise. To solve this problem, the gymnast should perform the *battement tendu simple* a few times to warm up.

Battement tendu jeté pointe (figure 9.13) is similar to *battement tendu jeté*, but in this exercise, the working leg is not closed into the first, third, or fifth position, and the toes touch the floor. The gymnast may perform the exercise two to seven times before she closes her working leg back to the starting position.

Grand battement jeté (figure 9.14) involves swinging the working leg forward, sideways, or backward. The gymnast executes this movement through the *battement tendu*, touching the floor with pointed toes. Then she lifts her working leg (leg straightened, toes pointed, and knee drawn in) to its maximum height and uses *battement tendu* again when she closes her leg back to the starting position by lowering it gradually with tight muscles and pointed toes, sliding her toes after touching the floor. The movement should be wide and without tension. Meanwhile, the gymnast should brace both her trunk and her turned-out supporting leg, keeping them motionless.

The gymnast must focus on keeping her trunk vertical when practicing this movement backward. We recommend that a gymnast begin by learning the *grand battement jeté* sideways from the first position facing the barre, then forward, and after this backward. It is better to not lift the leg maximally (not more than 90 degrees) when starting to learn this exercise.

One common difficulty encountered with the *grand battement jeté* backward is that when executing the swing, the gymnast tends to move her work-

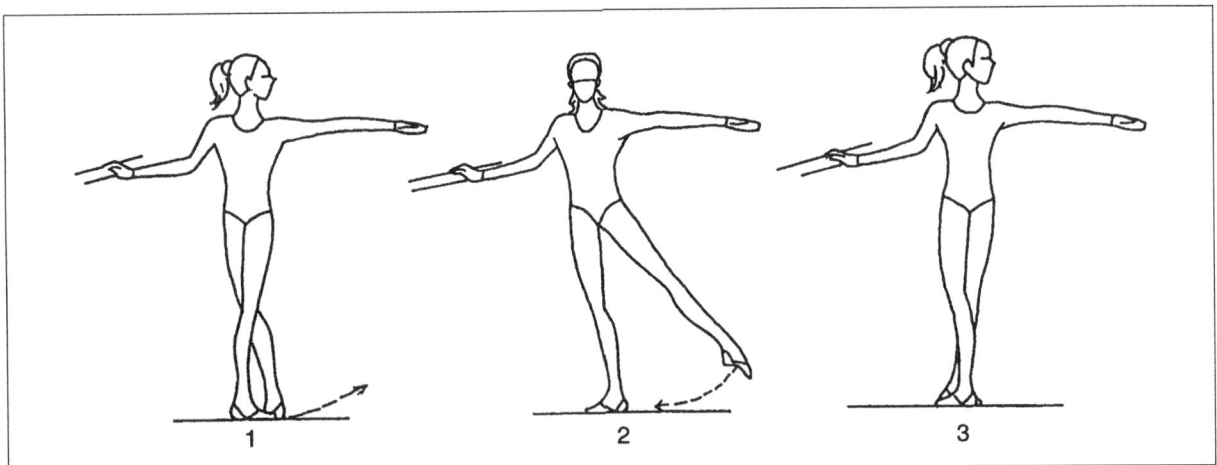

Figure 9.12 *Battement tendu jeté* sideways: (1) starting in fifth position, (2) moving the working leg sideways and downward, (3) starting position.

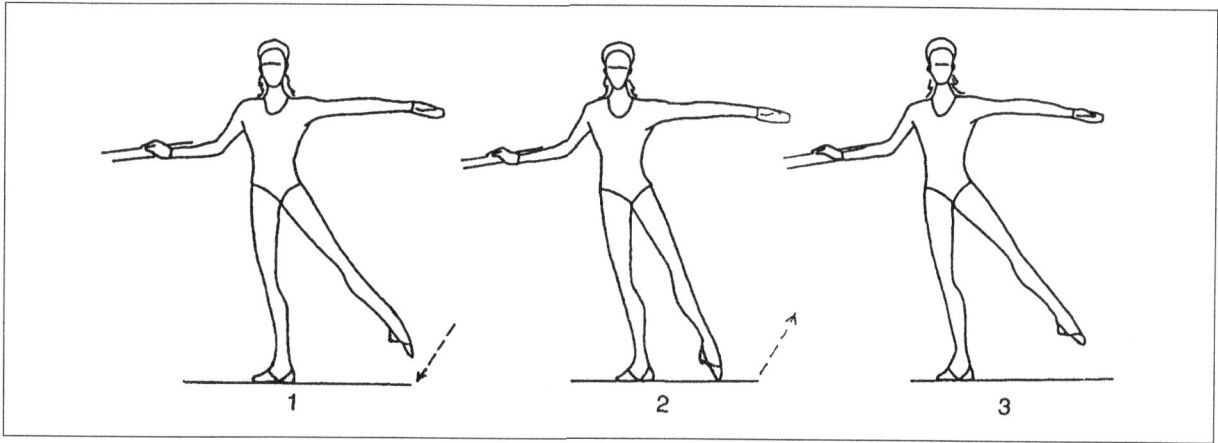

Figure 9.13 *Battement tendu jeté pointe* sideways: (1) move the working leg sideways and downward, (2) touch the toes to the floor, (3) return to the starting position.

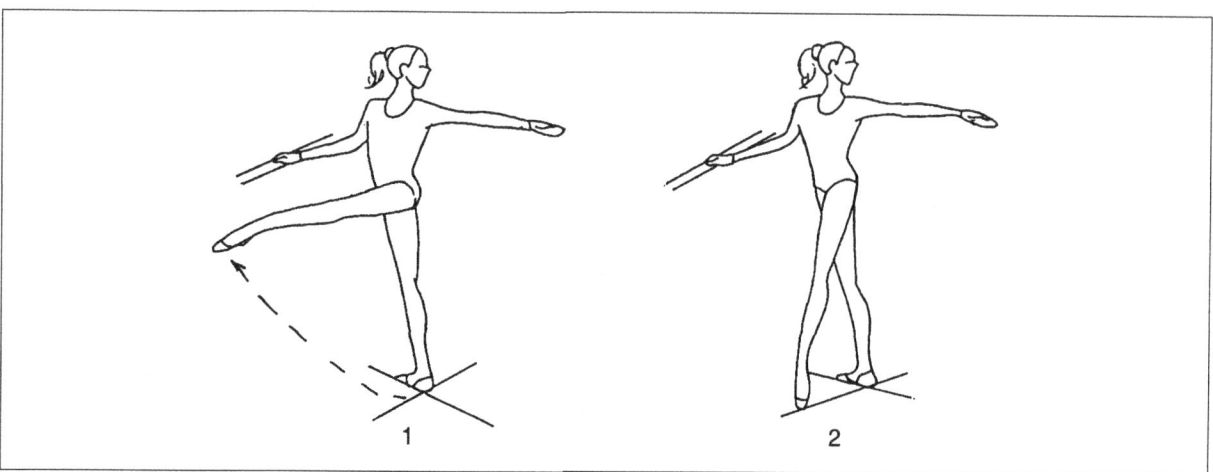

Figure 9.14 *Grand battement jeté* forward: (1) moving the working leg forward and upward, (2) *battement tendu*.

ing leg backward and sideways. To solve this problem, the gymnast should practice *battement tendu* and *grand battement jeté* backward while facing the barre. The second problem is performing the exercise without sliding movements by slightly bending the knee of her working leg. She should practice this movement with a smaller amplitude than usual while focusing on extending and straightening her knee.

Grand battement tendu jeté balance (figure 9.15) refers to swings forward and backward at an angle of 90 degrees or more through the first position.

The *grand battement jeté passé* is similar to *grand battement jeté* except for changing the position of the working leg through *passé*. The *passé* position (figure 9.16) is a position for which the gymnast bends her working leg and turns out her thigh. She should turn her working-leg knee sideways, keeping her toes level with the knee of her supporting leg.

The *grand battement jeté pointe* (figure 9.17) is similar to *grand battement jeté* except that the toes touch the floor (the *pointe*).

Battement développé (figure 9.18) involves a slow rising of the working leg. The gymnast slowly and smoothly slides the toes of her working leg along her supporting leg and up to the middle of the knee into the *passé* position (illustrations 1-2). Meanwhile, the gymnast must keep the thigh and knee of her working leg in line with her shoulders. She next moves her knee slightly upward, and then she straightens her working leg forward, sideways (illustration 3), or backward. Here, she fixes her leg at the desired height and, finally, she slowly lowers it into the starting position (illustration 4). It is very important that she move her leg gradually and finish

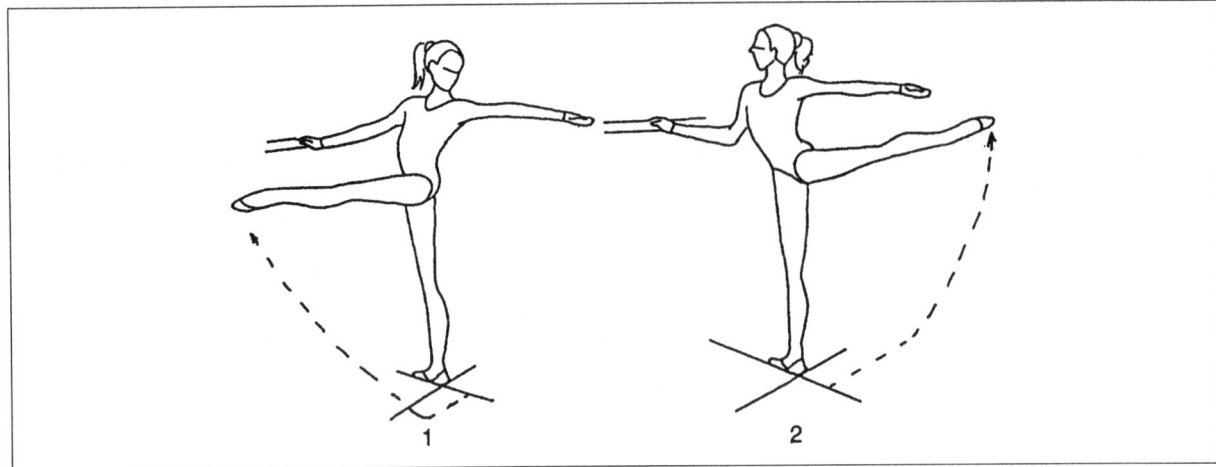

Figure 9.15 *Grand battement tendu jeté* balance: (1) forward, (2) backward.

Figure 9.16 *Passé* position.

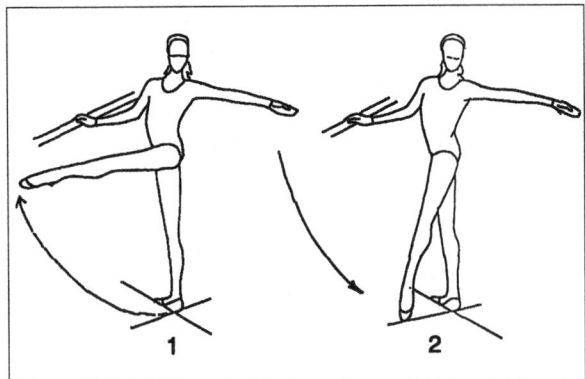

Figure 9.17 *Grand battement jeté pointe* forward: (1) *grand battement jeté*, (2) the working leg with the toes touching the floor.

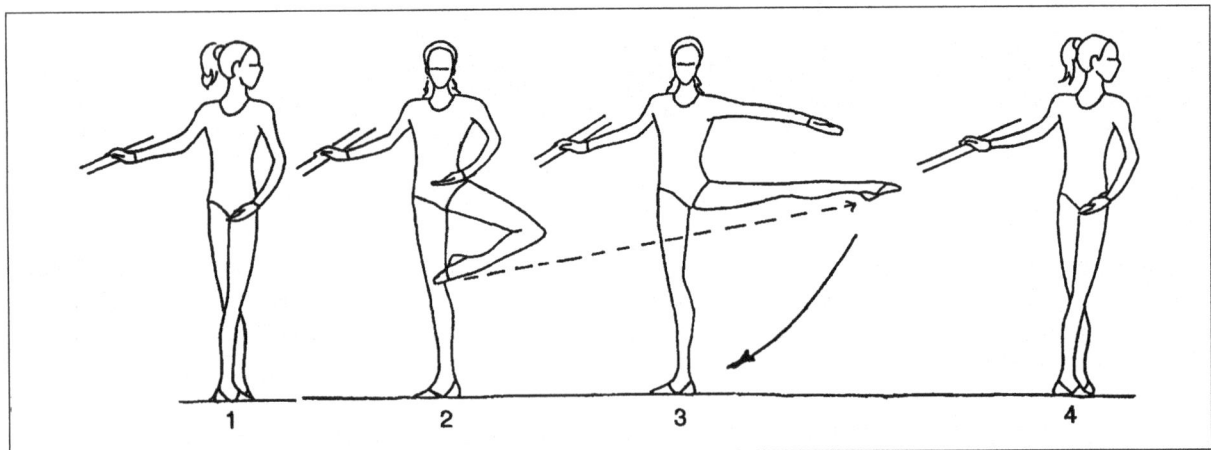

Figure 9.18 *Battement développé* sideways: (1) starting in fifth position, (2) *passé*, (3) *grand battement jeté* sideways, (4) starting position.

with pointed toes. Specifically, the gymnast touches her toes to the floor first and then slides her foot as in the *battement tendu*. Her thighs must be turned out to the maximum. Meanwhile, she must keep her supporting leg straight and immobile, and she must brace her trunk, holding it vertically. This exercise is the basis for *adagio*, for which the gymnast moves slowly and smoothly.

When moving the leg backward through *passé* position, the gymnast directs her thigh backward, raising it up as high as possible. Next, she stretches her working leg backward and fixes its height. Then, she moves her braced trunk slightly forward and returns to the vertical position while lowering her working leg.

We recommend that the novice start by learning the *battement développé* from the third position sideways, forward, and then backward, facing the barre. After this, she may try executing it from the fifth position. It is better if beginners fix the *passé* position while practicing in this exercise. The coach should check that the knee of the supporting leg is turned out and not lowered when the leg has been straightened.

Battement relevé lent is a slow raising of the working leg to an angle of 90 degrees or higher and then lowering it to the starting position. The gymnast slides her working leg forward, sideways, or backward onto pointed toes and then raises it up slowly. It must be braced and turned out. After the gymnast fixes its height, she lowers it, touches the floor with pointed toes, and slides her foot to the starting position. Meanwhile, the gymnast keeps her supporting leg straight and turned out and her trunk braced and vertical.

When practicing *battement relevé lent* backward, the gymnast should move her trunk slightly forward as in *battement développé*. The coach should check that the gymnast's shoulders are aligned with each other and her trunk muscles are tight. In addition, when the gymnast is practicing this exercise sideways, the coach should ensure that the same side of the trunk as the working leg remains erect as there is a tendency to turn the trunk toward the working leg. Finally, when the gymnast is practicing this exercise forward, the coach should check the position of the same side of the pelvis as the working leg because it may be moved forward.

We recommend that the novice begin by learning the *battement relevé lent* sideways from the first position, facing the barre. Then she can practice it forward from the first position with one hand holding the barre, then backward from the first position, facing the barre.

Rond de Jambe This group of exercises involves moving the working leg in an arc either on the floor or in the air. Exercises from this group will help to improve leg turn-out, ankle flexibility, and arch (instep) development.

Rond de jambe par terre refers to moving the stretched working leg in even movements in an arc while the toes touch the floor (figure 9.19). The exercise is started and finished by the same sliding movement as in *battement tendu simple*. The working leg may be moved outward (*en dehors*) or inward (*en dedans*), smoothly and evenly. The thigh of the working leg is turned out and the body weight is on the supporting leg. The gymnast must focus on maintaining the turn-out position of her free leg, especially at the heel.

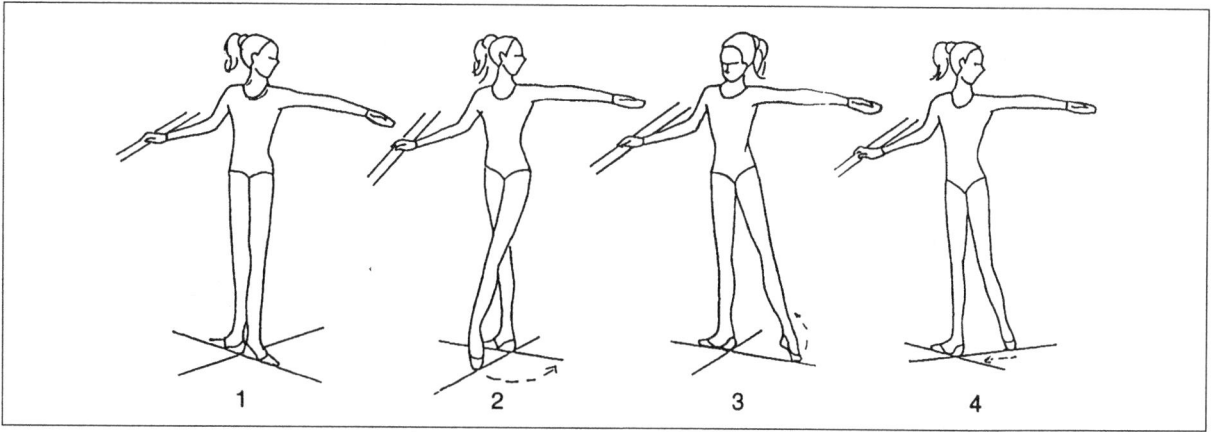

Figure 9.19 *Rond de jambe par terre*: (1) starting in first position, (2) *battement tendu* forward, (3) moving the working leg sideways in an arc, (4) moving of the leg backward in an arc.

When practicing this exercise *en dehors*, the coach should check the position of the gymnast's working leg at the finishing point behind before the gymnast returns her leg to the starting position. The finishing point in front must be under control, when practicing this exercise *en dedans*.

Rond de jambe en l'air (figure 9.20) refers to circular movements of the working leg in the air. The oval shape is formed by the shin of the working leg, which the gymnast has raised to an angle of 45 degrees or less. A gymnast may perform *rond de jambe en l'air* in two directions, either outward or inward. Either way, the pointed toes of the working leg touch the calf muscles of the supporting leg, while the thigh is turned out.

Port de bras involves leaning the trunk. The lean should be slow and smooth at an even pace with the shoulders aligned with each other. The knees should be straight. This exercise helps develop flexibility. Figure 9.21 demonstrates *port de bras* backward.

Classical Jumps and Leaps (Allegro) This group involves small, trailing jumps on the floor and large leaps in the air. This drill will strengthen the leg muscles, helping the gymnast master the techniques of taking off and landing.

The jumps and leaps of classical drills require the gymnast to perform the *demi-plié* before the jump or leap, stretch and turn out her knees, and point her toes during flight. She must strive to land softly by rolling from her toes to her heels in *demi-plié*.

We recommend that the novice begin by learning all ballet jumps at the barre. This will help the gymnast understand how flight is possible while pressing her hands on the barre during takeoff without shifting her body weight onto the barre. It is better if before learning ballet jumps and leaps, a gymnast can jump vertically loosely from the first half-turned-out position after the *demi-plié*. The coach should check that during flight the gymnast's toes are pointed and her trunk remains straight and without superfluous movements.

In RSG, the following jumps are typically used: *sote, changement de pied, pas échappé, pas assemblé,* and *jeté*.

Sote can begin in the first, second, or fifth position (figure 9.22). From a first, second, or fifth starting position, a gymnast should jump upward, stretching her legs and feet with pointed toes. In flight, the legs must be turned out. When landing, the gymnast returns to the starting position.

For *changement de pied* from the fifth position with a change of legs, the gymnast jumps from both legs and changes legs before landing in *demi-plié*.

Pas échappé (figure 9.23a) involves jumping from the fifth position into the second and from the second into the fifth, for example, two jumps from two legs onto two. The technique for this jump is the same as for the *sote*.

Pas assemblé (figure 9.23b) is a jump from one leg to two. Starting in the fifth position, the left leg is in front, as in *demi-plié* in which the gymnast transfers her body weight onto her left leg. Then she uses her left leg to take off. At the same time, the right leg slides sideways at an angle of 45 degrees. Then the gymnast forcefully stretches her left leg upward and then lifts her right leg to the left leg. At the end of the flight, the two legs come together in fifth position.

Jeté means to leap from one leg to the other. During the leap, the gymnast lifts one leg sharply

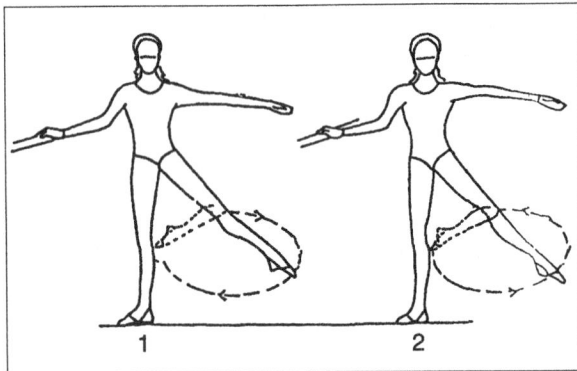

Figure 9.20 *Rond de jambe en l'air:* (1) inward (*en dedans*), (2) outward (*en dehors*).

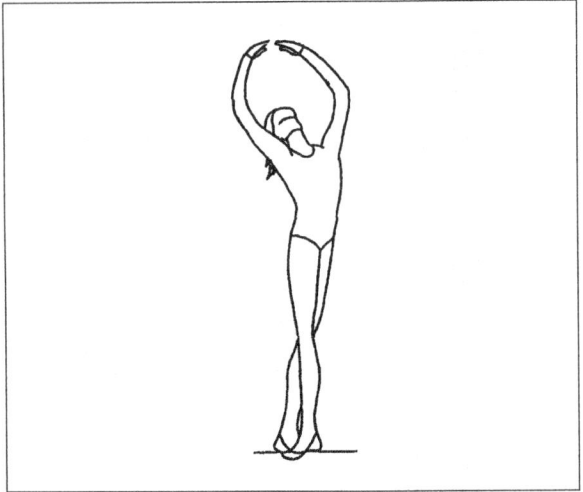

Figure 9.21 *Port de bras.*

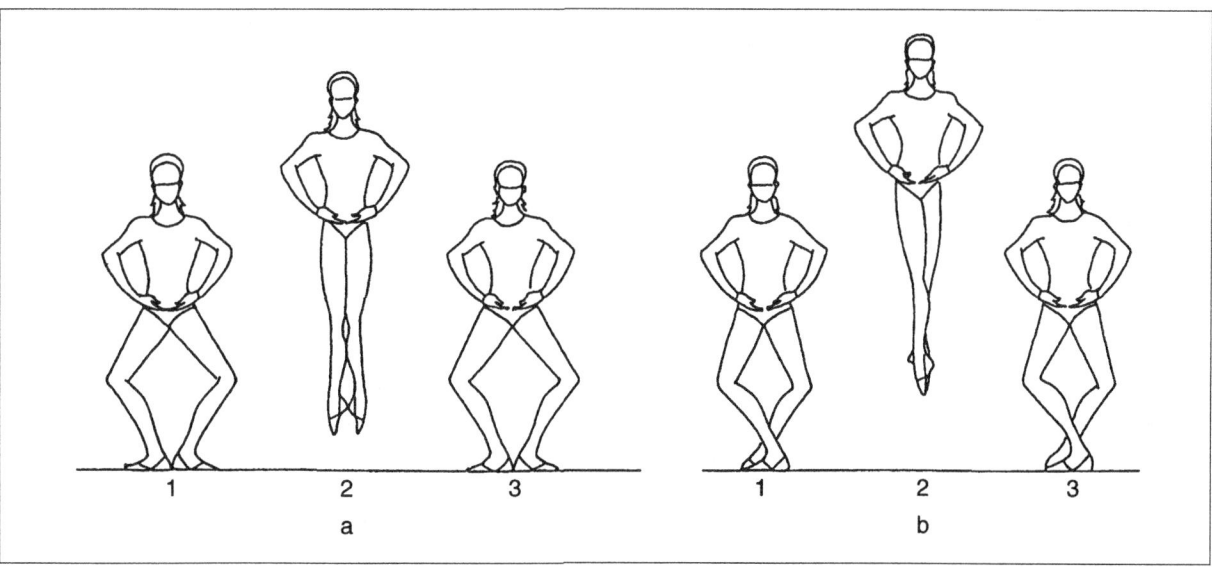

Figure 9.22 *Sote* jumps from (a) first position, (b) fifth position.

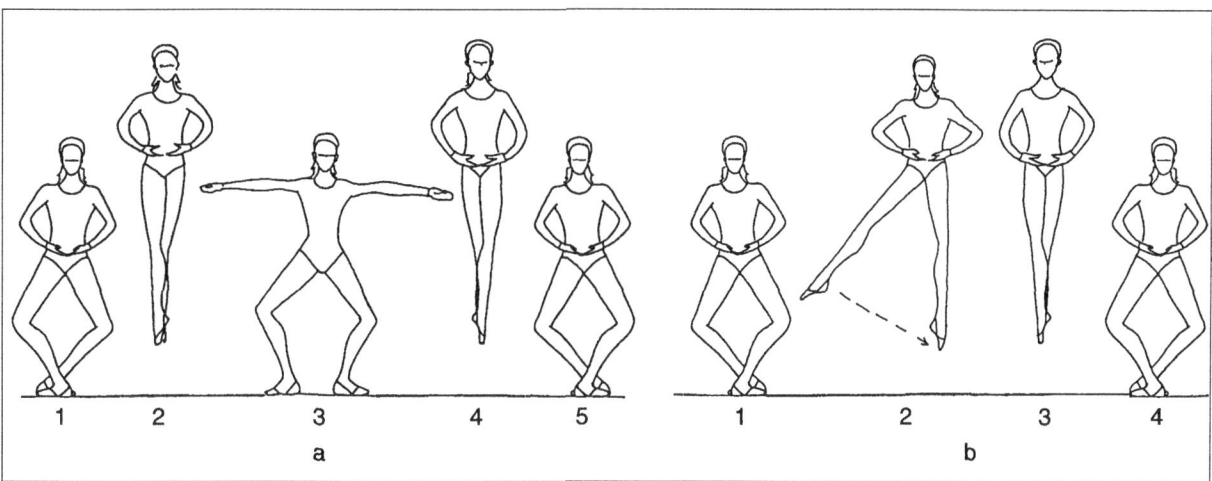

Figure 9.23 Classical ballet jumps: (a) *pas échappé*, (b) *pas assemblé*.

forward, sideways, or backward while extending the other leg into the air. Then the gymnast transfers her body weight from one leg to the other.

Classical Dance Drills Without the Barre

Exercises performed in the center of the gym have similar aims as those performed at the barre. Indeed, the movements are often the same. However, practicing the exercises in the center is more difficult because the turn-out of the legs and the stability of the body, especially on toes, must be maintained at all times—without the help of the barre.

The main conditions for mastering the body position are correctly distributing the body weight on one or both legs, tightening the body muscles, keeping the knee of the supporting leg straight, and keeping the thigh of the working leg straight and turned out.

The gymnast should not focus on only one part of her body when she practices in front of a mirror. Instead, she should concentrate on her entire body, noting if the shape of the movement and positions of her legs are correct. Other than visual aspects, the gymnast must also sense the tightening of her muscles.

When learning to work away from the barre, novices should begin by repeating the exercises they learned at the barre. More experienced gymnasts should do fewer exercises. A coach should schedule certain key movements practiced in the center in each session. These include *battements* (*tendu, jeté, fondu, grand*). Other movements such as *rond de jambe par terre*, *rond de jambe en l'air*, and *battement frappé* may be combined with the key movements. A gymnast should also perform arm exercises without the barre, such as moving the arms from one position to another and waving movements.

Dance combinations, which are made up of various kinds of *développé*, turns, and balances, are called *adagio*. *Adagio* means the combination of movements into one harmonious whole. For beginners, combinations help improve balance and coordination from one element to another and produce smooth, expressive movements of the arms. Moreover, *adagio* used by experienced gymnasts in technically difficult movements performed on the toes creates a reserve of complex body movements needed for successful competitive compositions.

A coach should introduce *adagio* gradually to learners. Beginners should start with elementary forms, such as *relevé lent* to an angle of 90 degrees, *développé*, and *port de bras*, performed at a slow tempo on a flat foot.

A more experienced gymnast can complicate *adagio* by adding pivots with her working leg in a high position, long balances on her toes, and transitions from one balance to another. The tempo is a little faster than for beginners.

Elite gymnasts may vary *adagio* not only by performing at a moderate tempo but also at an accelerated one. Variations at this level have different themes that include turns, pivots, jumps, and leaps.

Of all the classical drills, *adagio* is made up of the largest number of different movements, making musical choreography difficult. Short *adagios* are composed in musical phrases of not less than 4 bars in 4/4 time but more often than not in 8 or 12 bars. Long *adagios* are made up of 12 to 16 bars.

To construct an *adagio*, it is necessary to maintain the appropriate rhythm and tempo and observe the bar square (16, 32, or 64 counts). The turns, pivots, balances, and poses that should be included in an *adagio* must begin on an accented count (first and third counts in 4/4; first count in 3/4 time). Coordination between the music and movements should not start on the weak counts (second and fourth counts in 4/4 time; second and third counts in 3/4 time). Instead, a gymnast should perform linking and auxiliary movements, *passé*, and steps on the weak counts.

Jumps and leaps are the most difficult parts of the classical drill. At the barre or in the center of the gym, they depend on leg strength. Jumps and leaps also help to develop a gymnast's springiness. For ballet jumps that were previously learned at the barre, a gymnast should practice them in the following order: from two legs onto two, from one leg onto two, from one leg onto one, and so on. These jumps will help a gymnast train her legs for more difficult gymnastic jumps and leaps. The transition from ballet jumps to large leaps should be gradual. We recommend that the beginner start to expand her repertoire by combining simple gymnastic jumps with ballet movements.

Traditional and Modern Dances

All gymnasts must be able to dance; it is a compulsory skill they must master. Gymnasts frequently use dance steps in competitive compositions to connect various elements. Dance steps help gymnasts expressively portray the music. Thus, in RSG, it is wise to use dance elements that help a gymnast develop her expressiveness and dance habits as well as educate her about aesthetics.

The following are a few elementary dance movements from the most widely used dances, such as European and Latin dances and jazz.

European Dances

The European way of dancing requires the dancer to maintain a straight trunk and tight muscles in the stomach and back. Such a position allows the dancer to perform turns while maintaining stability, making it easier to execute clean and accurate movements.

Slide Step

The slide step (figure 9.24a) refers to the sliding movement of the foot on the floor, then shifting the body weight onto it and closing the other leg to the supporting leg. The gymnast may move forward, backward, or sideways on flat feet or on her toes. The slide step is the preparatory step for the gallop step (figure 9.24b).

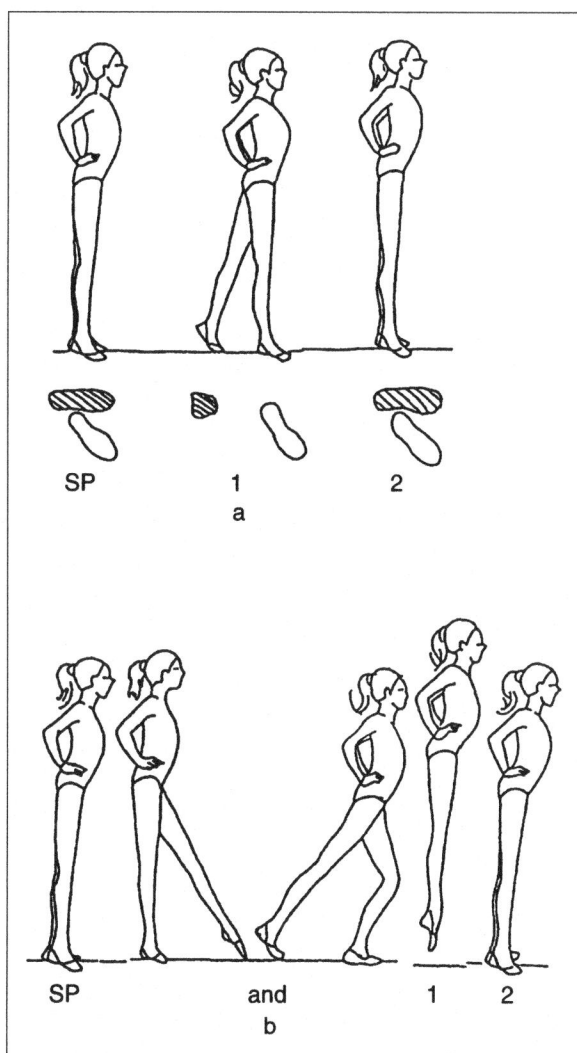

Figure 9.24 Slide steps and gallop: (a) slide step forward, (b) gallop forward.

Slide Step Forward Starting position—assume the third leg position with the right leg in front and place hands on the waist. Slide with the right foot forward, transfer the body weight onto it, and keep the left toes behind. Close the left foot behind into the third position with a sliding movement and transfer the body weight onto both feet. Turn out the legs, especially the knees and heels. The gymnast must keep an erect body posture and avoid turning her trunk sideways.

Pas de Grace **(Graceful Dance)** This dance is useful for beginners because it helps them acquire the "pointed toes" habit. The rhythm is 4/4 time at a moderate tempo. Starting position—stand in pairs in a circle with the left side to the center and legs in the third position with the right leg in front. Join nearest hands and stretch them forward, keeping the free hand on the waist.

1	Slide step to the right with the right foot.
2	Close the left leg to the third position behind the right leg and half-bend both knees.
3	Repeat count 1.
4	Rest the left toes in front.
5-8	Repeat counts 1-4 with the left foot.
9-11	Take three walking steps forward, starting with the right foot.
12	Rest the left toes in front.
13-15	Repeat counts 9-11 starting with the left foot.
16	Turn to face each other with hands on waists.
17-20	Repeat counts 1-4.
21-24	Repeat counts 5-8.
25-27	Partners join right hands and slide step three times along an arc to the right.
28	Rest the left toes at the side.
29-31	Repeat counts 25-27 to the left.
32	Return to the starting position.

Slide Changing Step Learning this step (figure 9.25) will prepare the gymnasts to learn the polka step. It consists of two parts: sliding from one foot, then changing the foot and sliding from the other foot. Starting position—assume the third leg position with the right leg in front.

1-2	Slide step forward with the right foot and close the left leg behind.
3	Step forward onto the right foot and stand with the left toes behind.
4	Move the left foot forward with a sliding movement on the floor, then close the right leg behind.
5-8	Repeat counts 1-4 from the left foot.

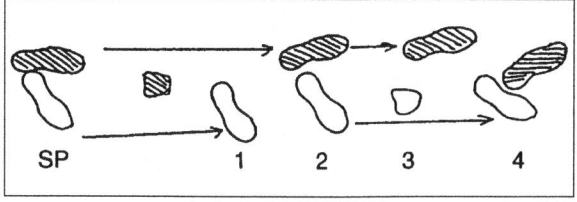

Figure 9.25 Slide changing step.

The slide changing step backward is done the same way as when moving forward, but the movement begins from the foot that is behind. The trunk and the head are slightly turned toward the stepping foot.

Slide Changing Step With a Turn to the Side
Starting position—assume the third leg position with the right leg in front, hands on the waist.

1-2	Slide step from the right foot to the right.
3	Step on the left foot to the right and half turn the body.
4	Place the right leg behind the left.
5-8	Repeat counts 1-4 from the left foot to the left.

We recommend that the dancer step from pointed toes and turn her trunk and head toward the stepping side.

Gallop Step

A gymnast can gallop step forward, backward, or sideways. The gallop step is dynamic and rapid. It begins with a sliding movement of the foot and slightly bent knees, followed by a takeoff and flight. During the flight, the gymnast joins and stretches her legs and points her toes. The landing is silent with rolling from the toes to the heels and a gentle half-bend of the knees. The musical accompaniment may be any polka of moderate tempo and merry nature.

The following is the dance exercise called gallop, which is suitable for beginners. The time signature is 2/4, and the tempo is moderately fast. Starting position—stand next to each other in pairs, forming a circle, with each gymnast's left side to the center, in the third leg position with the left leg in front, the arms sideways and downward, joining crossed hands.

1-2	Take two side gallop steps from the left foot toward the center.
3	Step on the left foot to the side.
4	Close the right leg into the third position in front of the right leg.
5-8	Repeat counts 1-4 from the right foot, moving out from the center.
9-12	Hop four times forward.
13	Step forward on the left foot, shifting body weight onto it.
14	Close the right leg behind the left leg.
15	Step backward onto the right foot.
16	Close the left leg in front of the right leg.

If desired, repeat entire sequence.

Polka Steps

Figure 9.26 shows polka steps, which consist of two gallop steps with a hop between to change feet, forward, backward, or with a turn. The rhythm is counted "and, one, two, three, four."

Polka Step Forward See figure 9.26a. Starting position—assume third leg position with the right leg in front, hands on the waist.

"And"	Hop on the left foot and raise the right leg slightly, pointing the toes.
1	Gallop step forward from the right foot.
2	Hop on the right foot and move the left foot to the front, pointing the toes.
3	Repeat count 1 from the left foot.
4	Repeat count 2, moving the right foot to the front.

The polka step backward is performed the same way, only backward.

Polka Step With a Turn See figure 9.26b. This polka step involves a slide changing step with a turn to the side, but with two hops when starting and turning.

Polka and Gallop Step Combinations It is possible to combine polka and gallop steps after learning the polka steps. The following is an example of a dance combination called polka, which is appropriate for beginners. The time signature is 2/4, and the tempo is moderately fast. Starting position—stand in pairs in a circle, with the left side to the center, assuming the third leg position with the right leg in front, partners holding each other's right and left hands, crossing their arms.

1	Hop on the left foot and place the right toes in front.
2	Hop on the left foot and place the right toes behind.
3-4	Hop twice on the right and left foot successively while lifting the free foot up, which is bent at the knee.
5-8	Repeat counts 1-4 from the right foot.
9-16	Do two sets of the polka step forward from the right foot.

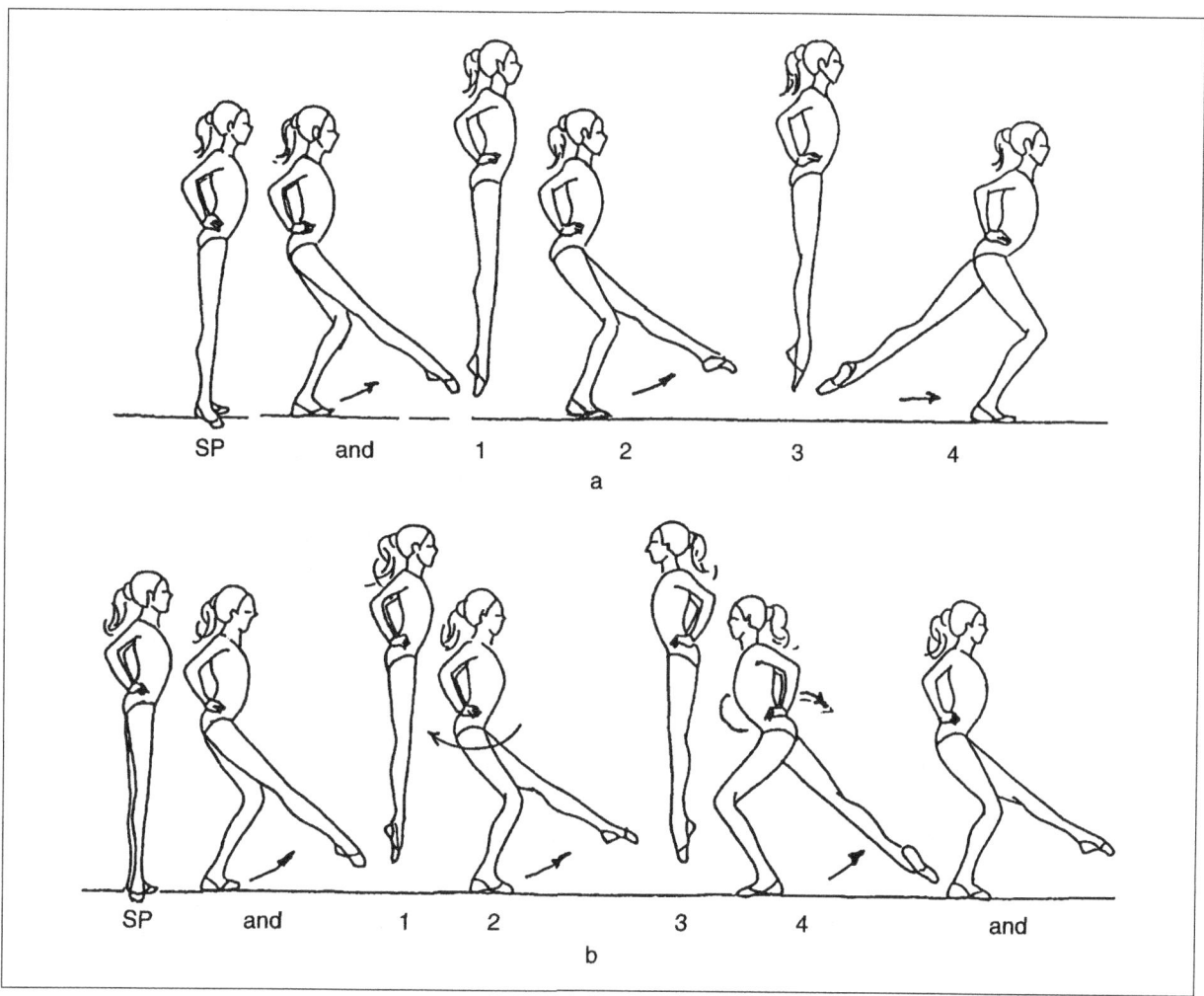

Figure 9.26 Polka steps: (a) forward, (b) with a turn.

17-20 Turn until standing face to face and gallop step four times from the right foot to the right.

21-24 Repeat counts 17-20 from the left foot to the left.

25-28 Perform four vertical jumps.

29-32 Do a set of polka steps forward from the right foot, side by side, with crossed arms.

If desired, repeat entire sequence.

Waltz Steps

Waltz steps in 3/4 time (figure 9.27) may be performed in a variety of styles, in any direction—forward, backward, sideways, or with a turn. Wave the arms in different directions, loosely and smoothly, when practicing waltz steps. The rhythm is counted "one, two, three."

Waltz Step Forward The waltz step forward, or walking waltz steps, is very common in RSG. It involves three small steps (figure 9.27a). Starting position—stand on toes, with knees, back, and shoulders held in alignment. On the first step, the gymnast must roll from her toes onto flat feet with her knee slightly bent on the first (accented) count of the bar. Then she takes two subsequent steps on her toes on the second and third counts. The waltz step backward follows the same pattern as the waltz step forward.

Waltz Step Sideways (Waltz Balance) See figure 9.27b. Starting position—stand on toes with weight evenly distributed between the feet. This is a rocking step. The gymnast must slide along the floor.

1 Step on the right foot to the right, rolling from the toes onto a flat foot with a slightly bent knee and a turned-out leg.

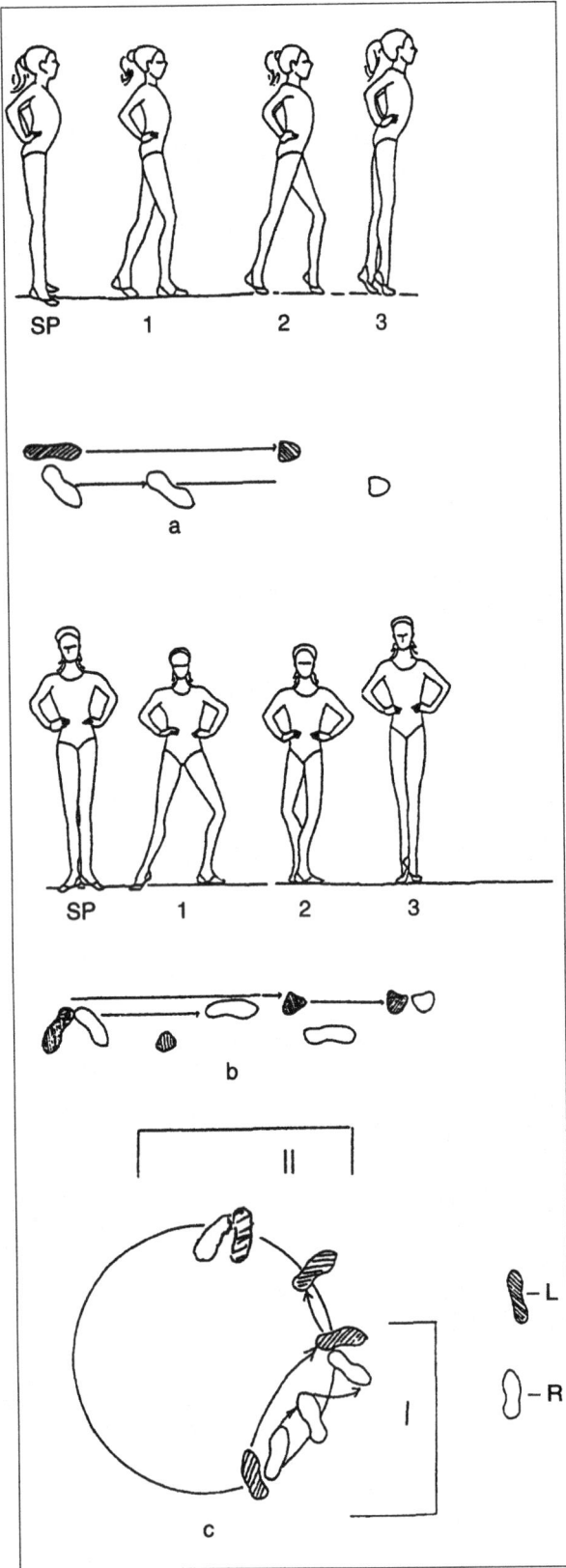

Figure 9.27 Waltz steps: (a) forward, (b) sideways, (c) with a turn (waltz turn).

2. Step on the right toes behind the left foot; the left leg should be turned out as well.
3. Shift the body weight onto the left toes, slightly rise off the right foot onto the toes in front of the left leg, and stretch the legs.

Repeat from the left foot to the left.

Waltz Turn See figure 9.27c. This is a waltz step forward with a turn to the right (right turn) or to the left (left turn) on two musical bars, consisting of six steps that may be divided into two parts. Each part ends in the third leg position.

Part I (one bar): Starting position—stand facing the center in the third leg position with the right leg in front, hands on the waist.

1. Step forward and to the right on the right foot.
2. Step on the left foot with a half-turn to the right and stand with the back to the center, shift the body weight onto the left foot, and fix the right foot in front.
3. Close the right foot to the left leg by turning to the right to face the center.

Part II (one bar):

1. Step backward on the left foot.
2. Step on the right foot with a half-turn to the right facing the center, shift the body weight onto the right foot, and rest the left toes behind.
3. Close the left foot behind the right foot.

It is best to perform the steps and turns softly, continuously, and slowly.

Figure Waltz This is a good dance combination for beginners. The time signature is 3/4, and the tempo is slow. Starting position—stand in pairs in a circle, facing each other, with arms out to the sides. The first gymnast stands with her back to the center and the second one faces it.

Bar 1 Waltz step sideways (waltz balance): the first gymnast starts from her left foot while the second one starts from her right foot. Each gymnast should lean her trunk slightly in the direction the pair will move.

Bar 2 Repeat bar 1 to the other side.

Bars 3-4 Waltz step forward with a turn and separate arms in counterclockwise direction.

Bars 5-8 Repeat bars 1-4.
Bar 9 Waltz step forward from the right foot with the overlapped nearest arms upward and the free arms to the sides.
Bar 10 Waltz step backward from the left foot, extending arms forward.
Bars 11-12 Repeat bars 3-4.
Bars 13-16 Repeat bars 9-12.

If desired, repeat entire dance combination.

Sirtaki

Sirtaki is a Greek dance in 2/4 time and a tempo of 60 bars, or 120 counts, per minute. The dancers stand in a line or form a circle with their hands placed on each other's shoulders. The main movements of this dance are the introduction, knocks, forward and backward step, and the side cross step.

Introduction: starting position—stand erect.

1 Half-bend the knees quickly.
2 Straighten knees quickly.
3-8 Repeat counts 1-2.

Knocks: starting position—stand erect.

1 Take a small step on the left foot to the left, moving it slightly and slowly. Raise the right leg.
2 Close the right foot slowly to the left foot.
3-4 Repeat counts 1-2 from the right foot slowly.
5-8 Repeat counts 1-4.

Forward and backward step: starting position—stand erect.

1 Stamp on the right heel.
2-3 Hop on the left foot and raise off the right one forward slowly.
4-5 Shift the body weight onto the right foot by slowly taking a small hop backward.
6-7 Step slowly backward onto the left foot, shifting the body weight onto it.
8-9 Step on the right foot to the right, shifting the body weight onto it.
10 Step on the left foot forward quickly, bending the knees.
11 Shift the body weight onto the right foot quickly.
12 Close the left leg toward the right one quickly while keeping the body weight on the right foot.
13 Move the left toes forward and right diagonally.
14 Repeat count 12.
15 Place the left foot forward and right diagonally, shifting the body weight onto it quickly.
16 Return to the starting position.

Side cross step (figure 9.28): starting position—stand erect.

1 Lift the right leg forward quickly.
2 Place the right foot forward, diagonal from the left one quickly.
3 Step on the left foot to the left quickly.
4 Place the right foot quickly, diagonal from the left one behind.
5 Step on the left foot to the left quickly.
6 Repeat count 2.
7-12 Repeat counts 1-6 from the left foot to the right.

Repeat the entire sequence twice.

Russian Dance

In Russian slow dances, the steps are executed with restraint, continuously and smoothly. In fast dances the steps are bold and merry, executed sharply and quickly. The time for Russian dances, as a rule, is 4/4. See figure 9.29. The rhythm is counted "one,

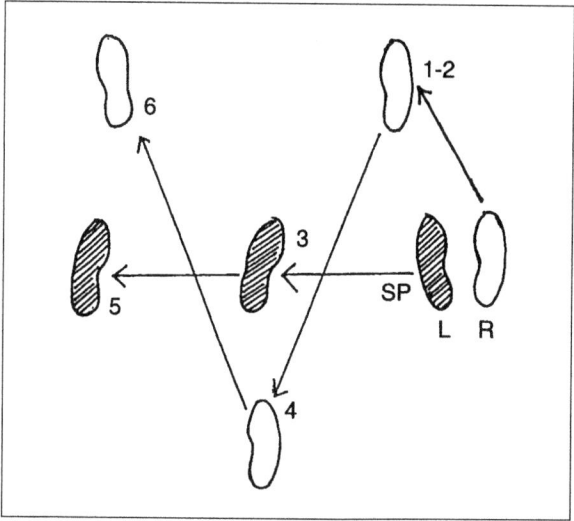

Figure 9.28 Side cross step from the dance "Sirtaki."

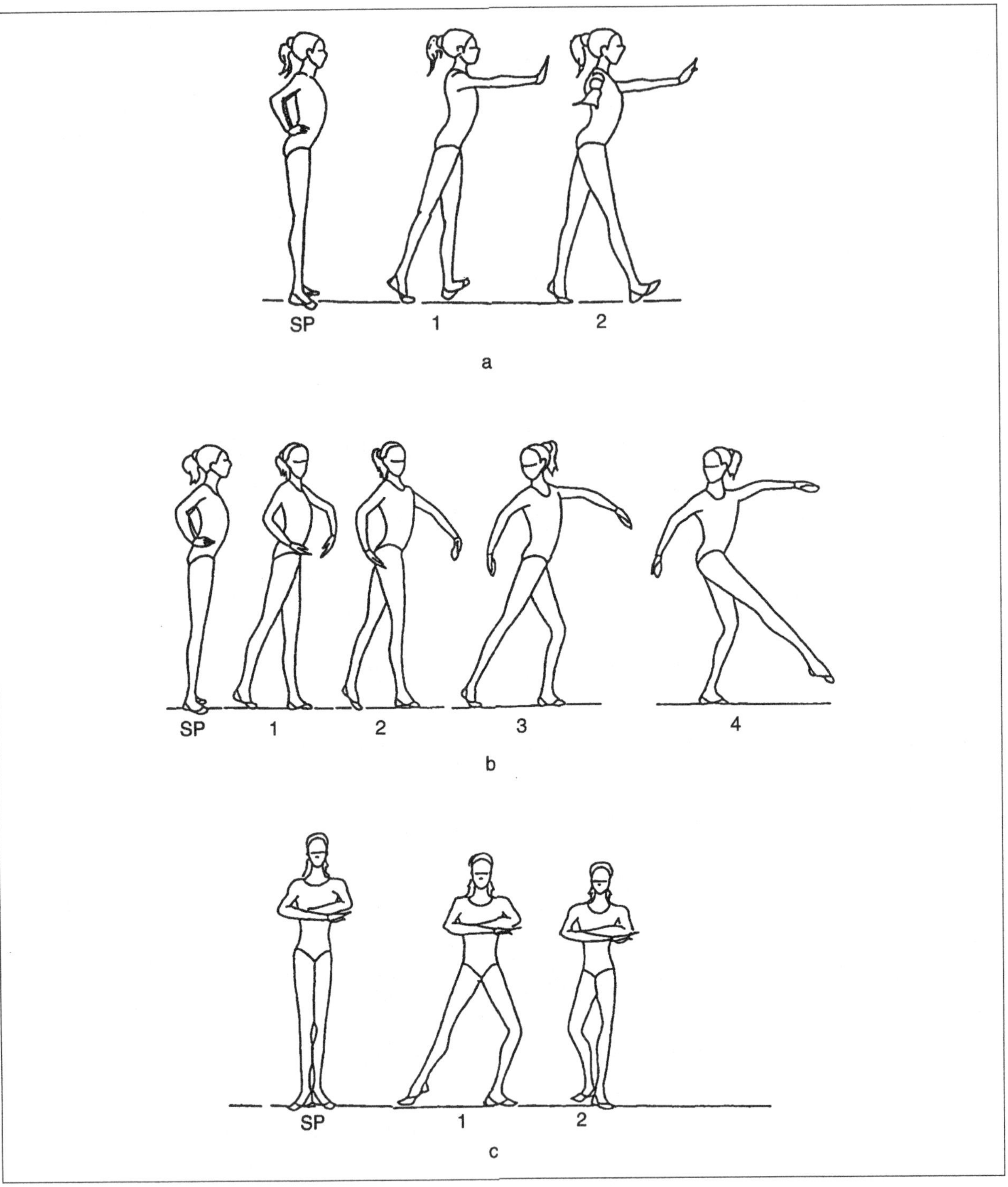

Figure 9.29 Russian dance steps: (a) heel step, (b) Russian walk, (c) dropping step.

two, three, four." Russian dances use many heel positions, for which the knee is straight and the foot and shin form a 90-degree angle.

Heel Step Perform the heel step in a relaxed manner, and with vigor (see figure 9.29a). The head must be turned toward the moving leg. The rolling from the heel to a flat foot should be done precisely and sharply, followed by the supporting leg bending slightly. The arms are slightly bent. Starting position—stand erect with feet together.

1	Step forward on the right foot by rolling from the heel to a flat foot while slightly bending the arms to the right.
2	Repeat count 1 from the left foot.
3-4	Repeat counts 1-2.

Russian Walk See figure 9.29b. Starting position—stand erect with the hands on the waist.

1	Step forward on the left foot.
2	Step forward on the right foot.
3	Step forward on the left foot and bend the knee halfway.
4	Lift the right foot forward with a sliding movement while turning the trunk and the head to the right.
5-8	Repeat counts 1-4 from the other foot.

Include the following arm movements as well: on counts 1-2, lift the arms forward with palms upward; on 3-4, move the arms to the right with palms upward. When performing the step from the other foot, the arm movements should be reversed: on 1-2, the arms move forward with the palms upward; on 3-4, turn the palms downward and place the hands on the waist.

Dropping Step See figure 9.29c. Perform the dropping step smoothly, conveying the nature of a slow dance. Starting position—stand erect on the right foot, raise off the left foot slightly to the left, and cross the arms at chest level.

1	Step on the left foot to the left, rolling from the toes to the heel and bending the knee halfway.
2	Place the right toes behind the left foot, while keeping the body weight on the right foot.
3-4	Repeat counts 1-2.

When practicing, the feet should be turned out, the legs should be bent, then gently straightened, the trunk should lean slightly in the direction of the movement, and the head should be turned toward the movement.

Latin Dances

The most typical movement in Latin dances is swinging the thighs, for which the dancer shifts her body weight gradually from one foot to the other, knees bent slightly toward one another and feet apart. Thus, to perform Latin dances, flexible ankles, knees, and hips are necessary. In addition, the feet should not slide when practicing these dances.

Pasodoble

Pasodoble means styling main movements executed by a bullfighter in the arena. The time signature is 2/4, and the typical tempo is 60 bars, or 120 counts, per minute, and each movement is performed on 1 count. The main pasodoble steps are the shifting step, deviation (ekar), and zigzag. See figure 9.30.

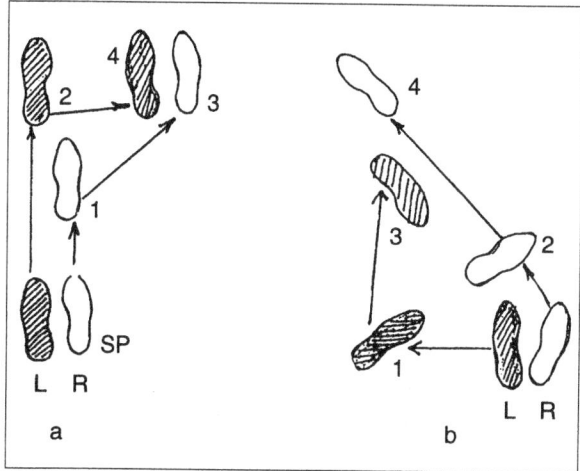

Figure 9.30 Pasodoble steps: (a) deviation (ekar), (b) zigzag.

Shifting Step Starting position—stand erect with feet together and elbows slightly bent and pointed sideways, with the hands on the hips.

1	Raise off the right foot slightly and shift body weight onto the left foot.
2	Place the right foot back, shifting the body weight onto it.
3-4	Repeat counts 1-2.

The feet are slightly apart and the heels stay off the floor slightly. The movement is done on the spot or with a half-turn to the left or right, four to eight times.

Deviation Step (Ekar) See figure 9.30a. The rhythm is counted "one, two." Starting position—stand erect with feet together.

1	(Count "one") step on the right foot forward.
2	(Count "two") step on the left foot forward.

3   (Count "one") step widely to the right on the right foot, bending the knees slightly.

4   (Count "two") close the left leg to the right one, rise on the toes, and straighten the body.

Zigzag   See figure 9.30b. Starting position—stand erect with feet together.

1   (Count "one") step on the left foot to the left.

2   (Count "two") step forward on the right foot.

3   (Count "one") step on the left foot to the left with a quarter-turn.

4   (Count "two") step backward on the right foot.

Repeat the entire sequence with the other foot.

Rumba

The rumba came from Cuba in the late 1920s (figure 9.31). It has different names when performed at different tempos. At a slow tempo it is called a bolero; at a fast tempo, a guarachs. Steps should be accompanied by the smooth swaying of the hips from side to side, known as "Cuban motion." The time signature is 4/4, and the tempo is 32 bars or 128 counts per minute. The rhythm is counted "one" (quickly), "two" (quickly), "three-four" (slowly).

Walk Forward   See figure 9.31a. Starting position—stand erect with feet together.

1   Step on the right foot to the right quickly.

2   Close the left foot to the right one quickly.

3-4   Step slowly forward on the right foot, shifting the body weight onto it.

5   Step on the left foot to the left quickly.

6   Close the right leg to the left one quickly.

7-8   Step forward on the left foot, shifting the body weight onto it.

Repeat the sequence from the other foot.

Box   See figure 9.31b. Starting position—stand erect with feet together.

1   Take a small step on the right foot to the right quickly.

2   Close the left leg to the right leg quickly.

3-4   Step forward slowly on the right foot, shifting the body weight onto it.

5   Take a small step on the left foot to the left to be parallel to the right foot.

6   Close the right leg to the left one quickly.

7-8   Step slowly backward on the left foot, shifting the body weight onto it.

Cuban Walk   Starting position—stand erect with feet together:

1   Step forward on the right foot quickly.

2   Step forward on the left foot quickly.

3-4   Step slowly forward on the right foot.

5-8   Repeat counts 1-4 from the left foot.

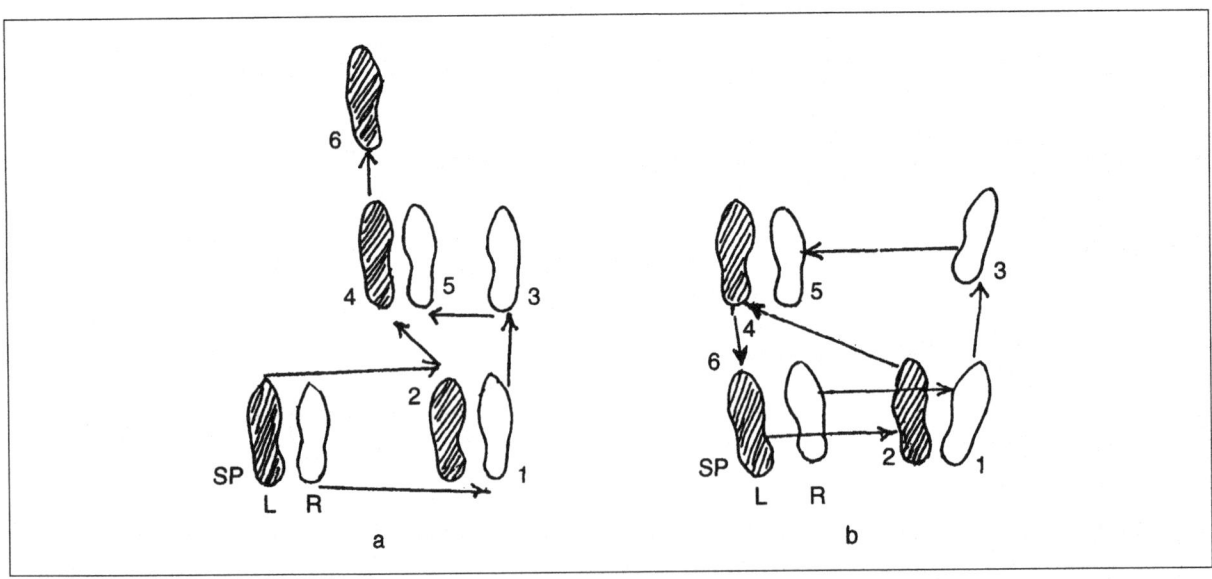

Figure 9.31   Rumba steps: (a) walk forward, (b) box.

Samba

The samba originated in Brazil. The time signature is 2/4, and the tempo is 53 bars, or 106 counts, per minute. The rhythm is "one" (quickly), "and" (quickly), "two" (slowly). In sambas, the thighs do not swing sideways, as in pasodobles but forward and backward. The balance is the main samba step.

Figure 9.32 shows the samba balance. Starting position—stand erect with the feet together.

1. (Count "one") step forward on the right foot quickly.
2. (Count "and") step forward on the left foot, closing it to the right foot without shifting the body weight onto it.
3-4. (Count "two") shift the body weight onto the right foot slowly.
5. (Count "one") step backward on the left foot quickly.
6. (Count "and") step backward on the right foot, closing it to the left foot without shifting the body weight onto it.
7-8. (Count "two") shift the body weight onto the left foot slowly.

Building on supple swings in the knees, when the gymnast moves forward, she should lean her body weight slightly backward, and when she moves backward, she should lean her body weight slightly forward.

Cha-Cha

The cha-cha is not connected with any particular folk dance, but it does emphasize rhythms from Cuban melodies (figure 9.33). The time signature is 4/4, and the tempo is 32 bars, or 128 counts, per minute.

The dance is performed without rising on toes; instead, all steps are performed by rolling the middle of the foot to the heel and the knees are relaxed alternately. The rhythm is counted "one, two, three, four, and" or "one, two, cha-cha-cha" in all four counts. Starting position—stand erect with feet together.

1. (Count "one") take a small step on the right foot to the right.
2. (Count "two") step forward on the left foot, shifting the body weight onto it.
3. (Count "three" or "cha") rise off the right foot, lower it next to the left leg on the spot, shifting the body weight onto it.

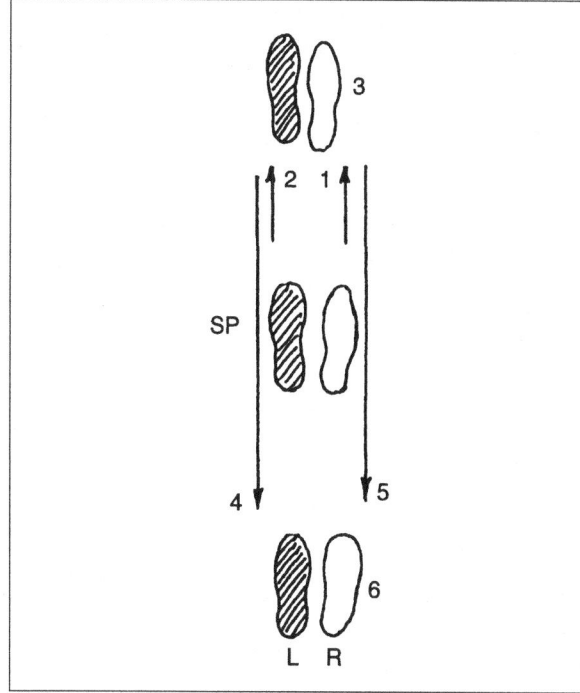

Figure 9.32 Samba balance.

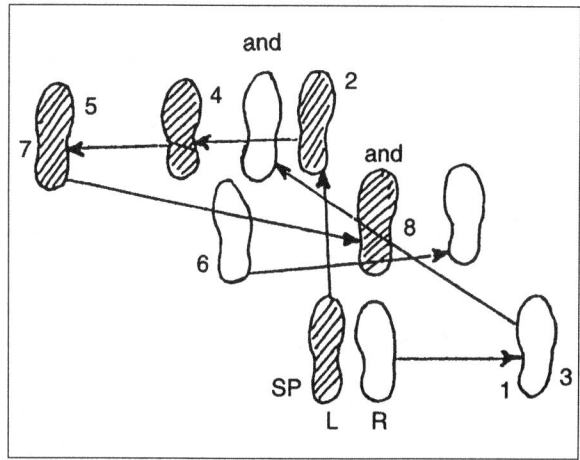

Figure 9.33 Main step of the cha-cha.

4. (Count "four" or "cha") take a small step on the left foot to the left.
5. (Count "and" or "cha") place the right foot next to the left foot, maintaining a distance between them.
6. (Count "one") take a small step on the left foot to the left.
7. (Count "two") step on the right foot backward and shift the body weight onto it;

8	(Count "three" or "cha") rise slightly off the left foot and lower it on the spot, shifting the body weight onto it.
9	(Count "four" or "cha") take a small step on the right foot to the right.
10	(Count "and" or "cha") move the left foot toward the right one, maintaining a distance between the feet.

Jazz Dances

The following are well-known jazz dances: boogie-woogie, bebop (jive), rock 'n' roll, the Charleston, and the twist.

Boogie-Woogie

This dance has a 4/4 time signature and a tempo of 40 bars, or 160 counts, per minute. The rhythm is counted "one, two, three, four, five, six." Starting position—stand erect with feet together.

1	Take a small step on the left foot behind the right foot (the right heel and the left toes in one line), shifting the body weight onto the left foot.
2	Shift the body weight back onto the right foot.
3	Return the left foot to the starting position and half support the body weight with it.
4	Shift the body weight entirely onto the left foot.
5	Shift half the body weight onto the right foot.
6	Shift the body weight entirely onto the right foot.

Bebop (Jive)

This dance has a time signature of 4/4, and a tempo of 40 to 50 bars, or 160 to 200 counts, per minute. The rhythm is counted "one, two, three, and, four, five, and, six." Starting position—stand erect with feet together.

1	(Count "one") take a small step backward on the left foot by crossing it behind the right leg, shifting the body weight onto it.
2	(Count "two") step on the spot on the right foot, shifting the body weight back onto it.
3	(Count "three") place the left foot slightly to the left of the right leg.
4	(Count "and") step on the spot on the right foot.
5	(Count "four") rise off the left foot and lower it slightly to the left of the right leg.
6	(Count "five") take a small step on the right foot to the right.
7	(Count "and") rise off the left foot and lower it slightly to the left of the right foot.
8	(Count "six") rise off the right foot and lower it slightly to the right of the left foot.

Rock 'n' Roll

This dance has the time signature of 4/4, and a tempo of 48 bars, or 192 counts, per minute, with the accent on the second and fourth beats. A rock 'n' roll rhythm is more syncopated. The rhythm is counted "one, two, three, four, five, six," accenting the second and fourth beats. The movements of this dance are executed on flat feet. Starting position—stand erect with feet together.

1	Take a small step backward, turning the left foot slightly to the left.
2	Shift the body weight onto the right foot while moving it parallel to the left foot.
3	Lift and bend the left knee and cross it in front of the right leg at knee level.
4	Move the left foot to the starting position.
5	Lift and bend the right knee and cross it in front of the left leg at knee level.
6	Move the right foot to the starting position.

Charleston

This dance has a time signature of 4/4, and a tempo of 50 bars, or 200 counts, per minute. The rhythm is counted "one, and, two, and, three, and, four, and," accenting the first beat. Most of the movements in this dance involve moving on the balls of the feet. To study the swiveling turns on the balls of the feet, we recommend that the gymnast practice the following exercises. The main movement starting position—stand erect with feet together and toes turned out.

1	(Count "one") turn on the balls of the feet while lifting the heels a little bit and separating the heels before the knees are joined.
2	(Count "and") lower the heels and return them to the starting position.

The next movement is performed on one leg. Repeat the main movement without moving the left leg from the floor on each count of "and." Other movements are changeable for which the left or right foot is moved from the floor. The double movement is performed in the following manner: "one, and, two, and," then two main movements of the Charleston, lifting the left leg higher and further bending the knee, and "three, and, four, and," then two main movements of the Charleston, lifting the right leg.

The Twist

This dance has a time signature of 4/4 and a tempo of 40 bars, or 160 counts, per minute. The rhythm is counted steadily "one, two, three, four, five, six, seven, eight." In this dance, the thighs must turn evenly from right to left as the trunk, shoulders, and arms move in different directions. The main movement's starting position—stand erect with feet together.

1. Maintain the body weight on the left foot and turn the right knee and the toes slightly outward.
2. Turn the right knee and the right toes inward.
3. Shift the body weight from the left foot onto the right leg.
4. Turn on the left heel to the left while raising its toes and turning the trunk to the left.
5. Bend the left knee over the right knee, turning the trunk to the right; the left foot must be on the right shin level.

Repeat the same procedure while maintaining the body weight on the right foot. Then repeat the movements, alternating the right and the left legs.

Summary

Dance is an important element in RSG. Properly executed dance steps unite a composition's technical and artistic components. Successful gymnasts learn to master the dance skills required in classical ballet. Steps are borrowed from ballet, traditional folk dances, and modern dances. Dance training can be done at the ballet barre or away from the barre.

In the next chapter, we will examine the elements involved in composing a rhythmic gymnast's routine.

Part III

Competition

The object of RSG competitions is to perform compositions. The most skillful and graceful gymnasts earn the highest scores.

In international competitions, compositions must comply with the FIG Code of Points. Judges evaluate a composition in conditional units (points), based on the Code of Points and their impressions of the accuracy and aesthetics (kinematics—the external picture) of the performance. Thus, a gymnast must perform a competitive composition according to the standards that are fixed by the Code of Points.

The FIG Code of Points is a book of rules for judging gymnastic competitions prepared by the International Gymnastics Federation, or Federation Internationale de Gymnastique (FIG). As RSG has developed, the Code of Points has changed as well. The latest edition was issued in 1997.

Competitions at national and lower levels may need to comply with additional requirements imposed by the governing national federation. Judges score according to the national federal documents, not only the FIG Code of Points. Since a gymnast's scores may depend on both sets of criteria, it is very important to follow all requirements exactly.

RSG judging is subjective. Of course, RSG organizers try to do their best to make judging as objective as possible, but RSG is by nature subjective. The gymnast's impression on the judges is therefore very important.

The coach should use a variety of training methods to help the gymnast perform at her best. Moreover, the coach must help the gymnast manage her behavior during competition very carefully. For example, the coach should help the gymnast reach an emotional peak when performing.

Only talented gymnasts can achieve the best results in RSG. This makes selecting gymnasts with the greatest potential very important. Understanding the steps of talent identification should help the coach evaluate his or her gymnasts accurately.

In this part of the book, we will describe how to compose a winning composition (chapter 10) and how to prepare for a competition (chapter 11).

Chapter 10

Composing a Routine

In RSG, a gymnast prepares her composition in advance, setting it to musical accompaniment. In competition, the judges evaluate her composition according to the criteria of technical mastery (execution score), difficulty, and aesthetics (composition score) specified in the FIG Code of Points. In this chapter, we will examine the components of an effective competitive composition. We will point out what makes a composition strong and which pitfalls to avoid. Coaches and gymnasts alike can use this information to create a composition that is both acceptable and successful.

Competitive Compositions

In RSG, the contents of a competitive composition depend on:

- the FIG Code of Points, which requires a gymnast to include elements of a certain level of difficulty and certain ways of handling the apparatus,
- subjective regularities, based on the emotional effect it has on the judges and spectators evaluating it,
- a gymnast's level of development and training, and
- trends in RSG's development as a sport.

To help the reader create a winning composition, we will look closer at exactly what the Code of Points requires. Then we will discuss specific aspects of effective choreography.

Composition Requirements

We can characterize a gymnast's composition both by how well it demonstrates technical mastery and how great an aesthetic impression it makes. There are two components of a composition score: technical value and artistic value. Technical value includes the composition's difficulty. Artistic value includes originality, musical accompaniment, choreography, and mastery of performance. Aesthetic impression includes the construction of the composition, the relationship between the music and the gymnast's movements, and expression of those movements. We will discuss each aspect in further detail in the following sections (see also chapter 9).

Technical Mastery

The Code of Points demands significant technical difficulty in competitive compositions. The difficulty of a composition is determined by the difficulty of its elements. The Code of Points sets several specific criteria for determining the difficulty of a composition: the number and level of difficult elements, the inclusion of specific technical elements (requirements) for the apparatus events, and the choice of elements (body movements and apparatus). Execution points are based on body technique and proper technique for each apparatus.

Original compositions go beyond the known traditional or classical framework to include novel elements, novel relationships between the gymnast and her apparatus, or a novel combination of well-known elements. Innovation advances the development of RSG as a sport. Therefore, as a rule, both spectators and judges highly value originality.

According to the Code of Points, mastery concerns mainly the composition, but also the skill of the gymnast. To receive a bonus, a gymnast should perform in such a manner that the apparatus is practically always in motion, displaying all possible shapes, showing the amplitude of the movements, and moving in all directions and at all levels.

The quality of virtuosity bonus requires performing a composition with perfect technique, great ease, flawlessness, and exceptional amplitude. This trait requires many hours of hard work and fine-tuning.

Expression

According to the Code of Points, expression is the aspect of performance displaying the ability of a gymnast to convey an idea. The RSG composition must satisfy aesthetic criteria. The artistic impression of a composition differs from its accuracy; instead, it corresponds to the current understanding of the aesthetic ideal, or what the judges feel represents beauty. Naturally, a gymnast aims for the best results. When she perfectly coordinates her movements in time and space, she displays beauty in the whole sequence. In this way, RSG uses the gymnast's body as an expressive instrument that facilitates creative freedom. Although this creative freedom is limited by the Code of Points, it can give movements expressive form, most of which conform with the aesthetic criteria and the musical accompaniment. Thus, successful RSG compositions rouse the gymnast's and the spectators' emotions.

Musical Accompaniment The essence of rhythmic gymnastics is the link between the musical accompaniment and the movements of the routine. The music must underline and bring forth the meaning of the exercise and convey a unified character from the beginning to the end. Even though the Code of Points allows a gymnast/group to use music with voice and words for only one routine, the emphasis is still on the coherence between the rhythm and personality of the music and the movements of the gymnast(s).

Choreography The Code of Points requires components of unity of composition, a balance between right/left-hand work, choice and variety of body movement elements, acrobatic elements, variety in the composition, and use of the whole floor area.

The following factors will largely influence the quality of choreography:

- The coach's ability to understand modern tendencies in RSG.
- The coach's musical and composition knowledge.
- The coach's capability to analyze compositions performed by top level gymnasts.
- The coach's and gymnast's knowledge of the most current Code of Points.
- The coach's and gymnast's creativity.
- The gymnast's capacity to understand the concept of the composition.
- The gymnast's level of development and training.

Thus, the quality of choreography depends significantly on the coach's abilities.

The principle of orienting young gymnasts with first-class samples, rather than encouraging them to copy them, is extremely valuable. In-depth study of leading gymnasts' compositions should help coaches and their gymnasts understand and comprehend the principles of choreography taught in RSG's various national schools. Therefore, it is useful to study the best samples in the world, but it is not worth copying them blindly.

Instead, from the very start, a coach should work creatively and independently. He or she should search for connections between various elements of body movements and apparatus handling as well as try to create original movements. Why? A successful search will make a composition much more interesting.

A coach should keep a record of the choreography of competitive compositions (both of his or her own gymnasts and of competitors and champions), perhaps by using a card file. Each card should include information about musical accompaniments, an outline of the arrangement of the elements on the floor area and their sequence, and a description of connections and poses.

Selecting Champion Gymnasts

To achieve the best competitive results, gymnasts selected for competitions should have morphologies with a special combination of natural physical and psychological abilities. Elite RSG gymnasts often have the following body proportions:

- Arm length from the point of the shoulder to the third finger, about 46 percent of body length.
- Leg length from the heel to the hip, at least 50 percent of body length.
- Shin length from the ankle to the knee, about 53 percent of leg length.
- Hand length from the wrist to the third finger, about 11 percent of body length.

Coaches should also pay attention to the girl's other physical features. Girls who have the following characteristics are often the most successful:

- A long neck.
- A cylindrical chest with small girth.
- A flat trunk and buttocks.
- Narrow, sloping shoulders.

- Slight muscle definition.
- A straight spine and legs.
- Arched insteps.
- A nice face with clear skin and even features.

Looking for candidates with championship potential in RSG is a complex and difficult process. Some additional relevant factors include the following:

- Health (no chronic illnesses, defects in posture or body parts).
- Body type (morphology and figure).
- Physical ability.
- Speed and ease of learning.
- Sense of music and expression.
- Motivation and persistence.

Architectonics

Architectonics (from the Greek *architektonike*—the art of building) involves the construction of a composition: alternating elements and distributing them within a specific time and space. Its goal consists of using movements and poses in the best duration of movement to reflect the music across the entire floor area. The duration of movement is from the spectator's viewpoint of a gymnast from the center of the main direction (see figure 10.1). There are two levels of architectonics: alternating elements and arranging elements over time in space.

Alternating Elements

The objective regularities of constructing a composition are based on producing a favorable impression on the spectators. When choreographing a composition, a coach should take the two objective regularities into account: integration and variety in the use of floor area and dynamics.

Integration

Understanding a composition as one art piece performed in one style will ensure its integrity. Unity should be evident from the beginning (introduction), through the middle, and through the last pose, all of which should be coordinated to create a uniform concept and style. The construction of a composition depends heavily on the musical accompaniment, which connects all movements and produces a certain mood. The experience of world champion gymnasts demonstrates that it is very important to achieve exact accents in a composition. These accents include a good start, graceful connection of all elements into a harmonious whole, and a brilliant finale (which is absolutely vital). Specifically, a gymnast should use original but mastered elements at both the start and the end of a composition.

Variety

Variety strengthens impressions through abruptly alternating movements by changing the amplitude, direction, and speed as well as the degree of muscular tension. Moreover, a strong composition will combine movements in different levels of space (required by the Code of Points): low (on the floor), average (stands), and high (jumps and leaps). A gymnast can also display variety by alternating intense motion with relaxation. For example, she might follow a ring leap with two legs with relaxation by standing on her knee or follow a body swing into a vertical balance by "trickling" (easing slowly) into a squat. Alternating fast tempos with slow tempos also displays variety. For example, a gymnast might begin with a set of fast movements by throwing the ball, making two cross turns and a forward roll, and catching the ball in a back balance, then slow down by standing on her toes and leaning back horizontally while rolling the ball from arm to arm across her chest.

Variety in dynamics strengthens the artistic impressions with a gradual increase or decrease in the amplitude and tempo of movements and degree of muscular tension. Increasing the tempo toward the end of the composition and simultaneously including original, more difficult elements should make a very strong impression on the judges and spectators.

Arranging Elements

Difficult elements should be evenly distributed throughout a composition. A coach should choose the main elements and establish an ideal sequence for their performance. According to research based on Soviet and Bulgarian gymnasts in the late 1980s, the difficult elements were distributed in 2- to 5-second intervals. Individual gymnasts showed considerable variation in these intervals, however.

The research revealed that the difficult elements were spaced from 2.12 to 5.17 seconds apart. Thus, a 60- to 90-second composition including 10 difficult elements should have 1 difficult element performed every 6 to 9 seconds to evenly distribute the difficult elements. Performing difficult elements well in the second half of the composition reveals both a gymnast's technical mastery and physical prowess.

Sequencing

The sequence of elements in a composition depends on the coach's tactical conception, the musical accompaniment, and the arrangement of certain elements on the floor area. The coach's tactical conception is based on her knowledge of the gymnast's abilities. The ability to perform an element correctly at different points in a composition is important as well. Moreover, it is important to take into account the gymnast's level of emotional maturity. For example, if a gymnast is able to perform the most difficult element at the start of a composition best, then her coach should place that element at the start. If a gymnast is unable to control her anxiety or nervousness at the start of a composition, then her coach should arrange the most difficult elements after those that may boost her self-confidence.

Rational Distribution

Rational distribution of a gymnast's strengths in a competitive composition assumes that performance is better when it is original and difficult elements are concentrated in the part of the composition with the most simple elements. This distribution is tactically superior because the contrast is more obvious. Increasing the tempo toward the end of the composition will emphasize a high level of mastery and fitness. If the gymnast's endurance is low, her coach should place the highest tempo and most difficult elements in the first part of the composition. In fact, it is very important to arrange elements according to their effect on the cardiovascular system. A coach must remember that jumps and leaps increase the pulse and respiration rates significantly, while balances and pivots can be used for "breathing space" because they do not.

The FIG Code of Points mandates the minimum level of difficulty in a composition. Of course, this minimum is not sufficient to win a competition. Therefore, the coach should build a certain "reserve of difficulty" into each composition. Difficult elements should be joined by the shortest modal (linking) elements that allow superior performance of the difficult elements, and connecting elements should vary, for instance by walking, then running, then a floor movement.

Finally, a winning composition emphasizes the best aspects of the gymnast—her physical abilities (coordination, flexibility, or power), her style of performance (relaxed or dynamic), or her original elements and connections.

Composition Framework

The framework consists of the introduction, the body, and the conclusion. Time limits on compositions mandate that the introduction and the conclusion be short—not more than two musical bars. The introduction usually includes a starting pose and either a difficult element or introductory steps. Normally, the conclusion consists of an effective difficult element and a final pose.

The body of a composition should include the climax of the musical accompaniment to avoid monotony. Ideally, each element of a composition has starting and finishing positions that differ from the linking ones between elements. Thus, we recommend that coaches and gymnasts select contrasting movements for the starting and finishing parts of a composition, especially if they coincide with the beginning or ending of musical themes.

The impression that a composition makes also depends on its rhythmic framework. Combinations of even and changing rhythms should help avoid monotony in a composition. Monotony may also result from uneven and broken rhythms. Yet, changing the rhythm of an element could also interfere with technique. We therefore recommend that changes in rhythm should occur primarily in modal elements and in the preparatory and finishing movements of difficult elements.

Traveling

Figure 10.1 shows the floor area for RSG competitions. The main direction is the front line where judges sit. Thus, a successful composition emphasizes the main direction, and a gymnast must perform all important movements facing the main direction.

When performing a composition, a gymnast should move in different directions. She may travel

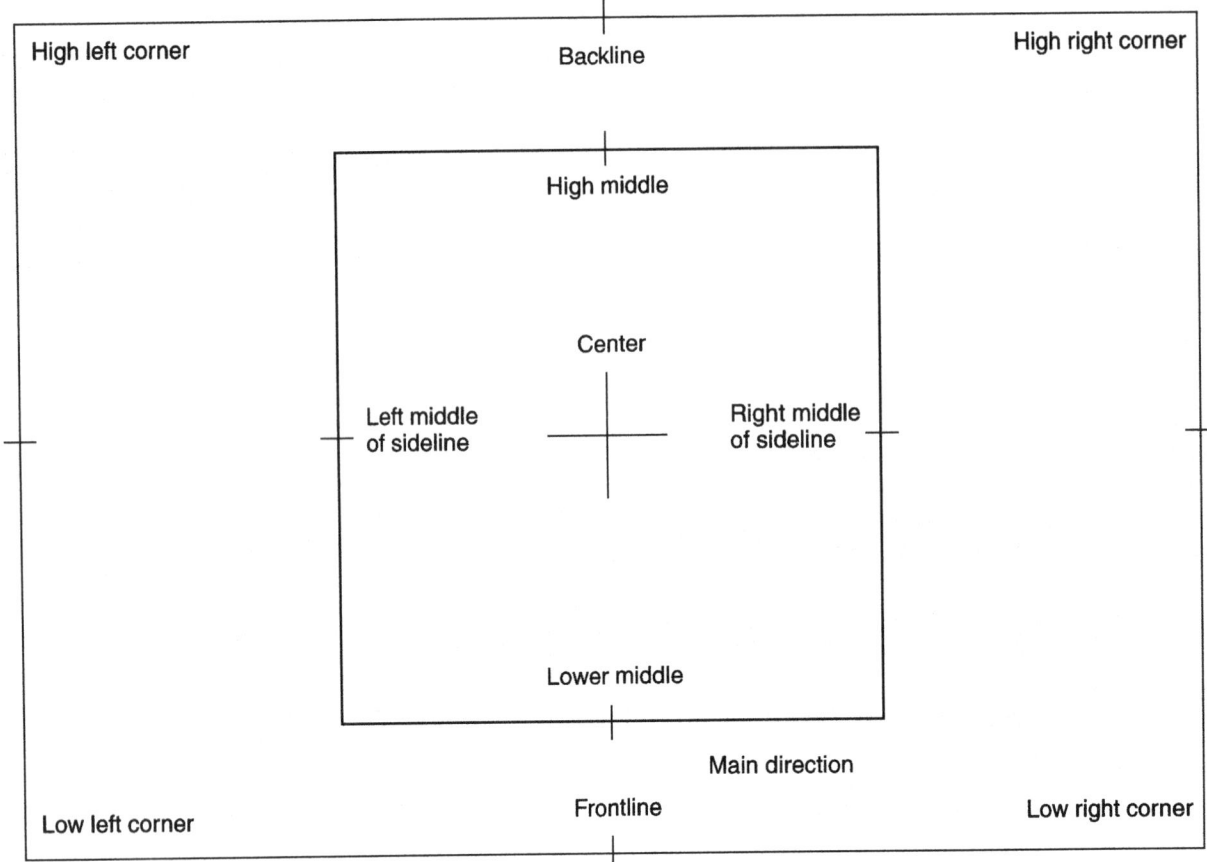

Figure 10.1 The competitive floor area in RSG.

about the floor area in, for example, circles, ellipses, parallel lines, diagonals, squares, triangles, and spirals.

Slow movements with a fixed body position (balances and bends) may be performed on the front- or backline, facing or in profile to the spectators. Gymnasts and coaches should arrange balances and leaps on these lines (split leaps, ring split leaps, and so on) so that they will begin in profile.

Gymnasts often use the diagonal line. It is very suitable for elements requiring rapid movement, such as fast pivots and wide leaps. The spectators can see the power of the takeoff, elevation, and amplitude of flight. These movements look best moving from the right rear corner to the left front corner.

The gymnast should move expressively when traveling perpendicular to the main direction. She should use slow elements, such as bending her arms in front of herself or opening them sideways or upward. If a gymnast moves perpendicularly from the back- to the frontline, she should perform facing forward while slightly turning out her shoulders and legs.

A gymnast should perform elements for which she turns her body on its axis (turns, pivots or jumps, leaps with a turn) while traveling in an arc.

A gymnast should perform the slow part of a composition in the center of the floor area, surrounded by free space or at the center of the backline. This will create the illusion of spaciousness.

The sidelines are the least desirable; thus, a gymnast should avoid them. If it is necessary to move on the sidelines, it is better to do it by using horizontal planes in the performance, for example, the "butterfly" leap. It is better to move from the center to the backline in an arc.

Choosing the Right Music

In contemporary RSG, music has been transformed from servant to master, playing a major role in how competitive compositions are choreographed. Music now forms the foundation of a composition. Gymnastic compositions result from the combined efforts of the coach, ballet master, pianist (musical editor), and gymnast.

Problems of Using Music in RSG

In a lesson, music not only provides the background and creates the mood but also helps to set the rhythm and dynamics of the elements. But this relationship is not easy. Gymnasts often commit the following errors:

- They do not understand how to use the music.
- They do not reflect the mood of the music in their movements.
- They commit rhythmic errors.
- They do not know how to connect the music to the movements.

There is a widespread, if somewhat mistaken, opinion that ballet classical drills accompanied by music are sufficient to develop a gymnast's musical sense. In these lessons, the coach selects music according to the movements and technical tasks he or she has set. But ballet lessons can help to develop the musical abilities of gymnasts only if the ballet master or coach specifically works on this aspect. Even this attention develops only a sense of rhythm, neglecting the other means and aspects of musical expression. But there are many opportunities to develop musical abilities in a competitive composition. However, many coaches encourage only very simple and even primitive connections of movements with the music.

Music Selection

According to the Code of Points, the music may be presented using one or several musical instruments. Music with voice and words may be used for one routine only. The musical accompaniment may be written especially for the composition, or it may be existing music. Regardless, the music should form a single harmonious piece, not a selection of unrelated musical fragments. A medly of different songs is acceptable as long as it logically flows together.

Musical editors should take care to preserve the tonality and phrasing of various musical themes. This is even more important when constructing an accompaniment from different existing musical pieces or when using two different instruments. Different musical themes must be linked or the music will appear to stop in the middle.

The coach and gymnast should define the genre and rhythm of the musical piece that they wish to use as they start to choreograph the composition. It is necessary to take into account the gymnast's individuality, including her appearance, age, temperament, artistic impression skills, technique (for both body movements and apparatus), as well as her physical abilities. The coach should recommend music that can emphasize the gymnast's strengths and disguise her weaknesses. The coach's aim is to help show the gymnast at her best, taking into account her individuality and her winning poses. The coach should objectively evaluate the gymnast's level of mastery. If her mastery of technique is low, then the coach should avoid choreography using popular classical works. The coach must use his or her skill to build a composition which expresses the nature of the music and shows the gymnast at her best.

Another problem that coaches face when choosing musical accompaniment is age-appropriateness. For example, the coach might develop a composition on "growing up" for young potential gymnasts. The musical accompaniment for such a composition should correspond with the age and the level of mastery of the gymnast after a year or two of RSG training. However, coaches must beware of creating a discrepancy between the music and the movements. For example, a coach might choreograph a composition for a preadolescent, and when the gymnast grows the coach changes her music, but not the movements. As a result, the gymnast will lose points during competition because she is only using the music as background.

When choosing music, the coach should determine if other gymnasts are going to use the same piece. The coach should find out if a top level gymnast has used this piece and, if so, if her performance is considered to have set the standard. If that is the case, it is best to choose another piece of music.

If the competition will occur in the country of a well-known composer, the coach may definitely consider choreographing a composition using that composer's music. This will help create a favorable response from the public, and it may make a good impression on the judges.

When choosing the music, the coach should consider how it will sound in a large gymnasium and whether the spectators can identify and understand it. Ideally, music should be familiar to the spectators, as this will also help create a positive response.

It is not easy to express difficult musical pieces through gymnastics. Difficult and unclear music will probably result in spectators and judges losing interest in the gymnast's performance. The coach should remember that the spectators and judges perceive a composition through both sight and sound. Thus, coaches should select musical pieces in which the composer's ideas can be expressed integrally and completely through the gymnast's movements.

Gymnastic movements and sounds have different natures. A gymnast who is trying to portray musical images should beware of confusing this with dramatic imagery. Indeed, a gymnast can only portray the main emotional points of the music and should not strive to create a dramatic image. Thus, coaches must choose musical parts from well-known ballets and operas with caution. For example, spectators have already formed a dramatic image (created by ballet dancers) of the Odett theme from Tchaikovsky's *Swan Lake*. A gymnast using this theme is doomed to failure unless she has exceptional technique and expression.

Many gymnasts try to use their national music for compositions. It is much clearer and simpler for them. In other cases, gymnasts prefer the traditional music of countries such as Spain and Hungary. Examples of these include hota, segidilia, and czardas. Gymnasts ought to study the unique characteristics of their national dances to explore the nature of the musical accompaniment. This dance music has the advantages of distinct rhythm and repeatability of any phrase. Even a gymnast who does not possess high qualifications can successfully perform using it. Therefore, we recommend that coaches choreograph a gymnast's first compositions using the gymnast's native dance. By starting with simple music and progressing to the more complex, coaches can ensure an intelligent musical progression.

When choreographing, a coach can include dance steps from different dances as connective elements in a composition with the aim of giving the composition a dance character. Sometimes it is enough to use simple movements of the head, arms, or legs; for example, a gymnast might raise her chin as in Spanish dances. When combined with music, such details will add a dash of color and authenticity to the composition.

Once the musical accompaniment has been chosen, the coach should listen to it carefully and divide it into parts with the help of a metronome. Slow parts of compositions work best with music that is 60 to 80 beats per minute. An average (moderate) tempo demands 90 to 140 beats per minute, and fast segments require 140 to 180 (and above) beats per minute. The coach should study the time signature of the musical accompaniment and the number of bars and phrases in the composition and in its significant themes.

Using Expressive Movements

Sometimes young gymnasts who fail to get proper guidance from their coaches will be carried away by the entertainment side of the composition. They overdo arm swings, smiles, and shoulder-jerking. They believe that by doing so they will create an artistic air. This is not true. As François Delsarte (1811-1871), a French singer and dramatic actor, wrote, it is absurd to include expressions at every possible point, regardless of appropriateness.

Elite gymnasts perform compositions with ease and grace by coordinating their excellent body movement and apparatus handling technique with the music. They leave redundant movements out of their compositions. Indeed, expressions of a performance in a competitive composition must be carefully chosen movements.

Some people believe that expressiveness is the ability to portray emotion. According to Delsarte, bad actors try too hard to express emotion, resulting in bad acting. In contrast, good actors convey emotion with only limited gestures. Indeed, greater expression with limited movement (gesturing) is more impressive.

Displaying an emotion is not expressiveness. It only becomes an expression when it is embodied in body movements such as a beautiful pose, soaring leap, or masterful handling of an apparatus. Expressiveness is a quality, a display of good techniques of elements, the correct school of body movements, good stability and tempo, elegance, and a clear conveyance of the emotional contents.

Technique and expressiveness are interconnected. The technique forms the necessary base on which a gymnast may build expressiveness. Properly considering the technical perfection of movements requires touching on motor habits. An expressive motor habit is the ability to give the movement a certain meaning and emotional feeling. Expressiveness has a significant influence on the judges' evaluation of a composition and may possibly comprise up to 15 percent of the score.

The arms are the most expressive part of movements. They express psychological and emotional nuances as well as complete movements. Agrippina Vaganova, a well-known Russian ballet teacher, remarked that the skill of coordinating arm movements shows that a dancer is from a good school. In RSG, arm movements in concrete compositions may vary along with the musical accompaniment.

Trunk movements may be expressive as well. The best Soviet gymnasts demonstrated mastery in the expressiveness of their trunk movements. Russian, Ukrainian, and Byelorussian gymnasts continue to build upon this tradition.

The legs play a different role from the arms. They serve a secondary expressive function because their primary function is support, and they merely accompany the arms.

Sometimes coaches and ballet masters create competitive compositions that are merely dances, overloading them with movements that are more suitable for classical, traditional, and modern dance. In reality, while both dance performers and gymnasts express their emotions through body movements, the languages of dance and RSG differ greatly in their themes and techniques. Therefore, the means of expression should also differ. RSG compositions may use only limited elements of a dance under the FIG Code of Points.

In RSG, expressiveness is founded on the richness of experiences and feelings as well as acquisition of a large reserve of movements capable of projecting these feelings. Expressiveness in RSG is displayed through technical mastery, poses, construction of a composition, and the traveling of a gymnast. Certainly, it is almost impossible for a poorly prepared gymnast to achieve a high level of artistry and a feeling for the music. Sadly, many gymnasts try to achieve these important qualities not through technique, but pretentiousness—unjustified movements of the arms, legs, and shoulders.

Gymnasts must be able to perceive poses and body positions in space. Neglecting the positioning of certain body parts in poses and movements reduces their expressiveness. Indeed, the precision of a pose has a huge impact on the expressiveness of movements in that pose. For example, when a gymnast stands on her toes with her arms raised and head thrown back, she creates the impression of looking upward. If she lowers her heels a little and rounds her body slightly or moves her arms to the side, that impression is lost. Then the position has a different emotional impact. Gymnasts should focus on these details, which affect their mastery of gymnastics. Thus, a coach should include special exercises requiring exact positioning of the arms, legs, shoulders, and other body parts in lessons. This should teach gymnasts the skill of controlling the position of different parts of the body in space.

The gymnast's traveling on the floor area is also an important factor in the expressiveness of movements. Movements on the diagonal have the greatest dynamics. Arches express softness and smoothness, while circles express unity, and spirals express tension. Abruptly changing direction conveys sharpness.

A gymnast learns how to properly express emotions through skillful training. Unfortunately, however, some coaches erroneously force girls to smile during performances. A smile is not necessarily wrong, but it is better not to hurry beginners' search for emotions. Expressiveness develops with experience, often after several years. The variety of movements acquired by an experienced gymnast enable her to express herself. With experience and maturity, she uses the energy in her body for her movements to create a visual image of the music. One of the main tasks of the coach, then, is to observe and note which movements the gymnast "feels" best and emphasize them in compositions.

Summary

In many cases, young gymnasts have rather good technique but are unable to demonstrate their mastery in competitions. They feel ignorant and constrained and do not know how to go about presenting all that they know easily and confidently. This is when an experienced ballet master is necessary; he or she can help by adding "color" to each movement. But first, a coach must know his or her gymnast's ability to express the nature of the music through the means that they have acquired. Ignorance of these abilities can cause some coaches to expect young gymnasts to create their own style from the very start. Remember that not all participants of the European and World Championships have their own style of performance in competitive compositions. The coach should use this chapter to help him or her develop effective, individualized compositions for gymnasts. In the next chapter, we will show the coach and gymnast how to deal effectively with the various types of actual competitions.

Chapter 11

Preparing for Competitions

Competition is the essence of sports. Competitions establish the goals, purpose, and development of gymnasts. In this chapter, we will examine how competitions can help a gymnast improve as she capitalizes on her training and how to schedule competitions with this goal in mind. We will explain how to deal with competitive conditions and mentally prepare for them and competition itself. Finally, we will outline how to handle the big day at the gym—from inspecting equipment, to choosing the right leotard, to warming up effectively.

Types of Competitions

In RSG, each type of competition has different goals, methods of calculating results, scope, and regulation.

RSG competitions have one of the following goals:

- Education. Some groups and clubs hold educational competitions under special RSG educational (classification) programs according to the grade or year of training (for example, a competition limited to gymnasts in the first year of training).
- Selection. Competitions are often used to select the best gymnasts to form a team to compete in future competitions.
- Testing. Competitions provide an excellent opportunity to examine a gymnast's mastery.
- Championships and cups. Championship and cup competitions are the traditional means of determining the best gymnast and team.
- Match. Match competitions both reveal the best gymnasts and teams and provide meaningful competitive experiences. They may be official and formal, or friendly in character.

Competition I

The first competition is a qualifying round. The results of Competition I determine the following:

- Team and individual gymnast qualification for competions II, III, and IV.
- Ranking of teams placed 9th or below.
- All-around rankings of individual gymnasts placed 31st or below.

- Ranking of individual gymnasts placed 9th or below on each apparatus.
- Qualification of individual gymnasts for the Olympic Games (in the year prior to the Olympics only).

The top 30 gymnasts from Competition I are qualified to compete in the individual all-around competition (Competition II). The best eight gymnasts on each of the four specified apparatus qualify to participate in the apparatus finals (Competition III). The top eight teams qualify for the team finals (Competition IV).

Team competition in Competition I follows these rules:

- A team is composed of 3 to 4 gymnasts.
- Each gymnast performs from 1 to 4 exercises.
- Each team performs 3 exercises, by different gymnasts, on each of the 4 specified apparatus, for a total of 12 exercises.
- Team classification is determined by adding the 10 best scores.

Competition II

Competition II is the individual all-around competition. The top 30 gymnasts from Competition I qualify for the individual all-around competition. Each country participating can be represented by no more than two gymnasts. Each gymnast performs four exercises with specified apparatus. Rankings are determined by adding the scores from each exercise.

Competition III

Competition III is the apparatus finals. The best eight gymnasts on each of the four specified apparatus compete against each other. Each country may be represented by no more than two gymnasts. Rankings are determined by scores.

Competition IV

Competition IV is the team finals. The top eight qualifying teams from Competition I participate in two rounds of competition: the semi-final round and the final round. All eight teams compete in the semi-final round. Each team performs two exercises on each of the four specified apparatus for a total of eight exercises per team. The four teams with the highest scores move on to the final round.

In the final round, the four top teams perform one exercise for each of the specified apparatus. The team's score in the final round is added to their score in the semi-final round to determine the team ranking.

The scope of a competition ranges from the group through the sport center or club, city, region, and country, and culminates in international competitions. Competitions are regulated as follows:

- Closed or open:
  — Closed competitions have no gymnasts from other cities or countries and do not allow spectators; their goal is to test gymnasts.
  — Open competitions allow all gymnasts to participate irrespective of city or country.
- System of judging:
  — According to the Code of Points.
  — Under other conditions, such as omitting special requirements or imposing temporary restrictions, requiring two repetitions of compositions, adapted judging must occur. This means the judges must overlook the standard set of rules and adjust their scoring to allow for the special conditions above.

Competitive Conditions

Many conditions can influence a gymnast's competitive results. These include fans, the gymnastic equipment and hall, the geographical location of the competition, the manner of judging, and the behavior of coaches and others. These factors become more prevalent as the gymnast's developmental level increases. For example, a higher level gymnast will most likely travel to many different locations where carpet, ceiling height, and other conditions may differ. An elite gymnast must also get used to the distractions and noise level that a greater number of fans attending the competitions can produce.

Fans can have a positive or negative psychological effect on competitors. Naturally, the relative level of support for the gymnast (and for her competitors), within the limits of normal behavior, influences the gymnast's confidence level.

When determining tactics and training for a competition, coaches and gymnasts should consider the following characteristics of the gym in which the competition will take place:

- Quality of the floor area (carpet and ceiling height).
- Time of performance (morning, afternoon, or evening).
- Schedule of competitions (normal or unusual).
- Character (natural or artificial), location, and quality of light.
- Quality of auxiliary premises, such as dressing and warm-up areas (convenient or inconvenient).
- Distance from the gym to the place where the gymnasts are staying.
- Availability and quality of places for rest and recovery.

The geographical location of the competition also influences the results, due to climate and time zone. The time zone can be very important; changing the gymnast's "daytime" too much or too quickly will hurt her performance. Coaches and gymnasts must consider climatic and temporal features when planning performances. So, for example, competitions in the middle of a mountain range require considering the influence of hypoxia (oxygen deficiency) on the gymnast. Temporary distinctions such as these influence the daily rhythm of activities and body functions. A coach should take all these factors into account during training and competition.

Organizers should provide qualified and objective judging. The judging itself may be somewhat subjective, however, and the judges' qualifications may be inconsistent. Despite measures taken by the FIG, the problem of disparate judging has not been solved. Therefore, when planning to participate in competitions, coaches need to consider—and anticipate—possible variations in the judges' evaluations.

Despite the portions of the FIG Code of Points that mandate the discipline of coaches, intense competition does affect their behavior. The behavior of a coach toward a gymnast can be supportive, negative, or neutral. The coach should plan in advance the effect she wishes to have on a gymnast during the competition, as competitive emotions can cause ill-considered decisions and undesirable situations.

Facing the Competitive Atmosphere

Competitions are significant in a gymnast's development. They are a means of monitoring the degree of training, a method of revealing winners, and a major motivation for increasing the level of training and mastery. Competing helps a gymnast adapt to competitive intensity and extreme conditions as well as develop willpower. This explains why many coaches want to include more competitions in their training programs.

Elite gymnasts compete for 25 to 35 days per year. A "start" is the performance of a composition in a competition. A gymnast may start up to 12 times per competition, or 210 to 250 times each year. Competitions play an important role in the gymnast's development. Indeed, a gymnast who seldom competes may lose her competitive edge.

Types of Competitions

As mentioned earlier in this chapter, a coach can systematically use competitions to enhance a gymnast's development. Here we will discuss in more detail control, preparatory (modeling), selecting, and main competitions.

Control Competitions

Control competitions allow great control over the gymnast's training. They reveal the gymnast's degree of mastery of compositions and tactics, the level of fitness, psychological readiness to compete, and efficiency of the past phase of training. An effective coach can correct the training process based on the results of control competitions. Control competitions can be specially organized as official competitions at various levels (city or regional).

Preparatory Competitions

The main goals of preparatory (modeling) competitions include perfecting rational technique and tactics for participating in main competitions, perfecting the skill of adapting to the conditions of intense competitions, increasing the degree of development, obtaining competitive experience, and allowing a gymnast to peak in main competitions for a year or a few years. These competitions can be specially organized in a gymnast's training as "official calendar" competitions. They should be completely or partially modeled on upcoming main competitions.

Selecting Competitions

These competitions help coaches select gymnasts for regional or national teams or choose the gymnast's level in individual competitions. They offer specific conditions for selection. They ensure gymnasts meet a certain level or a certain specification, which should allow them to perform adequately in main competitions.

Main Competitions

Major competitions, such as the RSG World Championships, Olympic Games, and the like, end the long stages of training and permit the coach a chance to evaluate the efficiency of the training program. Other competitions can help to decide the selection of gymnasts for participation in the main competitions. They are an effective means of increasing the specific training of the gymnasts. Main competitions are competitions in which gymnasts must show the best results of their stage of development. Each gymnast should display all her technical and functional abilities, the greatest desire to obtain the best possible results, and the highest level of psychological readiness.

The role and significance of competitions are distinguished by the stages of long-term training. At the initial stages, as a rule, coaches plan for such a gymnast to enter preparatory and control competitions. As the gymnast's qualifications increase, the number of competitions will also increase. Then, coaches should plan for such a gymnast to enter selecting and main competitions.

Stages of Selection for Elite Competition

The RSG selection process is difficult because it requires observation of a girl for one to three years of training. Not all children show or achieve their potential immediately, which results in different rates of RSG development. The coach must consider both the initial evaluations and the speed of development. When evaluating the development of a gymnast's abilities, the coach should remember that in some cases, a high rate of improvement may be due to rapid biological maturing. Therefore, when evaluating paces of developing abilities, the coach should take into account not only the calendar age, but also individual paces of biological maturing. This is especially important during puberty (12 to 15 years of age), when development of coordination and endurance can temporarily slow down.

The body development and functions, psychological characteristics, and maturation rates of people differ, so gymnasts will display different abilities and potential, even when they are coached by the same person. Patient teaching and different coaching methods are required to help gymnasts practice to reach the elite level in RSG. Selection for practice at the elite level should be conducted in four stages:

1. In the initial stage, the coach evaluates the health, body type, and the initial level of flexibility and coordination.
2. In the following stage, the coach evaluates physical, technical, and other development throughout the next one to three years of training.
3. In the main stage, the coach evaluates individual gymnasts and advises them whether they should continue training for the elite level in RSG or to train in a group, not aiming for the elite level.
4. In the specialization stage, conducted while preparing for championships, the coach helps gymnasts specialize either in individual or group exercises and selects teams.

Therefore, the selection process is a systematic process and increases the chance of choosing the best candidates for the elite level in RSG.

The coach should pay close attention to the gymnast's health, physical development, and posture during the first stage of selection. It may be best to choose girls with particular height and weight ranges. Between the ages of 6-7 years, girls with a height above 113 centimeters and weight of not more than 22 kilograms is preferred. Between the ages of 7-8 years, girls with a height above 117 centimeters and weight of not more than 25 kilograms are likely to be selected.

Scheduling Competitions

In modern practice, coaches use three methods to schedule competitions. The first method is connected to the desire of gymnasts to participate in competitions often as this is a way of achieving top results. It allows competitions to be used as a means and method of training and monitoring the efficiency of the training process. Gymnasts adapt to the conditions of competitions and can show consistent results. However, constant aspiration to achieve top sport results in all competitions has been associated with excessive psychological and physical fatigue. So, technical development may actually be limited, possibly leading to a decrease in success in main competitions.

The second way of scheduling competitions is where all the attention of the gymnast and coach is focused on training for the main competitions of a season. This way will probably deprive a gymnast of the opportunity to adapt to competitions. Indeed, insufficient competitive experience does not allow a gymnast to completely reach her technical and functional potential in main competitions.

The third way of scheduling competitions is to have the gymnast compete as usual, but with a different mind set. In other words, the gymnast should use preparatory and control competitions only as a means of training. The coach aims the entire training program at achieving top results in the main competitions. This approach is far better than the other two, as it has its advantages and simultaneously eliminates the defects of the first two ways. The gymnast still participates in enough competitions to better her ability to adapt, yet the emphasis is placed only on main competitions, lessening the chances for psychological and physical fatigue.

Competition Tactics

When planning competitions for the year, it is necessary to take training and competitive activities into account. In the following sections, we will look closely at the tactics of mental preparation, physical preparation, and the coach-gymnast relationship.

Tactics in sport are understood to be the art of managing competitive struggle. In RSG, the tactics are not so difficult and varied as in other sports. They are connected with the characteristics of RSG, in which gymnasts compete independently from one another. Therefore, tactics are determined by the sequence of gymnasts in competitions, that is, if a gymnast competes before or after the top contenders. Whether or not to include more difficult and risky elements in a composition also depends on the sequence of competitors.

Tactical training refers to the acquisition of tactics, that is, obtaining knowledge, skills, and habits that are necessary to perform tasks and make correct decisions in a competition. There are two types of tactical training: general and specific. General tactical training enables the gymnast to master the main principles of competing. Specific tactical training involves mastering the art of making correct decisions during actual competition.

Tactical conception is a part of specific tactical training, which is part of managing competitions. The coach and gymnast conceive the tactics before the start of competition with the purpose of achieving a certain result. To construct a tactical plan, it is best for coaches to know about real and potential competitors, their strong and weak points, the specifics of their training, their favorite tactics, their scores during previous competitions, and the conditions of upcoming competition (for example, which apparatus the best competitors will perform with first).

Mental Preparation

Unfortunately, there are many cases in which better prepared gymnasts have lost because they were weak psychologically or emotionally. Thus, when planning a gymnast's participation in competition, a coach must understand psychology very well.

Among top level gymnasts there are many individuals with strong, dynamic, and stable psychological traits, which are not affected by anxiety, excitement, or impulsiveness. Probably, on the way to the top level, some gymnasts with other traits decided to drop out. So, more often that not, gymnasts with strong psychological traits win. They can perform for a long period effectively and with good mental stability. Yet, as RSG is a highly emotional and expressive sport, many individuals with highly anxious, excitable, and impulsive traits are involved. Typically, these gymnasts can achieve top results in some competitions but are not able to maintain consistency over time. A detailed description of training and competitive psychological traits is given in table 11.1.

Mental preparation for an actual competition (specific psychological training) is based on the psychological readiness of a gymnast specifically for this competition. The main goals of a gymnast's psychological training for an actual competition may be as follows: deciding on the competitive goals, creating the desire to reach these goals, and instilling confidence in the gymnast in her ability to achieve her goals.

Consistent behavior (for example, following the same pre-performance ritual) of RSG gymnasts in competitions makes them mentally steady, thereby increasing their competitive reliability. This behavior is formed by early precompetitive training: participation in control competitions using mental training and mental imagery of competitive conditions.

The most important means of mental preparation for competition in RSG include rituals of competitive behavior, that is, certain preparations that are typical for a gymnast before she is called to the floor area. For example, standing on toes, tossing the apparatus, focusing her attention on a certain object, and mental imagery.

Preparation Details

On the big day, coaches and gymnasts must attend to many details to ensure that each start proceeds smoothly. Whether the detail is the best warm-up or the gymnast's underwear, each aspect of preparation is important.

Equipment

Gymnasts and coaches should check the condition of the apparatus before each competition. They should look for cracks in the hoop, clubs, and the ribbon's stick. They should choose the leotard color carefully. It should be in harmony with the colors of the apparatus and the venue's carpet. If the gymnast has not used the leotard for a long time, she should use it a few times during training while performing all elements so she can note any unusual or uncomfortable sensations. We also recommend that special attention be paid to choosing underwear. Underwear should be cut high enough so as not to stick out from under the leotard; depending on the color and thickness of the leotard's material, underwear with colorful prints may need to be avoided.

Warm-Up

Before leaving the house or hotel, a gymnast should check to make sure she has packed the musical tapes

TABLE 11.1

Comparison of Training and Competitive Psychological Traits*

Training conditions	Competitive conditions
Gymnasts with a high level of anxiety	
1. Have confidence in their capabilities
2. Perform all scheduled difficult connections, actively include risks and difficult elements and connections
3. Can repeat un-acquired elements a few times
4. Use variety in traveling on floor area; movements correspond to the tempo of the music and necessary amplitude	1. Often and easily lose confidence in their capabilities
2. Perform, as a rule, only minimum scheduled difficulty, not difficult and risky elements
3. Make frequent mistakes
4. Limit traveling on floor ("move on spot"), considerably advanced tempo of musical accompaniment ("bustle")
Gymnasts with a low level of anxiety	
1. Have confidence in their capabilities
2. Perform confidently and calmly; can perform 10-12 difficult elements in a composition
3. Stable balances and exact turns and pivots
4. Perform compositions easily with maximum amplitude	1. Perform confidently and calmly
2. Same confidence as in training sessions
3. Perform perfectly all static elements, including balances
4. Same as in training sessions, but without expression
Gymnasts with a high level of emotional excitability	
1. Have confidence in their capabilities
2. Can perform interesting, difficult, and original compositions
3. Can coordinate movements correctly and are inclined to improvise
4. Movements are emotionally expressive in conjunction with the music, leaving a good impression	1. Become very excited, do not have confidence in their capabilities
2. Like anxious gymnasts, can perform well with the minimum difficult elements
3. Commit errors, which negatively influences the performances of others
4. Perform compositions easily but cautiously while tense
Gymnasts with a low level of emotional excitability	
1. Have confidence in their capabilities
2. Use difficult elements in compositions, interesting handling of apparatus
3. Almost always perform elements without large or significant errors
4. Perform compositions with maximum amplitude but without expression	1. Have confidence in their capabilities, remain calm
2. Perform all scheduled difficult elements in the composition
3. Perform well without large or significant errors
4. Same as in training conditions

(continued)

TABLE 11.1 (continued)

Training conditions	Competitive conditions
Impulsive gymnasts	
1. Have confidence in their capabilities	1. Lose confidence in their capabilities
2. Perform compositions dynamically, easily, precisely, beautifully, and expressively, using difficult elements	2. Despite high difficulty of composition, perform movements without continuity and with too many interruptions
3. Despite significant errors in the performance, can concentrate and finish well	3. Perform significant errors in apparatus handling and can stop performance of composition independently
4. Quickly switch from one apparatus to another without loss of quality and necessary amplitude	4. Monotonous traveling on floor area with limited amplitude of movements while infringing on the tempo of the musical accompaniment
Non-impulsive gymnasts	
1. Have confidence in their capabilities	1. Have confidence in their capabilities
2. Perform the compositions freely with maximum amplitude	2. Perform the compositions with average amplitude of movement
3. Handle apparatus safely, but do not move well, relaxing when landing in jumps and leaps	3. Perform some elements and connections without thinking about their quality, but focus their attention on some details
4. Perform compositions without expression or emotion	4. Perform as well as when in training conditions

*Adapted from "Methodical Recommendations for Individualization of the Training Process in RSG According to Gymnasts' Psychological Traits" by R. Ziukova, Perm (1985).

she needs (if they are not collected before competition), her half-shoes, needle and thread, and other necessary articles. She needs to plan her time of arrival at the gym so that she will have enough time to warm up before the competition. Still, she should not arrive too early or she will probably start to worry. But if she is late, she may not have time for a good warm-up.

Upon arriving at the gym, the coach and gymnast should find out if there are any changes in the schedule of competitions. If so, the coach should help the gymnast alter her plans. If she ends up with a lot of time before warm-up, it is better to wait outside the gym; she should not watch the other gymnasts perform. Why? Although the other gymnasts' failures may increase the waiting gymnast's confidence, their successes may be upsetting. Moreover, she may also mentally perform the other gymnasts' actions, possibly confusing her own rhythm. Instead, the waiting gymnast should distract her mind from the competition.

Five to seven minutes before starting to warm up, the gymnast should enter the competitive gym for a short time, settle down, and become accustomed to the lights. She should also take a look at the spectators and judges. She must convince herself that everything is as she had expected. If she feels excited because of the large number of spectators and her reactions to others' performances, she should imagine that she is there simply for another lesson. Once she is accustomed to the gym, she can start her warm-up session.

Of course, the purpose of warming up before competition is to prepare the body for the upcoming performance. It should also help the gymnast concentrate on the compositions she is about to perform. Finally, it should help her mentally tune her performance.

The gymnast should start her general physical warm-up with different kinds of running (on the spot, on toes, with high knees, and so on) and jumps, warming up her entire body. Then she should do classical drills at the barre. After these, she should perform exercises to increase her sense of balance and stabilize her body position in space, stretch the ligaments and muscles for the upcoming work, and practice jump and leap takeoffs.

Next, she should start warming up with the apparatus. First, to "sense" them better, the gymnast should rotate, pass, do figure movements, and roll them. Then, she should toss, throw, and catch them. While doing these exercises, she should focus on her muscular sensations so she can feel her body and apparatus yield to being put into action.

After the general warm-up, the gymnast should turn her attention to the composition itself. At first, she should mentally imagine it and start to hum the music or count to herself. Then she should simulate the leg, arm, trunk, head, and apparatus movements so that these muscles are warmed up and ready to perform at full strength. At this point, the coach should focus the gymnast's attention on noting muscular senses, reminding the gymnast of key concepts, especially regarding amplitudes and expressiveness. If the excitement is not there, then the gymnast should repeat the composition. Then the gymnast should pay more attention to difficult elements, repeating them separately while concentrating on the rhythm of the performance in its main phases.

There are several types of specific warm-up, including warming up by performing:

- elements, connections, and favorite exercises,
- the entire composition,
- a part or parts of the composition, including elements and connections as they should be performed in the competition,
- the entire composition with fixed elements, but without using the gymnast's full strength and without certain important elements, or
- mental imagery, mentally going through the composition, mentally "feeling," thinking, and performing.

The contents of a warm-up and its tactics are primarily determined by the individuality of the gymnast and her competitive experience. It is important that it completely prepares her both physically and psychologically. Indeed, each gymnast has her own preferred style of warm-up in a rather set form. On the one hand, this approach has the necessary effect, especially in very tense situations. On the other hand, we recommend that a gymnast learn the various types of warm-ups so she can vary them according to the actual conditions of the competition.

A gymnast must mentally train herself to perform correctly. She should mentally convince herself that she is able to perform difficult elements well, as she has always done. She should firmly order herself to "Catch!" "Hold!" "Stand!" "Do!" This will help her control her excitement and reassure herself of her strength. A properly planned training program and a good warm-up will give her the confidence that she can succeed.

After the warm-up, the gymnast should wear a sport jacket and leggings so that she will not cool off. In this way, she should be prepared to warm up on the floor area (if she is allowed to do so).

Warming up on the floor area before the start of competition will help the gymnast maintain her confidence as well as orient herself to the floor area. This will also give her a chance to demonstrate to spectators, officials, and judges that she is prepared to perform her compositions well.

To warm up on the floor area, the gymnast should go through the standard warm-up she has practiced and polished during training, following the tactics we have already described. Thus, a coach should determine the elements, number of repetitions, and intervals of rest that will create an effective warm-up long before the day of the competition. The specific contents of a particular warm-up depend on the gymnast's composition and her starting number. If, for example, she performs first, her warm-up should be a little shorter so that her heart rate will recover before competition. In this case, she should not warm up at a high tempo or jump and leap very much. If possible, her warm-up should represent the composition she will perform—as long as she has time to recover from it.

When finishing her warm-up on the floor area, the gymnast should force herself to think that the floor area is good, the ceiling is high enough, and later she will repeat her performance just as successfully. In brief, she must tell herself firmly that "All is well!" A coach must remember, however, that it is unwise for the gymnast to watch the performances of the other gymnasts, listen to other musical accompaniments, or hear the points awarded. It is better if she goes somewhere else and practices handling the apparatus and does stretching exercises.

Immediately before being called to perform, some elite gymnasts mentally perform all or part of their composition. In addition at this time, the gymnast must maintain the correct rhythm of breathing and encourage herself to view the spectators as friends rather than enemies. These tactics and others we have mentioned are some of the many specific ways a gymnast may maintain her confidence. She can also control her emotions by firmly telling herself, for example, "Everything will be OK!" "I am the best!" "Forward to win!" and the like. Finally, posing in her starting position, her primary objective must be to focus on her composition, especially its first element. She should not, for example, focus on earning a 9.0; instead, she must focus on the means she must use to reach her goal, that is, the specific elements and connections of her composition.

After performing, the gymnast should go to the warm-up area and prepare for the next composition. Once again, she should perform some elements from the upcoming composition, practice handling the apparatus, and do stretching exercises.

The Relationship Between Coach and Gymnast

Good relationships must start on the first day of training. The relationship between the coach and gymnast can influence the result of the competition. Not surprisingly, good relationships produce good results, whereas bad relationships usually produce bad results.

Gymnasts with their various psychological traits will react differently in their relationships with their coaches. The highly anxious and impulsive gymnast who has a good relationship with her coach achieves good results because she is able to deliver a reliable performance, performing difficult elements boldly. In addition, her heart rate does not rise so high before starting as she is less likely to fear failure. In other words, a good relationship with her coach helps the high-strung gymnast overcome her anxiety. To a lesser degree, a gymnast who is not highly anxious and emotionally excitable improves her results if her relationship with her coach is good. See table 11.2 for suggestions on the coach's behavior toward the gymnast during competition.

If emotionally excitable and impulsive gymnasts have bad relationships with their coaches, they may not have confidence or they might display a "starting apathy." Moreover, their heart rates may be too high. They will not be able to concentrate on their compositions and may perform elements with lesser amplitude and without confidence. Naturally, their results may deteriorate.

Coaches can have a positive influence on their gymnasts by:

- offering encouragement,
- diverting a nervous gymnast's attention,
- stimulating willpower abilities,
- choosing important motivators,
- using positive gestures and signs, and
- guiding mental imagery.

Thus, improving the psychological readiness of a gymnast involves individualizing her warm-up to tailor it to the needs of her composition, creating conditions similar to actual competitions during training, and developing a good relationship between the coach and the gymnast so that the gymnast can achieve top results.

Summary

Competitions offer the gymnast the opportunity to demonstrate her skill and perform before an audience. Different competitions, from casual to the most competitive, can be used for gymnasts of all levels to showcase their talents, win awards, and build a competitive edge. Many factors influence how well a gymnast may perform at a competition: the physical environment, the intensity of the competition, the relationship between the coach and the gymnast, etc. Coaches must be prepared to guide their gymnasts through the trials of competition.

TABLE 11.2

Suggestions for Coach's Behavior During Competition, Depending on the Gymnasts' Psychological Traits

Psychological traits	Pedagogical approach
Gymnasts with a high level of anxiety	
1. Increased anxiety before competition 2. Inclined to premature tuning for performance 3. Underestimate self, do not have confidence in their capabilities 4. Premature anxiety regarding the scores before the performance	1. Offer an attentive and sympathetic attitude before performance (avoid critical remarks) 2. Limit excessive expenditure of energy during training and competitions 3. Build confidence 4. Give lessons and competitive tasks that are well within their powers; do not focus on possible (or probable) errors or loss of apparatus; teach methods of self-control; model the competitive conditions in training more often
Gymnasts with a low level of anxiety	
1. Are inclined to be late or not attend training 2. No desire to compete	1. Insist on and control attendance 2. Increase competitive interest; state goals and objectives
Gymnasts with a high level of emotional excitability	
1. Become increasingly excited before a competition 2. Underestimate the importance of competition, and their personal responsibility for performing 3. React painfully to the remarks of coaches and friends, and to their surroundings	1. Consciously divert thoughts from upcoming competitions 2. Increase the feeling of responsibility 3. Use gentle and tactful speech in competition; teach how to control emotions
Gymnasts with a low level of emotional excitability	
1. Underestimate their capabilities 2. Inactive during lessons and while preparing for competitions	1. Reinforce confidence 2. Include competitive motivation in the lessons with the purpose of increasing activity; develop the feel for music

(continued)

TABLE 11.2 *(continued)*

Psychological traits	Pedagogical approach
Impulsive gymnasts	
1. Underestimate the importance of competitions 2. Make hasty decisions 3. Think painfully of their failures, react negatively to the coach's remarks and then try to deny it	1. Decrease self-confidence 2. Require strict execution of scheduled volume of training load 3. State goals and objectives before training and competition; convince gymnasts that the coach is right
Non-impulsive gymnasts	
1. Slowly switch from one event of all-around to another 2. Underestimate their capabilities and are passive during competition	1. Limit the need to change tasks during training 2. State difficult goals and build self-confidence in their performances

*Adapted from "Methodical Recommendations for Individualization of the Training Process in RSG According to Gymnasts' Psychological Traits of Gymnasts" by R. Ziukova, Perm (1985).

Appendix: Barre Exercises

TABLE A

Set Number One of Barre Exercises for Beginners

N	Exercise	Time	Bar	Counts	Contents	Coach's tips
1	*Demi-plié*	4/4			SP—1st position, facing barre	The trunk should be braced; weight is supported on all toes; the knees are turned out
			1	1-4	Slow half-bending of the knees	
			2	1-4	Slow straightening of the knees	
2	*Battement tendu*	4/4			SP—1st position, facing barre	Supporting leg must be turned out; slide the working leg to turned out position; the trunk is motionless
			1	1-4	Slide the working leg to the side	
			2	1-4	Return leg to the SP	
3	*Sur le cou-de-pied*	4/4			SP—2nd position, facing barre	The working leg should be turned out to *sur le cou-de-pied* position
			1	1-2	Transfer body weight onto supporting leg; raise working leg to *sur le cou-de-pied*	
				3-4	Hold	
			2	1-2	Working leg to 2nd position on toes, lower heels	
				3-4	SP	
4	*Relevé lent*	4/4			SP—1st position, facing barre	The trunk should be straight; the working leg should be stretched and turned out
			1	1-2	*Battement tendu* to the side	
				3-4	Raise working leg up to 45°	
			2	1-2	Hold	
				3-4	Lower on toes and close to 1st position	
5	*Relevé*	3/4			SP—1st position, facing barre	The trunk should be straight; the legs should be turned out; the arms should not be tense
			1	1-2	Raise on toes	
				3	Hold	
			2	1-2	Lower the heels	
				3	Hold	

SP = Starting Position

TABLE B

Set Number Two of Barre Exercises for Beginners

N	Exercise	Time	Bar	Counts	Contents	Coach's tips
1	Demi-plié	4/4			SP—1st position, facing barre	Focus gymnast's attention on her leg turn out
			1	1-2	Demi-plié	
				3-4	Return to SP	
			2	1-2	Demi-plié	
				3-4	Return to SP	
			3	1-2	Demi-plié	
				3-4	Return to SP	
			4	1-2	Battement tendu to the side	
				3-4	Hold 2nd position	
			5	1-4	Repeat bar 1	
			6	1-4	Repeat bar 2	
			7	1-4	Repeat bar 3	
			8	1-2	Transfer body weight onto the supporting leg and the working one on toes	
				3-4	Working leg to 1st position	
2	Battement tendu	4/4			SP—1st position, facing barre	Slide the working leg forward; begin movement from the heel position; close movement from toes
			1	1-4	Slide the working leg forward to toes	
			2	1-4	Hold	
			3	1-4	Close the working leg to SP	
			4	1-4	Hold	
			5-8	1-4	Battement tendu to the side (see exercise 2 from table A)	
3	Rond de jambe par terre (demi)	4/4			SP—1st position, facing barre	The trunk is motionless; the legs are turned out
			1	1-4	Slide the working leg to the front on toes	
			2	1-4	Slide the working leg to the side in arch by toes	
			3	1-4	Slide the working leg to SP	
			4	1-4	Hold	
4	Battement frappé (warm-up exercise)	4/4			SP—sur le cou-de-pied position, facing barre	The trunk should be straight and the legs turned out
			1	1-4	Stretch the working leg to the side on toes	
			2	1-4	Bend the working leg to SP	
5	Relevé lent	4/4			SP—1st position, facing barre	The trunk should be straight; the working leg stretched and turned out
			1	1-2	Battement tendu forward by working leg	
				3-4	Raise it at 45°	
			2	1-2	Hold	
				3-4	Lower on toes and close to SP	
			3-4	1-4	Repeat bars 1-2 to the side	

N	Exercise	Time	Bar	Counts	Contents	Coach's tips
6	Relevé	3/4			SP—1st position, facing barre	The trunk should be straight and legs turned out
			1	1-3	Raise on toes	
			2	1-3	Hold	
			3	1-3	Lower heels	
			4	1-3	Hold SP	
			5	1-3	*Battement tendu* to the side	
			6	1-3	Lower the heel to 2nd position	
			7-10	1-3	Repeat bars 1-2	
			11	1-3	Slide the working leg to 1st position	
			12	1-3	Hold SP	
			13-16	1-3	Repeat bars 1-4	

SP = Starting Position

TABLE C
Set Number Three of Barre Exercises for Beginners

N	Exercise	Time	Bar	Counts	Contents	Coach's tips
1	Demi- and grand plié	4/4			SP—1st position, facing barre	The trunk should be straight and the legs turned out
			1	1-2	*Demi-plié*	
				3-4	Straighten to SP	
			2	1-4	Repeat bar 1	
			3	1-4	*Grand plié*	
			4	1-4	Straighten to SP	
2	Battement tendu	4/4			SP—1st position, facing barre	For *battement tendu* backward, the working leg should be turned out, the toes should be opposite the supporting heel; the shoulders should be parallel to the barre and not turned out or following the working leg
			1	1-4	Slide the working leg backward on toes	
			2	1-4	Hold	
			3	1-4	Slide the working leg to SP	
			4	1-4	Hold	
			5-8	1-4	Repeat *battement tendu* to the side	

(continued)

TABLE C (continued)

N	Exercise	Time	Bar	Counts	Contents	Coach's tips
3	Ronde de jambe par terre (demi)	4/4	1	1-2 3-4	SP—1st position, facing barre Side *battement tendu* Hold	The legs should be turned out; the buttock muscles should be tight; the trunk should be straight
			2	1-4	Slide the working leg backward in an arch	
			3	1-2 3-4	Hold Slide the working leg to 1st position	
			4	1-4	Hold	
4	Battement frappé forward (warm-up)	4/4			SP—*sur le cou-de-pied* position, facing barre	The trunk should be straight, and the legs should be turned out; the working leg should be turned out from the hips
			1	1-4	Straighten the working leg forward on the toes	
			2	1-4	Bend the working leg to SP	
5	Double frappé to the side	4/4	1	1-2	SP—1st position, facing barre Bend the working leg in *sur le cou-de-pied* position forward	The legs should be turned out from the hips
				3-4	Working leg in *sur le cou-de-pied* position behind	
			2	1-2 3-4	Working leg to the side on toes Close to 1st position	
6	Battement fondu	4/4	1	1-2 3-4	SP—1st position, facing barre Side *battement tendu* Hold	For *demi-plié*, the body weight is on the supporting leg; both legs are turned out from the hips
			2	1-2	*Demi-plié* with the supporting leg, bend the working leg to *sur le cou-de-pied* position behind	
				3-4	Hold	
			3	1-2 3-4	Hold Straighten the supporting leg, place the working leg on toes to the side	
			4	1-2 3-4	Close the working leg to 1st position Hold	
7	Relevé lent	4/4	1	1-2 3-4	SP—1st position, facing barre *Battement tendu* to the back Raise the working leg to 45°	The trunk should be straight, the working leg straight and turned out from the hips
			2	1-2 3-4	Hold Lower on toes and close to 1st position	
			3-4	1-4	Repeat bars 1-2 to the side	

SP = Starting Position

TABLE D

Set of Barre Exercises for Gymnasts at the Stage of Realization of Sport Possibilities

N	Exercise	Time	Bar	Counts	Contents
1	Demi- and grand plié	4/4			SP—1st position with the left side to the barre, the right arm in 2nd position
			1	1-4	Demi-plié
			2	1-3	Grand plié
				and	Slide the right leg on toes to the side
				4	2nd position
			3	1-2	Demi-plié
				3-4	Demi-plié
			4	1-3	Grand plié
				and-4	Slide the right leg to 5th position in front
			5	1-2	Demi-plié
				3-4	Demi-plié
			6	1-3	Grand plié
				and-4	Pass the right leg to 5th position behind
			7	1-2	Demi-plié
				3-4	Demi-plié
			8	1-3	Grand plié
				and-4	Pass the right leg to 1st position
			9-16	1-4	Repeat bars 1-8 for the left leg to the right side of the barre
2	Battement tendu	4/4			SP—5th position with the right leg in front, the left side to the barre, the right arm in 2nd position
			1	1	Battement tendu forward with the right leg
				2	Demi-plié in 4th position, the right arm to 3rd position
				3	Transfer body weight onto the left leg, the right leg on toes, with the right arm in 2nd position
				4	Return to SP
			2	1	Battement tendu to the side with the right leg
				2	Demi-plié in 2nd position, the right arm to 1st position
				3	Transfer body weight onto the left leg, the right leg on toes to the side, the right arm in 2nd position
				4	Close the right leg to 5th position behind the left leg
			3	1	Battement tendu backward with the right leg
				2	Demi-plié in 4th position, the right arm in 3rd position
				3	Transfer body weight to the left leg, the right leg behind on toes, the right arm in 2nd position
				4	Close the right leg to 5th position behind the left leg
			4	1-4	Repeat bar 2
			5-8	1-4	Repeat bars 1-4 with the left leg, the right side to the barre

(continued)

TABLE D *(continued)*

N	Exercise	Time	Bar	Counts	Contents
3	*Battement tendu jeté*	4/4			SP—5th position with the right leg in front, the left side to the barre, the right arm in 2nd position
			1	1-4	Two *battements tendu* forward with the right leg
			2	1-4	Repeat bar 1
			3	1-4	Two *battements tendu jeté pointe* with the right leg
			4	1-3	*Demi-plié* in 5th position with the right leg in front, the right arm in 2nd position
				4	Return to SP
			5-8	1-4	Repeat bars 1-4 to the side
			9-12	1-4	Repeat bars 1-4 backward
			13-16	1-4	Repeat bars 1-4 to the side
			17-18	1-4	Repeat bars 1-4 with the left leg, the right side to the barre
4	*Rond de jambe par terre*	4/4			SP—5th position with the right leg in front, the left side to the barre, the right arm in the preparatory position
			Prep	1	*Demi-plié* on the left leg, right leg forward on toes, right arm in 1st position
				2	Slide the right leg in an arc on toes to the side, move the right arm to 2nd position
			1	1-3	Three *rond de jambe par terre* forward with the right leg
				4	Move the right leg to 5th position behind the left leg, move the right arm to 3rd position
			2	1-2	Lean forward with a falling movement of the shoulders and the head
				3-4	Stand erect with the right leg to the side on toes, the right arm in 2nd position
			3-4	1-4	Repeat bars 1-2 with the right leg to the back
			5-8	1-4	Repeat bars 1-4 with the left leg, the right side to the barre
5	*Battement fondu*	4/4			SP—5th position with the right leg forward, the left side to the barre, the right arm in preparatory position
			Prep	1	The right arm in 1st position
				2	The right leg to the side on toes, the right arm in 2nd position
			1	1-2	*Battement fondu* forward with the right leg
				3-4	Stretch and raise the right leg forward at 45°
			2	1-2	*Relevé* on the left leg
				3-4	Lower the heel
			3-4	1-4	Repeat bars 1-2 to the side
			5-6	1-4	Repeat bars 1-2 backward
			7-8	1-4	Repeat bars 1-2 to the side
			9-16	1-4	Repeat bars 1-8 with the left leg, the right side to the barre

N	Exercise	Time	Bar	Counts	Contents
6	*Battement frappé*	4/4			SP—5th position with the right leg in front, the left side to the barre, the right arm in prep position
			Prep	1	The right arm to 1st position
				2	The right leg to the side on toes
			1	1-4	*Battement frappé* forward and to the side
			2	1-2	Double *battement frappé* with the right leg and *relevé* with the left leg
				3	Pivot 180° outward on the left leg and *sur le cou-de-pied* behind on the right leg
				4	5th position with the left leg forward, the right side to the barre
			3-4	1-4	Repeat bars 1-4 with the left leg, the right side to the barre
7	*Rond de jambe en l'air*	4/4			SP—1st position with the left side to the barre, the right arm in 2nd position
			1	1-3	Three *battements tendu jeté* to the side with the right leg
				and	Raise the right leg to the side at 45°
				4	Hold
			2	1-3	Three *rond de jambe en l'air* forward with the right leg
				4	Raise the right leg to the side at 45°
			3	1-4	Repeat bar 1
			4	1-4	Repeat bar 2 behind
			5-8	1-4	Repeat bars 1-4 with the left leg, the right side to the barre
8	Flexibility exercise	4/4			SP—1st position with the left leg, the right leg on the barre to the side; face the barre with hands on the barre
			1	1-2	*Demi-plié* with the left leg and return to SP
				3-4	Repeat counts 1-2
			2	1-4	Repeat bar 1
			3	1-2	Raise the left arm upward
				3-4	Lean to the right
			4	1-3	*Demi-plié* with the left leg
				4	Stand erect
			5	1-2	Raise the right arm
				3-4	Lean to the left
			6	1-3	*Demi-plié* with the left leg
				4	Stand erect
			7	1-2	Stand on the toes with the left leg; raise the right leg forward and upward
				3	Arch back
				4	Stand erect
			8	1-3	Repeat counts 1-3, bar 7
				4	Bend the right leg to *passé*

(continued)

TABLE D (continued)

N	Exercise	Time	Bar	Counts	Contents
8	Flexibility exercise (continued)	4/4	9	1-2	*Demi-plié* with the left leg and grip the right foot with the right hand
				3-4	Stretch the right leg forward
			10	1-4	Straighten the left leg
			11	1-4	Pass the right leg to the side
			12	1-4	Grip the right foot with the left hand with the right hand on the barre
			13-14	1-4	Four *demi-plié*
			15	1-2	Pass the right leg to the back
				3-4	Front balance, right hand on the barre and the left arm forward and down
			16	1-3	Hold
				4	Stand erect and close the right leg to 5th position behind, the left arm in preparatory position
			17-32	1-4	Repeat bars 1-16 with the other leg
9	*Grand battement jeté*	4/4			SP—1st position with the left side to the barre and the right arm in 2nd position
			1	1-4	Four *battement tendu jeté* balance forward-backward with the right leg
			2	1-4	Two *grand battement tendu jeté* balance forward-backward with the right leg
			3	1	*Grand battement tendu* forward with the right leg
				2-4	Hold
			4	1-2	Hold
				3-4	*Relevé* on the left leg
			5	1-4	Repeat bar 1 backward
			6-7	1-4	Repeat bars 2-3 backward
			8	1-2	Repeat counts 1-2 bar 4
				3-4	*Relevé* on the left leg, the right leg to 5th position behind, the left arm in 2nd position
			9-10	1-4	Repeat bars 1-2
			11	1	*Grand battement* forward with the right leg
				2	Grip the right foot with the right hand
				3-4	Hold
			12	1-4	Two *demi-plié* on the left leg
				and	Close the right leg to 1st position, the right arm to 2nd position
			13-14	1-4	Repeat bars 1-2 backward
			15	1	*Grand battement* backward with the right leg
				2	Grip the right shin with the right hand to arch balance
				3-4	Hold
			16	1-4	Two *demi-plié* on the left leg
				and	Lower the right leg, close to 1st position
			17-32	1-4	Repeat bars 1-16 with the left leg, the right side to the barre

SP = Starting Position

References

Arkaev, L., Kuzmina, N., Kirianov, Y., Lisitskaya, T., and Suchlin, N. *About model of long-term sport training in RSG.* 1989. Goskomsport: Moscow.

Balsevich, V. *Research of locomotor function in human post-natal ontogenes (5–65 years old).* 1977. Ph.D. diss., Moscow.

Biriuk, E. and Vlasova, L. *Using hand apparatus with asymmetrical weights in RSG.* 1985. Gymnastics, 2.

Borisov, I., Phendin, A., and Julinsky, L. *Nutrition and regulation of the gymnast's weight.* 1979. Gymnastics, 2.

Firiljeva, I. *Methodology of pedagogical control and perfection of fitness preparation of RSG gymnasts.* 1981. Pedagogical Gertsen's Institute: Leningrad.

Fomin, N. and Vavilov, Y. *Physiological fundaments of motor activities.* 1991. Physical Culture and Sports: Moscow.

Gudjalovsky, A., ed. *The bases of theory and methodology of physical culture.* 1986. Physical Culture and Sports: Moscow.

Jastrjembskaia, N. *Contents of the preparation for jumps and leaps at the base stage of training in RSG.* 1989. Ph.D. diss., Leningrad.

Kuramshin, Y. *Fitness preparation: Theoretical preparation of young athletes.* Edited by Y. Bujlin and Y. Kuramshin. 1981. Physical Culture and Sports: Moscow.

Lazarenko, T. *Quantitative evaluation of the qualitative parameters of jumps and leaps preparation in RSG.* 1991. Ph.D. diss., Moscow.

Matveev, A. *Developmental fitness abilities: Theory and methods for physical education.* Edited by B. Ashmarin and M. Prosveshenie. 1990.

Menhin, Y. *Physical preparation in gymnastics.* 1989. Physical Culture and Sports: Moscow.

Nochevnaya, N. *Using the conjunctive method of physical preparation in RSG group exercises.* 1990. Ph.D. diss., Moscow.

Shvartz, V. and Chrushev, S. *Medical and biological aspects of sports selection.* 1984. Physical Culture and Sports: Moscow.

Sobina, L. and Farfel, V. *Short-term effect of stretching exercises: Gymnastics.* 1979. Physical Culture and Sports: Moscow.

Volkov, V. and Filin, V. *Sports selection.* 1983. Physical Culture and Sports: Moscow.

Ziukova, R. *Methodical recommendations for individualization of the training process in RSG according to gymnasts' psychological traits.* 1985. Perm.

Index

A

acceleration 8, 37
Achilles tendon 14, 16-17
adagio 205, 208
aesthetic factors 7, 39, 127, 192, 224
allegro 206-207
ambidexterity 120-122
apparatus 1, 189
    competition preparation 224, 238
    types 64-65, 138
apparatus flight
    bounces 80-82
    catches 85-90
    physics 70-71
    rebounds 82-85
    throws 71-80
apparatus handling 4
    circular elements 90-108
    dynamic elements 66
    figure elements 108-113
    flight 70-90
    grips 66-70
    linking elements 113-118
    static elements 65-66
arabesques 26, 32-33, 43-45
architectonics 226-227
artistic impression 192, 224, 230-231
attitudes 32-33, 43-45

B

balances
    phases 27-28
    principles 27-29, 136
    techniques 30-37
ball 1-2, 64
    bounces 82
    catches 88-89
    figures 108
    grips 67-68
    linking 115
    rebounds 84
    rolls 92-94
    spins 96
    throws 75-76
    wrapping 98
ballet, classical
    arm positions 194-195
    at the barre 195-207
    leg positions 194-195
    rationale for 17, 151, 193-194, 229
    without the barre 207-208
Balsevich, V. 130
barre exercises
    battement 198-205
    jumps and leaps 206-207
    planning order 195-197
    pliés 197-198
    relevé 197
    rond de jambe 205-206
basic body movements 12
    balances 27-37
    floor elements 49-57
    jumps and leaps 15-27
    turns and pivots 37-45
    waves and swings 46-49
battement 151, 208
    barre exercises 198-205
battement développé 203, 205
battement fondu 201, 208
battement frappé 200, 208
battement relevé lent 205
battement tendu 198-200, 202, 208
bebop dance 218
Biriuk, E. 138
body movements 1, 4
    basic. *See* basic body movements
    classifications 12-14
    expressive 230-231
    modal. *See* modal body movements
    principles 13-15
boogie-woogie dance 218
boomerangs 80, 92
bounces 80-82
breathing space 227
butterfly jump 27
bypassing 86, 117

C

cabriole 26
calories 144
carbohydrates 144-145
cartwheels 53
catches
    grips in 85-86
    principles 85-86
    techniques 86-89

cat jump 26
center of gravity (CG) 64
    in body movements 14, 17, 28–29
    total (TCG) 7
cha-cha dance 217–218
chaîné turn 39–40
champion gymnasts. *See* elite gymnasts
changement de pied 206
Charleston dance 218–219
choreography
    competitive factors 225–226
    music coordination 229–230
circles, apparatus 99–103
circuit training 158, 166
circular apparatus elements
    circles 99–103
    physics 90–91
    proper rotations 103–108
    rolls 91–94
    spins 94–96
    wrapping 97–99
clubs 1–2, 64–65
    bounces 82
    catches 89
    figures 108–110
    grips 68–69
    linking 115–116
    rebounds 84
    rolls 94
    spins 96
    throws 76–78
    wrapping 98
coaches 1, 170, 225
    competition role 221, 237–238, 240, 242
    mastery analysis by 120–123
Code of Points
    body movement classifications 12
    as standard
        for apparatus 64–65, 224
        for apparatus handling. *See specific apparatus*
        for competition judging 221, 224–225
        for music selection 229
        for technique 1, 4, 6. *See also specific technique*
coefficient of asymmetry 121–122
competitions
    characteristics judged 4–5, 221
    compositions for. *See* compositions
    conditions influencing 235
    objectives 221, 234, 236
    Olympic. *See* Olympic competition
    scheduling methods 237
    scoring. *See* judging
    tactics. *See* tactics, competitive
    during training 170, 173–176, 179–182, 186
    types 2, 234–236
competitive floor area 227–228
compositions
    construction
        element arrangements 4–5, 120, 226–227
        framework for 227–228
    expression in 224–225, 228, 230–231
    main direction emphasis 226–228
    music for. *See* musical accompaniment
    preparation 124, 175, 179
    traveling design 227–228, 231
cool-down 189
coordination
    of movements 7
    physical
        methods of developing 136–139
        tests for 139–144
coordination barrier 137
Cossack jump 26
crossing
    in dance 195
    in turns 39–41
cues 7, 138, 148–149

D

dance
    artistic impression 192, 224, 230–231
    classical. *See* ballet, classical
    European 208–215
    gymnast's abilities 6, 127
    jazz 218–219
    Latin 215–218
    preparation methods 192–193
    Russian 213–215
deceleration 8
degree of difficulty 4–5
Delsarte, F. 230
demi-plié 17
duration, of movements 7, 17, 226

E

échapper 79
ekar dance 215
elements
    acrobatic. *See* floor elements
    characteristics judged 4–5, 120–124, 192, 224
    combinations. *See* compositions
    floor. *See* floor elements
    freehand. *See* body movements
    overview 4, 14–15
    techniques. *See* technique; *specific element*
    work. *See* linking elements
elite gymnasts
    features 225–226
    selection process 236–237
emotion
    expression in compositions 8, 230–231
    preparing for competition 235, 238–240
endurance
    general 132, 189
    specific 124
    tests for 156–158
    types 154–156
European dances 209–215

expression
    in compositions 224–225, 228, 230–231
    in modal body movements 60–62

F

Farfel, V. 132–133
fatigue. *See* endurance
fats 144
Fédération Internationale de Gymnastique (FIG) 1, 221
figure eight 108, 110–111, 113
figure elements, apparatus 108–113
Filin, V. 130
flexibility
    methods of developing 132–133
    tests for 133–136
flight
    apparatus. *See* apparatus flight
    body. *See* jumps and leaps
    horizontal distance. *See* range, of distance
    vertical elevation. *See* height
floor balancing 55
floor elements
    classifications 49–51
    techniques 51–57
folding, apparatus 113–114, 116–118
Fomin, N. 131–132
force factors
    in apparatus handling 71–73, 81, 90–91, 95–96, 103, 113–114
    in body movements 6, 8, 37
    centrifugal 38, 90–91
    rotational 37, 73, 90–91, 95–96, 103
fouetté pivot 45
freehand elements. *See* body movements
friction 8

G

gallop step dance 210
gesturing 230
grand battement jeté 202–203, 208
gravity 8, 17
grips
    in catches 85–86
    classifications 66–67
    techniques 67–70
grovels 54–55

H

height 17, 71–72, 85
hoop 1–2, 64
    bounces 82
    catches 87–88
    figures 108
    grips 67
    linking 114–115
    rebounds 84
    rolls 92
    spins 96
    throws 74–75
    wrapping 97

hops 15, 107
HRmax. *See* maximum heart rate

I

inertia 8, 37–38, 112
initial impulse 71, 96–98, 103
injury risks 19
isolations 60
isometrics 151–152, 156

J

Jastrjembskaia, N. 151
jazz dances 218–219
jeté 27, 206–207
judging
    characteristics considered 4–6, 120–124, 192, 221, 224
    standard for. *See* Code of Points
    as subjective 221, 235
jumps and leaps
    with apparatus 26, 106–108, 115, 150, 157
    characteristics 6, 8, 15, 151
    classical 206–208
    classifications 15, 19–20
    flight calculations 17
    phases 15–20
    poses during flight 20, 24
    techniques 20–27, 55

K

knocks 19
Kuramshin, Y. 151

L

Latin dances 215–218
Lazarenko, T. 17
leaps. *See* jumps and leaps
lessons
    density 166–168, 187
    goals and objectives 162–163, 186–189
    intensity 164–166, 175
    organization 165–166, 188
    overall programs. *See* training programs
    phases 163–164, 188–189
linking elements 113–118
long-term planning
    basic training stage 170–174, 183
    individualized 175–176
    realization of sport possibilities stage 174
    sport longevity stage 174–175
    top results 174–176
lying 55

M

macrocycles 176–180
manipulation. *See* apparatus handling
mass, as factor 71, 90–91
mastery, technical
    analysis by coaches 120–123
    characteristics judged 4–6, 120–124, 192, 224
Matveev, A. 130, 133, 137

maximum heart rate (HRmax) 156, 164–165, 168
maximum test (MT) 158
mesocycles 180–182
microcycles 182–186
mills 108–109, 113
mime 60
minerals 5, 144
modal body movements
    classifications 57–58
    expression in 60–62
    overview 12–13
    static 14, 58
    traveling 58–60
momentum 37–38, 71, 86
mood changes. *See* emotion
motor reactions 148–149
movements
    of apparatus. *See* apparatus handling
    of body. *See* body movements
    characteristics 6–8, 226
    tempo of. *See* tempo
moving trajectory 7
MT. *See* maximum test
musical accompaniment 4, 187
    problems with 7, 229
    selection 225, 228–230

N

nutrition factors 5, 144–145, 168

O

Olympic competition
    four-year training cycle 174
    historical champions 2, 160, 190
originality 4–5, 224

P

pas assemblé 206
pas de grace dance 209
pas échappé 206
pasodoble dance 215–216
passages through 113–115
passé position 30, 33, 203
    in turns 37–38, 137
passing 113, 115, 117
passing supports 53–54
physical exercise. *See* elements
physical fitness
    coordination 136–144
    endurance 154–158
    flexibility 132–136
    importance 4–6, 124, 127
    preparation factors 131–132, 158
    speed 148–150
    strength factors 1, 123–124, 138, 150–154
pivots. *See* turns and pivots
pliés 151, 206
    barre exercises 197–198
pointed toes 14
poised hand 14

polka dance 210–211
port de bras 206, 208
poses
    dynamic 14
    during flight 20, 24
    gymnast's perception 231
    on limited support. *See* balances
    progression of 6–7
    ring position 20
    split position 20
    stag shape 24
    static 14, 58
posture 14, 226
preliminary sport preparation 171, 173
proper rotations, apparatus 103–108
protein 144
psychological factors 4–5, 123, 179–180
    in competition 238–240, 243

R

radius of rotation 90–91, 99, 103, 107
radius of swing 113–114
range, of distance 72, 85
rationality 123–124, 136, 227
realization of sport possibilities stage 174
rebounds 82, 84
regrips 113–117
relevé 14, 37, 197, 208
rhythm 6, 8, 148
rhythmic sportive gymnastics (RSG) 1–2, 160, 190
ribbon 1–2, 65
    catches 89
    figures 110–112
    grips 70
    linking 116–117
    rebounds 84
    throws 79–80
    wrapping 99
rock 'n' roll dance 218
rolls
    apparatus 91–94
    body 51–53
rond de jambe 205–206, 208
rope 1, 65
    bounces 82
    catches 90
    figures 113
    grips 69–70
    linking 117–118
    rebounds 84
    spins 96
    throws 78–79
    wrapping 98–99
routines. *See* compositions
RSG. *See* rhythmic sportive gymnastics
rumba dance 216
running 60
Russian dances 213–215

S

sails 108, 113
samba dance 217
scissors jump 26
scoring. *See* judging
semisquat 15–17, 19, 72
sequencing 7–8, 227
shape. *See* poses
Shougourova's spins 96
Sirtaki dance 213
skipping 107
slide steps, dance 208–210
smiles 230–231
snails 108, 110
snakes 108, 111–113
Sobina, L. 132–133
sote 206
SP. *See* starting position
space orientation 72, 136–137
spectator's viewpoint 226, 228
speed 8, 39, 85
    developing abilities 148–149
    in jumps 16–17, 19
    tests for 149–150
spins, apparatus 94–96
spirals
    apparatus 108, 112–113
    in turns 41
split jumps and leaps 24, 26–27
sport longevity stage 174–175
sport specialization 171, 173
spotting 39
spring movement. *See* semisquat
squats. *See* pliés
stability 122–123, 136
stag jumps and leaps 24
stand on toes 14
starting position (SP) 6–7
static tension. *See* isometrics
stepping turn 39–40
steps
    for dance. *See* dance
    for traveling 58–60
straight line of the leg 14
strength
    methods for developing 151–152
    as performance factor 1, 123–124, 138
    proper versus speed 150–151
    tests for 152–154
supports 6–8, 12, 81
    role in balances 28–29
sur le cou-de-pied 41, 43, 201
swaying 108, 113
swings
    apparatus 113–118
    body. *See* waves and swings

T

tactics, competitive
    definition 237–238
    equipment preparation 238
    mental preparation 238–242
    physical preparation 238, 240–242
takeoffs 17, 19
TCG. *See* center of gravity, total
technique
    characteristics 6–8
    definition 1, 5–6
    developing 4–8, 124, 188
    mastery criteria 4–6, 120–124, 136, 192, 224
tempo 4, 7–8, 148
throws 6, 8, 38
    phases 73–74
    physics 71–73
    with rotations in flight 73, 86
    techniques 74–80
time factor
    in apparatus handling 71, 73, 114
    in elements 7, 17
tossing. *See* passing
training cycles
    macrocycles 176–180
    mesocycles 180–182
    microcycles 182–186
    Olympic based 174
training load 164, 166, 181, 183, 187–188. *See also* weights
training programs
    cycle planning 176–189
    evaluation 236
    lesson design. *See* lessons
    long-term planning 170–176
    setting objectives 162–163, 186–187
transferring 113–114, 116–117
traveling
    composition design 227–228, 231
    modal body movements 58–60
trickling 226
turn-out leg position 14
turns and pivots
    classifications 39–40
    phases 37–39
    techniques 40–45, 55
twist, dance 219

V

Vaganova, A. 231
Vavilov, Y. 131–132
velocity 71–73, 91
versatility 120–122
virtuosity 4–5, 224
visual marks 7
vitamins 144, 168
Vlasova, L. 138
Volkov, V. 130
volume, technique 120

W

walkovers 53
waltz dance 211–213

warm-up 188, 238, 240–241
waves and swings
   expressive 60–62
   principles 46–47
   techniques 47–49, 55
weights 132–133, 138, 151, 156. *See also* training load

work elements. *See* linking elements
workouts. *See* lessons
wrapping 97–99

Z

zigzagging 102, 216

About the Authors

Nadejda Jastrjembskaia has been involved in rhythmic gymnastics at many levels—as a scientist, educator, coach, administrator, judge, and gymnast. Born in the USSR, she graduated from P.F. Lesgaft's Academy of Physical Culture with a Candidate of Pedagogical Science degree. She coached for a Kaliningrad Regional RSG School and taught RSG courses at Kaliningrad State University. Most recently, she was the chief coordinator for Malaysia's RSG development program and a consultant for the Malaysian Gymnastic Federation. In 1998 she opened her own gymnastics center. Jastrjembskaia makes her home in Madison, Alabama.

Yuri Titov is the former president of the International Gymnastics Federation. He was a member of the USSR gymnastics team from 1956 to 1966. During that time, he participated in all Olympic Games and World Championships, winning a total of 33 medals, including 11 gold medals. Titov lives in Moscow, Russia.

We hope you enjoyed this title from Echo Point Books & Media

Before Closing this Book, Two Good Things to Know

Buy Direct & Save

Go to www.echopointbooks.com (click "Our Titles" at top or click "For Echo Point Publishing" in the middle) to see our complete list of titles. We publish books on a wide variety of topics—from spirituality to auto repair.

Buy direct and save 10% at www.echopointbooks.com

DISCOUNT CODE: EPBUYER

Make Literary History and Earn $100 Plus Other Goodies Simply for Your Book Recommendation!

At Echo Point Books & Media we specialize in republishing out-of-print books that are united by one essential ingredient: high quality. Do you know of any great books that are no longer actively published? If so, please let us know. If we end up publishing your recommendation, you'll be adding a wee bit to literary culture and a bunch to our publishing efforts.

Here is how we will thank you:

- A free copy of the new version of your beloved book that includes acknowledgement of your skill as a sharp book scout.
- A free copy of another Echo Point title you like from echopointbooks.com.
- And, oh yes, we'll also send you a check for $100.

Since we publish an eclectic list of titles, we're interested in a wide range of books. So please don't be shy if you have obscure tastes or like books with a practical focus. To get a sense of what kind of books we publish, visit us at www.echopointbooks.com.

If you have a book that you think will work for us, send us an email at editorial@echopointbooks.com

CPSIA information can be obtained
at www.ICGtesting.com
Printed in the USA
LVOW06s1210040916
503166LV00010B/314/P